CRUSADE TEXTS IN TRANSLATION

About the volume:

The Chronicle of Ibn al-Athīr (1160–1233 AD), entitled "al-Kāmil fī'l-ta'rīkh", is one of the outstanding sources for the history of the mediaeval world. It covers the whole sweep of Islamic history almost up to the death of its author and, with the sources available to him, he attempted to embrace the widest geographical spread; events in Iraq, Iran and further East run in counterpoint with those involving North Africa and Spain. From the time of the arrival of the Crusaders in the Levant, their activities and the Muslim response become the focus of the work.

A significant portion of this third part deals with the internal rivalries of the Ayyubid successors of Saladin, their changing relations with the Crusader states and in particular the events of the Damietta Crusade. As always, these events are portrayed against the wider background, with considerable emphasis on events in the eastern Islamic world, the fortunes of the Khwarazm Shahs and the first incursions of the Mongols.

About the series:

The crusading movement, which originated in the eleventh century and lasted beyond the sixteenth, bequeathed to its future historians a legacy of sources which are unrivalled in their range and variety. These sources document in fascinating detail the motivations and viewpoints, military efforts and spiritual lives of the participants in the crusades. They also narrate the internal histories of the states and societies which crusaders established or supported in the many regions where they fought, as well as those of their opponents. Some of these sources have been translated in the past but the vast majority have been available only in their original language. The goal of this series is to provide a wide ranging corpus of texts, most of them translated for the first time, which will illuminate the history of the crusades and the crusader-states from every angle, including that of their principal adversaries, the Muslim powers of the Middle East.

About the author:

D.S. Richards is retired as Lecturer in Arabic at the Oriental Institute, and is emeritus fellow of St Cross College, University of Oxford, UK.

Crusade Texts in Translation

Titles in the series include:

D.S. Richards
The Chronicle of Ibn al-Athīr for The Crusading Period
from *al-Kāmil fī'l-Ta'rīkh*. Part 1
The Years 491-541/1097-1146: The Coming of the Franks
and the Muslim Response

D.S. Richards
The Chronicle of Ibn al-Athīr for The Crusading Period
from *al-Kāmil fī'l-Ta'rīkh*. Part 2
The Years 541–589/1146-1193:
The Age of Nur al-Din and Saladin

Peter Jackson
The Seventh Crusade, 1244-1254
Sources and Documents

Colin Imber
The Crusade of Varna, 1443-45

Bernard S. Bachrach and David S. Bachrach
The *Gesta Tancredi* of Ralph of Caen
A History of the Normans on the First Crusade

Janet Shirley
The Song of the Cathar Wars
A History of the Albigensian Crusade

Peter W. Edbury
The Conquest of Jerusalem and the Third Crusade
Sources in Translation

The Chronicle of Ibn al-Athīr

for the Crusading Period

from

al-Kāmil fī'l-ta'rīkh

The Chronicle of Ibn al-Athīr for the Crusading Period from *al-Kāmil fī'l-ta'rīkh*

Part 3

The Years 589–629/1193–1231
The Ayyūbids after Saladin
and
the Mongol Menace

Translated by

D.S. Richards

ASHGATE

First published in paperback 2010.

Published by
Ashgate Publishing Limited
Wey Court East
Union Road
Farnham
Surrey, GU9 7PT
England

Ashgate Publishing Company
Suite 420
101 Cherry Street
Burlington
VT 05401-4405
USA

www.ashgate.com

British Library Cataloguing in Publication Data
Ibn al-Athir, Izz al-Din, 1160–1233
The Chronicle of Ibn al-Athir for the Crusading Period from al-Kamil i'l-Ta'rikh
Part 3: The Years 541–589/1146–1193: The Age of Nur al-Din and Saladin. – (Crusade Texts in Translation; 17)
1. Crusades – Early works to 1800. I. Title II. Richards, D. S. (Donald Sidney), 1935–.
940.1'82

Library of Congress Control Number: 2006926785

ISBN 9780754640790 (hbk)
ISBN 9780754669524 (pbk)

Mixed Sources
Product group from well-managed forests and other controlled sources
www.fsc.org Cert no. SA-COC-1565
© 1996 Forest Stewardship Council
FSC

Printed and bound in Great Britain by
MPG Books Group, UK

Contents

Preface

With this volume, which contains the last of three parts, we arrive at the end of Ibn al-Athīr's *al-Kāmil fi'l-ta'rīkh*, his great chronicle of Islamic history. Not that this translation has attempted to offer the whole work. The whole covers not only the full sweep of Islamic history up to the death of the author but also aspects of history prior to the rise of Islam, even venturing to take the record back as far as creation itself. The translation, consonant with its acceptance as part of the Ashgate series **Crusade Texts in Translation**, began with Ibn al-Athīr's account of the Crusaders' conquest of Antioch, the first indication of the prospect, or should one say the threat, of an attempt by Latin Christendom to recover the Holy Land, that is to say, with the annal for the year 491/1097–8. Part 1 ended with the death of Zankī in 541/1146 and was published in 2006. Part 2 followed in 2007 and was characterized in terms of the series as 'The Age of Nūr al-Dīn and Saladin'. However, in neither of the first two parts did the struggles with the Crusader states dominate the narrative.

This remains the case with the third and final part which is now presented. It begins with the state of the Ayyubid 'empire' as Saladin left it at his death and traces the subsequent relations of the members of the dynasty. The Damietta Crusade is quite naturally given a certain prominence but the main focus of events moves eastwards, far from Syria and Palestine. It will also be noticed that any account of the affairs of Islam in the west, in Spain and North Africa, practically disappears.

It has been enjoyable and challenging to spend this time getting to know the scope of the chronicle and becoming acquainted, as one fondly imagined, with the author, Ibn al-Athīr. Apart from any other consideration I have been provided with an engrossing occupation to fill the first few years of what is called retirement! One can only hope that the resulting translation will prove useful to a range of people, to those who have some Arabic but will appreciate a little help (for there are some tricky passages) and, above all, to those with no Arabic but an interest in the relevant history. All will, I trust, appreciate access to a thirteenth-century Muslim historian's view of the Crusades in the context of events in the wider Islamic world.

I am grateful to those people with Ashgate Publishing who have had a hand in the preparation and production of this volume, especially Kirsten Weissenberg and Dorothy Courtis, for their expertise, care and attention. I am also very grateful to Peter Rea for his production of the index for this, and the previous, volume. Once again I thank my former colleagues at the Oriental Institute for their assistance and encouragement, particularly Professor Geert Jan van Gelder, Dr. Emilie Savage-Smith and Dr. Judith Pfeiffer. I am especially grateful to Professor Peter Jackson of Keele University for reading my typescript with his customary care and precision, for making many valuable suggestions and corrections, and for bringing to my attention some relevant secondary literature of which I was unaware. As ever I owe to my wife Pamela, for her support and understanding, more than can be expressed.

Introduction

'Izz al-Dīn Abū'l-Ḥasan 'Alī ibn Muḥammad al-Jazarī, known as Ibn al-Athīr, was born in 555/1160 in the Mesopotamian town of Jazīrat Ibn 'Umar, modern Cizre. His family was well-to-do and closely connected in administrative capacities with the ruling dynasty of that region, that of the Zankids. Although his father and his two brothers followed bureaucratic careers in addition to engaging, in the case of his brothers, in scholarly and literary pursuits, Ibn al-Athīr, as far as can be known, held no office and was dedicated to the scholar's life.[1] He performed his pilgrimage to Mecca in 576/1181 and returned via Baghdad, where he continued his studies. During the year 584/1188–9 he spent some time in Syria and witnessed at first hand some of Saladin's campaigning, but whether he had any direct contact with Saladin is not known. He received patronage from the Atabeg Shihāb al-Dīn at Aleppo and consequently had some admiring words to say of him. At Mosul, where Ibn al-Athīr probably spent a good deal, if not the greater part, of his time, the Atabeg Badr al-Dīn Lu'lu' also acted as his patron and encouraged his work. This connection too is reflected in the author's favourable comments on that emir's rule and administration. It was at Mosul, which had been untouched by any direct depredations of the Mongols at this stage (although there had been alarms and panic), that Ibn al-Athīr died during Sha'bān 630/June 1233.[2]

For this part of the chronicle the identity of Ibn al-Athīr's sources remains a problem; indeed it is probably more acute than in the preceding parts. He names his written sources very seldom, a shortcoming that is stressed by many scholars. Those historians that have been identified as Ibn al-Athīr's important sources in Part 2 of this translation, such as Ibn al-Jawzī and 'Imad al-Dīn al-Isfahānī, were dead by the early years of the thirteenth century. Whether it will ever be possible to identify any of Ibn al-Athīr's sources among the minor and local historians, whose works have been preserved in scattered quotations in later compilations, is very doubtful. Similarly there is little hope of supplying names and book titles to match the anonymous historians whom Ibn al-Athīr refers to now and then,

---

[1] That he lived a comparatively privileged life may be inferred from a comment of his own. At a time of famine in Mosul he remarks that, since all the dogs and cats had disappeared, obviously consumed by the hungry people, the servant girls in his house no longer had to guard the meat. What strikes one in this snapshot is that Ibn al-Athīr's household clearly still had meat. See below, p. [**447**].

[2] For further biographical details, comment on the other writings of Ibn al-Athīr and background remarks on the *Kāmil* chronicle, see *Chronicle of Ibn al-Athīr (1)*, 1–6, and references there cited, and also *EIr*, vii, 671–2, s.v. Ebn al-Aṯīr.

particularly for events in the eastern Islamic lands. It is by far the easier task to list the historians, both younger contemporaries of Ibn al-Athīr and those of the early Mamluke period, who knew and used Ibn al-Athīr's work. Without hesitation one could name Sibṭ ibn al-Jawzī, Ibn Wāṣil, Ibn al-'Adīm, Abū Shāma, al-Yūnīnī and al-Nuwayrī. Another name to add is al-Nasawī's, who, although he made little or no direct use of his text, admired Ibn al-Athīr and his coverage of eastern affairs, while remaining puzzled about the identity of the sources that he might have had access to. This is significant in the light of the comments above.

If there is little to say about the written sources for this part of the chronicle, there is quite a lot of material and comment that derives from oral communications. As before, Ibn al-Athīr's older brother, Majd al-Dīn Mubārak, provided information from his direct experience of Zankid administration. Otherwise, our author's informants covered a wide range of people, including the likes of merchants, urban notables who were refugees from Daqūqa, envoys from the Georgian kingdom, slave girls, a villager who witnessed Mongol atrocities and a soldier who was a participant in a Khwārazmian expedition to Kirman and Sind but was unsure of the relevant dates.

As far as the progress of Ayyubid affairs is concerned, this part of the chronicle is initially a record of the rise to dominance of Saladin's brother, al-'Ādil Abū Bakr. Then follows the account of the Fifth Crusade against Damietta, which is presented in one of Ibn al-Athīr's continuous narratives that go beyond the basic annalistic framework. He comments on the cooperation and unusual mutual trust of the three sons of al-'Ādil, rulers of discrete entities, in their response to the Frankish threat. Ibn al-Athīr attributes to the Ayyubids the belief, which perhaps at one time he himself held, that the Crusaders were a greater danger to Islam than were the Mongols (see below) because their aim was lasting conquest. Of course, the Ayyubids were aware that the Damietta Crusade was a threat to Egypt, an attack on the basis of their power, which explains their willingness to cooperate to meet it. However, it is implicit in the narrative that this harmony weakens as rivalries develop. These rivalries had a significant effect on the response to the expedition of Frederick II and led to the cession of Jerusalem.

Events in the eastern lands of Islam loom large in this part of *al-Kāmil*. The narrative follows the complicated relations of the various states. We read of the fortunes of the Ghurids, their struggle with the Qarakhitay and their steady expansion into India. In lands to the west of the Jaxartes, in Transoxania, they gave way to the further rise of the Khwārazm Shāhs. Under Khwārazm Shāh Muḥammad this state achieved its widest expansion and dominance so that it came to threaten the Abbasid caliph in Iraq but was catastrophically swept away by the arrival of the Mongols. Ibn al-Athīr remarks that the very success of the Khwārazm Shāh in removing most of his rivals contributed to the completeness of his state's collapse.

The Mongols (or the Tatars as Ibn al-Athīr calls them throughout) are introduced, under the year 617/1220–21, in a well-known, extended section, which is rather more consciously crafted from the literary point of view. This section attempts to give their origins, describe their ways and follow the course of their astonishing early incursions. It portrays the shock and horror of the Mongols' arrival at a series of places. The younger historian, al-Nasawī, explicitly says that he does not intend to catalogue all those events in detail, because they are nothing but repeated slaughter and mayhem.[3] One wonders whether there is not an implicit criticism of Ibn al-Athīr here, who does recount massacre after massacre and horror after horror in a somewhat repetitive manner of expression.

One should note that Ibn al-Athīr records fluctuating views of the Mongol incursions. At one time he seems to regard them as a passing threat and not as permanent conquerors (see pp. [**398–9**]), even to the extent that he says under the year 614/1217–18, in the context of an expression of gratitude to God for saving the Muslims from the Franks at Damietta, 'He also saved them from the evil of the Tatars, as we shall record, God willing.' Ibn al-Athīr was, after all, at this stage of his chronicle recording ongoing events as information reached him. Al-Nasawī too, at one moment, appears to say that the Muslims must keep their heads down, as it were, and wait for the passing of the storm.[4] Later again in his narrative, Ibn al-Athīr hints at some return to normality and a revival of civic life under the Mongols in Transoxania, although Khurasan remains ruined and depopulated.[5] Nevertheless, Ibn al-Athīr in no way underestimates the destruction and loss of life that the Mongols did cause and is anxious that future generations should not accuse him and other historians of exaggeration and fail to give credence to their accounts. One must acknowledge that from his own point of view Ibn al-Athīr was correct to look upon the Mongol incursions as the first and only act of a tragedy that had fallen on western Iran, Iraq and Mesopotamia. The final act was to come after his death with Hulagu's invasion, the end of the Abbasid caliphate and the establishment of the Ilkhanid state.

Fluctuations are also evident in Ibn al-Athīr's reactions to the erratic career of Jalāl al-Dīn, the son of Khwārazm Shāh, who waged an ultimately unsuccessful war against the Mongols. He is praised for his victories for Islam, in particular against the Georgians, but his barbarous treatment of Muslims finally brings condemnation. Towards the end of the chronicle there are contradictory reports about his fate, although his death is confirmed in the end.

The uncertainties about Jalāl al-Dīn's fate are typical of an increasing sense of disorder in the latter parts of the chronicle. The scope of Ibn al-Athīr's vision shrinks and sources of information are more random. This mirrors the growing fragmentation of the Islamic polity around the author. There are more signs that the text was not fully revised and one or two promised cross-references are not followed up. The author appears to lose confidence in his narrative. Various

---

3 Nasawī, 116.
4 Nasawī, 111.
5 See p. [**495**].

material and its relevant dates that have been dealt with in the extended sections that range beyond the annalistic framework are repeated and the chronological thread is to some extent confused. We do not know enough about Ibn al-Athīr's situation when he was writing the final parts of his work but there are clearly indications of a lack of revision– and this is perhaps not surprising, given the general circumstances.

In a work of this relatively wide scope it is inevitable that the reader is assailed by many names of persons and names of places. Every effort has been made to identify them. I believe that this has been achieved for most of the names of dynasties and prominent figures, although it must be admitted that many of the less prominent individuals for whom Ibn al-Athīr provided an obituary notice, by a process of choice that remains inscrutable, remain empty ciphers. The notices of these religious scholars, for such most of them are, should be seen as a token acknowledgment of the ongoing tradition of learning. As for toponyms, among so many that are found over such a large geographical spread as is covered in this work, it is sadly the case that some remain unidentified, perhaps at times because they have been corrupted.

The same general practice has been followed as in the preceding two parts. The pagination of the Arabic text that has served as the base for the translation, that is, the Dār Ṣadir edition of Beirut, has been noted between square brackets in bold type. In addition, internal cross-references and references to material in Part 2 have been given to the pagination of the original. Square brackets are also used to mark text that has been added, normally for purposes of clarification or occasionally for stylistic reasons. However, when an original third-person pronoun has been turned for the sake of clarity into an appropriate personal name (one hopes correctly identified), this has not been noted.

As for dates in the text, Christian era equivalents for Hijra dates are given, again in square brackets. If the day of the week is mentioned, it may be understood that the Christian date is an exact match when no other indication is given. If, however, an equals sign (=) precedes the Christian date, this indicates that an adjustment has been made for the sake of congruity.

Although capable of presenting a telling narrative, Ibn al-Athīr, to my mind, is not an outstanding stylist. The translator hopes that he will be pardoned, if, in these present pages, he has allowed himself more latitude in the quest for readability and variety than was perhaps the case in the first two parts.

The Chronicle of Ibn al-Athīr

The Ayyūbids after Saladin and the Mongol Menace

The Year 589 [1193]

[97] Account of the circumstances of [Saladin's] family and children after his death

When Saladin died in Damascus, his eldest son al-Afḍal Nūr al-Dīn 'Alī was with him. While he was alive, Saladin had more than once made all his army swear an oath to al-Afḍal, so at his death al-Afḍal became ruler of Damascus, the coastal plain, Jerusalem, Baalbek, Ṣarkhad, Busrā, Baniyas, Hūnīn, Tibnīn and all the districts as far as Dārūm.

His son al-'Azīz 'Uthmān was in Egypt and he took control there, his rule becoming firmly based. Another son, al-Ẓāhir Ghāzī, was in Aleppo. He took control of it and all its dependencies, such as Ḥārim, Tell Bāshir, A'zāz, Barziyya, Darbsāk and others, [**98**] while Maḥmūd, son of Taqī al-Dīn 'Umar, who was in Ḥama, gave him allegiance and sided with him. Shīrkūh ibn Muḥammad ibn Shīrkūh, who was in Homs, gave his allegiance to al-Afḍal.

Al-'Ādil had already gone to Kerak, as we have mentioned,[1] and remained there securely, not presenting himself before any of his nephews. Al-Afḍal sent to him, requesting his presence. Although al-'Ādil promised to comply, he did not, so al-Afḍal repeated his message and tried to frighten him with al-'Azīz, the lord of Egypt, and with Atabeg 'Izz al-Dīn, lord of Mosul, for the latter had marched from Mosul into al-'Ādil's lands in the Jazīra, as we shall relate. Al-Afḍal said to him, 'If you come, I shall equip troops, march to your lands and keep them safe, but if you stay, my brother al-'Azīz will attack you because of your mutual hostility. If 'Izz al-Dīn takes your lands, there is nothing to protect Syria from him.' He also said to his envoy, 'If he comes back with you, [that is excellent], but if not, say to him, "I have my orders. If you come to him at Damascus, I shall return with you, but if you do not, I shall travel to al-'Azīz and swear to an alliance with him on terms of his choosing."'

When the envoy came to him, he promised to go with him, but when the envoy saw that he had nothing from him but his promise, he informed him of what he had been told about coming to terms with al-'Azīz. Thereupon al-'Ādil travelled to Damascus and al-Afḍal provided him with an army. He also sent to the lords of Homs and Hama and to his brother al-Ẓāhir Ghāzī in Aleppo, urging them to send troops with al-'Ādil to the Jazīra to defend those lands from the lord of Mosul and warning them of the consequences if they did not do so. Among other things he said the following to his brother al-Ẓāhir: 'You know the friendship[2] of the people

[1] See *Chronicle of Ibn al-Athīr (2)*, p. [**96**].

[2] Arabic *ṣuḥba*. One Ms. has *maḥabba* (love, affection).

of Syria for the Atabeg house. By God, if 'Izz al-Dīn takes Ḥarrān, the population of Aleppo will rise against you and you will surely be driven out before you know what is happening. The people of Damascus will do the same with me.' They therefore agreed to send troops with al-'Ādil. They equipped them and sent them to al-'Ādil, who had already crossed the Euphrates. [**99**] Their troops camped in the district of Edessa in the Meadow of Flowers.[3] We shall relate what al-'Ādil did, God willing.[4]

Account of Atabeg 'Izz al-Dīn's expedition to al-'Ādil's lands and his withdrawal on account of illness

When Atabeg 'Izz al-Dīn Mas'ūd ibn Mawdūd ibn Zankī, lord of Mosul,[5] heard of Saladin's death, he gathered his advisers, including Mujāhid al-Dīn Qaymāz, the great man of his state and commander of everyone in it, being his viceroy, and consulted them about what to do. They remained silent, but one of them, my brother Majd al-Dīn Abū'l-Sa'ādāt al-Mubārak, said to him, 'I think that you should set out quickly without a baggage train but with your lightly armed men and your special guard and order the rest to join you later. You should give anyone who requires anything to equip him what will allow him to set out and he should join you at Nisibis. You ought to write to the provincial rulers, such as Muẓaffar al-Dīn ibn Zayn al-Dīn, lord of Irbil, your nephew Sanjar Shāh, lord of Jazīrat ibn 'Umar and your brother 'Imād al-Dīn, lord of Sinjār and Nisibis, to inform them that you have taken the field and ask them for help and offer to swear to whatever they demand. When they see that you are on the march, they will fear you. If your brother, the lord of Sinjār and Nisibis, does not agree to cooperate, begin with Nisibis, seize it and leave someone there to hold it. Then go to Khābūr, which he also possesses, assign it [to someoneḥ] and leave its army facing your brother to prevent him from deploying, if [**100**] he has a mind to. Or you should move against Raqqa. It will not defend itself. Then proceed to Ḥarrān and Edessa. There is nobody there to hold it, neither lord nor army and no treasure. Al-'Ādil took both places from the son of Taqī al-Dīn but did not stay there to put their affairs in order. They were relying on their strength and did not expect this turn of events. When you have finished in this direction, return to deal with those who withhold allegiance and fight them. There is nothing to be fearful of in your rear, for your lands are great and there is no worry about all those behind you.' Mujāhid al-Dīn replied, 'The best course is for us to write to the provincial rulers, ask their opinion

3 Marj al-Rayḥān.

4 For a comprehensive account of the political and military situation at Saladin's death and subsequent developments, see Eddé, *Principauté ayyoubide*, 48–61.

5 The Zankid Atabeg dynasty continued to play a significant role in Mesopotamian affairs. For a breakdown of rulers and their dates, see Bosworth, *New Islamic Dynasties*, 190–91.

about action and win them over.'[6] My brother said, 'If they advise against acting, will you accept what they say?' 'No,' he said, and my brother went on, 'They will only advise against it, because they do not want our sultan to be strong because they fear him. I can just see them deceiving you as long as the Jazīra lands remain devoid of any lord or army. If someone comes here to hold on to them, they will declare their hostility to you.' He was unable to say more than this for fear of Mujāhid al-Dīn, since he saw that he favoured the view he himself had expressed. They broke up, intending to write to the provincial rulers, which they duly did and each of them advised no action until it was seen what Saladin's sons and their uncle would do. Thus they procrastinated.

Mujāhid al-Dīn repeated his messages to 'Imād al-Dīn, lord of Sinjār, with promises and blandishments. In this state of affairs they received a letter from al-'Ādil from his camp near Damascus, after he had set out from Damascus to return to his lands, in which he mentioned his brother's death and that the country was now firmly in the hands of his son al-Afḍal, as people had agreed to obey him, and that he himself was the guiding hand of al-Afḍal's state. Al-Afḍal had sent him with a large and numerous army to march to Mardīn, because he had heard that its lord had moved against some of his villages. He wrote a great deal in this vein. They thought it true and that there was no doubt about what he said, so they failed **[101]** to act and follow that [previous] plan. They sent out spies and news came to them that about 200 tents, no more, were outside Ḥarrān.[7] They then changed their minds and prepared to march, but before terms of an agreement could be decided between them and the lord of Sinjār, the Syrian troops, which al-Afḍal and others had sent, came to al-'Ādil, who was strengthened by them. Atabeg 'Izz al-Dīn moved to Nisibis, where he and his brother 'Imād al-Dīn joined forces and marched by way of Shabakhtān[8] towards Edessa. Al-'Ādil had camped near it at the Meadow of Flowers. They were greatly fearful of him.

When Atabeg 'Izz al-Dīn arrived at Tell Mawzan, he fell ill with dysentery. He stayed for a number of days too weak to move, losing a lot of blood. He feared he would die, so left the army with his brother 'Imād al-Dīn and returned without his baggage with 200 horsemen, accompanied by Mujāhid al-Dīn and my brother Majd al-Dīn. After he had reached Dunaysir, weakness overwhelmed him. He summoned my brother and wrote his last testament. Then he travelled on and entered Mosul, ill, on 1 Rajab [3 July 1193].

---

6 In *Bāhir*, 185, Mujāhid al-Dīn opposes any westward expedition in the Jazīra which would leave Sinjār, Jazīrat Ibn 'Umar and Irbil in their rear, still uncommitted and with their intentions unclear.

7 From Ḥarrān al-'Ādil made peace overtures to 'Izz al-Dīn, offering to hold Edessa, Ḥarrān and Raqqa as a fief from him, but this was not accepted (*Bāhir*, 186).

8 *Kāmil* reads Sinjār (a surprising route). In Arabic script without diacritics Sinjār could have been mistaken for Shabakhtān, which is specified as their route in *Bāhir*, 185 (cf. *Rawḍatayn*, iv, 415). Shabakhtān has been identified as an area east of Edessa and north of Ḥarrān, which included Tell Mawzan (*EI(2)*, ix, 153–4).

Account of the death of Atabeg ʿIzz al-Dīn and a little about his life

This year Atabeg ʿIzz al-Dīn Masʿūd ibn Mawdūd ibn Zankī ibn Āqsunqur, lord of Mosul, died at Mosul. We have mentioned how he returned ill. He continued ill until 29 Shaʿbān[9] [30 August 1193] and then died (God have mercy upon him). He was buried in the madrasa he had built opposite the seat of government. He had remained for more than ten days uttering nothing but the dual confession of faith and recitations from the Koran. If he spoke any other words, he asked pardon of God and then [**102**] reverted to his previous behaviour. He was granted a good end (may God be pleased with him!).

He was (God have mercy on him) of excellent character, a man of much goodness and kindness, especially to elders who had served his father. He treated them with reverence and kindness, liberality and respect, and paid attention to their words. He used to visit the pious, favour them and solicit their support. He was mild, little given to punishment and very shy. He did not speak to anyone next to him without lowering his gaze and he never said no to anything he was asked for, out of shyness and a generous nature. He performed the Pilgrimage and at Mecca (God guard it) donned the ragged garment of Sufism. He used to wear those rags every night, go out to the mosque he had built in his palace and there pray for about a third of the night.

He was tender-hearted and solicitous for his subjects. I have heard that one day he said, 'I lay awake a lot last night. The reason is that I heard the voice of a wailing woman. I thought that so-and-so's child had died, for I had heard that he was ill. I was upset and rose from my bed to walk around the roof. After a long time like this I sent a servant to the guards and he sent one of them to learn what had happened. He returned and mentioned a man I did not know. I calmed somewhat and went to sleep.' The man whose son he thought had died was not one of his own retainers but was just one of his subjects.

His death should have been mentioned later but we have treated it earlier to keep what is recorded about him as a consecutive narrative.

Account of the killing of Baktimur, lord of Khilāṭ

This year on 1 Jumādā I [5 May 1193] Sayf al-Dīn Baktimur, lord of Khilāṭ, was killed. Two months separated his killing and the death of Saladin. He made an excessive show [**103**] of exulting in Saladin's death, so God Almighty gave him no respite. When Saladin died, he rejoiced greatly. He fashioned a throne on which he sat and called himself Exalted Sultan Salaḥ al-Dīn. His title had been Sayf al-Dīn but he changed that and also took as his personal name ʿAbd al-ʿAzīz. He gave signs of being unbalanced and mad, making preparations to attack and besiege

[9] According to *Bāhir*, 186 (cf. *Rawḍatayn*, iv, 416), he died on 27 Shaʿbān/28 August.

Mayyāfāriqīn, but his death forestalled him.

His death came about as follows. Hazār Dīnārī, also one of Shāh Arman Ẓahīr al-Dīn's mamlukes, had become powerful and gathered a large following. He married Baktimur's daughter and was ambitious to rule. He arranged for someone to kill Baktimur and after his death succeeded him as ruler of Khilāṭ and its dependencies. Baktimur was a religious man, good and pious, much given to charity, good works and almsgiving, who loved the men of religion and the Sufis, to whom he was generous and much attached, as he was to all his subjects, beloved by them and just towards them. He was liberal, brave and just to his subjects and ruled them well.[10]

Miscellaneous events

This year Shihāb al-Dīn,[11] king of Ghazna, wintered in Peshawar.[12] He sent his mamluke [Quṭb al-Dīn] Aybak with many troops and ordered him to enter India to take booty and captives, and to conquer what lands he could. He did so and returned safely, he and his troops, with their hands full of spoils.

[**104**] In Ramaḍān this year [September 1193] there died Sulṭān Shāh,[13] ruler of Marv and other parts of Khurasan. His brother 'Alā' al-Dīn Tekesh succeeded, whom we shall mention under the year 590 [1194], God willing.

This year the Caliph al-Nāṣir li-Dīn Allāh ordered the building of the library in the Niẓāmiyya Madrasah at Baghdad and transferred there thousands of valuable books beyond compare. In Rabī' I [7 March–5 April 1193] the building of the hospice was completed which the caliph had also ordered to be erected at the Ṭāhirī Harem in West Baghdad on the Tigris. It was one of the most beautiful hospices and he brought to it many of the most handsome volumes.

The caliph conquered a castle in Khuzistan this year. The reason for this was that its ruler Sūsyān ibn Shumla[14] appointed a governor there who behaved badly towards its local troops. Some of them betrayed and killed him and proclaimed the caliph's watchword. The latter sent men there who took it over.

---

10 According to Ṣibṭ ibn al-Jawzī, 423, Baktimur, who left a young son, was killed by Ismā'īlīs. 'Imād al-Dīn tells that he also adopted Saladin's regnal title al-Malik al-Nāṣir, that he tried to stir up the lords of Mosul and Sinjār and that he was killed by Ismā'īlīs on 14 Jumādā I/18 May 1193 (in *Rawḍatayn*, iv, 412).

11 The Ghurid Ghiyāth al-Dīn Muḥammad ibn Sām (558–599/1163–1203) took Ghazna in 569/1173–4 and installed his younger brother there, Shihāb al-Dīn Muḥammad, who later changed his title to Mu'izz al-Dīn. This can cause confusion and it should be noted that Ibn al-Athīr calls him Shihāb al-Dīn throughout. See Jackson, *Delhi Sultanate*, 5–6.

12 Peshawar had been taken by the Ghurids in 575/1179–80; see *EI(2)*, viii, 299–300.

13 This is Sulṭān Shāh Muḥammad, son of the Khwārazm Shāh Īl Arslān.

14 Sūsyān ruled Khuzistan for twenty years until his death in 591/1195. See below, p. [**109**], and Bosworth, 'The Iranian World', 172.

Two great meteors came to earth and a great noise was heard. This was after dawn had broken and their light eclipsed the moon and the light of day.

This year Emir Dā'ūd ibn 'Īsā ibn Muḥammad ibn Abī Hāshim, emir of Mecca, died. The emirate of Mecca had continued to be held now by him and now by his brother Mukaththir up to the time he died.[15]

Also this year there died Abū'l-Rashīd al-Ḥāsib al-Baghdādī. The Caliph al-Nāṣir li-Dīn Allāh had sent him on a mission to Mosul and he died there.

---

[15] Ibn al-Qādisī says that Emir Dā'ūd, for whom he gives a fuller genealogy, died, out of office, at Nakhla in Rajab 589/July 1193 (in *Rawḍatayn*, iv, 296).

[105] The Year 590 [1193–1194]

Account of the conflict between Shihāb al-Dīn and the Indian king of Benares

Shihāb al-Dīn the Ghurid, king of Ghazna, had equipped his mamluke Quṭb al-Dīn Aybak and sent him to raid Indian lands. He entered them and killed, enslaved and plundered before returning. The king of Benares, one of the greatest kings of India, whose realm stretched from the borders of China to Malwa[1] in length and from the sea to ten days' journey from Lahore in breadth, a great kingdom, when he heard of this, assembled and mobilized his troops and set out towards the lands of Islam. The year 590 began and Shihāb al-Dīn the Ghurid marched with his troops against him. The two armies met at the Jumna,[2] a large river similar to the Euphrates, at Mosul. The Indian had 700 elephants and troops to the number, as is reported, of 1,000,000. Among his army were several Muslim emirs, who had been in those lands following their fathers and grandfathers since the days of Sultan Maḥmūd ibn Sabuktakīn, upholding the Shariah of Islam and observing their prayers and good deeds. When the Muslim and Indian armies met, a battle took place. The infidels held firm because of their great numbers and the Muslims did likewise because of their valour. However, the infidels were defeated and the Muslims gained a victory.[3] **[106]** Great was the slaughter among the Hindus, so that the land was full of their rotting corpses. Only boys and women were taken; the men were killed. Shihāb al-Dīn captured 90 elephants; as for the rest, some were killed and others fled. The king was slain. No one knew him, except that his teeth were weak at the roots and they had been fixed with a band of gold. By that token they identified him.

After the defeat of the Hindus, Shihāb al-Dīn entered Benares territory and carried away 1,400 loads of treasure. He returned to Ghazna with the elephants he had captured, including a white elephant.[4] Someone who saw it told me, 'When the elephants were taken and brought before Shihāb al-Dīn, they were ordered to kneel. All did so except the white one, for it did not kneel.' Let no one wonder at our saying that elephants kneel, for they understand what is said to them. I have witnessed an elephant in Mosul. When its mahout spoke to it, it did what it was told.

---

1 The edition has Malāwā. Malwa is a region east of Gujerat, north of the river Narmada.

2 For the location, see the following note. The edition reads Mājūn, that is, Mā-yi Jūn (Water of the Jumna or Yamuna).

3 For this victory over the Gāhaḍavālas' king, Jāyachandra, in the vicinity of Chandawār (near Etawah), which led to the occupation of Benares, see Jackson, *Delhi Sultanate*, 10.

4 For this campaign, see *Ṭabaqāt-i Naṣirī*, 470 and relevant notes.

Account of the killing of Sultan Ṭughril, Khwārazm Shāh's conquest of Rayy and the death of his brother Sulṭān Shāh

Under the year 588 [1192–3] we have mentioned how Sultan Ṭughril ibn Alp Arslān ibn Ṭughril ibn Muḥammad ibn Malikshāh ibn Alp Arslān the Saljuq got out of prison[5] and took Hamadhan and other places. There had been hostilities between him and Qutlugh Īnānj,[6] son of Pahlawān, in which the latter was defeated and took refuge in Rayy. Ṭughril then marched to Rayy and Qutlugh Īnānj sent to Khwārazm Shāh 'Alā' al-Dīn Tekesh, seeking his aid. He set out towards him in the year 588 and when they drew near to one another, Qutlugh Īnānj regretted his call to Khwārazm Shāh and feared for his own safety. He moved away and fortified himself in one of his castles. Khwārazm Shāh arrived at Rayy which he seized [**107**] and then besieged the castle of Ṭabarak, taking it in two days. Ṭughril made overtures to him and they came to a settlement. Rayy remained in Khwārazm Shāh's hands and he stationed a force there to hold it. He then returned to Khwārazm as he heard that his brother Sulṭān Shāh had attacked it. Fearful for it, he made a forced march but while on his way there news came to him that the people of Khwārazm had driven Sulṭān Shāh away and that he had been unable to approach but had withdrawn disappointed. Khwārazm Shāh wintered in Khwārazm and, when winter was over, set out for Marv to attack his brother in the year 589 [1193]. There was an exchange of envoys about making peace. While they were arranging peace terms, there came to Khwārazm Shāh an envoy from the governor of the citadel of Sarakhs belonging to his brother Sulṭān Shāh, inviting him to come so that he could surrender the citadel to him, because he had become estranged from his lord, Sulṭān Shāh. Khwārazm Shāh went to him with all speed, took over the citadel and the governor joined with him.

When Sulṭān Shāh learned of this, his strength ebbed away and his grief grew greatly. At the end of Ramaḍān 589 [29 September 1193] he died. Having heard of his death, Khwārazm Shāh immediately proceeded to Marv and took control there; indeed, he took over all his brother Sulṭān Shāh's kingdom and his treasures. He sent to his son, 'Alā' al-Dīn Muḥammad, who at that time had the title Quṭb al-Dīn, summoned him and appointed him governor of Nishapur. He also put his eldest son Malikshāh in charge of Marv. This was in Dhū'l-Ḥijja 589 [December 1193].

When the year 590 came [began 27 December 1193], Sultan Ṭughril marched to Rayy and attacked Khwārazm Shāh's men that were there. Qutlugh Īnānj fled and sent to Khwārazm Shāh, apologizing and asking a second time for his aid. This coincided with the arrival of the caliph's envoy, complaining of Ṭughril and requesting Khwārazm Shāh to attack his lands. He brought with him a diploma granting him those lands as a fief. Khwārazm Shāh left Nishapur for Rayy and was

---

[5] He had been held prisoner by Qizil Arslān, son of Īldikiz.

[6] He was a grandson of Īldikiz (1136–72), founder of the dynasty of Atabegs of Azerbayjan.

met by Qutlugh [**108**] Īnānj and his men, offering obedience. They joined forces with him. When Sultan Ṭughril heard of his arrival, his troops were scattered. He did not stop to gather them but moved against him with those he had. He was told, 'What you are doing is not the best plan. Your best course is to gather your armies.' He did not do so, for he was brave, and he completed his march. The two armies met near Rayy. Ṭughril personally charged the centre of Khwārazm Shāh's force. They encircled him, threw him from his horse and killed him on 24 Rabīʿ I [19 March 1194]. His head was carried to Khwārazm Shāh, who sent it that day to Baghdad. It was displayed there at the Nubian Gate for several days.[7]

Khwārazm Shāh proceeded to Hamadhan and took all that area. The Caliph al-Nāṣir li-Dīn Allāh had sent a troop to support Khwārazm Shāh and also sultanian robes of honour by his vizier Mu'ayyad al-Dīn ibn al-Qaṣṣāb. The latter camped a league from Hamadhan and Khwārazm Shāh sent to him, requesting his presence. Mu'ayyad al-Dīn replied, 'It is fitting that you should present yourself and don the robe in my tent.' Messengers went to and fro about this. Khwārazm Shāh was told, 'This is a plot against you, so that you attend and he arrests you', so he set out intending to seize him. Mu'ayyad al-Dīn withdrew and took refuge on a certain mountain where he could resist. Khwārazm Shāh returned to Hamadhan. When he took Hamadhan and those regions, he entrusted them to Qutlugh Īnānj. He assigned much of them to his mamlukes, command of whom he gave to Mayājuq,[8] and then returned to Khwārazm.

Account of how the caliph's vizier went to Khuzistan and took it

In Shaʿbān of this year [22 July–19 August 1194] the Caliph al-Nāṣir li-Dīn Allāh invested the deputy vizier, Mu'ayyad al-Dīn Abū 'Abd Allāh Muḥammad ibn 'Alī, known as Ibn al-Qaṣṣāb, with the office of [**109**] vizier and gave him full authority. He set out in Ramaḍān [20 August–18 September 1194] and marched to Khuzistan. The reason for this was that he had initially served in Khuzistan and administered districts there, where he acquired followers, friends and acquaintances. He got to know the country, which way to enter and conquer it. When he held the office of deputy vizier in Baghdad, he suggested to the caliph that he send him with an army to conquer Khuzistan for him. It was his plan, when he had taken the country and become established there, to remain, making a show of allegiance but monopolising authority to be personally secure.

---

7 Abū Shāma, *Dhayl*, 6, has further details. His head entered Baghdad on a pole in Jumādā I/24 April–23 May 1194 and was later entrusted to the 'Head Store' (*khizānat al-ru'ūs*). Although a rat ate the nose and ears, the head survived until 601/1204–5, when a fire at the store destroyed it and all other 'exhibits'.

8 So named in *Kāmil*, but called Mayanchuq in Juvainī, *History*, 304–7, 310–11 and Bosworth, 'The Iranian World', 182.

It happened that the local lord, the son of Shumla,[9] died. His children quarrelled after his death and one of them wrote to Mu'ayyad al-Dīn, seeking his aid because of the long-term friendship between them. His desire for the land grew strong, so troops were equipped and sent with him to Khuzistan. He arrived in the year 591 [1195] and between him and the local powers there followed negotiations and hostilities for which they were not strong enough. He took the castles of al-Nāẓir, Kākird, Lāmūj and other fortresses and castle and sent the Shumla clan, the rulers of Khuzistan, to Baghdad, where they arrived in Rabīʿ I [13 February–14 March 1195].[10]

Account of al-ʿAzīz's siege of Damascus

This year al-ʿAzīz ʿUthmān, son of Saladin, the lord of Egypt, came to Damascus and put it under siege. His older brother al-Afḍal ʿAlī was there and I myself was present in Damascus at that time.[11] He camped in the area of the Pebble Hippodrome. Al-Afḍal sent to his uncle, al-ʿĀdil Abū Bakr ibn Ayyūb, the lord of the Jazīra lands, asking him for support, for he trusted him greatly and relied upon him. Evidence of this has already been given. [**110**] Al-ʿĀdil set out for Damascus, he and also al-Ẓāhir Ghāzī, a son of Saladin and lord of Aleppo, Nāṣir al-Dīn Muḥammad ibn Taqī al-Dīn, lord of Hama, and Asad al-Dīn Shīrkūh ibn Muḥammad ibn Shīrkūh, lord of Homs, along with the army of Mosul and elsewhere. All these gathered at Damascus and agreed to defend the place, in the knowledge that, if al-ʿAzīz took it, he would seize their lands.

When al-ʿAzīz saw their unity, he realized that he did not have the ability to take the city. Thereupon envoys were exchanged to discuss peace, and an agreement was made that Jerusalem and the neighbouring parts of Palestine should be for al-ʿAzīz, that Damascus, Tiberias and its dependencies and the Jordan Valley should remain al-Afḍal's as they were, that al-Afḍal should give Jabala and Lattakia on the Syrian coast to his brother al-Ẓāhir and that al-ʿĀdil should have his original fief in Egypt. They all concurred in this. Al-ʿAzīz returned to Egypt and every [other] one of the princes went back to his lands.

---

9 i.e. Sūsyān ibn Shumla, lord of Khuzistan. See above, p. [**104**].

10 According to Sibṭ ibn al-Jawzī, 445, Sūsyān and ʿAlī, sons of Shumla, entered Baghdad in Ṣafar 591/ 15 January–12 February 1195.

11 Perhaps not unconnected with his brother Ḍiyā' al-Dīn's being al-Afḍal's vizier and at that time a dubious influence on him and one which al-ʿĀdil tried to remove (see Sibṭ ibn al-Jawzī, 441–2).

Miscellaneous events

This year there was an earthquake during Rabīʿ I [24 February–25 March 1194] in the Jazīra, Iraq and many of the lands. It caused the ruin of the cemetery which is by the shrine of the Commander of the Faithful ʿAlī (peace be upon him).[12]

In Jumādā II [24 May–21 June 1194] the Zughb and other Arab tribes united and attacked Medina, the city of the Prophet (may God bless him and give him peace). Hāshim ibn Qāsim, the brother of the emir of Medina, went out against them and fought, but he was killed. The emir of Medina had gone to Syria. That was why the Arabs were tempted to attack.

This year in Shaʿbān [22 July–19 August 1194] the Cadi Abū'l-Ḥasan Aḥmad ibn Muḥammad ibn ʿAbd al-Ṣamad al-Ṭarsūsī al-Ḥalabī died. He was one of the righteous servants of God (may God Almighty have mercy on him).

---

[12] The mausoleum of the Imam ʿAlī ibn Abī Ṭālib is situated at Najaf in Iraq.

[111] The Year 591 [1194–1195]

How the caliph's vizier took Hamadhan and other parts of the lands of the 'Ajam

We have related how Mu'ayyad al-Dīn ibn al-Qaṣṣāb took Khuzistan. After he had done so, he went to Maysān[1] in Khuzistan. He was joined by Qutlugh Īnānj ibn Pahlawān, the ruler of the country (it has already been mentioned how Khwārazm Shāh conquered it) along with a number of emirs. The caliph's vizier gave [Qutlugh Īnānj] a generous and friendly reception. The reason for his coming was that battles had taken place between him and Khwārazm Shāh's army, led by Mayājuq, at Zanjān. They had fought and Qutlugh Īnānj and his troops were defeated. He sought out the caliph's forces to seek refuge with Mu'ayyad al-Dīn, the vizier, who gave him horses, tents and other things he needed. He gave him and the emirs with him robes of honour and they departed for Kirmānshāhān.[2] From there they went to Hamadhan, where were Khwārazm Shāh's son, Mayājuq, and the army they had. When the caliphal army drew near, the Khwārazmian troops left and went to Rayy, so the vizier took control of Hamadhan in Shawwāl of this year [8 September–6 October 1195]. Later he departed, followed by Qutlugh Īnanj, and they took over every town they passed, for example Kharraqān, Mazdaqān, Saveh and Āveh.[3] They went on towards Rayy, which the Khwārazmians also abandoned to go to Khuwār of Rayy. Again the vizier sent an army after them and the Khwārazmians left for [**112**] Dāmghān, Bisṭām and Jurjān. The caliphal troops returned to Rayy, where they remained. Qutlugh Īnānj and the emirs with him agreed to disobey the vizier and the caliphal troops because they saw the land devoid of Khwārazm Shāh's forces and were eager to seize it. They entered Rayy, which the caliph's vizier then besieged and, after Qutlugh Īnānj had abandoned it, seized control there. The troops sacked it and the vizier ordered a proclamation that plundering should cease.

Qutlugh Īnānj and the emirs with him proceeded to Āveh, where there was a prefect of the vizier, who barred their entry. They moved away and the vizier set out on their tracks towards Hamadhan. He heard, while on his way, that Qutlugh Īnānj had gathered an army and made for Karaj, where he camped in a pass. The

---

1 A district, the chief town of which is al-Madhār, between Wāsiṭ and Basra (Krawulsky, 493).

2 Otherwise known as Kirmānshāh or Qarmīsīn (Krawulsky, 371).

3 Kharraqān is the name of a district in Iraq al-'Ajam and also a town in the neighbourhood of Hamadhan (Krawulsky, 264; Yāqūt, ii, 424–5). For Mazdaqān, see Krawulsky, 371. Āveh is both a district and a town on the highway from Sulṭāniyya to Isfahan; see Krawulsky, 233–4 and *EI(2)*, i, 756, s.v. Āwa.

vizier followed them and, after drawing near, they met in a fierce battle. Qutlugh Īnānj was defeated but himself escaped. The vizier left the battlefield for Hamadhan, outside which he camped and remained for about three months. The envoy of Khwārazm Shāh Tekesh came to him. He had sought him to protest at his seizure of the land from his forces and demand its restitution and the settlement of peace terms. The vizier did not accept this, so Khwārazm Shāh Tekesh set out for Hamadhan on forced marches.

The vizier, Mu'ayyad al-Dīn ibn al-Qaṣṣāb, died at the beginning of Sha'bān [592] [July 1196]. A pitched battle followed between [Khwārazm Shāh] and the caliphal army in the middle of Sha'bān 592 [15 July 1196] and many were killed from both armies. The caliphal army was defeated and the Khwārazmians took much booty from them. Khwārazm Shāh, after he had conquered Hamadhan, dug up the vizier from his grave, cut off his head and sent it to Khwārazm, claiming that he had killed him in battle. Subsequently Khwārazm Shāh received news from Khurasan that necessitated his return there, so he left these territories and returned to Khurasan.

[113] Account of Ibn 'Abd al-Mu'min's expedition against the Franks in Andalusia

In Sha'bān this year [11 July–8 August 1195] Abū Yūsuf Ya'qūb ibn Yūsuf ibn 'Abd al-Mu'min,[4] the lord of the Maghrib and Andalusia, attacked Frankish territory in Andalusia. The reason was that Alfonso,[5] the Frankish king there, whose capital was the city of Toledo, wrote a letter to Ya'qūb, the text of which is as follows:[6]

> In Your name, O God, creator of the heavens and the earth. Now, O emir, it is not unknown to every man of solid intelligence nor to a man of understanding and keen mind that you are the emir of the true Islamic community, as I am the emir of Christendom and that you are one who is not unaware of the Andalusian leaders' state of feebleness, lack of commitment, neglect of their subjects and abandonment to ways of ease, while I humiliate them, empty the lands, enslave the offspring, mutilate the middle-aged and slay the young men. You have no excuse for failing to come to their aid. Your arm is powerful enough to allow you and you believe that God has made it your duty to fight ten of us with one of you. Now God has lightened your task, knowing that there is a weakness in you. He has made it your duty to

4 A Ms of *Kāmil* correctly supplies 'ibn Yūsuf', as 'Abd al-Mu'min (1130–63), the founder of the Almohad empire, was Abū Yūsuf's grandfather. His father was Abū Ya'qūb Yūsuf (1163–84).

5 i.e. Alfonso VIII of Castile.

6 A version of this letter is in Sibṭ ibn al-Jawzī, 446–7.

> fight two of us with one of you. We shall now fight a number of you with one of us and you will be unable to defend yourselves and incapable of resistance.
>
> I have been told of you that you have begun to assemble [troops] and you have looked upon the mount of battle and yet you procrastinate year after year. You advance one step and take another backwards. I am not sure whether cowardice has delayed you more or distrust in what has been revealed to you. Moreover I have been told of you that you do not find a path to war in case perhaps you cannot stomach involvement [**114**] in it. Here I say to you what will give you comfort and I excuse you. Now it is for you to swear truly to me with compacts, undertakings and oaths that you will come with all your men in ships and galleys or I will cross to you with all mine and challenge you in whatever spot is dearest to you. If the day is yours, then great booty shall came to you and a gift will be presented you; if the day is mine, my hand shall be dominant over you. I shall claim the leadership of both communities and the command of both peoples. God will facilitate His will and bring the blessing of good fortune by His favour. There is no lord but He and no good but His good.

When his letter arrived and Ya'qūb had read it, he wrote this [Koranic] verse at the head of it: 'Return to them, for we shall surely come to them with troops that they are powerless to withstand and we shall surely drive them out, abashed and humbled.'[7] He then sent it back, gathered together great armies from the Muslims and crossed the straits to Andalusia.

It is said that the reason for his crossing to Andalusia was the following. When Ya'qūb fought the Franks in the year 586 [1190] and made peace with them, one Frankish party remained discontented with the peace, as we have mentioned.[8] At the present time this party gathered a body of Franks and invaded Islamic territory, killing, enslaving, plundering and taking captives, and caused severe disruption. This came to Ya'qūb's attention, so he gathered troops and crossed the straits into Andalusia with an army that no open plain could contain. The Franks heard of this and brought together their men from far and near, who came eager for the fight, trusting in victory because of their numbers. They met on 9 Sha'bān [19 July 1195] north of Cordoba at the castle of Rabāḥ,[9] in a place known as the Meadow of Iron, and fought a fierce battle. Fortune initially went against the Muslims but then it turned against the Franks, who fled [**115**] in a most terrible rout. The Muslims were victorious over them. 'He made the word of the infidels the most lowly and the word of God the most exalted. God is powerful and wise.'[10] The number of the Franks who were killed was 164,000 and 13,000 were taken prisoner. The Muslims

---

[7] Koran, xxvii, 37.

[8] See *Chronicle of Ibn al-Athīr (2)*, p. [**58**].

[9] In the district of Toledo, west of that city (Yāqūt, ii, 747).

[10] Koran, ix, 40.

took much booty, 143,000 tents, 46,000 horses, 100,000 mules and 100,000 donkeys. Ya'qūb had proclaimed to the army, 'Whoever takes any booty may keep it, apart from weapons and armour.' A count was made of what was brought to him and there were more than 70,000 cuirasses. Among the Muslims about 20,000 were killed.[11]

Abū Yūsuf pursued the Franks when they fled in defeat. He saw they had taken the castle of Rabāḥ but had left it in fear and terror. He took it and placed a governor there and a force to hold it, and then returned to Seville.

As for Alfonso, after his defeat he shaved his head, inverted his cross and took to riding a donkey. He swore that he would not ride a horse or a mule until Christendom was victorious. He assembled great hosts, news of which reached Ya'qūb, who sent to the Maghrib, Marrakech and elsewhere, calling people to arms without compulsion. A great crowd of volunteers and enlisted men came to him. They met again in battle in Rabī' I 592 [February 1196] and the Franks were badly defeated. The Muslims seized as booty what money, weapons and mounts they had with them. Ya'qūb then marched to Toledo which they put under siege and attacked fiercely. He cut down its trees and carried out raids on the surrounding districts, where he conquered several fortresses and killed the men, enslaved the women, destroyed the houses and razed the walls. Christendom was weakened at that time and the cause of Islam in Andalusia grew strong. Ya'qūb returned to Seville, where he stayed a while.

[116] When the year 593 [1196–7] arrived, he marched out into Frankish lands and acted as he had on the first and second occasions. The Franks found their territory squeezed and they were humiliated. Their princes gathered and sent asking for peace. He granted their request, having first intended to refuse, wishing to persist with the Jihad until he finished with them. However, he received news of 'Alī ibn Isḥāq, the Almoravid from Majorca, that he had perpetrated the dreadful deeds in Ifrīqiya that we shall relate. He therefore abandoned his purpose, made peace with them for five years and returned to Marrakech at the end of the year 593 [ended November 1197].

Account of the doings of the Almoravid in Ifrīqiya

When Abū Yūsuf Ya'qūb, lord of the Maghrib, crossed to Andalusia, as we have mentioned, and remained waging the Jihad for three years, information about him was cut off from Ifrīqiya. The ambitions of 'Alī ibn Isḥāq,[12] the Almoravid from Majorca, increased. He was in the desert with the Arabs and he reverted to his

[11] This was the battle of Alarcos, in which Alfonso VIII of Castile was defeated (O'Callaghan, *Medieval Spain*, 243–4).

[12] One of the Banū Ghāniya, the Almoravid governors of Spain (lost in 1148) and the Balearics. 'Alī had deposed his brother Muḥammad, who favoured submission to the Almohads, and had invaded Ifrīqiya. For more details, see Abun-Nasr, *Maghrib*, 114–16.

attacks on Ifrīqiya. His troops spread throughout the land, ruined it and perpetrated many wicked acts there. The culture of these lands was effaced and underwent a great change. The lands became devoid of civilized life, 'collapsed on its roof timbers'.[13]

He wished to go to Bougie and besiege it because Ya'qūb was preoccupied with the Jihad. He declared that, when he had control of Bougie, he would proceed to the Maghrib. News of this reached Ya'qūb, so he made peace with the Franks, as we have related, and returned to Marrakech, intending to attack him and expel him from the land, as he had done in the year 581 [1185–6][14] and we have already told of that.

[117] How the caliph's army took Isfahan

During this year the Caliph al-Nāṣir li-Dīn Allāh equipped an army and sent it to Isfahan. Its commander was Sayf al-Dīn Ṭughril, the fief-holder of Liḥf in Iraq. At Isfahan there was an army of Khwārazm Shāh with his son. The people of Isfahan disliked them, so Ṣadr al-Dīn al-Khujandī, the head of the Shāfi'īs in Isfahan, wrote to the Diwan at Baghdad, offering on his own initiative to surrender the city to any troops that might arrive from[15] the Diwan. He had authority over the whole population of Isfahan.

Troops were dispatched and, when they arrived at Isfahan, camped outside the city. Khwārazm Shāh's troops departed and returned to Khurasan. Some of the caliph's force followed them, harassing them and snatching those they could from their rearguard. The [main] force of the caliphal army entered Isfahan and took possession of it.

Account of the beginning of the career of Kūkjeh and his taking power in Rayy, Hamadhan and elsewhere

After Khwārazm Shāh had returned to Khurasan, as we have mentioned, the mamlukes who belonged to Pahlawān and the emirs came to an agreement and placed Kūkjeh[16] in command of themselves, he being one of the leading mamlukes of Pahlawān. They seized control of Rayy and the neighbouring lands and then went to Isfahan to expel the Khwārazmians. When they drew near, they heard that the caliph's army was there, so Kūkjeh sent to the caliph's mamluke, Sayf al-Dīn

---

13 Koran, xxii, 45.

14 For this earlier conflict which lasted until 583/1187, recorded in the annal for 581/1185–6, see *Chronicle of Ibn al-Athīr (2)*, pp. [**519–22**].

15 The preposition *min* is missing in the text before *al-Dīwān*. Cf. *Kāmil* (Thornberg), xii, 76.

16 In Bosworth, 'The Iranian World', 183: Gōkche.

Ṭughril, offering himself as a servant of the Diwan and pretending [**118**] submission and that he had only moved against Isfahan to pursue the Khwārazmian forces and, seeing that they had left Isfahan, he followed their tracks but failed to overtake them. The caliph's army then left Isfahan to go to Hamadhan.

As for Kūkjeh, he followed the Khwārazmians to Ṭabas, part of Ismā'īlī territory, then returned, made for Isfahan and took control of it. He sent to Baghdad, requesting that he might have Rayy, Khuwār of Rayy, Saveh, Qumm, Qāshān and what pertains to them up to the border of Mazdaqān, while Isfahan, Hamadhan, Zanjān and Qazwin would belong to the caliph's Diwan. This was granted, and a diploma for what he requested was engrossed. He became an important figure and his power great. His troops increased in number and he lorded it over his comrades.

Account of al-Azīz's second siege of Damascus and his defeat

This year al-'Azīz 'Uthmān, the son of Saladin, marched with his troops from Egypt to Damascus, intending to besiege it, and withdrew defeated.

The reason for this was that his father's mamlukes in his service, known as the Ṣalāḥiyya, Fakhr al-Dīn Jarkas, Sirā Sunqur, Qarājā and others, had turned against al-Afḍal 'Alī, another son of Saladin, because he had driven away some of their number in his service, such as Maymūn al-Qaṣrī, Sunqur the Elder, Aybak and others. They continually warned al-'Azīz of his brother, saying, 'The Kurds and the Asadī mamlukes in the Egyptian army want your brother. We fear that they will lean towards him and oust you from the country. Your best plan is to take Damascus.' He therefore made the expedition of the past year but withdrew, as we have related. This present year he made his preparations for an expedition. News of this reached al-Afḍal, who left Damascus to go to his uncle al-'Ādil. He joined him [**119**] at Qal'at Ja'bar and called on him for aid. Leaving him, he went to Aleppo to his brother al-Ẓāhir Ghāzī and asked him for aid too. Al-'Ādil marched from Qal'at Ja'bar to Damascus, preceded al-Afḍal and entered the city. Because of his trust in him al-Afḍal had instructed his lieutenants to allow him access to the citadel. Later al-Afḍal returned to Damascus from Aleppo and al-'Azīz arrived near Damascus. The commander of the Asadiyya, namely Sayf al-Dīn Ayāzkūsh, and some others and also some of the Kurds, including Abū'l-Hayjā' the Fat, sent to al-Afḍal and al-'Ādil, announcing that they sided with them and were of their party, and bidding them join them against al-'Azīz and leave Damascus so that they could give him up to them.

The reason why they turned against al-'Azīz and favoured al-Afḍal was that the former, when he became ruler of Egypt, favoured the Nāṣirī mamlukes,[17] promoted and trusted them and paid no attention to those [other] emirs, who resented this

[17] i.e. the mamlukes of Saladin. Nāṣirī is an adjectival form derived from his regnal title al-Nāṣir (the Victorious). The collective form is al-Nāṣiriyya.

and inclined to his brother. So they sent to al-Afḍal and al-ʿĀdil, who agreed to this. A settlement was reached in the presence of envoys from the emirs, that al-Afḍal would rule Egypt and hand Damascus to his uncle al-ʿĀdil. They both came out of Damascus and those whom we have named joined them. Al-ʿAzīz's position was untenable, so he returned in flight, making forced marches for fear of pursuit and hardly crediting his escape. His followers fell away one by one until he reached Egypt.

As for al-ʿĀdil and al-Afḍal, they sent to Jerusalem, where al-ʿAzīz had a governor, and he surrendered the city to them. They then both set out for Egypt with the Asadiyya and the Kurds in their service. Al-ʿĀdil saw the army's support for and unity behind al-Afḍal and feared that he might take Egypt and not hand over Damascus to him, so he thereupon sent secretly to al-ʿAzīz ordering him to be steadfast and put men in the city of Bilbays to hold it. He guaranteed that he would stop al-Afḍal and others from engaging the men there. Al-ʿAzīz placed the Nāṣiriyya and their commander Fakhr al-Dīn Jarkas there along with others. Al-ʿĀdil and al-Afḍal came to Bilbays and besieged the Nāṣiriyya within. **[120]** Al-Afḍal wanted to engage them or to leave them and proceed to Cairo, but was allowed neither course by al-ʿĀdil, who said, 'These are the soldiers of Islam. If they fight with one another, who will repel the infidel enemy? There is no need for this. The lands are yours and under your authority. If you attack Fustat and Cairo and take them by force, the awe felt for this land will be lost and the enemy will be ambitious for it. It holds no one who can keep you at bay.'

He followed this sort of line with him and the days passed by. He sent secretly to al-ʿAzīz, ordering him to send Qāḍī al-Fāḍil, who was much respected by the house of Saladin because of the high standing he had held with Saladin. He attended on them and held peace talks. The discussion waxed and waned, and all plans were nullified. It was agreed that al-Afḍal should have Jerusalem, all of Palestine, Tiberias, the Jordan and all he already possessed, and that al-ʿĀdil should have his old fief and be resident in Egypt with al-ʿAzīz. Al-ʿĀdil chose this just because the Asadiyya and the Kurds did not want al-ʿAzīz but were united behind him, so al-ʿAzīz would be unable to stop him doing what he wanted. When this settlement had been reached and mutual oaths sworn, al-Afḍal returned to Damascus and al-ʿĀdil stayed in Egypt with al-ʿAzīz.

Miscellaneous events

On 19 Dhū'l-Qaʿda [25 October 1195] a great fire broke out in Baghdad at the Arcade of the Cistern. The quarter opposite it was burnt down, as was the shop of Ibn al-Bakhīl, the *harīsa*[18] seller. It is said that the fire began in Ibn al-Bakhīl's house.

[18] A dish made of meat and burghul (cracked wheat).

[121]

The Year 592 [1195–1196]

Account of Shihāb al-Dīn's conquest of Thangīr and other Indian territory

This year Shihāb al-Dīn the Ghurid, lord of Ghazna, went to India and besieged the fortress of Thangīr,[1] a large, strongly fortified castle. After a period of siege those within asked for terms to surrender the place. He granted them and received its surrender. He remained with them for ten days until he had organized its troops and affairs, and then departed for the fortress of Gwalior,[2] a distance of five days' journey away. On the way there is a large river, which he crossed and came to Gwalior, a vast, strong and well-defended fortress on a high hill beyond the range of either a trebuchet's stone or an arrow. He spent the whole of Ṣafar [January 1196] besieging it, without achieving any objective. Then the defenders made contact with him about making peace. He agreed on the basis that the fortress should remain in their hands in return for their paying a tribute. They brought him an elephant with a golden howdah. He departed for the lands of Āy Waswar (?), which he raided and plundered. He took more prisoners and captives than any person could manage to count and then returned safely to Ghazna.

How al-'Ādil took Damascus from al-Afḍal

On 27 Rajab this year [26 June 1196] al-'Ādil Abū Bakr ibn Ayyūb took the city of Damascus from his nephew al-Afḍal 'Alī, son of Saladin.[3]

[122] The most telling reason for this was al-Afḍal's trust in al-'Ādil. His trust went so far as to allow him to enter his city when he himself was absent. His brother al-Ẓāhir Ghāzī, lord of Aleppo, had sent to him to say, 'Exclude our uncle from our affairs, for no good will come to us from him. I shall follow you in whatever you wish. I know him better than you and am closer to him. He is my uncle as he is yours, but I am married to his daughter. If I knew that he wished you well, I would be friendlier to him than you are.' Al-Afḍal replied, 'You have a bad opinion of everybody. How does it benefit our uncle to damage us? If our word is united and we send troops with him from all of us, he will conquer lands greater than ours. Otherwise we shall gain evil repute.'[4]

---

1 Thangīr or Tahangarh is the necessary emendation for the edition's B.h.n.k.r. See Jackson, *Delhi Sultanate*, 10–11

2 See *EI(2)*, ii, 1143–4, s.v. Gwāliyār.

3 According to 'Imād al-Dīn (*Rawḍatayn*, iv, 406) al-'Ādil took control of Damascus in Sha'bān/July 1196.

4 Since the 'otherwise' is somewhat forced here, one might emend the verb by changing the

Of the reasons this was the most telling, although not everyone knows what they were. As for another, we have mentioned al-ʿĀdil and al-Afḍal's expedition to Egypt and their siege of Bilbays, the peace they made with al-ʿAzīz and al-Ādil's remaining in Egypt with him. When he stayed with him, he won him over and planned with him to march to Damascus, take it from his brother and hand it over to him. He set out along with him from Egypt to Damascus, which they put under siege. They won to their side an emir of al-Afḍal's, called ʿIzz al-Dīn ibn Abī Ghālib al-Ḥimṣī, to whom al-Afḍal was very kind and whom he relied on and trusted greatly. To him he entrusted one of Damascus's gates, called the East Gate, to hold it. However, he inclined towards al-ʿAzīz and al-ʿĀdil, and promised to open the gate to them, through which their army could make a surprise entry into the city. He opened the gate on 27 Rajab [26 June] at early evening and allowed al-ʿĀdil with a detachment of his men to enter. Before al-Afḍal had any inkling of this, his uncle was already in Damascus and al-ʿAzīz had mounted up and taken a position at the Green Hippodrome, west of Damascus.

When al-Afḍal realized that the city had fallen, he went out to his brother at sunset, [**123**] met with him and then both entered the city, where they met al-ʿĀdil, who had taken up residence in the [former] house of Asad al-Dīn Shīrkūh, and they held talks. Al-ʿĀdil and al-ʿAzīz had agreed to give al-Afḍal the impression that they would leave the city in his hands, because they feared that he might gather the troops he had, turn on them with the mob also on his side and drive them out of the city, for al-ʿĀdil did not have a large force. He sent al-Afḍal back to the citadel, himself spent the night in Shīrkūh's house, while al-ʿĀziz went out to the camp and spent the night there.

The next day al-ʿĀdil went out to his pavilion. He stayed there while his troops were in the city and every day al-Afḍal would come out and meet with both of them. Thus matters continued for some days and then they both sent to him and ordered him to vacate the citadel and surrender the city in return for being given the castle of Ṣarkhad but surrendering all the dependencies of Damascus. Al-Afḍal came out and lodged in a pavilion outside the city to the west. Al-ʿAzīz took over and entered the citadel and remained there for several days. One day he held a drinking session and after wine had taken effect on him he suggested in a remark that he would restore the city to al-Afḍal. This was immediately reported to al-ʿĀdil, who came to the session straightaway, while al-ʿAzīz was still drunk and importuned him until he yielded the citadel to him. Al-ʿAzīz left and returned to Egypt, while al-Afḍal travelled to Ṣarkhad. Al-ʿĀḍil was claiming that al-Afḍal had plotted to kill him and that that was the reason why he took Damascus. Al-Afḍal denied this and declared his innocence. 'And God will judge between them on the Day of Resurrection concerning that in which they differ.'[5]

---

diacritical points to *nuzīḥ*. The translation would then be: 'and we shall do away with evil repute'.

[5] Koran, ii, 113.

Miscellaneous events

In Muḥarram of this year [6 December 1195–4 January 1196] a violent wind blew in Iraq, all the sky became black and red sand fell. The people were greatly disturbed and proclaimed 'God is great!' Lights were lit during the day.

[124] This year Ṣadr al-Dīn Maḥmūd ibn 'Abd al-Laṭīf ibn Muḥammad ibn Thābit al-Khujandī, the head of the Shāfi'īs in Isfahan, was killed. He was killed there by Falak al-Dīn Sunqur the Tall, the prefect of Isfahan. He came to Baghdad in the year 588 [1192], settled there and became inspector of the Niẓāmiyya Madrasah in Baghdad. When Mu'ayyad al-Dīn Ibn al-Qaṣṣāb went to Khuzistan, he accompanied him and then, when the vizier became ruler of Isfahan, Ibn al-Khujandī resided there in his house, his power and his office. Some dispute occurred between him and Sunqur the Tall, the prefect of Isfahan, who put him to death.

In Ramaḍān [August 1196] Mujīr al-Dīn Abū'l-Qāsim Maḥmūd ibn al-Mubārak al-Baghdādī, the Shāfi'ī lawyer, lectured in the Niẓāmiyya Madrasah at Baghdad.

In Shawwāl [September 1196] Naṣīr al-Dīn Nāṣir ibn Mahdī al-'Alawī al-Rāzī was appointed deputy vizier in Baghdad. He had come to Baghdad when Ibn al-Qaṣṣāb became ruler of Rayy.

This year Abū Ṭālib Yaḥyā ibn Sa'īd ibn Ziyāda took charge of the Chancery in Baghdad. He was an outstanding secretary and the author of excellent poetry.

The following died this year:

Fakhr al-Dīn Maḥmūd ibn 'Alī al-Qūfānī, the Shāfi'ī lawyer, in Ṣafar [January 1196] at Kufa when returning from the Pilgrimage. He was one of the leading pupils of Muḥammad ibn Yaḥyā.[6]

Abū'l-Ghanā'im Muḥammad ibn 'Alī ibn al-Mu'allim, the poet from Hurth,[7] so written, which is a village in the district of Wāsiṭ, at the age of ninety-one.

The vizier, Mu'ayyad al-Dīn Abū'l-Faḍl Muḥammad ibn 'Alī ibn al-Qaṣṣāb on 4 Sha'bān [3 July 1196] at Hamadhan. We have already related sufficient to indicate his competence and his ability.[8]

---

6 Emend *aṣḥābi-hi* to *aṣḥāb*. Muḥammad ibn Yaḥyā al-Nīsābūrī, a student of al-Ghazālī, was killed by the Oghuz in 548/1153 (*Wāfī*, v, 197).

7 Ten leagues below Wāsiṭ on the Ja'farī Canal. He died in Rajab/June 1196 (Sibṭ ibn al-Jawzī, 451–2).

8 Originally from Shiraz, he came to Baghdad in 584/ 1188–9, began employment in the Chancery and was also skilled in warfare (Sibṭ ibn al-Jawzī, 450–51).

[125] The Year 593 [1196–1197]

Account of how Emir Abū'l-Hayjā' was sent to Hamadhan and what he did there

In Ṣafar of this year [24 December 1196–21 January 1197] a great Egyptian emir, called Abū'l-Hayjā', who was known as the Fat because he was very corpulent, arrived at Baghdad.[1] He was one of the greatest emirs of Egypt, whose fief had recently been Jerusalem and other neighbouring places. When al-'Azīz and al-'Ādil seized Damascus from al-Afḍal, Jerusalem was taken from him, so he left Syria, crossed the Euphrates to Mosul and then went down to Baghdad, because he was invited by the caliph's Diwan. On his arrival he was received with great honour, and ordered to make preparations and march to Hamadhan as commander of the Baghdad armies. He set out and there met with Prince Uzbek, son of Pahlawān, Emir 'Alam and the latter's son and Ibn Saṭmas and others, who had written offering their allegiance to the caliph. After his meeting with them, they trusted him and were not wary of him but he arrested Uzbek, Ibn Saṭmas and Ibn Qarā with the agreement of Emir 'Alam. When news of this came to Baghdad, Abū'l-Hayjā' was criticized for this affair and he was ordered to release them all. Robes of honour were sent to them from Baghdad to placate them but after this event they were not at ease, nor did they feel secure. They broke with Abū'l-Hayjā' the Fat, who was then fearful of the Diwan and did not return to it. He was also unable to stay [where he was] but set out to go back to Irbil, as he was from there, but he died before he reached it. He was one of the Ḥakamī Kurds from the area of Irbil.

[126] Account of al-'Ādil's taking Jaffa from the Franks, the Franks' taking Beirut from the Muslims, the Franks' siege of Tibnīn and their withdrawal

In Shawwāl [17 August–14 September 1197] al-'Ādil Abū Bakr ibn Ayyūb conquered Jaffa on the Syrian coast, which was in the hands of the Franks (God curse them). This came about as follows. The Franks were now ruled by Count Henry, as we have mentioned before, and peace had been agreed between the Franks and the Muslims in the days of Saladin (God have mercy on him). When Saladin died and his sons succeeded, as we have said, al-'Azīz renewed the treaty with Count Henry, the Franks' ruler, and lengthened the period of the truce, which remained [in force] until now.

[1] Sibṭ ibn al-Jawzī, 452, tells how, in his youth, he saw this emir in Baghdad and how a local potter made clay jugs to resemble him (Toby jugs!).

In Beirut there was an emir called Usāma, who was the fief-holder.[2] He used to send out galleys to interrupt Frankish shipping. More than once the Franks complained of this to al-ʿĀdil at Damascus and to al-ʿAzīz in Egypt, but they did not stop Usāma. The Franks sent to their rulers over the sea, complaining of what the Muslims were doing to them and saying, 'If you do not help us, the Muslims will take our lands', so the Franks supplied them with many troops, most of whom were from the king of the Germans, commanded by a priest known as the Chancellor.[3] When news of this came to al-ʿĀdil, he sent to al-ʿAzīz in Egypt, asking for troops, and he sent to the Jazīra and Mosul, also asking for troops. The reinforcements came to him and assembled at Goliath's Spring.[4] [**127**] They remained there during Ramaḍān and part of Shawwāl[5] and then marched to Jaffa. They took the city but the defenders in the citadel held out. The Muslims destroyed the city and invested the citadel, which they took by force of arms that same day, a Friday. Everything and everybody within was seized as booty or as captives. The Franks marched from Acre as far as Caesarea to prevent the fall of Jaffa to the Muslims, but while they were there they heard that the city had fallen, so they retired. The reason for their being too late was that their ruler, Count Henry, had fallen to his death from a high place in Acre.[6] There was confusion in their affairs and that is why they were delayed.

The Muslims returned to Goliath's Spring and then they heard that the Franks intended to attack Beirut. Al-ʿĀdil and the army moved to Marj al-ʿUyūn in Dhū'l-Qaʿda [15 September–14 October 1197] and a detachment of the army went to Beirut with the intention of demolishing it. They razed the city wall on 7 Dhū'l-Ḥijja [21 October] and embarked on the destruction of the houses, but Usāma stopped them and undertook to hold the city. The Franks marched from Acre to Sidon. The Muslim troops left Beirut and met the Franks in the district of Sidon, where a skirmish took place in which several on both sides were killed before night separated them. On 9 Dhū'l-Ḥijja [23 October] the Franks set out for Beirut. When they drew near, Usāma and all the Muslims that were there fled, so the Franks took it with no effort without any fighting. It was easy prey. Al-ʿĀdil sent men to Sidon who demolished what remained of it, as Saladin had already demolished most of it. The Muslim forces then went to Tyre, where they cut down the trees and destroyed the villages and towers that remained. Learning of this, the

---

2 Sibṭ ibn al-Jawzī, 453, calls him Usāma al-Jabalī (of the Mountain).

3 The German crusade, sent by Emperor Henry VI, was led by the imperial marshall, Henry of Kalden, and the imperial chancellor (*kh.n.ṣ.līr*), Conrad of Querfurt, bishop of Hildesheim (Mayer, *The Crusades*, 148).

4 Arabic: ʿAyn al-Jālūt. Situated in the Jezreel Valley, north of Mt Gilboa, it was the site of the battle in which the Mamlukes defeated the Mongols in Ramaḍān 658/September 1260.

5 Ramaḍān began 18 July and Shawwāl on 17 August 1197.

6 Henry of Champagne, who had succeeded the Marquis Conrad as king of Jerusalem in April 1192, had this fatal accident in September 1197. Cf. *The Chronicle of Ibn al-Athīr (2)*, p. [**79**].

Franks left Beirut and moved to Tyre, where they stayed.

[**128**] The Muslims camped at the castle of Hūnīn and al-'Ādil gave permission for the eastern armies to return home, thinking that the Franks would stay in their own territory. He also wished to give the Egyptian forces leave to depart but in the middle of Muḥarram [27 November 1197] news reached him that the Franks had invested the fortress of Tibnīn, so he sent a force to guard and defend it. The Franks set out from Tyre and descended on Tibnīn on 1 Ṣafar 594 [13 December 1197] and engaged the defenders in fierce fighting. They mined it on all sides. Having learnt this, al-'Ādil sent to al-'Azīz in Egypt, asking him to come in person and saying, 'If you do not come, it will be impossible to hold this frontier', so al-'Azīz set out, making forced marches with the troops that remained with him.

As for the defenders in Tibnīn, when they saw that the mining had destroyed the castle's hill and all that remained was for it to be overrun by force of arms, some of them descended to the Franks to ask for guarantees for their lives and property in return for surrendering the castle. The person they applied to was the priest, the Chancellor, one of the German king's men. Some of the Franks of the Syrian coast said to these Muslims, 'If you surrender the castle, this man will seize and kill you. Defend yourselves.' They returned, as though they would consult those in the castle about surrendering it and, when they had gone back up, they maintained their resistance and fought as men fighting for their lives. They held out until al-'Azīz arrived at Ascalon in Rabī' I [11 January–9 February 1198]. When the Franks heard of his arrival and the gathering of the Muslims, and as the Franks had no king to unite them, their affairs being in the hands of a woman, the queen, they came to an agreement to send to the king of Cyprus, named Aimery.[7] They summoned him, the brother of the king who had been captured at Ḥaṭṭīn, as we have related, and arranged his marriage to the queen, the widow of Count Henry. He was a wise man, who loved peace and the good life. After he had taken power, he did not resume the siege and assaults on the castle.

[**129**] Al-'Azīz's arrival fell on 1 Rabī' II [10 February 1198]. He and his forces came to the mountain of Hebron, known as Mount 'Āmila, and camped for several days under incessant rain, remaining until 13 Rabī' II [22 February]. He broke camp and approached the Franks. He sent his archers forward, who shot at them for a while and then withdrew. He drew up his troops to attack the Franks and engage them fiercely, so the latter departed towards Tyre during the night on 15 Rabī' [23 February] and then moved on to Acre. The Muslims went to Lajūn and camped. Letters about peace were exchanged and discussions dragged on. Al-'Azīz returned to Egypt before the situation was resolved.

The reason for his departure was that several emirs, namely Maymūn al-Qaṣrī, Usāma, Sirā Sunqur, al-Ḥajjāf,[8] Ibn al-Mashṭūb and others, had determined to kill

---

7 In Arabic Haym.rī, i.e. Aimery II, who had succeeded his brother, Guy of Lusignan, as king of Cyprus in 1194.

8 In the year 595/1202–3 al-Afḍal 'Alī tried to arrest several of Saladin's former emirs, one of whom was called Fakhr al-Dīn al-Ḥajjād (Ibn Wāṣil, iii, 93). Is this in fact the same man?

him and Fakhr al-Dīn Jarkas, the guiding hand of his state. Al-'Ādil put them up to this. When al-'Azīz heard of it, he left but al-'Ādil remained. Envoys went to and fro between him and the Franks about peace, and terms were agreed that Beirut should remain in Frankish hands. Peace was made in Sha'bān 594 [8 June–6 July 1198]. After the conclusion of peace al-'Ādil returned to Damascus and from there went to Mardīn in the Jazīra. What then happened we shall relate, if God Almighty wills.

Account of the death of Sayf al-Islām and his son's succession

In Shawwāl of this year [17 August–14 September 1197] Sayf al-Islām Ṭughtakīn ibn Ayyūb, Saladin's brother and lord of Yemen, died at Zabīd. We have already mentioned how he came to power. [**130**] He was a stern ruler, harsh to his subjects, one who used to buy merchants' goods for himself and sell them at whatever price he wished. He wanted to take Mecca (may God Almighty guard it) and the Caliph al-Nāṣir li-Dīn Allāh wrote on the matter to his brother Saladin, who prevented that. He collected an untold quantity of money. He had so much that he even used to melt down the gold and make of it what looked like millstones and store it away.[9]

When he died, his son Ismā'īl came to power after him. He was a hare-brained, very disturbed man, in that he claimed that he was a Qurayshī of the Umayyad line. He proclaimed himself caliph with the title al-Hādī.[10] When his uncle al-'Ādil heard of this, it grieved and worried him. He wrote him letters of censure and reprimand, ordering him to reinstate his genuine lineage and give up his fabrications that made him a laughing stock. However, he paid no attention, did not recant but kept on as he was indeed in addition to this he behaved badly towards his troops and emirs. They therefore attacked and slew him, then put on the throne as successor an emir, one of his father's mamlukes.[11]

Miscellaneous events

The following died this year:

Abū Bakr 'Abd Allāh ibn Manṣūr ibn 'Imrān al-Bāqillānī al-Muqrī[12] from Wāsiṭ,

---

9 When the Fatimid army led by Jawhar invaded Egypt in 969, 'nombreux chameaux portaient ostensiblement des lingots d'or, fondus en forme de meules, "pour impressioner les populations"' (Wiet, *L'Egypt arabe*, 153).

10 i.e. the Guiding One.

11 Al-Mu'izz Ismā'īl was killed on 30 Rajab 598/17 January 1202. Sayf al-Dīn Sunqur, the atabeg of Ismā'īl's young brother, al-Nāṣir Ayyūb, seized power (*Simṭ al-ghālī*, 81–4).

12 Born in 500/1106–7, he first came to Baghdad in 520/1126 and for the last time in 576/1180–81, and died the last day of Rabī' II/ 21 March (Abū Shāma, *Dhayl*, 12; Sibṭ ibn al-Jawzī, 453–4).

who died there in Rabīʿ II [March 1197] aged 93 years, three months and a few days. He was the last surviving student of al-Qalānisī.[13]

Chief Cadi Abū Ṭālib ʿAlī ibn ʿAlī ibn al-Bukhārī in Jumādā II [21 April–19 May 1197] at Baghdad. He was buried in his mausoleum at the Shrine of the Straw Gate.[14]

Malikshāh, son of Khwārazm Shāh Tekesh, in Rabīʿ II [21 February–21 March 1197] at Nishapur. His father had installed him there, assigned to him the armies of all his lands in Khurasan and appointed him [**131**] the heir apparent to his kingdom. He left a son called Hindūkhān, but when Malikshāh died his father Khwārazm Shāh placed in Nishapur his other son Quṭb al-Dīn Muḥammad and he was the person who succeeded his father. Between the two brothers there was an inveterate enmity which led to Hindūkhan ibn Malikshāh's flight from Muḥammad when he came to power after his father, as we shall relate.

Our teacher, Abū'l-Qāsim Yaʿīsh ibn Ṣadaqa ibn ʿAlī al-Furātī, the blind Shāfiʿī lawyer. He was a leading scholar of Islamic law, a sound teacher of great piety, with whom I studied much. I never saw his like (God have mercy on him).[15]

I witnessed from him a wonderful proof of his religion and his desire to seek the face of God in all he did. I was studying under him at Baghdad the *Sunan* of Abū ʿAbd al-Raḥmān al-Nasāʾī, which is a large book.[16] Time was short because I was with the pilgrims after having returned from Mecca (God protect it). While we were listening to him along with my older brother Majd al-Dīn Abū'l-Saʿādāt, one of the leading men of Baghdad came to him and said, 'The order has been issued that you should attend for such-and-such a matter.' He replied, 'I am busy teaching these gentlemen and they do not have much time, and what is required of me will not be missed.' The other said, 'I cannot very well say this in response to the caliph's command.' 'Never mind! Say that Abū'l-Qāsim said, "I cannot come until the study session is over."' We asked him if we could walk with him but he refused and said, 'Read', so we read. The next day a servant of ours came and mentioned that the emir of the Mosul pilgrims was on the point of setting out. We were dismayed at this but he said, 'Why are you upset to return to your family and your home?' We answered, 'On account of completing this book.' 'If you set out,' he said, 'I will hire an animal to ride and go with you while you continue your reading. When you have finished, I shall return.' Our servant went off to buy provisions while we continued to read. He came back and reported that the pilgrim caravan had not yet departed, so we did complete the book. Just consider this steadfast faith that refuses the caliph's order, though he fears and courts him, and his willingness to travel with us, strangers though we were, whom he neither fears nor from whom he has anything to hope.

---

[13] His teacher in Wāsiṭ, Abū'l-ʿIzz Muḥammad ibn al-Ḥusayn ibn Bandār al-Qalānisī, who died in 521/1127 (Sibṭ ibn al-Jawzī, 453-4).

[14] The text has Bāb al-Tīn (Fig Gate) in error. For Bāb al-Tibn, see Yāqūt, i, 443. The shrine in question is the tomb of the seventh Imam Mūsā al-Kāẓim.

[15] Cf. the short entry in *Wāfī*, xxix, 37.

[16] For Sunnīs one of the six canonical collections of Ḥadīth.

[132] The Year 594 [1197–1198]

Account of the death of 'Imād al-Dīn and the succession of his son, Quṭb al-Dīn Muḥammad

This year in Muḥarram [13 November–12 December 1197] the lord of Sinjār, Nisibis, Khābūr and Raqqa, 'Imād al-Dīn Zankī ibn Mawdūd ibn Zankī ibn Āqsunqur, died. We have previously mentioned his coming to power in the year 579 [1183–84]. He was succeeded by his son Quṭb al-Dīn Muḥammad, whose father's mamluke, Mujāhid al-Dīn Yarunqush, took over the direction of his state.

['Imād al-Dīn] was pious, good and just, one who ruled his subjects well and respected their wealth and property. He was a retiring man who loved and respected men of learning and religion, and used to join their sessions and defer to what they said. He was (God have mercy on him) very prejudiced against the school of al-Shāfi'ī,[1] very critical of the Shāfi'ī [lawyers]. An example of his partisanship is that he built a madrasah for the Ḥanafīs at Sinjār and made it a condition that those of his children who were Ḥanafīs should be overseers to the exclusion of any Shāfi'īs. He also stipulated that the doorkeeper and caretaker (*farrāsh*) should follow the Ḥanafī school and that the law students should have food cooked for them every day. This is indeed excellent provision (God have mercy on him).

How Nūr al-Dīn took control of Nisibis

In Jumādā I [11 March–9 April 1198] Nūr al-Dīn Arslān Shāh ibn Mas'ūd ibn Mawdūd, lord of Mosul, marched to the city of Nisibis and took control, taking it from **[133]** his cousin Quṭb al-Dīn Muḥammad. This came about as follows. His uncle, 'Imad al-Dīn [Zankī II], possessed Nisibis but his lieutenants became high-handed there and appropriated several villages in the district of Bayn al-Nahrayn, in the Mosul province, which were close to Nisibis. News of this came to Mujāhid al-Dīn Qāymāz, the regent of Nūr al-Dīn at Mosul and its dependencies, and the chief authority there. He did not inform his master Nūr al-Dīn of this, since he knew his lack of firmness to bear such a thing and feared that a dispute would arise. On his own initiative he sent an envoy to 'Imād al-Dīn on the matter without any order to do so and expressed his disapproval of this action which his lieutenants had taken. He said, 'I have not informed Nūr al-Dīn of the situation, lest

[1] The text reads *al-Ḥanafiyya* here, which is against the sense of the passage. I have adopted the variant given in *Kāmil* (Thornberg), xii, 86, for which cf. *Bāhir*, 191.

it go out of your control.' The reply came back, 'They have only done what I ordered them. These villages belong to Nisibis.'

Envoys were exchanged but 'Imād al-Dīn did not cancel the appropriation. Thereupon Mujāhid al-Dīn informed Nūr al-Dīn of the situation, who sent an envoy,[2] one of the elders of his state who had served their ancestor the Martyr Zankī and his successors, and made him the bearer of a message that contained a certain harshness. The envoy on arrival found 'Imād al-Dīn ill. When he heard the message, he paid no attention to it and said, 'I will not give back what is mine.' The envoy, on his own initiative, since he was an elder of their state, advised abandonment of obstinacy and the surrender of what he had taken and warned of the possible consequences. 'Imād al-Dīn addressed rough words to him and made critical and demeaning comments about Nūr al-Dīn. The envoy returned and told Nūr al-Dīn the plain facts of the situation. He was furious at this and resolved to march to Nisibis to take it from his uncle.

However, it came about that his uncle died and was succeeded by his son.[3] [Nūr al-Dīn's] eagerness to act grew greater. Mujāhid al-Dīn restrained him but with no success. He made his preparations and marched to Nisibis. When its lord, Quṭb al-Dīn, heard this, he marched there from Sinjār with his army and camped around it to defend it from Nūr al-Dīn. The latter arrived and advanced towards the city. There was a river between them, which one of Nūr al-Dīn' emirs[4] crossed and engaged those facing him [**134**] who did not stand firm. All of Nūr al-Dīn's army then crossed and Quṭb al-Dīn's rout was complete. He and his lieutenant Mujāhid al-Dīn Yarunqush went up into the citadel of Nisibis. Night fell and they fled away to Ḥarrān. They wrote to al-'Ādil Abū Bakr ibn Ayyūb, lord of Ḥarrān and other places, who was in Damascus, and offered him large sums of money to help them recover Nisibis.

Nūr al-Dīn remained in possession of Nisibis but his army dwindled away because of the prevalence of sickness and their returning home to Mosul. Many of them died. Al-'Ādil arrived in the Jazīra and then Nūr al-Dīn abandoned Nisibis and himself returned to Mosul in Ramaḍān [7 July–5 August 1198]. After he had left, Quṭb al-Dīn took it over.

Among the emirs of Mosul who died were 'Izz al-Dīn Jūrdīk, Shams al-Dīn 'Abd Allāh ibn Ibrāhīm, Fakhr al-Dīn 'Abd Allāh ibn 'Īsā al-Mihranī, Mujāhid al-Dīn Qāymāz, Ẓahīr al-Dīn Yavlaq ibn Balankirī, Jamāl al-Dīn Muḥāsin and others. When Nūr al-Dīn returned to Mosul, al-'Ādil attacked the citadel of Mārdīn, put it under siege and closely blockaded the population, as we shall relate, God willing.

---

2 Named in *Bāhir*, 192, as Bahā' al-Dīn 'Alī ibn al-Shukrī.

3 i.e. Quṭb al-Dīn Muḥammad.

4 A Kurdish emir, Fakhr al-Dīn 'Abd Allāh ibn 'Īsa al-Mihrānī (*Bāhir*, 192).

Account of the Ghurids' taking of the city of Balkh from the infidel Khitay

This year the ruler of Bāmiyān, Bahā' al-Dīn Sām ibn Muḥammad ibn Mas'ūd, the nephew of Ghiyāth al-Dīn and Shihāb al-Dīn, the two rulers of Ghazna and other parts, took Balkh. Its ruler had been a Turk, called Azyeh, who had been paying tribute annually to the Khitay in Transoxania. He died this year and Bahā' al-Dīn Sām went there, seized it and became firmly established there. He cut off the tribute to the Khitay and made the khutbah for Ghiyāth al-Dīn. Balkh became a part of Islamic territory after having been in allegiance to the infidels.[5]

[135] Account of the defeat of the Khitay at the hands of the Ghurids

This year the Khitay crossed the Oxus into Khurasan, where they caused mischief and destruction. The army of Ghiyāth al-Dīn the Ghurid met them in battle and the Khitay were defeated.

This came about as follows. Khwārazm Shāh Tekesh had marched to Rayy and to Hamadhan and Isfahan and the lands between and taken control of them. He clashed with the caliph's army and proclaimed his demand for the sultanate and the khutbah at Baghdad. The caliph sent to Ghiyāth al-Dīn, the ruler of the Ghur and Ghazna, ordering him to attack Khwārazm Shāh's territory to make him withdraw from Iraq. He duly withdrew to Khwārazm and wrote to Ghiyāth al-Dīn deploring what he had done and threatening to attack and seize his lands. Khwārazm Shāh sent to the Khitay complaining of Ghiyāth al-Dīn and saying that, if they did not act soon against him by sending troops, Ghiyāth al-Dīn would take his lands, as he had taken Balkh, and would then attack their lands, that they would be incapable of stopping him, too weak and powerless to drive him out of Transoxania. The Khitay ruler dispatched a large army and appointed as commander a man known as Ṭāyankū,[6] who was like a vizier for him. They set out and crossed the Oxus in the winter in Jumādā II [April 1198]. Shihāb al-Dīn the Ghurid, Ghiyāth al-Dīn's brother, was in India with his forces and Ghiyāth al-Dīn was suffering from gout that left him unable to move. He was carried about in a litter. The one who led the army and took part in the battles was his brother Shihāb al-Dīn.

When the Khitay came to the Oxus, Khwārazm Shāh proceeded to Ṭūs, with the intention of attacking and besieging Herat. The Khitay crossed the river and came to Ghurid lands, such as Kurzabān,[7] Sarqān and the like, where they killed, took prisoners, plundered and enslaved untold numbers. The people appealed for help

---

[5] For the Ghurid capture of Balkh and the subsequent events recounted in the following section, see Barthold, *Turkestan*, 344ff; Biran, *Empire of the Qara Khitai*, 65–6.

[6] See Juvainī, *History*, i, 322 and note 14: 'Tayangu in Old Turkish means "chamberlain".' It is probably a title here, rather than the name of the commander.

[7] Yāqūt, iv, 258–9: 'a town in the mountains near Ṭāliqān, which are connected to the mountains of Ghūr. It is also a village of Marv al-Rūdh.'

to Ghiyāth al-Dīn but he did not have [**136**] enough troops to confront them. The Khitay made contact with Bahā' al-Dīn Sām, lord of Bāmiyān, ordering him to vacate Balkh or to pay the money that those before him used to pay. He did not comply. A great misfortune came upon the Muslims because of what the Khitay did.

Emir Muḥammad ibn Kharnak[8] al-Ghūrī, the fief-holder of Ṭaliqān appointed by Ghiyāth al-Dīn, a brave man, took it upon himself to write to al-Ḥusayn ibn Kharmīl, who was in the citadel of Kurzabān, and Emir Kharwash[9] al-Ghūrī also joined with these two. With their troops they marched against the Khitay and made a surprise attack on them at night. It is the custom of the Khitay to stay in their tents at night and not leave them. These Ghurids came and fought them and did much slaughter among them. The survivors fled but where could they fly with the Ghurid army in their rear and the Oxus before them? The Khitay thought that Ghiyāth al-Dīn with his troops had attacked them. When morning came, they realized who their enemy was and understood that Ghiyāth al-Dīn was still in his [same] position. Their spirits were strengthened and they stood firm, fighting most of that day. Large numbers were killed on both sides. Volunteers joined the Ghurid men and reinforcements from Ghiyāth al-Dīn came to them while they were in battle. The Muslims stood firm and great was the damage done to the infidels. Emir Kharwash charged the centre of the Khitay. He was an old man and was wounded fatally. Then Muḥammad[10] ibn Kharnak and Ibn Kharmīl charged with their followers. They proclaimed, 'Let no one shoot with his bow or thrust with his spear.' They took clubs, charged the Khitay and put them to flight. They caught them up at the Oxus and those who still resisted were slain, while those that cast themselves into the water drowned.

The news came to the ruler of the Khitay and he was greatly upset. He sent to Khwārazm Shāh, saying, [**137**] 'You have killed my men. I want 10,000 dinars for every man slain.' The dead were 12,000 in number. He sent men to bring him back to Khwārazm and to force him to present himself. At that, Khwārazm Shāh sent to Ghiyāth al-Dīn to inform him of his situation with the Khitay, addressing his complaints to him and attempting to win him over more than once. In the reply that was sent back he was ordered to obey the caliph and to restore the Islamic territory that the Khitay had taken. There was no settlement made between them.[11]

---

8 His father's name is routinely spelt as J.r.b.k in the text. Kharnak is taken from *Ṭabaqāt-i Nāṣirī*, 471, note 5.

9 The edition has Ḥ.r.w.sh. Cf. *Chronicle of Ibn al-Athīr (2)*, p. [**166**].

10 The text has Maḥmūd, but Muḥammad is given above and repeated a little further below.

11 Biran, *Empire of the Qara Khitai*, 66: 'It seems that Tekesh agreed to these terms.' See especially note 48, where Ibn al-Athīr's narrative is called into question.

How Khwārazm Shāh took the city of Bukhara

When the envoy of the Khitay ruler came to Khwārazm Shāh with the message we have mentioned, he sent back the reply, 'Your army's sole intention was to recover Balkh. They did not come to my aid, nor did I meet with them, nor did I order them to cross over. If I had done that, I would produce the money demanded of me, but since you have been unable to deal with the Ghurids, you have turned on me with this accusation and this demand. I have made peace with the Ghurids and entered into their allegiance. I owe you no allegiance now.'

The envoy returned with this answer. The ruler of the Khitay equipped a great army and sent them to Khwārazm, which they put under siege. Every night Khwārazm Shāh made sallies against them and killed a large number. A great crowd of volunteers came to him and he kept up his operations against the Khitay until he destroyed most of them. The rest entered their own territory, pursued by Khwārazm Shāh. He made for Bukhara and put it under siege but the population resisted him and fought him along with the Khitay. They even took a one-eyed dog, dressed it in a *qabā'*-gown and skullcap and said, 'Behold Khwārazm Shāh', because Tekesh was indeed one-eyed. They paraded it around the city wall and then hurled it into the [enemy] army from a trebuchet, [**138**] saying, 'Here is your sultan.' The Khwārazmians [in their turn] were abusing them, saying, 'Troops of the infidels, you have apostatized from Islam.' They continued in this fashion until Khwārazm Shāh took the city after a few days by force of arms. He pardoned the inhabitants and treated them well, distributing much money among them. He remained there for a while and then returned to Khwārazm.

Miscellaneous events

In Dhū'l-Ḥijja this year [October 1198] Abū Ṭālib Yaḥyā ibn Sa'īd ibn Ziyāda, the head of Chancery in the caliph's Diwan, died. He was a learned and cultured man, with a good grasp of the secretarial art. He was an intelligent and good man, who benefited people much and wrote some excellent poetry.[12]

This year al-'Ādil Abū Bakr besieged the citadel of Mardin in Ramaḍān [7 July–5 August 1198] and fought the defenders. Its ruler was Ḥusām al-Dīn Yavlaq Arslān ibn Īlghāzī ibn Alpī ibn Timurtāsh ibn Īlghāzī ibn Artuq. All of these [ancestors] were princes of Mārdīn. We have mentioned enough of their history for their importance to be understood. This one was a young boy and the real authority in his lands and state was his father's mamluke Niẓām al-Dīn Yarunqush. His master had not the slightest authority in any affairs. When al-'Ādil besieged Mārdīn and remained there, some of the inhabitants surrendered the suburbs to

[12] He was born in 522/ 1128 and served the caliphate in various capacities (Abū Shāma, *Dhayl*, 14).

him by a plot agreed between them. However, the army plundered the population most shamefully and did some terrible unheard-of things to them. After the suburbs had been taken over, he was able to press hard on the citadel and cut off its supplies. He continued the siege until he departed in the year 595 [1198–99], as we shall relate, if God wills.

This year the following died:

Shaykh Abū 'Alī al-Ḥasan ibn Muslim ibn Abī'l-Ḥasan al-Qādisī, [**139**] the ascetic, resident of Baghdad. Qādisiyya, after which he was named, is a village on the Īsā Canal in the district of Baghdad. He was one of the righteous servants of God who do good works and he was buried in his village.[13]

Abū al-Majd 'Alī ibn Abī'l-Ḥasan 'Alī ibn al-Nāṣir ibn Muḥammad, the Ḥanafī lawyer, professor of the students [at the shrine] of Abū Ḥanīfa in Baghdad.[14] He was a descendant of Muḥammad ibn al-Ḥanafiyya,[15] the son of the Commander of the Faithful 'Alī ibn Abī Ṭālib (God be pleased with him).

[13] He died on the day of 'Āshūra/ 22 November 1197, reputedly having spent forty years without speaking to anyone and having had a rapport with wild animals (Sibṭ ibn al-Jawzī, 456–7).

[14] Born 515/1121-2 and died in Rabī' I/11 January–9 February 1198 (Abū Shāma, *Dhayl*, 14).

[15] Alī's son (born 16/ 637) by Khawla of the Banū Ḥanīfa tribe. Although not descended from the Prophet, he became a figure-head for extremist Shiites in early Umayyad times; see *EI(2)*, vii, 402–3.

The Year 595 [1198–1199]

Account of the death of al-'Azīz and his brother al-Afḍal's taking power in Egypt

On 20 Muḥarram this year [22 November 1198] al-'Azīz 'Uthmān, son of Saladin and lord of Egypt, died. His death came about as follows. He went hunting and his expedition took him to Fayyum. He caught sight of a jackal and spurred his horse in pursuit, but his horse stumbled and he fell to the ground.[1] A fever ensued, so he returned ill to Cairo and remained so until his death. When he died, the man who dominated affairs was his father's mamluke, Fakhr al-Dīn Jahārkas, who held authority in the country. He summoned one of al-'Ādil Abū Bakr's men who was with them, showed him al-'Azīz dead and sent him to al-'Ādil who was besieging Mardin, as we have mentioned, to summon him to be given the reins of power. The messenger set out with all speed. When he was in Syria, he saw one of al-Afḍal 'Alī's men and said to him, 'Tell your master that his brother al-'Azīz is dead. There is no one in the land to defend it. Let him proceed there, for there is no one to keep him out.'

Al-Afḍal was beloved by the people and their favourite, but he paid no attention to this suggestion. However, there arrived envoys from the emirs in Egypt, inviting him to come to be made ruler. The reason was that the commander of the Asadiyya, Emir Sayf al-Dīn Yāzkuj, the Asadiyya regiment [**141**] and the Kurdish emirs were in favour of al-Afḍal and leaned in his direction, while the Nāṣirī mamlukes, who had been his father's, disliked him. Sayf al-Dīn, the Asadiyya commander, and Fakhr al-Dīn, the Nāṣiriyya commander, met to agree about whom to instal as ruler. Fakhr al-Dīn said, 'We should instal the son of al-'Azīz,' to which Sayf al-Dīn replied, 'He is a child. This land is the front line of Islam. It needs someone to exercise power, gather armies and lead them in battle. Our best course is to make this young child ruler but put alongside him one of Saladin's sons to act as his regent until he grows up, for the army will give allegiance to no others and will not obey an emir.' They agreed on this and Jahārkas said, 'Who will take on this office?' Rather than al-Afḍal, Yāzkuj suggested someone else, with whom Jahārkas was at odds, to avoid suspicion and so that Jahārkas would not baulk at al-Afḍal. He refused to appoint this person, so Sayf al-Dīn continued to name Saladin's sons one after another until he finally mentioned al-Afḍal. Jahārkas said, 'He is far away from us.' Since Damascus had been taken from him he was

[1] Ibn al-Qādisī (quoted by Sibṭ ibn al-Jawzī, 460–61) says that the sultan was chasing a gazelle, fell from his horse and broke his neck and died after four days. Sibṭ ibn al-Jawzī disputes this and claims that the pommel of his saddle 'entered' his heart and he survived in Cairo (sic) for two weeks.

residing in Ṣarkhad. Yāzkuj replied, 'We shall send someone to fetch him post-haste.' Jahārkas began to make specious counter-arguments, so Yāzkuj said, 'Let us go to Qāḍī al-Fāḍil and consult him.' This was agreed. Yāzkuj sent to forewarn him and advise the appointment of al-Afḍal. When the two met with him and explained the situation, he recommended al-Afḍal. Immediately Yāzkuj sent off messengers to fetch him. He set out from Ṣarkhad when two nights remained of Ṣafar [29 December 1198], in disguise and with nineteen men, because it was al-'Ādil's territory whose officers were patrolling the highways to stop his crossing into Egypt so that al-'Ādil could come and rule there.

When al-Afḍal approached Jerusalem, having diverged from the direct route there, two horsemen, who had been sent to him from Jerusalem, met him and told him that the men in Jerusalem had declared their allegiance to him. He made forced marches and arrived at Bilbays on 5 Rabī' I [5 January 1199] and was met by his brothers, [**142**] several Egyptian emirs and all the notables. It so happened that his brother al-Mu'ayyad Mas'ūd prepared a banquet for him, as did Fakhr al-Dīn, his father's mamluke. He commenced with his brother's feast because his brother had sworn an oath that he would have his first. [Fakhr al-Dīn] Jahārkas imagined that he did this as a slight and because he did not trust him. His attitude changed and he determined on flight. He came to al-Afḍal and said, 'Some Arabs have taken up arms. If you do not go and make peace between them, this will lead to trouble.' Al-Afḍal gave permission for him to go, so he left him and went with all speed to Jerusalem, which he entered and took control of. He was joined by a group of the Nāṣiriyya, including Qarāja al-Zardkash and Sirā Sunqur. They summoned to them Maymūn al-Qaṣrī, lord of Nablus, also one of the Nāṣiriyya mamlukes, who added greatly to their strength. They were united in their opposition to al-Afḍal and wrote to al-'Ādil at Mardin, asking him to come to them, so that they could enter Egypt with him and make him ruler. However, he did not come because his ambition to take Mardin had grown strong, the defenders had become too weak to hold it and he was of the opinion that he would surely take it and that he would also not fail to gain what the [emirs] were wishing for him.

Al-Afḍal entered Cairo on 7 Rabī' I [7 January 1199]. He heard of Jahārkas's flight, which worried him. Envoys went to and fro between him and the emirs to get them to come back to him but they only became more estranged. A group of the Nāṣiriyya also joined them. Al-Afḍal became alienated from the rest and arrested them, namely Shuqayra, Aybak Faṭīs and Albakī al-Fāris, each of whom was a famous hero and a reputed commander, besides others unrivalled in leadership and high status. Al-Afḍal remained in Cairo, set affairs aright and established his regime. The person looked to in all matters was Sayf al-Dīn Yāzkuj.

[143] Account of al-Afḍal's siege of Damascus and his withdrawal

Al-Afḍal had become ruler in Egypt and was well established, associated with his nephew,[2] al-'Azīz's son, who was only nominally ruler because of his young years. While support united behind al-Afḍal, the envoy of his brother al-Ẓāhir Ghāzī, lord of Aleppo, came to him, as did the envoy of his cousin Asad al-Dīn Shīrkūh ibn Muḥammad ibn Shīrkūh, lord of Homs, urging him to march to Damascus and take advantage of al-'Ādil's absence. They offered him support with money, morale and men. He left the capital the middle of Jumādā I [15 March 1199] with the intention of going to Damascus. He remained outside Cairo until 3 Rajab [1 May], when he set out but met hindrances on his march. Had he made haste with forced marches, he would have taken Damascus, but he was delayed. He reached Damascus on 13 Sha'bān [10 June] and made camp at the Wooden Bridge one and a half furlongs from the city. Al-'Ādil had already received messengers from his lieutenants in Damascus to inform him of al-Afḍal's plan to attack them. He abandoned Mardin and left his son al-Kāmil Muḥammad with all his troops to pursue the siege. He set out lightly equipped, made forced marches and forestalled al-Afḍal, arriving at Damascus two days before him.

The next day, 14 Sha'bān [11 June], al-Afḍal advanced towards the city. That very same day a small detachment of his army from[3] Ascalon entered Damascus by the Gate of Peace. The reason for that was that some of his troops, whose houses were near the gate, met with Emir Majd al-Dīn, the brother of the Lawyer 'Īsā al-Hakkārī, and suggested to him that he go to the gate, he and his troops, so that they could open it for them. Majd al-Dīn wanted to keep the opening of the gate as his own special operation, so he did not inform al-Afḍal nor did he take with him any of the emirs. He set off quite independently, accompanied by about fifty mounted men of his own. The gate was opened for him and in he went [**144**] with his men. When the city's common people saw them, they proclaimed the watchword of al-Afḍal and the troops there surrendered and came down from the walls. This news came to al-'Ādil and he almost gave up but he held on.

Meanwhile, those who had entered the city came to the Gate of the Post and, when al-'Ādil's force in Damascus saw how few they were and that support for them was cut off, they attacked and drove them out. Al-Afḍal had pitched his tents at the Green Hippodrome and his troops approached the New Gate, one of the citadel's gates. God Almighty decreed that al-Afḍal was advised to transfer to the Pebble Hippodrome, which he did. The defenders' morale was stiffened but the spirits of the Egyptian army weakened. Then the Kurdish emirs swore mutual oaths and became a single unit, willing to support each other either in anger or in satisfaction. Al-Afḍal and the rest of the Asadiyya thought that they did this by some agreement between them and the Damascenes, so they broke camp and retired on 20 Sha'bān [17 June]. Asad al-Dīn Shīrkūh, lord of Homs, reached al-Afḍal on 25 Sha'bān [21 June] and al-Ẓāhir, lord of Aleppo, arrived after him

---

2 i.e. al-Manṣūr Muḥammad, born 10 Jumādā I 585/26 June 1189 and therefore aged about ten years (*Rawḍatayn*, iv, 110, 445).

3 The text has the preposition *ilā* ('towards') here. *Min* ('from') is the reading of *Kāmil* (Thornberg), xii, 94.

on 12 Ramaḍān [8 July]. They wanted to make an assault on Damascus, but al-Ẓāhir prevented them out of envy and ill will towards his brother. His brother al-Afḍal was not aware of this.

As for al-'Ādil, when he saw the large size of the army and that reinforcements came continuously to al-Afḍal, he was dismayed and sent to the Nāṣiriyya mamlukes in Jerusalem to summon them to join him. They set out the last day of Sha'bān [26 June] and news of them reached al-Afḍal. He sent Asad al-Dīn, lord of Homs, with a number of emirs to intercept and halt them, but they took a different route and those troops arrived and entered Damascus on 5 Ramaḍān [1 July]. They greatly strengthened al-'Ādil. Al-Afḍal and his men despaired of Damascus. The Damascus troops left the city in Shawwāl [27 July–24 August] and [attempted] a surprise attack on the Egyptian army but they found them already forewarned, so they withdrew, disappointed.

[**144**] The [besieging] army remained at Damascus between strength and weakness, victory and despair, until al-'Ādil sent after his son al-Kāmil Muḥammad. He had moved from Mardin, as we shall relate, God willing, and was at Ḥarrān. Al-'Ādil summoned him with his army and he came by the desert route. He entered Damascus on 12 Ṣafar 596 [3 December 1199] and thereupon the army abandoned Damascus to go to the skirt of the Kiswa hill on 17 Ṣafar [8 December]. It was agreed that they should stay in the Ḥawrān until the end of winter. They moved to Ra's al-Mā', which is a very cold place, and they changed their minds about staying. They agreed that each of them should return to his own land, so al-Ẓāhir, lord of Aleppo, and Asad al-Dīn, lord of Homs, returned home and al-Afḍal returned to Egypt. The sequel we shall relate, if God Almighty wills.

Account of the death of Ya'qūb ibn Yūsuf ibn 'Abd al-Mu'min and the accession of his son Muḥammad

On 18 Rabī' II [17 February 1199], or some say Jumādā I [18 March 1199], Abū Yūsuf Ya'qūb ibn Abī Ya'qūb Yūsuf ibn 'Abd al-Mu'min, ruler of the Maghrib and Andalusia, died in the city of Salé.[4] He had gone there from Marrakech and had previously built a city over against Salé, which he called Mahdiyya, one of the most beautiful and delightful cities. He went there to view it and it was there he died.

His reign had lasted fifteen years and he was a man of Jihad against the enemy, of religion and good rule. He made public adherence to the Ẓāhiriyya[5] school and

4 Both Sibṭ ibn al-Jawzī, 467, and Abū Shāma, *Dhayl*, 16, put his death in Rabī' I/January 1199

5 The Ẓāhiriyya was a school of law, founded by Dā'ūd ibn Khalaf (d. 270/884) and based on the *ẓāhir*, the literal text of the Koran and Sunna (see *EI(2)*, xi, 394–6; Schacht, *Islamic Law*, 63–5).

rejected the Mālikī school. During his days the Ẓāhiriyya's status was high. There was a great multitude of them in the Maghrib, called the Jurramiyya, named after Ibn Muḥammad ibn Jurram, the leader of the Ẓāhiriyya [in his time[6]], although they were all deluded [**146**] totally. In [Ya'qūb's] lifetime they openly proclaimed their beliefs and spread widely, but then at the end of his life he appointed Shāfi'ī judges in some of his lands and inclined towards them. When he died his son Abū 'Abd Allāh Muḥammad became ruler. His father had declared him heir apparent during his lifetime and his rule became firmly established and the people obeyed him. He equipped a number of Arabs and sent them to Andalusia as a precaution against the Franks.

Account of the rebellion of the people of Mahdiyya against Ya'qūb and their allegiance to his son Muḥammad

When Abū Yūsuf Ya'qūb, lord of the Maghrib, returned from Ifrīqiya, as we have related under the year 581 [1185–6], he gave office to Abū Sa'īd 'Uthmān and Abū 'Alī Yūnus, sons of 'Umar Īntī. These two and their father too were leading men in his state. He made 'Uthmān governor of Tunis and his brother governor of Mahdiyya, and the command of the army in Mahdiyya he gave to Muḥammad ibn 'Abd al-Karīm, a man of renowned bravery. He did a good deal of damage to the Arabs, not one of whom was left who did not fear him.

It came about that he received news that a group of the 'Awf were besieging a certain place, so he took the field against them. He moved around them until he had passed beyond their present position and then turned to come back and attack them. They heard news of his moves and fled from him but they found him in front of them, so fled, leaving their property and their families without a fight. He seized everything, returned to Mahdiyya and gave their families to the governor. Of the spoils and the booty he took what he wanted, then gave the remainder to the governor and the army.

The Arabs of the Banū 'Awf sought out Abū Sa'īd ibn 'Umar Īntī and proclaimed the Almohad creed, [**147**] becoming part of the Almohad movement, and they sought his protection for the restoration of their families and their property. He summoned Muḥammad ibn 'Abd al-Karīm and ordered him to give back the booty he had taken from them. He said, 'The troops have taken it and I cannot get it back.' Abū Sa'īd addressed harsh words to him and had a mind to crush him, but he asked for a respite until he could return to Mahdiyya and recover from the troops what he could find with them. Whatever was missing, he undertook to replace from his own resources. This delay was granted and he returned to Mahdiyya in fear. On his arrival he gathered his men, told them what had happened with Abū Sa'īd and asked them to swear to stand by him, which they did. He arrested Abū 'Alī Yūnus

[6] This addition is found in one Ms.

and took control of Mahdiyya. Abū Sa'īd sent to him about releasing his brother Yūnus, which he did in return for 12,000 dinars. When Abū Sa'īd sent him this money, he distributed it among the troops and released Yūnus. Abū Sa'īd gathered his armies and wished to attack and besiege him. Muḥammad ibn 'Abd al-Karīm then sent to 'Alī ibn Isḥāq the Almoravid with whom he became a sworn ally and whose protection he gained. Abū Sa'īd refrained from attacking him.

Ya'qūb died and was succeeded by his son Muḥammad, who sent an army by sea with his uncle and another by land with his cousin al-Ḥasan ibn Abī Ḥafṣ ibn 'Abd al-Mu'min. When the sea-borne force arrived at Bougie and the land army at Qusanṭīnat al-Hawā, ['Alī ibn Isḥāq] the Almoravid and the Arabs with him fled from Ifrīqiya into the desert. The fleet came to Mahdiyya and Muḥammad ibn 'Abd al-Karīm complained about what he had met with from Abū Sa'īd, saying, 'I am a loyal subject of the Commander of the Faithful Muḥammad. I shall not surrender the city to Abū Sa'īd. I shall only surrender it to someone who comes from the Commander of the Faithful.' Muḥammad then dispatched someone to take it over from him and he returned to his allegiance.

[148] Account of the departure of al-'Ādil's army from Mardin

This year the siege of Mardin was raised and al-'Ādil's army marched away with his son al-Kāmil. This came about because, when he besieged Mardin, Nūr al-Dīn, lord of Mosul, and other princes of Diyār Bakr and the Jazīra were greatly disturbed. They feared that, if he conquered it, he would not allow them to survive. However, their inability to resist him brought them to submit to him. When al-'Azīz, lord of Egypt, died and al-Afḍal, as we have related, became ruler of Egypt, between whom and al-'Ādil a difference existed, al-Afḍal sent and took[7] the Egyptian troops from him. He made contact with Nūr al-Dīn, ruler of Mosul, and other princes, inviting them to ally themselves with him. They agreed to this and, when al-'Ādil departed from Mardin, as we have mentioned, Nūr al-Dīn Arslān Shāh ibn Mas'ūd ibn Mawdūd emerged from Mosul on 2 Sha'bān [30 May 1199] and proceeded to Dunaysir, where he camped. His cousin, Quṭb al-Dīn Muḥammad ibn Zankī ibn Mawdūd, lord of Sinjār, and another cousin, Mu'izz al-Dīn Sanjar Shāh ibn Ghāzī ibn Mawdūd, lord of Jazīrat Ibn 'Umar, were in agreement with him and all gathered at Dunaysir until they had celebrated the end of Ramaḍān [ended 26 July]. They then left on 6 Shawwāl [1 August] and stopped at Ḥarzam. The troops advanced to below the mountain to scout for a place to pitch camp.

The citizens of Mardin were short of provisions and sickness increased among them, so that many of them were incapable of standing. When Niẓām al-Dīn, the real authority in the ruler's state, saw this, he sent to al-'Ādil's son about

[7] *Kāmil* (Thornberg), xii, 97, reads *arsala akhadha*.

surrendering the citadel by a fixed time which he stated, on condition that he would allow them to take in enough food to sustain them and nothing more. He agreed to this and they swore oaths to one another. They raised their banners to the top of the citadel and al-ʿĀdil's son posted **[149]** at the citadel's gate an emir who was to allow them to introduce only enough food to satisfy them day by day. However, the men in the citadel gave this emir something and he permitted them to take in many supplies.

While this situation continued, they received news of the arrival of Nūr al-Dīn, ruler of Mosul. Their morale rose and they determined to hold out. When his army advanced to the skirt of Mardin's mountain, God decreed that al-Kāmil, al-ʿĀdil's son, descended with his troops from the suburb of Mardin to confront and fight Nūr al-Dīn. Had he remained in the suburb, neither Nūr al-Dīn nor anyone else would have been able to climb up to them and dislodge them. However, he moved down 'in order that God might achieve his foreordained plan'. When he came down from the mountain to the plain, battle was joined. It is strange to relate that Quṭb al-Dīn, lord of Sinjār, had concerted a plan with al-ʿĀdil's troops to retreat when the fighting began but he did not inform any of [his] troops. God ordained that, when al-ʿĀdil's troops came down and the battle lines were drawn up, necessity obliged Quṭb al-Dīn to crowd together, so that he stood at the foot of Mardin mountain's scrubland with no way for al-ʿĀdil's troops to come to him. He could not see the battle taking place between them and Nūr al-Dīn and he missed his opportunity for the [feigned] flight that he planned. When the two armies met and fought, Nūr al-Dīn charged in person that day and fought bravely. His men threw themselves before him and al-ʿĀdil's force gave way and climbed the mountain to the suburb. Many were taken prisoner and taken before Nūr al-Dīn, who treated them well and promised to release them if they disbanded.

He did not think that al-Kāmil and his men would leave Mardin quickly but then they were faced with a situation they had not counted on. When al-Kāmil climbed up to the suburb, he saw that the citadel's defenders had descended on those troops he had stationed in the suburb, engaged them and inflicted damage on them and taken booty. God had injected panic in the hearts of all. Having formed their plan to abandon the suburb at night, they departed the eve of Monday 7 Shawwāl [2 August 1199], leaving much of their baggage, their saddlebags and what they had prepared. This the men in the citadel took. Had al-ʿĀdil's troops remained firm **[150]** in their position, no one would have been able to get near them.

After their departure the lord of Mardin, Ḥusām al-Dīn Yavlaq ibn Īlghāzī, came down to Nūr al-Dīn and then returned to his fortress. The Atabeg withdrew to Dunaysir and from there went to Ra's ʿAyn with the intention of attacking and besieging Ḥarrān. However, an envoy came to him from al-Ẓāhir, demanding the khutbah, his name on the coinage and other things. Nūr al-Dīn's attitude underwent a change and his eagerness to help them lessened. He expressed his intention to return to Mosul and was hesitating about this when he was struck by an illness.

His intention to return was confirmed and he left. He sent an envoy to al-Afḍal and al-Ẓāhir apologizing for his return on account of his illness. The messenger reached them on 2 Dhū'l-Ḥijja [25 September 1199], when they were at Damascus.

Nūr al-Dīn's withdrawal was due to al-'Ādil's good fortune. He and all his men were waiting to see what news of him they would hear. The defenders of Ḥarrān were ready to give up but God Almighty decreed that Nūr al-Dīn withdrew. When he did so, al-Kāmil came to Ḥarrān, after he had already moved from Mardin to Mayyāfāriqīn. He came to Ḥarrān after Nūr al-Dīn's departure and then proceeded to his father at Damascus, as we have related. This greatly added to the latter's strength, while al-Afḍal and his men became weaker.

[151] Account of the disturbance at Fīrūzkūh [spread] from Khurasan

This year there was much discord in the army of Ghiyāth al-Dīn, king of Ghūr and Ghazna, when he was at Fīrūzkūh,[8] which was general among the subjects, the princes and the emirs. This came about because Fakhr al-Dīn Muḥammad ibn 'Umar ibn al-Ḥusayn al-Rāzī, the famous scholar and Shafi'ī lawyer, had come to Ghiyāth al-Dīn, leaving Bahā' al-Dīn Sām, the ruler of Bāmiyān, who was Ghiyāth al-Dīn's nephew. Ghiyāth al-Dīn received him with honour and respect, indeed went to great lengths to honour him. He built a madrasah for him at Herat near the Friday mosque. Lawyers from far and wide sought him out, which annoyed the Karrāmiyya,[9] of whom there were many in Herat. The Ghūr were all Karrāmīs, so they disapproved of him. The most hostile was Prince Ḍiyā' al-Dīn, the cousin of Ghiyāth al-Dīn and his son-in-law. It so happened that lawyers from the Karrāmiyya, the Ḥanafīs and the Shāfi'īs, came before Ghiyāth al-Dīn at Fīrūzkūh to debate. Fakhr al-Dīn al-Rāzī and the Cadi Majd al-Dīn 'Abd al-Majīd ibn 'Umar, known as Ibn al-Qudwa, a member of the Hayṣamiyya branch of the Karrāmīs, who was much revered by them because of his asceticism, his learning and his lineage, were both present. Al-Rāzī put forward a position and Ibn al-Qudwa attacked it. The debate was lengthy and Ghiyāth al-Dīn rose [and left]. Fakhr al-Dīn behaved outrageously and abused and upbraided [Ibn al-Qudwa], insulting him beyond measure, while Ibn al-Qudwa did no more than say, 'May our lord do nothing but let God take you. God help me!' They parted at that juncture.

Ḍiyā' al-Dīn took up this matter and complained to Ghiyāth al-Dīn with criticism of Fakhr al-Dīn. He called him a *zindīq*[10] and a philosopher but Ghiyāth al-Dīn paid no attention to him. On the following day the cousin of Majd al-Dīn

---

8 The centre of Ghurid power, 'identified by André Maricq in 1957 with ruins at Jām on the middle Hari Rūd, some 200 km. east of Herat' (Jackson, *Delhi Sultanate*, 6).

9 The Karrāmiyya, 'a pietistic and ascetic form of Sunni Islam', founded by Abū 'Abd Allāh Muḥammad ibn Karrām (d. 255/869), spread widely among the Ghūr. See Nizami, 'Ghurids', 178 and 190; *EI (2)*, iv, 667–9.

10 i.e. a man of heretical views directly dangerous to the state.

ibn al-Qudwa gave a sermon in the Friday mosque. On ascending the pulpit he said, after praising God and blessing the Prophet (God bless him and give him peace), 'There is no god but God. "Our lord! We believe [**152**] in what You have revealed and we follow the Prophet. Write us down with those who bear witness to him."[11] O people, we only say what we hold to be right on the authority of the Prophet (God bless him and give him peace). As for the learning of Aristotle, the blasphemies of Ibn Sīnā and the philosophy of al-Fārābī, we know nothing of them. For what reason was a shaykh of Islam upbraided yesterday for defending God's religion and the Sunna of His Prophet?' He wept and the people raised a clamour. The Karrāmīs wept and called for help, and they were supported by those whose main aim was to separate Fakhr al-Dīn al-Rāzī from the sultan. The people rose on every side and the city was taken over by rioting. They were on the point of fighting and bringing about the death of large crowds. This reached the ears of the sultan, who sent some of his own men to calm the people and promise them the expulsion of Fakhr al-Dīn. He commanded him to return to Herat, which he did.

Account of Khwārazm Shāh's march to Rayy

In Rabī' I [January 1199] Khwārazm Shāh 'Alā' al-Dīn Tekesh marched to Rayy and other parts of the Uplands because he had heard that his deputy there, Mayājuq, had changed his loyalties. He set out and Mayājuq, fearful of him, began to flee from his advance. Khwārazm Shāh pursued him and called upon him to present himself, but he refused. Most of his men asked for terms from Khwārazm Shāh but he himself fled and ended up taking refuge in a castle in the district of Mazandaran. Troops came after him and he was seized there and brought before Khwārazm Shāh, who ordered his imprisonment after his brother Aqche had interceded for him.

Robes of honour were sent from the caliph to Khwārazm Shāh and his son Quṭb al-Dīn Muḥammad, [**153**] and also a diploma for the lands he held. He donned the robe of honour and busied himself with fighting the Bāṭinīs.[12] He conquered a castle at the gates of Qazwin, called Arslān Kushād,[13] and then moved to besiege Alamut, where Ṣadr al-Dīn Muḥammad ibn al-Wazzān, the head of the Shāfi'īs at Rayy, was killed. He had become very prominent in his service, so the 'deviators' slew him. Khwārazm Shāh retired to Khwārazm. Then the 'deviators' surprised and assassinated his vizier Niẓām al-Dīn Mas'ūd ibn 'Alī in Jumādā II 596 [19 March–16 April 1200], so Tekesh ordered his son Quṭb al-Dīn to attack them. He proceeded to the castle of Turshīsh,[14] one of their fortresses, and put it under siege.

---

[11] Koran, iii, 53.

[12] Here they are called, as not infrequently, *al-mulāḥida* (literally 'the deviators').

[13] A slight correction is made to the name as given in the edition. See Hodgson, *Order of Assassins*, 212.

[14] Krawulsky, 132–3, s.v. Torshīz; also *EI(2)*, x, 737. It was located in the region of Bust in

They announced their submission and made peace on payment of 100,000 dinars. Quṭb al-Dīn departed, having only made peace because he heard news that his father was ill. They had been making overtures of peace, which he was not accepting. However, when he heard of his father's illness, he did not leave until he had made peace with them in return for the sum mentioned and their submission, then he left.

Miscellaneous events

In Rabīʿ I [January 1199] Mujāhid al-Dīn Qāymāz died in the citadel of Mosul (God have mercy on him).[15] He was the strong man of Nūr al-Dīn's state, to whom all deferred. His period as governor of the Mosul citadel began in Dhū'l-Ḥijja 571 [11 June–9 July 1176]. He took charge of Irbil in the year 559 [1163–4]. When Zayn al-Dīn ʿAlī Kūchuk died in the year 563 [1167–8] he was left as sole authority there along with the sons of Zayn al-Dīn whom he selected, although none of them had any power. He was intelligent, religious, charitable and learned, with an understanding of law according to the school of Abū Ḥanīfa. He knew by heart a good deal of history, poetry and collections of tales. He was given to much **[154]** fasting, every year keeping fast for about seven months. He had many beautiful prayers for his nightly use and gave away a lot in alms. He possessed an excellent insight into who deserved alms, and was able to recognize the deserving poor and give them charity. He built several mosques, for example the mosque outside Mosul at the Bridge Gate. He also built hospices, madrasahs and caravanserais on the highways. He did much good work (God have mercy on him) and was one of the ornaments of this world.

This year Ghiyath al-Dīn, ruler of Ghazna and part of Khurasan, abandoned the Karrāmiyya school and became a Shāfiʿī. The reason for this was that there was in his service a man called Fakhr al-Dīn Mubārak Shāh, who wrote poetry in Farsī and was a master in many branches of learning. He brought Ghiyāth al-Dīn into contact with Shaykh Waḥīd al-Dīn Abū'l-Fatḥ Muḥammad ibn Maḥmūd al-Marwarūdhī, the Shāfiʿī lawyer, who expounded the Shāfiʿī school to him and explained the wickedness of the Karrāmiyya school. He therefore became a Shafiʿī and built madrasahs for the Shāfiʿīs. In Ghazna he also built a mosque for them and showed them a lot of concern. The Karrāmiyya strove to undermine Waḥīd al-Dīn but God Almighty did not allow them to do that. [Alternatively] it is said that Ghiyāth al-Dīn and his brother Shihāb al-Dīn, when they came to power in Khurasan, were told that the people in the whole country ridiculed and despised the Karrāmiyya and that it would be best if they gave up their beliefs, so they both

Quhistan, northeastern Persia, to the west of present Kashmar. An older form of the name was Turaythīth.

[15] Sibṭ ibn al-Jawzī, 458, puts his death under the year 594/1197–8, as does Abū Shāma, *Dhayl*, 14.

became Shāfi'īs. It is claimed, however, that Shihāb al-Dīn was a Ḥanafī. God knows best.

This year Abū'l-Qāsim Yaḥyā ibn 'Alī ibn Faḍlān, the Shāfi'ī lawyer, died.[16] He was a learned imam who taught at Baghdad, and one of the outstanding students of Muḥammad ibn Yaḥyā[17] al-Nīsābūrī.

---

[16] Born in 515/1121–2, he studied at the Baghdad Niẓāmiyya, then travelled to Nishapur where he studied with Muḥammad ibn Yaḥyā (see the note to p. [**124**] above), then spent ten years in Baghdad, returned to Nishapur, from where he fled the Oghuz and died at Baghdad in Sha'bān/June 1199 (Abū Shāma, *Dhayl*, 15; *Wāfī*, xxviii, 233–5).

[17] The 'Najī' given in the edition after his father's name appears to be a corruption of 'Yaḥyā'.

The Year 596 [1199–1200]

Account of al-'Ādil's taking power in Egypt

Under the year 595 [1198–9] we have mentioned how al-Afḍal and al-Ẓāhir, two sons of Saladin, besieged Damascus and withdrew to Ra's al-'Ayn with the intention of remaining in the Ḥawran until the end of winter. After a time there the troops experienced intense cold, because that place was cold in summer, and certainly so in winter! They changed their minds about staying and agreed that everyone should return home and assemble again later. They broke up on 9 Rabī' I [29 December 1199]. Al-Ẓāhir and the lord of Homs returned to their lands and al-Afḍal went to Egypt. The latter came to Bilbays and camped there. News came to him that his uncle al-'Ādil had left Damascus to go to Egypt, accompanied by the Nāṣirī mamlukes, who had got him to swear that the son of al-'Azīz should be lord of the country, with himself as regent until his majority. They set out on that basis.

Al-Afḍal's army in Egypt had already parted from him at al-Khashabī[1] and every man had gone to his fief to put his horses on the spring grass. Al-Afḍal wished to gather them together from all parts of the country but the situation developed too quickly for this. Only a small detachment of those whose fiefs were nearby assembled before al-'Ādil arrived. Some people advised al-Afdal to demolish Bilbays's wall and to remain at Cairo, but others advised an advance to the frontier. That was what he did. He left Bilbays and camped at a place called al-Sāniḥ[2] on[3] the frontier. He and al-'Ādil met on 7 Rabī' II [= 25 January 1200]. Al-Afḍal was defeated and entered Cairo by night.

[156] That same night Qāḍī al-Fāḍil 'Abd al-Raḥīm ibn 'Alī al-Baysānī, Saladin's head of chancery and vizier, died. Al-Afḍal attended for his funeral prayers. Then al-'Ādil came, descended upon Cairo and put it under siege. Al-Afḍal gathered the emirs who were with him and consulted them but met with defeatism. He therefore sent an envoy to his uncle about making peace, surrendering the country to him and receiving a place in exchange. He asked for Damascus but got no response from al-'Ādil. He then was ready to accept Ḥarrān and Edessa but still had no response. He lowered his sights to Mayyāfāriqīn, Ḥānī and Jabal Jūr, and this was granted. They swore mutual oaths and al-Afḍal left Cairo the eve of Saturday 18 Rabī' II [= 5 February 1200], met with

[1] On the main route to Palestine, situated three days' journey from Cairo at the beginning of the sands of the Sinai (see Yāqūt, ii, 90 and 445).

[2] The edition has al-Sā'iḥ. Cf. *Rawḍatayn*, iv, 455.

[3] The edition has *ilā* (towards) here. *Kāmil* (Thornberg), xii, 102, has *fī* and its reading has also been adopted for the immediately following sentence, which is suspect in the edition.

al-'Ādil and then went to Ṣarkhad. Al-'Ādil made his entry into Cairo on that Saturday.

After al-Afḍal had reached Ṣarkhad, he sent people to take over Mayyāfāriqīn, Ḥānī and Jabal Jūr. However, Najm al-Dīn Ayyūb ibn al-'Ādil refused to give up Mayyāfāriqīn, although he surrendered the others. There was an exchange of messengers between al-Afḍal and al-'Ādil about this. The latter asserted that his son had rebelled against him but al-Afḍal refrained from communicating with him about this because he knew that it had been done on al-'Ādil's orders.

When al-'Ādil's foot was well established in Egypt, he dropped the khutbah in the name of al-Manṣūr, al-'Azīz's son, in Shawwāl of this year [15 July–12 August 1200] and had it made in his own name. He carried out an audit of the army's fiefs and examined them about their personal companies and the established troops they had to maintain. For this reason their attitude towards him underwent a change and the result was what we shall relate under the year 597 [1200–1201], God willing.

Account of the death of Khwārazm Shāh

During this year on 20 Ramaḍān [4 July 1200] Khwārazm Shāh Tekesh ibn Īl Arslān,[4] lord of Khwārazm, Rayy and other parts [**157**] of the Uplands, died in Shahristāna[5] between Nishapur and Khwārazm. He had travelled from Khwārazm to Khurasan, while suffering from quinsy. His doctors advised him not to travel but he refused [to listen] and went. When he drew near Shahristāna, his illness worsened and he died. When his illness grew serious, they had sent for his son, Quṭb al-Dīn Muḥammad, telling him of his father's serious situation. He set out to come to them but his father had already died. He succeeded him and took the title of 'Alā' al-Dīn, his father's title, after having been titled Quṭb al-Dīn. He ordered his father to be carried to Khwārazm to be buried in a tomb chamber he had constructed in a large, magnificent madrasah he had built. He was a just and good ruler, of excellent understanding and learning, being knowledgeable in law according to the school of Abū Ḥanīfa and in the fundamentals[6] [of Islamic jurisprudence].

His son 'Alī Shāh was in Isfahan. Having been sent for by his brother, Khwārazm Shāh Muḥammad, he went to him and the people of Isfahan plundered his treasury and his baggage. His brother, after he had come, made him military governor of Khurasan,[7] gave him command over its army and assigned him

---

4 Correct the text's 'Alp Arslān'.

5 Shahrastān (sic) is a small town in Khurasan three 'miles' from Nasā. It is on the edge of the sand desert between Nishapur and Khwārazm. See Yāqūt, iii, 343, lines 2ff, who adds that he saw the place, already in decay and with most of its population leaving, in the year 617/1220–21, when he himself was fleeing Khwārazm to escape the Mongols.

6 The four *uṣūl* are the Koran, Sunna, *qiyās* (analogy) and *ijmā'* (consensus).

7 Following *Kāmil* (Thornberg), xii, 103: *wallāhu ḥarb Khurasān*, and omitting the *ahl* that

Nishapur. Hindūkhān ibn Malikshāh ibn Khwārazm Shāh Tekesh was fearful of his uncle Muḥammad and fled from him. When his grandfather Tekesh had died, he plundered much from his treasure chests, for he was with him. He now went to Marv.

When Ghiyāth al-Dīn, king of Ghazna, heard of the death of Khwārazm Shāh, he ordered that his ceremonial music should not be sounded for three days and held a session of condolence, despite the enmity and hostility between them. He acted thus out of wisdom and a sense of honour.

Later Hindūkhān gathered a large force in Khurasan, so his uncle Khwārazm Shāh Muḥammad sent an army against him, led by Jaqar the Turk. When Hindūkhān heard that they had set out, he fled from Khurasan and went to Ghiyath al-Dīn to seek his aid against his uncle. He was honourably received and lodged, given upkeep and promised help. He remained at his court, while Jaqar entered the city of Marv, where were Hindūkhān's mother and children. He seized their persons and informed his master, who ordered that they be sent to Khwārazm in honoured state. When he heard this, Ghiyāth al-Dīn sent to Muḥammad ibn Kharnak,[8] **[158]** lord of Ṭāliqān, ordering him to send threats to Jaqar. He did this and he marched from Ṭāliqān and took Marv al-Rūdh and the five villages, called in Farsī Panj Deh. He sent to Jaqar ordering him to make the khutbah in Marv for Ghiyāth al-Dīn or to leave the city. The reply came with threats and menaces for Ibn Kharnak but Jaqar also wrote to him secretly to ask him to procure him a safe conduct from Ghiyāth al-Dīn so that he could present himself to serve him. He passed on this message to Ghiyāth al-Dīn, who, when he read the letter, knew that Khwārazm Shāh had no power and that this was why Jaqar requested to join him. His territorial ambitions grew and he wrote to his brother Shihāb al-Dīn with orders to invade Khurasan so that they could both act together to seize the lands of Khwārazm Shāh Muḥammad.

Miscellaneous events

In Jumāda II [19 March–16 April 1200] the Ismā'īlī 'deviators' set upon Niẓām al-Mulk Mas'ūd ibn 'Alī, the vizier of Khwārazm Shāh Tekesh, and assassinated him. He was a righteous and very charitable man, of good conduct and Shāfi'ī by law school. For the Shāfi'īs in Marv he built a mosque that overlooked the Ḥanafīs' mosque. The Shaykh al-Islam in Marv, who was the head of the Ḥanbalīs there, a man of an ancient leading family, acting out of fanaticism, assembled the mob and burnt it down. Khwarazm Shāh sent and summoned before him the Shaykh al-Islam and several others who took the lead in this. He fined them a large sum of

---

the edition inserts.

[8] This leading emir is called Muḥammad Kharang in Juvainī, *History*, i, 316, 319–20. The edition generally has 'ibn J.r.b.k'.

money. The vizier also built a large madrasah in Khwārazm and a mosque, in which he set up a library. There are other good works of his that survive in Khurasan.

At his death he left behind a young son, whom Khwārazm Shāh appointed as vizier, [**159**] out of regard for the merits of his father. He was advised to tender his resignation, so he sent to say, 'I am a youth, unfit for this prestigious office. Let the sultan appoint someone fit for it until I grow up. If I prove fit, I am his humble servant.' Khwārazm Shāh replied, 'I shall not release you. I am *your* vizier. Be the person to whom I have recourse in the affairs of state, for none of them will falter.' This [reply] was widely admired. However, the youth's days did not last long. He died a little before Khwārazm Shāh.

During Rabīʿ I this year [21 December 1199–19 January 1200] our teacher Abū'l-Faraj ʿAbd al-Munʿim ibn ʿAbd al-Wahhāb ibn Kulayb al-Ḥarrānī, resident of Baghdad, died at the age of 96 years and two months. His informants had high authority in the field of Ḥadīth and he was a reliable and sound transmitter.[9]

In Rabīʿ II [January 1200] Qāḍī al-Fāḍil ʿAbd al-Raḥīm al-Baysānī, the celebrated government secretary, died.[10] In his time there was no one better than he at the secretarial art. He was buried outside Cairo at Qarāfa. He was pious, much given to almsgiving and worship. Many charitable trusts to provide alms to ransom captives were set up by him. He performed many pilgrimages and pious retreats despite his busy life in the service of the sultan. Sultan Saladin revered, respected and rewarded him, and listened to what he had to say (God have mercy on him).

9 See Abū Shāma, *Dhayl*, 18.

10 He was born in 529/1134–5 (Sibṭ ibn al-Jawzī, 472). ʿImād al-Dīn specifies his death date as Tuesday 6 Rabīʿ II/ 25 January 1200 (*Rawḍatayn*, iv, 472) and gives a fulsome assessment of al-Fāḍil and an acknowledgment of his own debt to him (op. cit., 472–7). For a summary of his career and other references, see *EI(2)*, iv, 376–7).

[160] The Year 597 [1200–1201]

How al-Ẓāhir, lord of Aleppo, took Manbij and other places in Syria and how he and his brother al-Afḍal besieged the city of Damascus and then withdrew

We have previously mentioned that al-'Ādil took control of Egypt, dropped the khutbah for al-Manṣūr, the son of al-'Azīz 'Uthmān, Saladin's son, and that, when he did this, the Egyptian emirs were not pleased with him and their feelings of loyalty towards him changed for the worse. They made contact with ['Uthmān's] brothers, al-Ẓāhir in Aleppo and al-Afḍal in Ṣarkhad, and letters and messages went to and fro between them, inviting them both to attack and besiege Damascus to make al-'Ādil move against them. When he left Egypt, they would give him into their hands and join with them to make them rulers of the lands.

This [conspiracy] grew until knowledge of it became widespread and it came to al-'Ādil's ears. In addition to this, the Nile in Egypt did not reach its full flood which prepares the land for people to plant crops. Food was short and prices high, so the army was weakened. Fakhr al-Dīn Jahārkas along with a body of Nāṣirī mamlukes had left Egypt to besiege Bānyās to take it for himself on the orders of al-'Ādil. It was held by a great Turkish emir called Bishāra, whom al-'Ādil suspected, so he gave this order to Jahārkas.

One of al-'Ādil's emirs, called Usāma, went on pilgrimage this year. When **[161]** he returned and drew near Ṣarkhad, al-Afḍal came down and met him respectfully and invited him to join him. Usāma agreed and swore an oath to him. Al-Afḍal then informed him of the full details of the plot. Usāma was an intimate of al-'Ādil and only swore to have the whole affair uncovered. After leaving al-Afḍal he sent to al-'Ādil, who was in Egypt, to tell him the whole story. Al-'Ādil sent to his son in Damascus, ordering him to besiege al-Afḍal in Ṣarkhad, and he wrote to Iyās Jahārkas[1] and Maymūn al-Qaṣrī, the lord of Bilbays, and other members of the Nāṣiriyya, ordering them to join with his son in the siege of al-Afḍal.

Hearing this, al-Afḍal set out to his brother al-Ẓāhir in Aleppo on 1 Jumādā I [7 February 1201] and arrived at Aleppo on the 10th of the month [17 February]. Al-Ẓāhir had sent one of his great emirs to his uncle al-'Ādil but the latter refused to receive him and ordered him to write what he had to communicate. He did not do this but returned immediately. At that al-Ẓāhir made his move, assembled his army and went to Manbij, which he seized on 26 Rajab [2 May 1201]. He then proceeded to Qal'at Najm, which he besieged and took over on the last day of Rajab [6 May].

---

1 It is unclear why Fakhr al-Dīn is given this extra name and what its significance is.

As for al-'Ādil's son who was based in Damascus, he proceeded to Buṣrā and sent to Jahārkas and those with him, who were besieging Bānyās, to summon them to join him. They did not respond to him but kept him guessing. After he had spent a long time at Buṣrā, he returned to Damascus and sent Emir Usāma to them to summon them to come to his aid. It happened that there occurred between him and Ilbakī al-Fāris, one of the senior Nāṣirī mamlukes, an altercation in which Ilbakī used very harsh language and they came to blows. The whole army rose against Usāma, who sought protection with Maymūn. The latter gave him safe conduct and sent him back to Damascus. They all gathered around al-Ẓāfir Khiḍr, a son of Saladin, and brought him out of Ṣarkhad. They sent messages to urge al-Ẓāhir and al-Afḍal to come to them, but al-Ẓāhir waited prudently and pleaded difficulties. He later came from Manbij to Hama in twenty days [**162**] and remained besieging Hama, where was its lord Nāṣir al-Dīn Muḥammad ibn Taqī al-Dīn, until 19 Ramaḍān [23 June 1201]. They both then came to terms and Taqī al-Dīn's son paid him 30,000 Tyrian dinars. From there they went to Homs and then on to Damascus by way of Baalbek. At Damascus they camped by the Mosque of the Foot.[2] After they had made camp, the Nāṣirī mamlukes came to them with al-Ẓāfir Khiḍr, son of Saladin. It had been agreed between al-Ẓāhir and his brother al-Afḍal that, when they took Damascus, it should be held by al-Afḍal. They would march to Egypt and when they took it, al-Ẓāhir would take over Damascus and the whole of Syria should remain his, while Egypt should remain al-Afḍal's. [In the meantime] al-Afḍal gave over Ṣarkhad to Zayn al-Dīn Qarāja, his father's mamluke, that he might be present at his service, and moved his mother and his family out and had them conveyed to Homs, where they resided with Asad al-Dīn Shīrkūh, its lord.

Al-'Ādil had already travelled from Egypt to Syria, stopped at Nablus and sent a detachment of his army to hold Damascus. They arrived there before al-Ẓāhir and al-Afḍal. Fakhr al-Dīn Jahārkas and other members of the Nāṣiriyya came to al-Ẓāhir and made an armed assault on Damascus on 14 Dhū'l-Qa'da [16 August 1201]. The fighting was fierce but the infantry were able to reach the wall. Night came on and they withdrew. However, their eagerness to take the city had been strengthened. They returned to the assault a second and a third time and its fall was imminent, as the troops had climbed onto the roof of the caravanserai of Ibn al-Muqaddam, which was adjacent to the wall. Had not night overtaken them, they would have gained the city, but when night fell, leaving them determined to attack in the morning as there was no one to hold the city against them, al-Ẓāhir became jealous of his brother al-Afḍal and sent to him, saying [**163**] that Damascus should be his and held by him and that he would send the armies with [al-Afḍal] to Egypt. Al-Afḍal replied, 'You know that my mother and family, who are your family too, are homeless.[3] They have no place to take refuge in. Consider that this city is

---

2 i.e. *masjid al-qadam*. It was an ancient, endowed mosque with a minaret, situated to the west of Damascus (see Ibn Shaddād, *Damas*, 155–6).

3 *Kāmil* has '[they are] on the ground' (*'alā'l-arḍ*).

yours, but that you are lending it to us to be a home for my family for this period until Egypt is taken.'

Al-Ẓāhir did not agree to this but persisted [in his demand]. When al-Afḍal saw this, he said to the Nāṣiriyya and all the fighting men who had come to them, 'If you have come to me, I give you permission to return to al-'Ādil. If you have come to my brother al-Ẓāhir, then you and he know best.' All in fact wanted al-Afḍal and said, 'We want only you but we prefer al-'Ādil to your brother.' He then allowed them to go back. Fakhr al-Dīn Jahārkas and Zayn al-Dīn Qarāja, to whom al-Afḍal had given Ṣarkhad, fled and some there were who entered Damascus and others who returned to their fiefs. When their [original] plan collapsed, they turned again to making a new peace with al-'Ādil. Envoys went to and fro and the settlement reached was that al-Ẓāhir should have Manbij, Apamea, Kafarṭāb and certain specified villages of Ma'arrat [al-Nu'mān], and that al-Afḍal should have Sumaysāṭ, Sarūj, Ra's 'Ayn and Jamalīn. They departed from Damascus on 1 Muḥarram 598 [1 October 1201], al-Afḍal going to Homs where he took up residence and al-Ẓāhir going to Aleppo. Al-'Ādil reached Damascus on 9 Muḥarram [9 October] and al-Afḍal came to him from Homs. He met with him outside Damascus and then parted from him to return to Homs, from where he went to take over Sumaysāṭ. He duly took over it and the rest of what was assigned to him, Ra's 'Ayn, Sarūj and elsewhere.

[164] How Ghiyāth al-Dīn and his brother took what Khwārazm Shāh held in Khurasan

We have already mentioned Muḥammad ibn Kharnak's[4] march from Ṭāliqān, his conquest of Marv al-Rūdh and the request of Jaqar al-Turkī, 'Alā' al-Dīn Muḥammad Khwārazm Shāh's deputy in Marv, to be part of Ghiyāth al-Dīn's army. When Ibn Kharnak's letter came to Ghiyāth al-Dīn on the subject of Jaqar, he understood that the only thing that prompted him to join with them was the weakness of his master. He sent to his brother Shihāb al-Dīn to summon him to Khurasan. He accordingly set out from Ghazna with his regular troops, his levies, his retinue and whatever he needed.

Emir 'Umar ibn Muḥammad al-Marghanī was in Herat, acting as lieutenant for Ghiyāth al-Dīn. He disapproved of Ghiyāth al-Dīn's incursion into Khurasan. The latter summoned him for consultation and he advised him to give up his planned expedition. Ghiyāth al-Dīn found fault with him for this and had it in mind to banish him but later left him alone. Shihāb al-Dīn arrived with his troops and the armies of Sijistan and elsewhere in Jumādā I of this year [7 February–8 March 1201]. When they reached Maymana, a village between Ṭāliqān and Kurzabān, Shihāb al-Dīn received a letter from Jaqar, the castellan of Marv, asking for him,

[4] The edition now reads 'ibn Kharmīl' here and just below.

so that he could surrender it to him. He asked his brother Ghiyāth al-Dīn for permission, which was granted, and he made his way there. The population along with the Khwārazmian troops issued forth and engaged him. He ordered his men to charge them and fight them fiercely. This they did and forced them back into the city. They attacked with elephants until they drew close to the wall and then the citizens asked for terms. He gave them guarantees and stopped his men doing them harm. Jaqar came out to Shihāb al-Dīn and was given fair promises.

[**165**] After its fall, Ghiyāth al-Dīn came to Marv, took Jaqar and sent him to Herat with all honour. He entrusted Marv to Hindūkhān ibn Malikshāh ibn Khwārazm Shāh Tekesh, whose flight from his uncle Khwārazm Shāh Muḥammad ibn Tekesh to Ghiyāth al-Dīn we have already mentioned, and he enjoined him to treat its people well.

Then Ghiyāth al-Dīn went to Sarakhs, which he took on terms and handed over to Emir Zankī ibn Mas'ūd, a cousin of his, to whom he gave Nasā and Abīward as a fief in addition to it. With his troops he then marched to Ṭūs, and the emir there wished to resist and not surrender. He closed the city gate for three days. Bread reached three *manns*[5] for a Ruknī dinar and the citizens raised a clamour against him, so he sent to Ghiyāth al-Dīn, asking for terms, which were granted. When he came out, he was given a robe of honour and sent to Herat. After this success Ghiyāth al-Dīn sent to 'Alī Shāh, son of Khwārazm Shāh Tekesh, who was his brother 'Alā' al-Dīn Muḥammad's lieutenant in Nishapur, ordering him to abandon the city and warning him, if he stayed, of his brother Shihāb al-Dīn's onslaught. An army from Khwārazm Shāh was with 'Alī Shāh and they agreed to refuse to surrender the city. They fortified it, demolished the constructions outside and cut down the trees. Ghiyāth al-Dīn set out for Nishapur and arrived early in Rajab [began 7 April 1201]. The troops of his brother Shihāb al-Dīn advanced to do battle and when Ghiyāth al-Dīn saw this, he said to his son Maḥmūd, 'The army of Ghazna beat us to the conquest of Marv and they want to conquer Nishapur and gain the renown. Attack the city and do not retire until you reach the wall.' He attacked along with the Ghūr notables and no one drove them back from the wall until they had raised Ghiyāth al-Dīn's banner on it. Seeing his brother's banner on the wall, Shihāb al-Dīn said to his comrades, 'Attack this sector with us and climb the wall here', and he indicated a part of it. The wall fell in ruins and the people cried aloud 'God is great.' The Khwārazmians and the citizens were left in dismay and the Ghūrs entered and seized the city by force of arms and sacked it [**166**] for an hour of daytime. The news reached Ghiyāth al-Dīn, who ordered the proclamation, 'Whoever plunders property or harms any person, his blood may be shed with impunity.' Men restored what they had plundered to the very last item.

A friend of mine, a merchant who was in Nishapur for this episode, told me the following:

---

5 The *mann*, theoretically two *raṭls*, differed greatly according to time and place. It ranged from the equivalent of 833 gm. to about 1,000 gm. (for details for Iran, see Hinz, 16–21).

Some of my goods were plundered, including some sugar. When the troops heard the proclamation, they gave back everything they had taken from me. There remained a carpet and some sugar outstanding. I saw a group had the sugar, but when I asked them for it, they said, 'The sugar, we've eaten it. We ask you not to let anyone hear of this. If you want what it cost, we shall give it you.' 'You can forget that,' I said. These men did not have the carpet. I walked to the city gate with the onlookers and caught sight of my carpet thrown down by the gate. Nobody dared to take it. I took it and said, 'This is mine.' They asked me for someone to vouch for this, so I fetched someone who gave testimony for me and then took it away.

The Khwārazmian troops fortified themselves in the Friday mosque but the citizens drove them out and the Ghurid troops seized them and their property. 'Alī Shāh, Khwārazm Shāh's son, was taken and brought before Ghiyāth al-Dīn on foot. He censured those who brought him for this and was very upset. A nurse who had been 'Alī Shāh's came before Ghiyāth al-Dīn and said to him, 'Is this how the sons of kings are treated!' He replied, 'No, but rather like this,' and he took his hand, gave him a seat with him on the throne and put his mind at rest. Several Khwārazmian emirs he sent under supervision to Herat. He summoned his cousin and son-in-law, Ḍiyā' al-Dīn Muḥammad ibn Abī 'Alī al-Ghūrī, and appointed him military and financial governor of Khurasan and gave him the title 'Alā' al-Dīn, installing alongside him some Ghurid notables. He departed for Herat and handed 'Alī Shāh to his brother Shihāb al-Dīn. He treated the people of Nishapur with kindness and distributed much money among them.

After him Shihāb al-Dīn left for the district of Quhistān. He came to a village and it was mentioned [**167**] to him that the people there were Ismā'īlīs. He ordered the killing of the men who could bear arms, plundered their possessions and enslaved the women. He destroyed the village and left it a ruined waste. He then went to Gunābād,[6] one of the cities wholly inhabited by Ismā'īlīs. He descended on it and began a siege. The lord of Qūhistān sent to Ghiyāth al-Dīn to complain of his brother Shihāb al-Dīn, saying, 'There is a treaty between us. What have we done that you besiege my city?'

The Ismā'īlīs in the city feared Shihāb al-Dīn greatly and asked for terms to allow them to leave. He gave them terms, sent them out and took the city which he gave to one of the Ghūrs, who instituted prayers there and normative practices of Islam. Shihāb al-Dīn then departed and besieged another fortress of the Ismā'īlīs. A messenger from his brother Ghiyāth al-Dīn came to him and said, 'I have a command from the sultan. Do not be furious if I act on it.' 'No [I will not],' he replied, so the other said, 'He says, "What are you doing with my subjects? Depart!"' 'I shall not depart,' said Shihāb al-Dīn. The messenger went on, 'Then I

---

6 Situated about 80 km. north-west of Qāyīn, it is the modern Juymand (see Yāqūt, ii, 120–21; Cornu, *Atlas*, 156).

shall do what he ordered me,' and he drew his sword and severed the guy-ropes of Shihāb al-Dīn's pavilion and said, 'Depart on the sultan's command.' Shihāb al-Dīn along with his troops left reluctantly. He went to India and did not stay at Ghazna, angry at what his brother had done to him.

Account of Nūr al-Dīn's attack on al-'Ādil's lands and the peace they made

During this year Nūr al-Dīn Arslān Shāh, lord of Mosul, made his preparations, assembled his troops and marched against the lands of al-'Ādil in the Jazīra, Ḥarrān and Edessa. The reason for this move was that, when al-'Ādil became ruler of Egypt, as we have previously related, Nūr al-Dīn and al-Ẓāhir, lord of Aleppo, and the lord of Mardin and elsewhere agreed that they should be [**168**] a single force, united to stop al-'Ādil attacking any one of them. When al-Afḍal and al-Ẓāhir began their new action, they sent to Nūr al-Dīn to invade the Jazīran lands. He left Mosul in Sha'bān of this year [7 May–4 June 1201], accompanied by his cousin Quṭb al-Dīn Muḥammad ibn 'Imād al-Dīn Zankī, lord of Sinjār and Nisibis, and the lord of Mardin. He reached Ra's 'Ayn when the weather was extremely hot and sickness was rife among his troops.

At Ḥarrān was al-'Ādil's son called al-Fā'iz with a force to hold the city. When Nūr al-Dīn arrived at Ra's 'Ayn, envoys from al-Fā'iz and the senior emirs who were with him came to him eagerly seeking a settlement. Nūr al-Dīn had already heard that moves to conclude peace had already begun between al-'Ādil, al-Ẓāhir and al-Afḍal, and in addition to that there was the great amount of sickness in his army, so he gave a favourable response. He got al-Fā'iz and the senior emirs with him to swear to the terms that were agreed and they swore that they would secure al-'Ādil's oath for him. If he refused, they would join with Nūr al-Dīn against him. He gave his oath to al-'Ādil. The envoys left him and his son to seek an oath from al-'Ādil. The latter agreed and gave his oath. The settlement was made and security prevailed in the lands. Nūr al-Dīn returned to Mosul in Dhū'l-Qa'da [3 August–1 September 1201].

[169] How Shihāb al-Dīn took Nahrawāla

When Shihāb al-Dīn left Khurasan, as we have mentioned, he did not stay at Ghazna but made for India. He sent his mamluke Quṭb al-Dīn Aybak to Nahrawāla, where he arrived in the year 598 [1201–2]. He was met by the Hindu army which fought him fiercely but Aybak defeated them and ransacked their camp, taking their mounts and other property. He advanced to Nahrawāla and took it by storm. Its ruler fled but proceeded to raise troops, of whom a large number gathered.

Shihāb al-Dīn realized that he was unable to hold the city unless he himself took up residence there and emptied it of its inhabitants. This was impossible for it was a great city, one of the greatest in India, and the most populous. He therefore made peace with its ruler in return for tribute, part paid immediately and part delayed. He withdrew his troops and gave it back to its lord.

Account of Rukn al-Dīn's taking of Malaṭya from his brother and [his taking of] Erzurum

In Ramaḍān this year [June 1201] Rukn al-Dīn Sulaymān ibn Qilij Arslān[7] took Malaṭya, which belonged to his brother Mu'izz al-Dīn Qayṣar Shāh. He marched there and after a siege of some days he took it. From there he went to Erzurum, which was held by the son of Prince [Malikshāh] ibn Muḥammad ibn Ṣaltuq,[8] of an ancient house that ruled Erzurum for a long time. When he drew near on his march, its ruler came out to meet him, trusting in him, to arrange peace on terms acceptable to Rukn al-Dīn. However, he arrested and imprisoned him and took his city. He was the last of his line to rule. Blessed be the ever-living, eternal God whose kingdom lasts for ever and ever.

[170] Account of the death of Suqmān, lord of Āmid, and the succession of his brother Maḥmūd

This year Quṭb al-Dīn Suqmān ibn Muḥammad ibn Qarā Arslān ibn Dā'ūd ibn Suqmān, lord of Āmid and Ḥiṣn Kayfā, died. He fell from the roof of a pleasure pavilion he had outside Ḥiṣn Kayfā and died. He had a strong dislike for his brother and an aversion to him. He banished him and kept him in Ḥiṣn Manṣūr[9] in a remote part of their lands. He took up a mamluke called Iyās, married him to his sister and was greatly enamoured of him, making him his heir apparent. On his death, Iyās became ruler for a number of days and threatened a former vizier of Quṭb al-Dīn's and other emirs of the state. They sent secretly to Suqmān's brother Maḥmūd to summon him. He set out post haste but came to Āmid after Iyās, his brother's mamluke, had already arrived there. However, Iyas dared not refuse to obey and so Maḥmūd took over all the lands and became ruler. The mamluke was

---

7 The Saljuq sultan of Rūm, who was in the process of reconstituting the unitary state (Cahen, *Pre-Ottoman Turkey*, 115), which his father Qilij Arslān II had divided among his many sons (see *Chronicle of Ibn al-Athīr (2)*, p. **[88]**.

8 The history of the late Salṭuqids is obscure. According to Cahen, *Pre-Ottoman Turkey*, 107, the anonymous son in the text was 'Alā al-Dīn Abū Manṣūr, who had replaced his father, al-Muẓaffar Malikshāh ibn Muḥammad, by 593/1197. A different version makes al-Muẓaffar himself the last of his line who was imprisoned by Sulaymān II. See *EI(2)*, viii, 1001, s.v. Saltuḳ Oghulları.

9 i.e. Manṣūr's Castle, west of the Euphrates and south of Malaṭya at the site of the modern Adiyaman. See Yāqūt, ii, 278–9 and Krawulsky, 612.

imprisoned and remained confined for a while, but then the ruler of Anatolia[10] interceded for him and he was released. He went to Anatolia and became one of the state's emirs.

Miscellaneous events

This year famine became serious in Egypt because of the failure of the Nile's inundation. Provisions were impossible to come by, so that people ate carrion and even one another. Later a plague came upon them and high mortality destroyed the population.

In Sha'bān [7 May–4 June 1201] there was an earthquake at Mosul and the whole of the Jazīra, Syria, Egypt and elsewhere. It had a terrible effect in Syria. It destroyed many buildings in Damascus, Homs and Hama. A village of Buṣrā was engulfed and the effect **[171]** was also great on the Syrian coast. Destruction overwhelmed Tripoli, Tyre, Acre, Nablus and other castles. It was felt as far as Anatolia but was insignificant in Iraq and did not destroy buildings.[11]

In Baghdad a child was born with two heads; that is to say, its forehead was divided enough to insert a surgical probe in it.

In Ramaḍān [June 1201] Abū'l-Faraj 'Abd al-Raḥmān ibn 'Alī ibn al-Jawzī, the Ḥanbalī preacher, died in Baghdad. His writings are celebrated. He was very censorious of people, especially of the ulema, both those of opposing schools of law and those of his own. He was born in the year 510/1116–17.[12]

In the same month there died 'Īsā ibn Nuṣayr al-Numayrī, the poet. He was an excellent poet, a man of culture and learning. He died in Baghdad.

This year 'Imād al-Dīn Abū 'Abd Allāh Muḥammad ibn Muḥammad ibn Ḥāmid ibn Muḥammad ibn Aluh died, known as 'Imād al-Dīn, the secretary from Isfahan.[13] He served as administrator for Nūr al-Dīn Maḥmūd ibn Zanki and for Saladin (God be pleased with them both). He was an outstanding government secretary and a master of words.

During this year the person who had seized control of the mountains of Yemen, 'Abd Allāh ibn Ḥamza al-'Alawī, gathered large forces, consisting of 12,000 cavalry and more infantry than could be counted. Some of the troops of al-Mu'izz[14] Ismā'īl ibn Sayf al-Islām Ṭughtakīn ibn Ayyūb, the ruler of Yemen, had joined him

---

[10] i.e. Rukn al-Dīn Sulaymān.

[11] It seems that Ibn al-Athīr mistook the year of this major earthquake which, according to Frankish sources, occurred on 20 May 1202 (Mayer, 'Syrian Earthquake', 302).

[12] This was the prolific author and preacher, author of the chronicle *al-Muntaẓam*, used extensively by Ibn al-Athīr. He died on the eve of Friday 12 Sha'ban/18 May 1201. Sibṭ ibn al-Jawzī, 481–503, has a long section on his grandfather.

[13] The celebrated historian and administrator died on Monday 1 Ramaḍān/Monday = 4 June 1201. See Abū Shāma, *Dhayl*, 27; *Wafāyāt*, v. 147–53; EI(2), iii, 1157–8.

[14] The text incorrectly inserts an 'ibn' after al-Mu'izz.

because they feared him. They were certain that they would conquer the land and they divided it up among themselves. The son of Sayf al-Islām was greatly fearful of them. The generals of Ibn Ḥamza's army gathered together at night to agree on a plan which they could act on. They were twelve generals in number. However, a thunderbolt fell on them and destroyed them [**172**] all. In what remained of that night news of this reached the son of Sayf al-Islām, who moved against them with all haste and fell upon the assembled forces. They did not hold firm but fled before him. Among them 6,000 or more were slain. His rule became firm and well-established in that land.

This year in the land of Shirā between the Hijāz and Yemen a serious plague fell upon the Banū 'Anaza.[15] They dwelt in twenty villages and the plague afflicted eighteen, where not a single person survived. If a person approached one of those villages, he died the moment he drew near. People quarantined them. Their camels and flocks were left with no guard. As for the two other villages, no one died there. They did not in any way experience what those others suffered.

---

[15] An important tribal grouping; see *EI(2)*, i, 482.

[173]

The Year 598 [1201–1202]

Account of Khwārazm Shāh's reconquest of his lands that the Ghurids had taken

We have previously mentioned under the year 597 [1200–1201] how Ghiyāth al-Dīn and his brother Shihāb al-Dīn took what had belonged to Khwārazm Shāh Muḥammad ibn Tekesh in Khurasan, Marv, Nishapur and elsewhere, how they returned after having distributed the lands in fiefs and how Shihāb al-Dīn marched into India. When Khwārazm Shāh 'Alā' al-Dīn Muḥammad ibn Tekesh heard that the Ghurid armies had withdrawn from Khurasan and that Shihāb al-Dīn had entered India, he sent a reprimand to Ghiyāth al-Dīn, saying, 'I believed that you swore an oath to me after my father, that you would aid me against the Khitay and repel them from my lands. Since you have not done so, then the least you can do is not to harm me and seize my lands. What I would like is for you to restore to me what you have taken from me. If you do not, I shall ask for the support of the Khitay and other Turks against you. If I am unable to take my lands, it is only my preoccupation with mourning for my father and settling my lands that distracts me from resisting you. Otherwise I would not be unable to deal with you and seize your lands in Khurasan and elsewhere.' Ghiyāth al-Dīn wrote a temporizing answer to draw out the negotiations to give time for his brother Shihāb al-Dīn to leave India with his troops, for Ghiyāth al-Dīn was incapacitated by overwhelming gout.

When Khwārazm Shāh had read Ghiyāth al-Dīn's letter, he sent to 'Alā' al-Dīn al-Ghūrī,[1] **[174]** Ghiyāth al-Dīn's lieutenant in Khurasan, ordering him to withdraw from Nishapur and threatening him if he failed to do so. 'Alā' al-Dīn wrote to Ghiyāth al-Dīn to tell him of this and to inform him that the population there inclined to the Khwārazmian regime. Ghiyāth al-Dīn replied, stiffening his morale and promising him aid and protection.

Khwārazm Shāh gathered his troops and marched from Khwārazm in the middle of Dhū'l-Ḥijja 597 [16 September 1201]. When he approached Nasā and Abīward, Hindūkhān, his brother Malikshāh's son, fled from Marv to Ghiyāth al-Dīn at Fīrūzkūh. Marv was taken by Khwārazm Shāh, who marched to Nishapur, where 'Alā' al-Dīn was, and put him under siege, making fierce assaults. The siege lasted a long time and more than once he made contact about the surrender of the city but no response was forthcoming as 'Alā' al-Dīn was expecting help from Ghiyāth al-Dīn. He continued so for about two months and then, when relief was slow to come, he sent to Khwārazm Shāh asking for terms for himself and the

[1] i.e. Muḥammad ibn Abī 'Alī. See below, p. [**181**].

Ghurid troops with him, that they should not be exposed to imprisonment or any other harm. This was agreed and sworn to, so they left the city and Khwārazm Shāh treated them kindly, giving then substantial sums and many gifts. He asked 'Alā' al-Dīn to act as go-between to make peace between himself and Ghiyāth al-Dīn and his brother. To this he agreed.

'Alā' al-Dīn went to Herat and from there to his fief. He did not go to Ghiyāth al-Dīn because he blamed him for the delay in his relief. When the Ghurid troops left Khurasan, Khwārazm Shāh was generous to al-Ḥusayn ibn Kharmīl, one of their senior emirs, more than to anyone else and paid him very great respect. It is reported that from that day he made him his sworn ally, to be with him after Ghiyāth al-Dīn and his brother Shihāb al-Dīn.

Khwārazm Shāh went to Sarakhs, where Emir Zankī[2] was, and besieged him for forty days. There were many engagements between the two sides and the inhabitants suffered from lack of supplies, especially of firewood. Zankī sent to Khwārazm Shāh asking him to draw back from the gate [**175**] of the town, so that he and his followers could depart and leave the town to him. Khwārazm Shāh wrote to him suggesting a meeting to show kindness to him and those with him, but he did not agree to that, pleading his close kinship to Ghiyāth al-Dīn. Khwārazm Shāh duly withdrew with his troops some distance from the town gate and Zankī came out and took the grain and other things in the [enemy] camp that he wanted, especially firewood. Then he returned to the town and expelled those for whom the situation had already become difficult. He wrote to Khwārazm Shāh, 'To go back is more praiseworthy.' The latter regretted what he had done when regret was useless. He departed from the town, leaving a group of his emirs to continue the siege.

After Khwārazm Shāh had moved far away, Muḥammad ibn Kharnak, one of the Ghurid emirs, set out from Ṭaliqān and sent to Zankī, emir of Sarakhs, that he was planning to make a surprise attack on the Khwārazmians, so that he would not be anxious when he heard of the conflict. However, the Khwārazmians heard this news and abandoned Sarakhs. Zankī came out and met Muḥammad ibn Kharnak and a force at Marv al-Rūdh. He took the land tax from it and its neighbouring places. Khwārazm Shāh sent an army led by his maternal uncle against them. Muḥammad ibn Kharnak met and fought them. Mace in hand, he charged the Khwārazmian standard-bearer, struck and killed him. He threw down their standard and broke their drums. When the beat was no longer audible to their troops and they could not see the standards, they fled. The Ghurids pursued them for about two leagues, killing and taking prisoners. They were about 3,000 horse, while Ibn Kharnak led 900 horse. All their camp was ransacked. When Khwarazm Shāh heard this news, he returned to Khwārazm and sent to Ghiyāth al-Dīn about peace. He responded to this diplomatic mission by sending a great Ghurid emir, called al-Ḥusayn ibn Muḥammad al-Marghanī (Marghan is a settlement of the

---

2 This was Tāj al-Dīn Zankī ibn Fakhr al-Dīn Mas'ūd, a cousin of Ghiyāth al-Dīn.

Ghūr), whom Khwārazm Shāh arrested.

[176] Account of Khwārazm Shāh's siege of Herat and his withdrawal

When Khwārazm Shāh sent to Ghiyāth al-Dīn on the subject of peace and he answered his mission by sending al-Ḥusayn al-Marghanī to play for time, Khwārazm Shāh arrested al-Ḥusayn and marched to Herat to besiege it. Al-Ḥusayn wrote to his brother 'Umar ibn Muḥammad al-Marghanī, emir of Herat, to tell him of this, so he prepared for the siege.

That Khwārazm Shāh planned to besiege Herat came about as follows. Two brothers, men who had served Sulṭān Shāh Maḥmūd,[3] joined with Ghiyāth al-Dīn after the death of Sulṭān Shāh. He honoured and showed them both favour. One was called Emir al-Ḥājjī. They later wrote to Khwārazm Shāh, whetted his appetite for the city and undertook to surrender it to him. Therefore he set out and descended upon it and put it under siege. Emir 'Umar al-Marghanī, the city's emir, entrusted the keys of the gates to the two of them and put them in charge of the defence as he trusted them and believed that they were enemies of Khwārazm Shāh Tekesh and his son Muḥammad after him. It chanced that one of the Khwārazmians told al-Ḥusayn al-Marghanī, who was a prisoner with Khwārazm Shāh, about the two brothers, that they were the ones who were guiding Khwārazm Shāh and ordering him what to do. He did not believe it, so he brought him a note in Emir al-Ḥājjī's hand. He took it and sent it to his brother 'Umar, emir of Herat, who seized and imprisoned them both and arrested their followers.

Subsequently, Alp Ghāzī, Ghiyāth al-Dīn's nephew, arrived with a force of Ghurid troops and camped five leagues from Herat. He prevented supplies reaching the army of [**177**] Khwārazm Shāh. The latter sent a force to the district of Ṭāliqān on a raid. They were met by al-Ḥusayn ibn Kharmīl, who fought and overcame them. Not one of them escaped.

Ghiyāth al-Dīn marched with his troops from Fīrūzkūh to Herat and camped at the hospice of Razīn, near Herat. He did not advance against Khwārazm Shāh because his troops were few, as most of them were with his brother in India and Ghazna. Khwārazm Shāh remained before Herat for forty days and then determined to withdraw because he had heard of the defeat of his men at Ṭaliqān and that Ghiyāth al-Dīn was close and likewise that Alp Ghāzī was nearby. He heard also that Shihāb al-Dīn had left India for Ghazna, where he arrived in Rajab of this year [28 March–26 April 1202]. He feared that he would arrive with his troops and it would be impossible to maintain the siege, so he sent to the emir of

---

3 The text has Muḥammad incorrectly. An Ms. variant has 'his uncle Sultān Shāh'. Sultān Shāh Maḥmūd, son of Khwārazm Shāh Arslān ibn Atsiz, died in Ramaḍan 589/September 1193 (see p. [**104**]). He was the brother of Khwārazm Shāh Tekesh and hence the uncle of Khwārazm Shāh Muḥammad.

Herat, ‘Umar al-Marghanī, about making peace. He agreed to this on payment of some tribute and Khwārazm Shāh left the city.

As for Shihāb al-Dīn, after he came to Ghazna, he was told of what Khwārazm Shāh had done in Khurasan and how he had taken it. He marched to Khurasan and came to Balkh and from there to Bāmiyān and then to Marv, intending to bring Khwārazm Shāh to battle, as he was residing there. The advance guards of both armies met and fought. Large numbers were killed on both sides. Then Khwārazm Shāh left his position as though in rout. He breached the dykes and killed Emir Sanjar, lord of Nishapur, because he suspected him of treachery. Shihāb al-Dīn moved to Ṭūs, where he spent that winter, with the intention of marching to Khwārazm to besiege it. However, news came to him of the death of his brother Ghiyāth al-Dīn, so he went to Herat and abandoned that plan.

[178] Miscellaneous events

This year Majd al-Dīn Abū ‘Alī Yaḥyā ibn al-Rabī‘, the Shāfi‘ī lawyer, lectured in the Niẓāmiyya at Baghdad in Rabī‘ I [December 1201].

The following died this year:

Banfasha (Amethyst), the concubine of the Caliph al-Mustaḍī’ bi-Amr Allāh. He showed her much favour and loved her greatly. She was devoted to what was good and was very kind and charitable.[4]

The preacher, ‘Abd al-Malik ibn Zayd al-Dawla‘ī, the preacher of Damascus. He was a Shāfi‘ī lawyer who came from al-Dawla‘iyya, a village in the district of Mosul.[5]

---

4 She died in Rabī‘ I/December 1201. At Baghdad she built hospices, a mosque and ‘the bridge’ and gave much to ‘the ulema, Sufis and the poor’ (Sibṭ ibn al-Jawzī, 510–11).

5 Born 507/1113–14, he studied in Baghdad, settled in Damascus and died in Rabī‘ I/December 1201 (Sibṭ ibn al-Jawzī, 511).

The Year 599 [1202–1203]

Account of the siege of Mardin by al-'Ādil's army and the agreement reached with its ruler

In Muḥarram this year [20 September–19 October 1203] al-'Ādil Abū Bakr ibn Ayyūb, lord of Damascus and Egypt, sent an army with his son al-Ashraf Mūsā to Mardin.[1] They besieged the town and appointed prefects[2] over its dependencies. The army from Mosul, from Sinjār and elsewhere joined them and they camped at Ḥarzam below Mardin. A force descended from the castle of al-Bāri'iyya, which was held by the lord of Mardin, to cut the supply route of al-'Ādil's army. A detachment of the latter moved against them, engaged them and put the force from al-Bāri'iyya to flight.

The Turkomans rose up and cut the highway in that region, causing much disturbance. Travel on the route was impossible except for a sizeable number of armed men. A detachment of al-'Ādil's force went to Ra's 'Ayn to improve the situation on the roads and prevent the damage of the troublemakers. Al-'Ādil's son remained there but achieved nothing. The ruler of Aleppo, al-Ẓāhir Ghāzī, Saladin's son, entered the peace talks between them and made contact with his uncle al-'Ādil on the matter, who agreed to the settlement that the lord of Mardin should pay him 150,000 dinars (one dinar being rated at eleven *qīrāṭ*s of *amīrī*s), that he should make the khutbah for him in his lands, strike coins in his name and that his troops should be at his service any time he asked for them. Al-Ẓāhir took 20,000 [**180**] dinars of the cash mentioned and the village of al-Qurādī[3] in the district of Shabakhtān. Al-'Ādil's son then departed from Mardin.

Account of the death of Ghiyāth al-Dīn, king of the Ghūr, and a little about his life

Ghiyāth al-Dīn Abū'l-Fatḥ Muḥammad ibn Sām al-Ghūrī, lord of Ghazna, part of Khurasan and elsewhere, died in Jumādā I of this year [16 January–14 February 1203]. His demise was concealed. Shihāb al-Dīn, his brother, was in Ṭūs, planning to attack Khwārazm Shāh, when news of his brother's death reached him. He set out for Herat and, when he arrived there, he held sessions of condolence for his

---

1 Mardin was held by the Artuqid Nāṣir al-Dīn Arslān; see Eddé, *Principauté ayyoubide*, 78.

2 This is a speculative translation of *shaḥḥana*, taking it as a denominative verb from *shiḥna* (prefect, garrison commander). Cf. its use below, p. [**479**].

3 See Elisséef, 140.

brother during Rajab [16 March–14 April 1203] and at that time his death was made public. Ghiyāth al-Dīn left a son named Maḥmūd, who took the title Ghiyāth al-Dīn after his father's death. We shall be narrating a good deal of his history.

When Shihāb al-Dīn left Ṭūs, he left as deputy in Marv Emir Muḥammad ibn Kharnak. Several of the Khwārazmian emirs came against him but Muḥammad went out to them at night and took them by surprise. Only a few survived, and the captives and the heads were sent to Herat. Shihāb al-Dīn ordered preparations to invade Khwārazm by the desert route and Khwārazm Shāh equipped a force and sent them with Barfūr the Turk to fight Muḥammad ibn Kharnak, who heard news of them, moved out and encountered them ten leagues from Marv. After a fierce battle in which many on both sides were killed, the Ghurid troops were defeated and Muḥammad ibn Kharnak entered Marv with ten horsemen. The Khwārazmians came and besieged the city for fifteen days. Muḥammad was too weak [**181**] to hold it and sent a request for terms. They swore that, if he came out willing to accept whatever they decided, they would not kill him. He did surrender to them but they killed him and took all he had.

Shihāb al-Dīn heard this news and was outraged. There was an exchange of envoys between him and Khwārazm Shāh but no peace was arranged. He wished to return to Ghazna, so he appointed his nephew Alp Ghazī over Herat and Falak al-Mulk 'Alā' al-Dīn Muḥammad ibn Abī 'Alī al-Ghūrī over the city of Fīrūzkūh. He also made him military commander of Khurasan and responsible for all affairs of state. His brother Ghiyāth al-Dīn's son, Maḥmūd, came to him and he made him governor of Bust, Isfizār and that region. He kept him detached from all sovereign power and did not bestow on him nor on any other member of his family the succession to his father. One of the things he did was the following. Ghiyāth al-Dīn had a wife, who had been a singing girl, whom he fell in love with and married. When he died, Shihāb al-Dīn arrested her and gave her a violent beating. He also beat her son Ghiyāth al-Dīn [Maḥmūd[4]] and her sister's husband, seized their money and their property, then sent them to India. They were in the worst possible situation. She had built a madrasa, where she buried her father, mother and brother. He demolished it, dug up their graves and threw away their bones.

As regards Ghiyāth al-Dīn's manner of life and his character, he was successful and victorious in his battles. Never was a banner of his defeated, although he was himself seldom directly engaged in warfare. He was simply cunning and wily. He was generous and his creed was sound. His alms and his charitable endowments in Khurasan were numerous. He built mosques and madrasahs in Khurasan for the followers of al-Shāfi'ī and also caravanserais on the highways. He cancelled [**182**] the non-canonical taxes and laid hands on nobody's property. If anyone died without an heir, he gave his estate away in alms. If anyone from a known place died in his city, he would hand his property to merchants who were his compatriots and, if he could not find anybody, he would entrust it to the cadi and keep it

---

4 Her son took the title Ghiyāth al-Dīn after the death of his father (see p. [**180**]).

under seal until someone came who could take it in accordance with the Shariah.

When he came to a town, his liberality encompassed its people, the lawyers and the scholars. He would bestow robes of honour on them and assign them annual pensions from his treasury. He would also distribute money to the poor and show proper regard to all Alids, poets and such-like who came to his court. He was a man of abundant learning and literary culture, in addition to having an excellent hand and a gift of eloquence. He used (God have mercy on him) to make Koran copies in his own hand and present them in perpetual trust to the madrasahs that he built. He did not reveal partisanship for any school of law but would say, 'Partisanship for law schools in a ruler is reprehensible.' However, he was himself of the Shāfi'ī school. He inclined towards the Shāfi'īs without encouraging them at the expense of others and did not give them more than they were due.

How al-Ẓāhir took Qal'at Najm from his brother al-Afḍal

This year al-Ẓāhir Ghāzī took Qal'at Najm[5] from his brother al-Afḍal. It was part of what he had received from al-'Ādil when he made peace with him in the year 597 [1200–1201].

When this year came al-'Ādil took from al-Afḍal Sarūj, Jamalīn and Ra's 'Ayn, and Sumaysāṭ and Qal'at Najm were left in his possession. Al-Ẓāhir sent to him to ask him for Qal'at Najm and undertook to intercede with his uncle al-'Ādil for the restoration of what had been taken from him. He refused to give it up, so al-Ẓāhir threatened that he would join those hostile to him. Envoys continued to go to and fro until he surrendered the castle to him in Sha'bān [15 April–13 May 1203] and asked him [**183**] to give him some villages or money in exchange. He did not do so. This was one of the most shameful things reported of a prince, to pressure his brother for the like of Qal'at Najm, although it was insignificant and paltry, while he had many lands and his brother lacked them.

As for al-'Ādil, after he had taken Sarūj and Ra's 'Ayn from al-Afḍal, the latter sent his mother to him to request their return but he did not accept her intercession and sent her back disappointed. The house of Saladin was punished for the way their ancestor had treated the Atabeg house, for when he planned the siege of Mosul in the year 580 [1184–5], the lord of Mosul sent his mother and the daughter of his uncle Nūr al-Dīn to Saladin to request that he withdraw. He did not accept their intercession.[6] Now his sons had this experience and his own wife was sent away disappointed, as he had treated others.

When al-Afḍal saw that his uncle and his brother had taken what had been his, he sent to Rukn al-Dīn Sulaymān ibn Qilij Arslān, lord of Malaṭya and Konya and

---

5 This was a strong fortress on the east bank of the Euphrates at an important crossing place not far from Manbij (Yāqūt, iv, 165; Le Strange, *Caliphate*, 107; Krawulsky, 614).

6 For this incident, in fact in 581/1185, see *Chronicle of Ibn al-Athīr (2)*, p. [**512**].

the territory between, offering to be obedient to him and at his service and to make the khutbah for him and strike coins in his name. Rukn al-Dīn accepted this and sent him a robe of honour, which al-Afḍal donned. He made the khutbah in his name at Sumaysāṭ in the year 600 [1203–4] and became an ally of his.[7]

Account of the king of the Georgians' conquest of Dvin

This year the Georgians took possession of the city of Dvin in Azerbayjan, which they plundered and gave up to be sacked, killing most of the inhabitants. It and all the land of Azerbayjan had been held by Emir Abū Bakr ibn Pahlawān. Normally he was preoccupied in drinking night and day, never recovering and being sober, and not looking into the affairs of his realm, his subjects and his army. He had cast all this from his mind and followed the path of someone who has no affiliation or bond. The local population had frequently called upon him for help and informed him of the incursions of the Georgians with raids time after time. It was as though they were appealing to a deaf rock. When during this year the Georgians besieged the city of [**184**] Dvin, many citizens came seeking help but he gave none. Several of his emirs warned him of the result of his neglect and feebleness and his persistence in his present course, but he did not listen to them. After this continued for a long time, the inhabitants became weak and incapable. The Georgians then violently overwhelmed them with the sword and did what we have mentioned.

After their position was well established there, the Georgians treated the remaining inhabitants well. Truly God Almighty will consider the Muslims and provide for their frontier lands someone to guard and protect them, for they are open to spoliation, especially this region. We are God's and to Him do we return. What we heard about the killing, enslavement and subjection that the Georgians imposed on the people of Dvin is enough to make one's skin creep.

Miscellaneous events

This year al-'Ādil summoned Muḥammad, the son of al-'Azīz the lord of Egypt, to Edessa. The reason for this was that, when he cancelled the khutbah for him in Egypt in the year 596 [1199–1200], as we have mentioned, he feared that his father's supporters might combine against him and that he might have trouble with them. So he expelled him in the year 598 [1200–1201] and then during this year brought him to Edessa, where he remained with all his brothers and sisters, his mother and his personal retainers.

In Rajab [16 March–14 April 1203] Shaykh Wajīh al-Dīn Muḥammad ibn Maḥmūd al-Marwarūdhī, the Shāfi'ī lawyer, died. He is the person who gave the

---

7 For these events, see Eddé, *Principauté ayyoubide*, 78.

instigation for Waḥīd al-Dīn to become a Shāfi‘ī.[8]

In Rabī‘ I [18 November–17 December 1202] Abū'l-Futūḥ ‘Ubayd Allāh ibn Abī'l-Mu‘ammar, the Shāfi‘ī lawyer, known as al-Mustamlī, died in Baghdad. He had an excellent hand.

In Rabī‘ II [18 December 1202–15 January 1203] Zumurrud Khātūn, the mother of the Caliph al-Nāṣir li-Dīn Allāh, died. Her bier was brought forth publicly and vast crowds of people prayed for her. She was buried in the mausoleum that she built for herself. She was a person of many good deeds.[9]

---

[8] He was also instrumental in making a Shāfi‘ī of the Ghurid Sultan Ghiyāth al-Dīn; see *Chronicle of Ibn al-Athīr (2)*, p. [**384**].

[9] According to Sibṭ ibn al-Jawzī, 513–14, she died in Jumādā I/ 16 January–14 February. The caliph walked before her bier, crossed the Tigris in a fleet of boats and then there was a long walk to the mausoleum near that of Ma‘rūf al-Karkhī. The vizier who was fat had to sit down several times and nearly died.

[185] The Year 600 [1203–1204]

Account of Khwārazm Shāh's second siege of Herat

This year on 1 Rajab [5 March 1204] Khwārazm Shāh Muḥammad came to Herat, where Alp Ghāzī, nephew of Shihāb al-Dīn al-Ghūrī, the ruler of Ghazna, was, and subjected the city to a siege after an exchange of missions between him and Shihāb al-Dīn about making peace, which was not concluded. Shihāb al-Dīn had left Ghazna for Lahore, planning to raid India. Khwārazm Shāh continued to besiege Herat until the end of Sha'bān [2 May 1204].

The fighting was continuous and the deaths on both sides numerous. Among those killed was the headman of Khurasan, a man of great standing who resided in the shrine at Ṭūs. Al-Ḥusayn ibn Kharmīl was in Kurzabān, which was his fief, and he sent to Khwārazm Shāh, saying, 'Send us a force to which we may surrender the elephants and the treasury of Shihāb al-Dīn.' He duly sent him at Kurzabān 1,000 cavalry, his leading troops. Al-Ḥusayn and al-Ḥusayn ibn Muḥammad al-Marghanī moved out to meet them and killed them all but a few. When the news reached Khwārazm Shāh, he was crestfallen and regretted sending his troops. He made contact with Alp Ghāzī to ask him to come to him out of the city and to salute him as sultan so that he could then depart. He did not agree to this but it happened that he fell ill and his illness became serious. He feared that he would be distracted by his illness and that Khwārazm Shāh would take the city. He therefore agreed to what was requested, got him to swear to peace terms and presented him with a magnificent gift. He left the city to attend on him but then collapsed to the ground, dead. No one was aware that this had happened and Khwārazm Shāh withdrew from the city, burned his siege engines and departed to Sarakhs, where he took up residence.

[186] Account of Shihāb al-Dīn's return from India, his besieging Khwārazm Shāh and his defeat by the Khitay

This year in Ramaḍān [May 1204] Shihāb al-Dīn al-Ghūrī returned to Khurasan from his Indian expedition. The reason for this was that he heard of Khwārazm Shāh's siege of Herat and the death of Alp Ghāzī, his own lieutenant there. He returned, furious with Khwārazm Shāh, and when he reached Maymand, he turned aside on to another route to go to Khwārazm. Khwārazm Shāh sent to him saying, 'Return to me so that I may bring you to battle, otherwise I shall go to Herat and from there to Ghazna.' Khwārazm Shāh had left Sarakhs to go to Marv, where he remained outside. Shihāb al-Dīn replied, 'Perhaps you will be defeated as happened on that other occasion. No, we shall meet at Khwārazm.' Khwārazm Shāh then divided his troops, burnt the fodder that he had gathered and set out to get to Khwārazm before Shihāb al-Dīn. He did arrive first and blocked the route by flooding it. Shihāb al-Dīn was unable to proceed and waited for forty days to repair the route so that he could reach Khwārazm. The two armies met at Qarāsū,[1] which means 'Black Water', and a fierce battle ensued in which there were many dead on both sides. Among those killed on the Ghurid side was al-Ḥusayn al-Marghanī, along with others. Several of the Khwārazmians were taken prisoner and Shihāb al-Dīn ordered them killed, which was done.

Khwārazm Shāh sent to the Khitay Turks to seek their aid, they being at that time the masters of Transoxania. They made their preparations and set out for Ghurid territory. Having heard this, Shihāb al-Dīn retired from Khwārazm and encountered their advance guard in the desert of Andkhūd on 1 Ṣafar 601 [28 September 1204]. He killed and captured many of them. However, on the following day he was crushed [**187**] by a force of the Khitay that he could not withstand. The Muslims suffered a dreadful defeat. The first to flee was al-Ḥusayn ibn Kharmīl, lord of Ṭaliqān. The army followed him and Shihāb al-Dīn was left with a small band. With his own hand he killed four [of his] elephants because they were exhausted, but the unbelievers captured two. Shihāb al-Dīn entered Andkhūd with the men he still had. The unbelievers besieged him but came to terms with him, on condition that he give them another elephant. He did so and gained his freedom.

Reports that he was dead spread throughout his lands and rumours of that multiplied. Later, however, he arrived at Ṭāliqān with seven persons. Most of his men had been killed and all his treasury plundered. Nothing of it remained. Al-Ḥusayn ibn Kharmīl, lord of Ṭāliqān, sent out to him some tents and everything he needed. He then went to Ghazna, taking al-Ḥusayn ibn Kharmīl with him, because he was told that Ḥusayn was extremely fearful since he had fled and that he said, 'When the sultan leaves, I shall run away to Khwārazm Shāh.' So he took him with him and made him emir-chamberlain.

When the rumour of his death spread, Tāj al-Dīn Yildiz, a mamluke whom Shihāb al-Dīn had purchased, gathered his followers and made an attempt to gain access to the citadel of Ghazna. The castellan resisted him, so he returned to his house and remained there. He stirred up the Khalaj and all other troublemakers, interrupted travellers on the roads and killed many. After Shihāb al-Dīn had returned to Ghazna, he heard what Yildiz had done and wished to kill him, but all the other mamlukes interceded for him, so he let him go and he later apologized. Shihāb al-Dīn travelled around his lands and put to death a large number of troublemakers of the races mentioned.

---

[1] 'A canal of the Oxus east of Gurganj' (Biran, *Empire of the Qara Khitai*, 67). *Kāmil* inverts the elements and calls it Sūqarā.

He also had another mamluke, whose name was Aybak Bāk(?).[2] He survived the battle and made his way to India, entering Multan. He killed the sultan's lieutenant there, took power in the town and seized the sultan's monies. He behaved very badly towards the subjects and seized their goods. He said, 'The sultan has been killed and I am sultan.' He was urged and encouraged in this by a man called 'Umar ibn Yazān, who was a *zindīq*. He did what this man told him, gathered troublemakers, seized property [**188**] and made the roads dangerous. Information about him reached Shihāb al-Dīn, who set out for India. He sent troops against him, who took him together with 'Umar ibn Yazān and put both to a very ugly death. During Jumādā II 601 [24 January–21 February 1205] Shihāb al-Dīn also killed those who had acted with them. When he saw them dead, he recited 'The reward of those who wage war on God and His prophet and strive to make mischief on the earth is to be killed or crucified.'[3] Shihāb al-Dīn commanded that it should be proclaimed throughout his lands that preparation should be made to fight and attack the Khitay and take revenge on them.

[In another version] it is said that the reason for his defeat was as follows. When he went back to the Khitay from Khwārazm, he divided his army in the desert that was on his route because of the shortage of water. The Khitay had camped on the route from the desert. As each detachment of his men emerged, they destroyed them, killing and taking prisoners. Any of his troops that survived fled towards their homeland and not one of them returned to him to acquaint him with what was happening. Shihāb al-Dīn then arrived in the rearguard, leading 20,000 cavalry and unaware of the situation. When he emerged from the desert, the Khitay, fresh and rested, met him. He and his men were tired and exhausted. The Khitay were several times more numerous than his men, but he fought them throughout the day and defended himself from them. They blockaded him in Andkhūd and during several days there were fourteen engagements between them, one of which lasted from late afternoon till morning on the following day. Later he sent away a detachment of his army secretly by night and ordered them to return to him in the morning, as though they were reinforcements, come from his territory. After this move, the Khitay feared him. The lord of Samarqand,[4] who was a Muslim but subject to the Khitay and one who feared for Islam and the Muslims if Shihāb al-Dīn were vanquished, said to them, 'You will never find this man weaker than he was when he came out of the desert, but despite his weakness, his fatigue and the fewness of his followers we did not overcome him. He has now received reinforcements. You can imagine his troops [**189**] that have set out from every direction. At this time let us seek to be free of him, for we cannot overcome him.

---

2 The edition has Aybak Bāl T.rā (with a variant: Bāk), an unexplained name. Below on p. [**209**] the same man, it seems, is called Aybak Bāk. That simpler form has been adopted here, but only tentatively.

3 Koran, v, 33.

4 i.e. the Qarakhanid sultan, 'Uthmān (see *Ṭabaqāt-i Nāṣirī*, 479; Biran, *Empire of the Qara Khitai*, 68).

The right course is for us to make peace with him.' They agreed to this and sent to him to discuss peace.

The ruler of Samarqand had already sent to Shihāb al-Dīn and secretly informed him of the situation. He asked him to make a show of refusing peace at first and eventually to agree. When the envoys came to him, he resisted and made a show of strength because he was expecting reinforcements. Discussions lasted a long time but they reached agreement on condition that the Khitay should not cross the river to attack his lands and that he too should not cross into their lands. The Khitay withdrew and he escaped and returned to his lands. The rest [of this account] is similar to what has already been mentioned

Account of the killing of a group of Ismāʿīlīs in Khurasan

During this year a messenger came to Shihāb al-Dīn al-Ghūrī from the leader of the Ismāʿīlīs in Khurasan with a communication which did not meet with his approval. He ordered ʿAla' al-Dīn Muḥammad ibn Abī ʿAlī, the governor of the Ghūr lands, to march with some troops against them and blockade their lands. He duly set out with many troops to Quhistan. The lord of Zūzan heard of his coming, sought him out and joined with him, leaving the service of Khwārazm Shāh. ʿAlā' al-Dīn camped before the city of Qā'īn, which belonged to the Ismāʿīlīs, put it under siege and pressed hard on the inhabitants. News arrived of the death of Shihāb al-Dīn, as we shall mention, so he made peace with the inhabitants on their payment of 60,000 Ruknī dirhams and then departed. He attacked the fortress of Kākhk,[5] took it and killed the fighting men and enslaved the children. Then he went to Herat and from there to Fīrūzkūh.

[190] How Constantinople was taken from the Byzantines

In Shaʿbān of this year [April 1204] the Franks took Constantinople from the Byzantines and removed it from Byzantine sovereignty.[6] This came about as follows. The emperor had married the sister of the king of the French, one of the greatest kings of the Franks, and a male child was born to him from her. A brother of his seized power, arrested him and took the city from him. He blinded him and put him in prison, but his son fled and went to his maternal uncle to seek help against his father's brother.[7] This took place after many Franks had gathered to

[5] A large settlement in the province of Gunābad within Quhistan (see Krawulsky, 126, and reference there cited).

[6] For an account of the so-called Fourth Crusade, its background and consequences, see Runciman, iii, 109–31; Queller and Madden, *Fourth Crusade*; Phillips, *Fourth Crusade*.

[7] Ibn al-Athīr's version is incorrect. The Emperor Isaac II Angelus married his daughter Irene to Philip of Swabia, king of Germany, shortly before he was blinded, deposed and

leave for Syria and recover Jerusalem from the Muslims. They took the emperor's son with them and took their route by Constantinople with the intention of repairing relations between him and his paternal uncle. He himself had no ambition beyond that. When they arrived, his uncle came forth with the armies of Byzantium to fight them. They met in battle in Rajab 599 [16 March–14 April 1203] and the Greeks were defeated. They entered the city and the Franks did so too, along with them. The emperor fled to the limits of his territory. It is said that the emperor did not engage the Franks outside the city. He was only besieged within.

In Constantinople there were Greeks who were in favour of the boy, so they set fire to the city. This distracted the populace. They then opened one of the city gates and the Franks entered through it. The emperor left in flight and the Franks invested that boy with the imperial rank but he had no authority at all. They released his father from prison, although the Franks were the only powers in the city. They applied burdensome pressure on the inhabitants and demanded monies from them that they could not produce. They seized the wealth of the churches, the gold and silver and such-like that were in them, even that which was on the crosses and on images of the Messiah (upon Him be peace) and the disciples, and also what was on copies of the New Testament.

The Greeks were outraged at this and endured great anguish at it. They sought out that boy emperor, killed him and expelled the Franks from the city, locking the gates. This was in [**191**] Jumādā I 600 [6 January–4 February 1204]. The Franks remained outside, besieging the Greeks, engaging them continously night and day. The Greeks became very weak and sent to Sultan Rukn al-Dīn Sulaymān ibn Qilij Arslān, lord of Konya and other lands, asking for his aid but he found no way to respond.

In the city there were many Franks who were resident, approaching 30,000 in number. Because of the great size of the city their presence was not obvious. They and the Franks outside the city conspired together. They rose up and started fires a second time, so that about a quarter of the city was burnt down. They opened the gates, allowing the others to enter. For three days they put the sword to work and destroyed the Greeks, killing and plundering. All the Greeks were left either dead or impoverished, possessing nothing. A number of leading Byzantines entered the great church known as [Agia] Sophia. The Franks moved against it and several priests, bishops and monks emerged, carrying the Gospel and the cross as a way of appealing to the Franks to spare them. They paid no attention to them but slew them all and sacked the church.

There were three princes: the Doge of Venice, who was the master of warships and in whose ships they had sailed to Constantinople, a blind old man, whose horse

---

imprisoned by his brother Alexius III in 1195. His son, another Alexius, was also imprisoned but escaped in late 1201 and fled to his sister and brother-in-law in Germany (Runciman, iii, 111–12; Vasiliev, *Byzantine Empire*, ii, 439–40).

was led when he rode; the second was called the Marquis, the commander of the French, and the third was called Count of Flanders, who had the largest following.[8] When they took possession of Constantinople, they cast lots to choose a ruler and the lot fell to the Count of Flanders. They cast lots a second and a third time but he won, so they made him ruler. God gives kingship to whomsoever He wishes and takes it from whomsoever He wishes.[9] When he won the lot, they made him ruler of the city and the neighbouring lands. The Doge of Venice was to have the large islands, such as Crete, Rhodes and others, while the Marquis [**192**] of the French was to have the lands east of the straits such as Nicaea and Laodicaea.[10] None of them actually acquired anything apart from the person who took Constantinople. As for the remainder [of the territory], none of the Greeks there survived, and as for the lands that had been the emperor's, east of the straits, which were neighbouring the territory of Rukn al-Dīn Sulaymān ibn Qilij Arslan, including Nicaea and Laodicaea, they were seized by a great Byzantine patrician, named Lascaris, in whose hands they are to this day.[11]

Account of the defeat of Nūr al-Dīn, lord of Mosul, by the forces of al-ʿĀdil

On 20 Shawwāl [21 June 1204] Nūr al-Dīn Arslān Shāh, lord of Mosul, was defeated by the forces of al-ʿĀdil. This came about as follows. Between Nūr al-Dīn and his cousin[12] Quṭb al-Dīn Muḥammad ibn Zankī, lord of Sinjār, there was initially an entrenched aversion, but they came to an agreement. They went together to Mayyāfāriqīn in the year 595 [1198–9], as we have mentioned. At the present time al-ʿĀdil Abū Bakr ibn Ayyūb, lord of Egypt, Damascus and the Jazīra, sent to Quṭb al-Dīn and tried to win him over. He did incline to him and made the khutbah in his name. When Nūr al-Dīn heard of this, he went to Nisibis, which was held by Quṭb al-Dīn, at the end of Shaʿbān [2 May 1204] and besieged it. He took the city but the citadel held out, so he invested it for a number of days. While the siege was continuing and he was on the point of taking it, he received the report that Muẓaffar al-Dīn Kūkbūrī ibn Zayn al-Dīn ʿAlī, lord of Irbil, had attacked the Mosul district, plundered Nineveh and burnt its crops. Having heard this news from his deputy installed in Mosul to protect it, Nūr al-Dīn left Nisibis to go to Mosul with the intention of crossing the river into the territory of Irbil and

---

8 These three are the Doge Enrico Dandolo (1192–1205), Boniface Marquis of Montferrat, who had been elected leader of the Crusade after the death of Tibald of Champagne, and Baldwin IX of Hainault, Count of Flanders.

9 A reference to Koran, iii, 26.

10 In Arabic Lādhīk, 9 km. from modern Denizli (Krawulsky, 398–9; *EI(2)*, ii, 204–5).

11 This was the ancestor of a future imperial dynasty, Theodore Lascaris, the husband of Anna, daughter of Alexius III. For details concerning the distribution of territory, see Runciman, iii, 124–7.

12 The text has *ʿammi-hi* (his uncle). It should read *ibn ʿammi-hi* (his cousin).

ravaging it to requite what its ruler had done in his lands. He arrived at Balad and Muẓaffar al-Dīn retired to Irbil. Nūr al-Dīn realized that what he had been told had been exaggerated. From Balad he marched to Tell A'far, besieged it and, having taken it, organised its affairs and remained there for seventeen days.

[**193**] Al-Ashraf Mūsā, son of al-'Ādil, had gone from Ḥarrān to Ra's 'Ayn to aid Quṭb al-Dīn, lord of Sinjār and Nisibis. He, along with Muẓaffar al-Dīn, lord of Irbil, and the lord of Ḥisn [Kayfā] and Āmid, and the lord of Jazīrat Ibn 'Umar and others, had agreed on that and on preventing Nūr al-Dīn from taking any of his lands. All of them feared him but were unable to meet while he was at Nisibis. When Nūr al-Dīn departed, al-Ashraf proceeded there and the lord of Ḥisn [Kayfā],[13] the lord of Jazīrat [Ibn 'Umar] and the lord of Dārā joined him and they moved from Nisibis towards the district of al-Baq'ā[14] near Būshrā. Nūr al-Dīn went from Tell A'far to Kafar Zammār[15] and decided to play a waiting game to bring about their dissolution. He received a letter from one of his mamlukes, called Jurdīk, whom he had sent to spy on them. He played down their strength to him and encouraged him to attack them, saying, 'If you give permission, I shall face them on my own.' Thereupon Nūr al-Dīn marched to Būshrā and arrived at noon on the following day when his mounts and his men were tired and had experienced hardship because of the heat. He camped near the enemy for less than an hour.

News came to him that the enemy troops had mounted up, so he and his men did the same and moved towards them but saw no trace of them, so returned to his camp. He and his men dismounted and many of them scattered in the villages to get fodder and things they needed. Someone came with the news that the enemy were on the move and coming his way, so he and his troops mounted up and advanced to meet them. There were about two leagues between them. They halted, now more tired than ever, while the enemy was rested. They met and fought but the conflict did not last long before Nūr al-Dīn's army fled.[16] He too fled and made for Mosul, where he arrived with four persons. His men caught up little by little. Al-Ashraf and his men came to camp at Kafar Zammār. They sacked the area in a terrible fashion and destroyed whatever was no use to them, especially at Balad, for the way they plundered there was atrocious.

[**194**] A strange thing we heard is that a woman was cooking and when she saw the pillaging, she threw two bracelets she had on her arms into the fire and fled. A soldier came and ransacked the house. He saw some eggs there, took them and put them on the fire to make a meal. He stirred the fire, caught sight of the bracelets there and took them.

---

13 i.e. the Artuqid Nāṣir al-Dīn Maḥmūd ibn Muḥammad ibn Qarā Arslān.

14 According to Yāqūt, i, 701, a large district in the territory of Mosul, the chief town of which is Barqa'īd.

15 Tell A'far is a fortress and settlement between Sinjār and Mosul (Yāqūt, i, 863–4), and Kafar Zammār an extensive area, part of the districts of Qurdā and Bāzandā, four or five leagues from Barqā'īd (Yāqūt, iv, 288).

16 The battle took place on Saturday 19 Sha'bān/= 24 April 1204 (Sibṭ ibn al-Jawzī, 518).

They remained for a long time, while envoys went to and fro about peace. Talks were stalled over the return of Tell A'far and whether the settlement should be on the original basis. Nūr al-Dīn was reluctant to give Tell A'far back, but after lengthy negotiation he gave it up to them. Peace was agreed early in the year 601 [began 29 August 1204]. The armies departed their separate ways.

Account of the Franks' incursion into Islamic territory in Syria and the peace made with them

This year many Franks came to Syria by sea. It was an easy matter for them to do this because of their conquest of Constantinople. They anchored at Acre and planned to attack Jerusalem (God protect it) and recover it from the Muslims. When they had rested at Acre, they set out and plundered much territory of Islam in the region of the Jordan. They took captives and did much slaughter among the Muslims.[17]

Al-'Ādil was at Damascus and he sent messages for the gathering of his troops from Syria and Egypt. He moved to a camp at Ṭūr near Acre to prevent the Franks from invading Muslim territory. The Franks camped in the plain of Acre and raided Kafar Kannā,[18] seizing everyone there [**195**] and their property. The emirs were urging al-'Ādil to invade and ravage their lands but he did not do so. They remained as they were until the year had ended, that is, the year 601 [ended 17 August 1205]. Al-'Ādil made peace with the Franks for Damascus and its dependencies and for what he held in Syria. He ceded to them all the shared revenues for Sidon, Ramla and other places, gave them Nazareth and elsewhere and then set out towards Egypt. The Franks attacked Hama, whose ruler, Nāṣir al-Dīn Muḥammad ibn Taqī al-Dīn 'Umar ibn Shāhinshāh ibn Ayyūb, met and fought them. He was leading a small force, so they defeated and pursued him to the town. The common people came out to engage them but the Franks killed several of them and then withdrew.

Account of the killing of Kūkjeh in the Uplands

We have already mentioned that Kūkjeh, Pahlawān's mamluke, had seized control of Rayy, Hamadhan and the Uplands and continued until this present time. He had

---

17 Many members of the Fourth Crusade declined to join those who were diverted to Constantinople to support the cause of the young prince Alexius and eventually to sack the city (April 1204). For example, a Flemish fleet arrived at Acre in April 1203, but activities were constrained by the truce that King Aimery II maintained until its end in November 1203. See Queller et al., 'The neglected majority'.

18 i.e. Cana of Galilee.

shown special favour to another mamluke who had been Pahlawān's, called Aydughmish, and promoted him, was generous to him and trusted him. However, Aydughmish assembled bands of mamlukes and other followers and then attacked Kūkjeh. The two parties fought a pitched battle in which Kūkjeh was slain, so Aydughmish took control of the lands and secured the person of Uzbek ibn Pahlawān, who was titular ruler while Aydughmish directed him and undertook all the affairs of state. He was resolute, brave and tyrannical, whereas Kūkjeh had been a just and good ruler (God have mercy on him).

Account of the death of Rukn al-Dīn ibn Qilij Arslān and the succession of his son

On 6 Dhū'l-Qa'da [6 July 1204] there died Rukn al-Dīn Sulaymān ibn Qilij Arslān ibn Mas'ūd ibn Qilij Arslān ibn Sulaymān ibn Qutlumish ibn Saljūq, lord of [**196**] Anatolia, the lands between Malaṭya and Konya. He died of colic within seven days. Five days before he fell ill he had behaved treacherously to his brother, the lord of Ankara, an impregnable city. His brother was in dispute with Rukn al-Dīn, so the latter besieged him for several years until he became weak and his provisions ran short. He agreed to surrender on condition that he receive some place in exchange. Rukn al-Dīn offered him as replacement a castle on the confines of his lands and gave him his oath to that. His brother left Ankara and yielded it up. Two sons of his were with him. Rukn al-Dīn arranged for men to seize him along with his children and put him to death. Before five days had passed he was stricken by colic and died. After his death people gathered around his son Qilij Arslān, who was young. He remained ruler until part-way through the year 601 [1204–5] but then he was deposed, as we shall narrate at that point.

Rukn al-Dīn was fierce against his enemies and active in the business of the state. However, people used to attribute to him corrupt beliefs. It used to be said that it was believed that his doctrine was that of the philosophers. All those people who were accused of such a doctrine used to seek refuge with him. This group received much kindness from him, although he was himself clever, preferring to conceal this belief so that people would not turn away from him.

I was told of him that he had in his entourage a man, a relative of his, who was accused of being a *zindīq* and holding the doctrines of the philosophers. A canon lawyer came to court one day and they both disputed. When the man declared some part of the philosophers' creed, the lawyer stood up, stepped toward him and slapped and cursed him while Rukn al-Dīn was present but keeping silent. The lawyer went out and the other said to Rukn al-Dīn, 'Something like that happens to me in your presence and you do not express disapproval!' He replied, 'If I had spoken up, we would all have been killed. It is impossible to profess openly what *you* want,' and he left him.

[197] Account of the massacre of Bāṭinīs at Wāsiṭ

This year in Ramaḍān [May 1204] there was a massacre of Bāṭinīs at Wāsiṭ. Their being there and their slaughter came about because a man called Zakī al-Dīn[19] Muḥammad ibn Ṭālib ibn ʻUṣayya, originally from al-Qārūb, a village of Wāsiṭ, who was a heterodox Bāṭinī, arrived there and settled in the vicinity of the dwellings of the Banū al-Harawī. People flocked to him and his followers became numerous. Among those who frequented him was a man called Ḥasan al-Ṣābūnī. It happened that he passed through the Little Market (*al-Suwayqa*) and a carpenter tackled him about their beliefs. Al-Ṣābūnī gave him a rough reply, so the carpenter attacked and killed him. The report of this spread among the people and they rose up and massacred all they could find who belonged to this sect. They singled out the house of Ibn ʻUṣayya, where many of his followers had gathered and locked the door . They went up on the roof and fought off the people but they climbed up to them from one of the houses via the roof. Those left in the house attempted to make themselves secure by shutting the doors and the ventilation openings, but the people broke them down. They came down and slew and burnt those they found in the house. Ibn ʻUṣayya was killed. The [main] door was opened and several fled out through it but were killed. News of this reached Baghdad and Fakhr al-Dīn Abū'l-Badr ibn Amsīnā al-Wāsiṭī travelled down to settle the situation and calm the disturbance.

How Maḥmūd seized power at Mirbāṭ and elsewhere in the Hadramawt

This year a man called Maḥmūd ibn Muḥammad al-Ḥimyarī seized Mirbāṭ, Ẓafār and other places in the Hadramawt. His career began as follows. He had a ship that he used to hire out [**198**] to sea-going merchants. Then he acted as vizier for the ruler of Mirbāṭ as he possessed generosity, bravery and good conduct. When the ruler of Mirbāṭ died, he became ruler of the city after him and people obeyed him because they loved him for his generosity and his conduct. His period of rule lasted a long time and when it was the year 619 [1222] he demolished Mirbāṭ and Ẓafār and built a new city on the coast near Mirbāṭ. There was a large freshwater spring close by, which he brought by conduit into the city. He constructed a city wall and a moat and made the city strong, calling it al-Aḥmadiyya. He was a lover of poetry and gave large prizes to reward it.

Miscellaneous events

This year a Frankish fleet attacked Egypt and sacked the town of Fūwa. They

---

19 The text reads al-Z.k.m, although the index entry has al-Zakī. *Kāmil* (Thornberg), xii, 129, has al-R.k.m.

stayed for five days, taking captives and plundering, while the Egyptian forces were facing them across the Nile. They had no way of reaching them because they had no ships.

There was a large earthquake which affected most of Egypt, Syria, the Jazīra, Anatolia, Sicily and Cyprus, reaching as far as Mosul, Iraq and elsewhere. It destroyed the city wall of Tyre and left its mark on much of Syria.

In Rajab [5 March–3 April 1204] a company of Sufis gathered in the hospice of the Chief Shaykh at Baghdad. Amongst them was a Sufi called Aḥmad ibn Ibrāhīm al-Dārī, a follower of Chief Shaykh ʻAbd al-Raḥīm ibn Ismāʻīl (God have mercy on them) and with them was a singer who sang the following verses:

> My little reprover, desist! That's enough blame for my hoary age.
> It's as though youth never was and grey hairs have always been.
> By the nights of union, their ends and beginnings,
> And the lover's pale complexion when he hears blame,
> If my life is restored through you,
> Sweet and lasting will life be for me.

[**199**] The company was in ecstasy as is customary for Sufis during their musical sessions and the aforementioned shaykh was lost in rapturous transport. He then collapsed in a faint. They tried to rouse him but found he was dead. Prayers having been said over him, he was buried. He was a pious man.

This year Abū'l-Futūḥ As'ad ibn Maḥmūd al-ʻIjlī, the Shāfiʻī lawyer, died at Isfahan in Ṣafar [10 October–7 November 1203]. He was a learned imam.

In Ramaḍān this year [May 1204] the cadi of Herat died, ʻUmdat al-Dīn al-Faḍl ibn Maḥmūd ibn Ṣāʻid al-Sāwī.[20] His son Ṣāʻid succeeded him in the office.

---

[20] On p. [**225**] below his son Ṣāʻid is given the *nisba* al-Sayyārī, which could be confused with al-Sāwī in Arabic script. It has not been possible to discover which is correct.

The Year 601 [1204–1205]

How Kaykhusro ibn Qilij Arslān took Anatolia from his nephew

This year during Rajab [22 February–23 March 1205] Ghiyāth al-Dīn Kaykhusro ibn Qilij Arslān took Anatolia, which had been in the hands of his brother Rukn al-Dīn Sulaymān and which, after the latter's death, was transferred to his son Qilij Arslān.

How Ghiyāth al-Dīn came to rule there was as follows. Rukn al-Dīn had taken what his brother Ghiyāth al-Dīn held, which was the city of Konya. The latter had fled and made his way to Syria to al-Ẓāhir Ghāzī, son of Saladin and lord of Aleppo, but he found no welcome with him; on the contrary he was disdained, so he left him and travelled from country to county until he came to Constantinople. The emperor showed him kindness, assigned him upkeep and received him with respect, so he remained with him and married the daughter of a great patrician.[1] This patrician had a castle in the Constantinople region and when the Franks conquered Constantinople, Ghiyāth al-Dīn fled to his father-in-law at his castle. He gave him a home and said, 'We shall share in this castle and live satisfactorily on its revenues.' Ghiyāth al-Dīn remained with him.

When his brother died in the year 600 [1204], as we have mentioned, the emirs gathered around his son but they were opposed by [an emir of][2] the Ivaj Turks, who were numerous in those lands. He scorned to follow them and sent to Ghiyāth al-Dīn to ask him to come [**201**] so that he could make him ruler. He set out and came to meet with him in Jumādā I [25 December 1204–23 January 1205]. His forces became numerous and he proceeded to lay siege to the city of Konya, where were Rukn al-Dīn's son and his troops. They sent out a detachment against him and in the following engagement Ghiyāth al-Dīn was routed. This left him at a loss, not knowing where to go. He made for a small town called Ūkaram near Konya.

God Almighty decreed that the inhabitants of Aksaray rebelled against their governor, expelled him and proclaimed the watchword of Ghiyāth al-Dīn. When the people of Konya heard of this, they said, 'We are the more appropriate ones to act thus, for he was a good ruler among us when he was our king.' So they also proclaimed his name, expelled the men they had and summoned him to come, which he did and took the city, arresting his nephew and his followers. God gave

1 He was Manuel Maurozomes, who became after the events at Constantinople a vassal of the Turks at Chonae and Laodicaea (Cahen, *Pre-Ottoman Turkey*, 115–16).

2 Added here on the basis of a variant reading, which the following singular verbs support. According to Cahen, *Pre-Ottoman Turkey*, 115, the Turkomans on the west frontier and 'certain notables in the Anatolian State itself, in particular three Dānishmendids', plotted against Qilij Arslān III, son of Rukn al-Dīn, and recalled Ghiyāth al-Dīn.

him sovereignty and all at one moment united all the country under him. Glory be to Him who, when He wishes a matter, supplies the means.

His brother Qayṣar Shāh, lord of Malaṭya, when Rukn al-Dīn took it from him in the year 597 [1200–1201], had departed and sought out al-ʿĀdil Abū Bakr ibn Ayyūb, because he was married to his daughter, to seek his help. He ordered him to reside at Edessa, which he did. When he heard that his brother Ghiyāth al-Dīn had come to power, he went to him but did not find a welcome with him. He merely gave him something and ordered him to depart, so he returned to Edessa and continued living there. When Ghiyāth al-Dīn's rule was well established, al-Afḍal, the ruler of Samosata, went to him and met with him at Caesarea. He was also visited by Niẓām al-Dīn,[3] ruler of Khartbirt, who became an ally. Ghiyāth al-Dīn became great and powerful.

[202] How the lord of Āmid besieged Khartbirt and then withdrew

Khartbirt had been held by ʿImād al-Dīn ibn Qarā Arslān but he died and his successor was his son Niẓām al-Dīn Abū Bakr.[4] He sought the protection of Rukn al-Dīn ibn Qilij Arslān and after him of the latter's brother Ghiyāth al-Dīn as a defence against his cousin, Nāṣir al-Dīn Maḥmūd ibn Muḥammad ibn Qarā Arslān.[5] He secured this protection.

The lord of Āmid, who was under the protection of, and subject to, al-ʿĀdil, was present with the latter's son al-Ashraf at the battle against the lord of Mosul on condition that al-Ashraf would join him with his troops and take Khartbirt for him. It was the death of Rukn al-Dīn that gave him this ambition. After this year had begun, he demanded what had been agreed upon, so al-Ashraf and the troops of the Jazīra from Sinjār, Jazīrat Ibn ʿUmar, Mosul and elsewhere set out with him and descended upon Khartbirt in Shaʿbān [24 March–21 April 1205]. During Ramaḍān [22 April–21 May] they gained the suburb.

The lord of Khartbirt had met with Ghiyāth al-Dīn after he had taken control of the Anatolian lands and became his loyal ally. When the lord of Āmid descended upon Khartbirt, he made contact with Ghiyāth al-Dīn to ask him to help with troops to raise the siege. He equipped a large force which numbered 6,000 cavalry and sent them with al-Afḍal ʿAlī, Saladin's son, who was lord of Samosata. When this force arrived at Malaṭya, the lord of Āmid and his allies left Khartbirt and entered the desert. They blockaded the lake known as the Lake of Sumnīn,[6] in which were two castles, one of which belonged to the lord of Khartbirt. After a

---

3 An Artuqid prince; see the next section.

4 According to the family tree in *EI(2)*, i, 663, his personal name was Ibrāhīm. His father ʿImād al-Dīn was Abū Bakr.

5 This is 'the lord of Āmid', who ruled 597–619/1201–22.

6 Sumnīn itself is, according to Yāqūt, iii, 146, a town in the frontier zone of Rūm (Anatolia).

siege and an assault, they took it on 2 Dhū'l-Ḥijja [21 July 1205].

The lord of Khartbirt came with the Anatolian army to Khartbirt and the lord of Āmid left the lake, having strengthened the castle he had taken there and supplied it with everything necessary. [**203**] He withdrew one day's journey and made camp. Envoys were exchanged, while the Anatolian force demanded [the return of] the lake and the lord of Āmid resisted that. After long discussions the castle remained in the hands of the lord of Āmid and the two armies departed, each side returning to their lands.

Account of riots at Baghdad

On 17 Ramaḍān [8 May 1205] there was a disturbance between the inhabitants of Azaj Gate and those of al-Ma'mūniyya. The cause was that the people of Azaj Gate had killed a lion[7] and wanted to parade it around but the al-Ma'mūniyya people stopped them. Rioting broke out between them at the Great Garden and many people were wounded and several killed. The Master of the Gate (*ṣāḥib al-bāb*) rode out to calm the riot but his horse was wounded, so he withdrew.

On the following day the inhabitants of al-Ma'mūniyya moved against those of Azaj Gate and serious rioting ensued between them, a battle using swords and bows and arrows. The situation worsened and the nearby houses were sacked. Rukn al-Dīn ibn 'Abd al-Qādir and Yūsuf al-'Uqāb did their best to calm people. The Turks were mobilized and took to keeping a night-watch below the Belvedere. The rioters were prevented from gathering and so quietened down.

On 20 [Ramaḍān] [11 May] rioting occurred between the inhabitants of Quṭuftā and al-Qarya, districts of the West Bank, also because of the killing of a lion. The people of Quṭuftā wanted to assemble and parade with it but the inhabitants of al-Qarya prevented them from taking it through their area, so they came to blows and a number were killed. A force was sent to them from the Dīwān to repair the situation and stop the people rioting. They did stop in due course.

On 9 Ramaḍān [29 April] there was rioting between the people of Sultan's Market and al-Ja'fariyya. It arose from the fact that two men from the two quarters had a dispute and each one threatened the other. [**204**] Both districts gathered together and fought in the Ja'fariyya cemetery. Men were sent from the Dīwān to settle and calm the affair. After there had been these many riots, a senior emir, one of the caliph's mamlukes, was appointed, with a large company, and he patrolled the city. He put to death several persons who were suspect and calm prevailed.

Account of the Georgian incursion into Islamic territory

During this year the Georgians invaded Islamic territory through the province of

[7] The meaning of this incident and the one that follows is not clear.

Azerbayjan and caused much trouble, destruction and pillage, and enslaved many. They raided the region of Khilāṭ in Armenia, penetrating deeply even as far as Malāzgird. No Muslims took the field to oppose them. They reconnoitred the lands, while pillaging and taking prisoners and captives, and whenever they advanced, the Muslim forces retreated, until they returned home. May God Almighty consider Islam and its folk and supply them with someone to protect their lands, guard their frontiers and wage war on their enemies.

When the Georgians invaded Khilāṭ this year, they came to Arjīsh[8] and its districts, where they plundered, took captives and ruined the country. They proceeded to Figs' Castle,[9] a district of Khilāṭ, neighbouring Erzurum. The lord of Khilāṭ gathered his army and went to the son[10] of Qilij Arslān, lord of Erzurum, to ask for his aid against the Georgians. He sent all his army with him and they moved towards the Georgians. They met in a pitched battle and [**205**] the Georgians were defeated. Zakarī[11] 'the Little', one of their greatest commanders, was slain. He was the commander of this Georgian army and their leader in battle. The Muslims plundered all their goods, weapons, mounts and such-like and killed a large number of them, taking prisoners likewise, before returning to their lands.

Account of conflict between the emir of Mecca and the emir of Medina

This year there was also conflict between Emir Qatāda al-Ḥasanī, emir of Mecca, and Emir Sālim ibn Qāsim al-Ḥusaynī, emir of Medina. Each of them had a large following and they fought a fierce battle. It took place at Dhū'l-Ḥulayfa[12] near Medina. Qatāda had attacked Medina to besiege and conquer it. Sālim met him, after he had visited the [Prophet's] chamber (peace and blessing upon its occupant), prayed there and made his private devotions. He then moved to face him and Qatāda was defeated. Sālim pursued him to Mecca and besieged him there, but Qatāda sent to the emirs with Sālim and suborned them. They inclined to him and swore oaths to him. When he saw this, Sālim departed back to Medina and Qatāda's position became strong again.

Miscellaneous events

This year on Friday 14 Jumādā II [= 4 February 1205] the khutbah for the

---

8 According to Yāqūt, i, 196, it was near Khilāṭ and mostly Christian in population. Krawulsky, 419, states that it was about two km. south of modern Erciş.

9 In Arabic: Ḥiṣn al-Tīn.

10 This was Mughīth al-Dīn Ṭughril Shāh. For a summary of his career, see *EI(2)*, x, 555.

11 His name appears as Zakharé, alongside another member of the Mkhargrdzei family, Iwané, in *EI(2)*, v, 490a.

12 One of the sites where pilgrims don the *iḥrām*, the pilgrim garb (Yāqūt, ii, 324).

heir-apparent was cancelled. A document was made public and read in the palace of the vizier, Naṣīr al-Dīn Nāṣir ibn Mahdī al-Rāzī. It proved to be a document written by the heir-apparent, Emir Abū Naṣr, son of the caliph, addressed to his father al-Nāṣir [**206**] li-Dīn Allāh, Commander of the Faithful, stating his inability to undertake the position of heir-apparent and requesting to be released. Two witnesses witnessed that it was his hand and that the caliph duly released him. A report to this effect was drawn up, which was witnessed by the cadis, the notaries and the lawyers.

This year a woman in Baghdad gave birth to a child with two heads, four legs and two arms. It died that same day.

There was a fire that broke out in the Armaments' Store belonging to the caliph. Very much was burnt there. The fire lasted for two days. The story of this fire travelled throughout the lands and various rulers supplied a large quantity of armaments to Baghdad.

At Herat snow fell for a whole week. After it stopped, it was followed by a flash flood from the mountain through Palace Gate,[13] which destroyed much of the city and threw down a large part of the citadel. Heavy rain came after this which ruined the fruit, although there was only little there this year.

In Sha'bān [24 March–21 April 1205] a Ghurid army, commanded by Emir Zankī ibn Mas'ūd, marched towards the city of Marv and was met at Sarakhs by Khwārazm Shāh's lieutenant, namely Emir Jaqar, who prepared an ambush for them. When they reached it, he put them to flight and seized the Ghurid leaders as prisoners. Only a few of them escaped and their emir, Zankī, was taken and put to death in cold blood. Their heads were exposed at Marv for several days.

In Dhū'l-Qa'da [20 June–19 July 1205] Emir 'Imād al-Dīn 'Umar ibn al-Ḥusayn al-Ghūrī, lord of Balkh, marched to Tirmidh, which was held by the Khitay Turks, and took it by force of arms. He put his eldest son in charge and slaughtered the Khitay that were there. He moved the Alids from there to Balkh. Tirmidh became Islamic territory, one of the most impregnable and powerful fortresses.

This year Ṣadr al-Dīn al-Sajzī, the shaykh of the sultan's Sufi centre (*khānkāh*) at Herat, died.

[**207**] In Ṣafar [October 1204] Abū 'Alī al-Ḥasan ibn Muḥammad ibn 'Abdūs, the poet from Wāsiṭ, died. He was one of the outstanding poets and I met him at Mosul. He had come there as an encomiast for the ruler Nūr al-Dīn Arslān Shāh and other leading men. He was an excellent man and a good sociable companion.

During this year two blind men at Baghdad together attacked another blind man and killed him in a mosque, eager to steal something from him, but they found he had nothing to take. Morning came and they fled in fear, intending to go to Mosul. The man was discovered dead and it was not known who had killed him. It so chanced that one of the prefect's men came out of the Harem about some dispute

---

13 In text Bāb Sarā, sc. Bāb Sarāy. It was a northern gate of Herat on the Balkh road (Le Strange, *Caliphate*137

that had occurred. He saw the two blind men and said to those with him, 'These are the ones who killed the blind man,' speaking in jest. At that one of them said, 'By God, this is the man who killed him,' and the other said, 'No, you killed him.' They were both taken to the Master of the Gate and they confessed. One was put to death and the other was crucified at the entrance of the mosque where they had killed the man.

[208] The Year 602 [1205–1206]

Account of civil disorder at Herat

In Muḥarram of this year [18 August–16 September 1205] the common people rose up at Herat and major disorder occurred between the people of two markets, the blacksmiths' and the coppersmiths'. Several persons were killed, property ransacked and houses demolished. The emir of the city rode out to restrain them but one of the mob struck him with a stone, which gave him serious pain. The rabble gathered against him, so he was taken up into the Fīrūzī Palace, where he lay low for some days until the disorder quietened down and then he reappeared.

Account of Shihāb al-Dīn's battle with the Khokars

We have mentioned the defeat of Shihāb al-Dīn Muḥammad ibn Sām al-Ghūrī, lord of Ghazna, at the hands of the infidel Khitay and that news spread in his lands that he was lost in the battle and his men had heard no word of him. When this report became widely known, troublesome elements rose up on the borders. One of those was Dāniyāl, lord of Mount Jūdī.[1] He had converted to Islam but on hearing this report he apostatized and joined with the Khokars. They were among those that had rebelled. They dwelt in the impregnable and formidable mountains between Lahore and Multan. They had been subject to Shihāb al-Dīn and paid him tribute. When they heard news of his death, they rose up with the tribes and peoples that followed them. [**209**] The lord of Mount Jūdī and others who lived in those mountains gave them allegiance and blocked the road to Ghazna from Lahore and elsewhere.

After Shihāb al-Dīn had managed to kill his mamluke Aybak Bāk, whom we have mentioned before,[2] he sent to his lieutenant in Lahore and Multan, Muḥammad ibn Abī 'Alī, ordering him to supply the revenue for the year 600 and the year 601 [1203–1205], so that he could use it to prepare for war with the Khitay. He replied that the Khokars had cut the road and he was unable to send the money. Some merchants presented themselves and reported that a large caravan had been seized by the Khokars and only a few people had escaped. Shihāb al-Dīn then ordered his mamluke [Quṭb al-Dīn] Aybak, the commander of the Indian

[1] Otherwise known as the Salt Range, south of Rawalpindi, between the Indus and the Jhelum rivers. This range is not to be confused with Mount Jūdī, situated south of Sirnak on the Turkish frontier with Syria and Iraq and identified in Muslim tradition as the mountain where the Ark came to rest (Koran, xi, 44).

[2] See above, p. [**187**].

armies, to make contact with the Khokars to call them to allegiance and to threaten them if they did not respond. This he did and the leader of the Khokars said, 'What is the idea that the sultan did not send us an envoy?' The envoy replied, 'What is your status that he should treat with you? It's merely his mamluke who will make you see your right course and threaten you.' 'If Shihāb al-Dīn were alive,' said the other, 'he would write to us and we would be paying him tribute. Since he is dead, tell Aybak to abandon Lahore, the adjacent lands and Peshawar to us and we shall make peace with him.' Thus he paid no attention to his words and sent him away. The envoy returned and reported what he had heard and seen. Shihāb al-Dīn ordered his mamluke Quṭb al-Dīn Aybak to return to his lands and gather troops to fight the Khokars. He returned to Delhi and ordered his troops to prepare. Shihāb al-Dīn remained in Peshawar until the middle of Sha'bān 601 [7 April 1205] and then returned to Ghazna, where he arrived on 1 Ramaḍān [22 April]. He ordered proclamations among the army to prepare for war with the Khitay and that they should march on 1 Shawwāl [22 May]. They duly prepared for this.

It happened that there were many complaints about the Khokars and their actions, for example, their making the roads dangerous **[210]** and their sending a prefect to the land. Most of the Indians joined with them and cast off obedience to the emir of Lahore, Multan and other places. The governor's letter arrived telling of what he had suffered from them, that the Khokars had expelled his officials and had collected the taxes, and that their chief had sent to him telling him to abandon Lahore, those regions and his elephants, saying that he should go to Shihāb al-Dīn, otherwise he would kill him. The governor said, 'If Shihāb al-Dīn does not come in person with his armies, the country will pass from his control.'

People spoke of the large hosts with them and the strength they possessed, so Shihāb al-Dīn changed his plan and gave up his attack on the Khitay. He prepared his tents and left Ghazna on 5 Rabī' I 602 [20 October 1205]. After he had travelled some distance, his people in Ghazna and Peshawar were deprived of news about him and eventually there were rumours that he had been defeated.

When Shihāb al-Dīn had left Peshawar, he received news that the Khokar leader was camped with his troops between Jhelum and Sūdara. He made forced marches and surprised him before the time at which he had calculated his arrival. They fought a fierce battle on Thursday five days remaining of Rabī' II [10 November 1205] from morning until evening. While this battle was raging fiercely, Quṭb al-Dīn Aybak came up with his troops. They proclaimed the watchword of Islam and made an all-out charge. The Khokars and their allies fled and were slain at every turn. They made for some thickets, where they gathered and lit fires. A man would say to his comrade, 'Do not let the Muslims kill you,' and then threw himself on the flames. His comrade would follow his example. Destruction came upon them all, slain or burnt. 'Away with you, wicked people!'[3] Their families and their possessions were with them. They had not left them behind. The Muslims took

3 Koran, xi, 44.

unheard-of amounts of booty. Slaves were sold for five Ruknī dinars or thereabouts. Their leader escaped [**211**] after killing his brothers and his womenfolk.[4]

As for Dāniyāl,[5] the lord of Mount Jūdī, he came by night to Quṭb al-Dīn Aybak and asked for his protection, which he granted. He interceded with Shihāb al-Dīn for him and this too was accepted, but he took the citadel of al-Jūdī from him. Having dealt with them, he set out to Lahore to give guarantees to its inhabitants and to calm their fears. He ordered his men to return to their lands and to prepare for war with the Khitay. Shihāb al-Dīn remained at Lahore until 16 Rajab [26 February 1206] and then set out back to Ghazna. He sent to Bahā' al-Dīn Sām, lord of Bāmiyān, to tell him to prepare to march to Samarqand and to construct a bridge that he and his troops could cross over.

Account of the victory over the Tīrāhīs

Among the troublemaking rebels against Shihāb al-Dīn were the Tīrāhīs,[6] for they emerged into the confines of Sūrān and Makrahān[7] to raid the Muslims. The lieutenant of Tāj al-Dīn Yildiz, Shihāb al-Dīn's mamluke, in that area, who was known as al-Khaljī, soundly defeated them and slew a great number of them. He brought the heads of people of note to where they were displayed in Muslim territory.

The trouble caused by these Tīrāhīs in Islamic lands was great in both old and recent times. Whenever a Muslim prisoner fell into their hands, they used to torture him in all sorts of ways. Owing to them the inhabitants of Peshawar suffered great hardship because they surrounded that province on all sides, especially at the end of the reign of the house of Sabuktakīn.[8] While those rulers became weak, these people grew stronger than them and used to raid their outlying lands. They were infidels with no religion to refer to and no teaching to rely on. When a daughter was born to one of them, he would stand at the door of his house and cry out, 'Who will marry this one? Who will accept her?' If he had a response [**212**] from anyone, he would spare her, but otherwise kill her. Each woman had several husbands and if one of them was with her, he would place his boots by the door. Then, if another of her husbands came, he would see the boots and withdraw. They continued in this fashion until a group of them converted to Islam at the end

4 This is quite probably an example of the 'honour' strategy called *jauhar*.

5 The text has 'Ibn Dāniyāl' here.

6 The inhabitants of the Tīrāh, the mountainous region at the north-west frontier, west of Kohat and south of the Khyber Pass.

7 Prof. Peter Jackson has suggested that Sūrān (S.w.rān) is probably a corruption of Shinwarān (see *Chronicle of Ibn al-Athīr (2)*, note to p. [**168**]) or S[h]unqurān, a region often linked with Kurram, and that Makrahān may be a corruption of Nangrahār on the middle Kabul River (see *EI(2)*, vii, 957).

8 i.e. the Ghaznavid dynasty.

of the reign of Shihāb al-Dīn al-Ghūrī. They then left his lands unmolested.

The reason for their conversion was that they had captured a man from Peshawar, who, although they tortured him, did not die. He lived a long time among them. One day their leader summoned him and questioned him about the lands of Islam. He said to him, 'If I were to attend upon Shihāb al-Dīn, what would he give me?' The teacher replied, 'He would give you money, a fief and restore to you the government of all your lands.' So he sent this man to Shihāb al-Dīn about becoming a Muslim and the latter sent him back with an envoy bearing robes of honour and the diploma for a fief. After the arrival of the envoy, he and a number of his family travelled to Shihāb al-Dīn, accepted Islam and returned home. The people now enjoyed peace with them. However, when this trouble occurred and the country was disturbed, most of them came down from the mountains and this group did not have the strength to hold them in check. They caused much mayhem and did what we have mentioned.

Account of the assassination of Shihāb al-Dīn al-Ghūrī

This year, the eve of 1 Sha'bān [13 March 1206] Shihāb al-Dīn Abū'l-Muẓaffar Muḥammad ibn Sām al-Ghūrī, lord of Ghazna and part of Khurasan, was killed after his return from Lahore at a staging post called Damyal at the time of the evening prayer.[9]

The reason for his death was that a body of infidel Khokars dogged his army, determined to slay him, because of the killing and taking of prisoners and captives that he had inflicted on them. When this night came, his men separated from him. [**213**] He had returned with untold quantities of money, for he planned to attack the Khitay and to enlist many troops and distribute the money among them. He had ordered his troops in India to join him and had ordered the Khurasanian troops to prepare and [wait] until he came to them. God came for him from a quarter he had not anticipated and all the money, weapons and men he had assembled profited him nothing, yet he was engaged in a goodly plan to fight the infidel.

When his men had left him and he remained alone in a tent, this group sprang into action. One of them killed one of the guards at the entrance to Shihāb al-Dīn's pavilion. When he was killed, he cried out and his comrades rushed to see what was wrong with him and left their posts. There was a great commotion and the Khokars took advantage of this neglect of their watch. They went in to Shihāb al-Dīn in his tent and struck him with their daggers twenty-four blows and slew him. His men came in and found him on his prayer mat dead, in a position of prostration. They seized these infidels and killed them. Two of their number were circumcised men.

9 See Juvainī, *History*, i, 326 and note 27 and sources there quoted. The date of his death is given as 3 Sha'bān/15 March and the place as Damyak (unidentified). Damyak is also the spelling found in *Ṭabaqāt-i Nāṣirī*, i, 484.

It is claimed that it was the Ismāʿīlīs who killed him because they feared his expedition into Khurasan. He had an army that was besieging one of their fortresses, as we have related.[10]

After his assassination the emirs gathered aound his vizier, Mu'ayyad al-Mulk, son of the Khwāja of Sijistan,[11] and swore to preserve his treasury and his authority, and to maintain calm until it was clear who would succeed him. They put Shihāb al-Dīn on a seat, sewed up his wounds, put him in a litter and set off with him. The vizier organized affairs and kept the people peaceful, so that not a drop[12] of blood was shed and there was no disturbance. The litter was surrounded by attendants, the vizier and the troops, while the parasol was borne aloft as it was during his life. The vizier commanded the justicer of the army to apply the state's code[13] and to keep discipline [**214**] in the army. The treasury which accompanied him comprised 2,200 loads. The young Turkish mamlukes rioted, intending to plunder the money, but the vizier and the great mamluke emirs, that is Savinj, Yildiz's son-in-law, and others, prevented them. They ordered everyone who held a fief from Quṭb al-Dīn Aybak, Shihāb al-Dīn's mamluke in India, to return to it. Large sums of money were distributed among them and they went back.

The vizier and those who had a fief and family at Ghazna continued on their way. They knew that there would be fierce struggles between Ghiyāth al-Dīn Maḥmūd, the son of Shihāb al-Dīn's elder brother Ghiyāth al-Dīn, and Bahā' al-Dīn, lord of Bāmiyān, who was Shihāb al-Dīn's sister's son. The vizier, the Turks and others favoured Ghiyāth al-Dīn Maḥmūd, while the Ghūrī emirs inclined to Bahā' al-Dīn Sām, lord of Bāmiyān. Each group sent to the one they favoured to inform him of Shihāb al-Dīn's death and give a clear account of affairs. Some troublemakers, people of Ghazna, came and said to the mamlukes, 'Fakhr al-Dīn al-Rāzī killed your master, because he is the one who sent the assassins, instigated by Khwārazm Shāh.' They rose up against him, meaning to kill him, but he fled and sought Mu'ayyad al-Mulk, the vizier. After he had told him of his situation, the vizier sent him secretly to a safe place.

When the army and the vizier reached Peshawar, a difference arose. The Ghūrī emirs were saying, 'Let us go to Ghazna by the Makrahān route,' their aim being to approach Bāmiyān to call out its ruler, Bahā' al-Dīn Sām, to take control of the treasury, while the Turks said, 'No, let us go by the Sūrān route,' their plan being to draw near to Tāj al-Dīn Yildiz, Shihāb al-Dīn's mamluke and the lord of

---

[10] For a discussion of the identity of the attackers, see *Ṭabaqāt-i Nāṣirī*, 485, note 3.

[11] This was Muḥammad ibn 'Abd Allāh. He himself is referred to as Khwāja (otherwise Khoja), which is a title for a vizier or other high dignitary; see *Ṭabaqāt-i Nāṣirī*, 504–5, where he is also described as Sanjarī. This should be emended to Sijzī, i.e. 'of Sijistan' (cf. below, p. [**304**]).

[12] Literally 'not a cupping-glass of blood'.

[13] The term in Arabic is *al-siyāsa*, a complicated concept that denotes the customary governance and jurisdiction that is parallel to, but distinct from, the religious law, the Shariah, and responds primarily to *raisons d'état*.

Kurramān [K.r.mān],[14] a city between Ghazna and Lahore and not the [province of] Kirman which borders Fars, to allow Yildiz to keep the treasury and themselves to send to Ghiyāth al-Dīn from Kurramān and summon him to Ghazna to make him ruler. The dissension between them increased, until they almost came to blows. Mu'ayyad al-Mulk managed to persuade [**215**] the Ghūrī emirs to allow him and the Turks to take the treasury and the litter in which Shihāb al-Dīn was and to go to Kurramān. They travelled on the Makrahān route and the vizier and those with him encountered great hardship. The peoples in those mountains, the Tīrāhīs, Ūghān and others, waylaid them and attacked the flanks of the army until they arrived at Kurramān. Tāj al-Dīn Yildiz went out to receive them and when he caught sight of the litter with Shihāb al-Dīn dead inside, he dismounted and kissed the earth, as was his practice when Shihāb al-Dīn was alive. He drew back the curtains and when he saw the corpse, he tore his garments, cried out and wept, reducing those present to tears. It was a day to remember.

Account of what Yildiz did

Yildiz was one of the first of Shihāb al-Dīn's mamlukes, the greatest and oldest and the one held in the highest esteem, so much so that Shihāb al-Dīn's family used to attend on him and apply to him for their business affairs. When his master was killed, he was ambitious to control Ghazna. The first thing he did was to ask Vizier Mu'ayyad al-Mulk about the money, weapons and mounts. Informed of what had been issued and what remained with the vizier, he disapproved of the state of affairs and answered him impolitely, saying, 'The Ghūrī emirs have written to Bahā' al-Dīn Sām, ruler of Bāmiyān, to make him ruler of Ghazna. Ghiyāth al-Dīn Maḥmūd, my master, has written to me, ordering me not to allow anyone to approach Ghazna and he has appointed me his deputy there and in all the neighbouring district, because he is occupied with Khurasan.' He further said to the vizier, 'He has also ordered me to take over the treasury from you.' The vizier was unable to refuse because the Turks inclined to Yildiz, who, having taken it over, proceeded with the litter, the mamlukes and the vizier to Ghazna. Shihāb al-Dīn was buried in the tomb in the madrasah which he had built and where he had buried his daughter. He arrived there on 22 Sha'bān this year [3 April 1206].

[216] Some account of the conduct of Shihāb al-Dīn

He was (God have mercy on him) brave and bold, a frequent campaigner in India, just to his subjects and a good ruler among them, who judged them according to

[14] If correctly vocalized (cf. modern Kurram in Pakistan and see *Chronicle of Ibn al-Athīr (2)*, p. [**164**]), it is rather to be placed between Ghazna and Peshawar. In Yāqūt, iv, 266, it is spelt as Karmān and said to be four days' journey from Ghazna.

the dictates of the pure Holy Law. The cadi in Ghazna used to attend at his palace each week on Saturdays, Sundays, Mondays and Tuesdays, accompanied by the emir-chamberlain, the justicer and the head of the postal service. The cadi would decide cases and the sultan's men carry out his decisions for young and old, noble and commoner. If one of the litigants demanded to appear before the sultan, he would summon him, hear what he had to say and apply the rule of the Shariah either against him or for him.

I have been told about him that an Alid boy of about five years of age came before him, blessed his name and said, 'For five days I have eaten nothing.' The sultan returned immediately from his ride, taking the boy with him, and lodged him in his palace. He fed the Alid in his presence with the finest food and then gave him some money. Afterwards he had his father fetched and restored the boy to him. He distributed a large sum of money among all the Alids.

It has been told of him that a merchant from Marāgha was in Ghazna and was owed by one of Shihāb al-Dīn's mamlukes a debt that amounted to 10,000 dinars. The mamluke was killed in one of his wars. The merchant reported his situation and the sultan ordered that the mamluke's fief should be registered in the possession of the merchant until his debt was fully paid. This was duly done.

It has also been related that the ulema used to attend his court and discuss questions of canon law and others. Fakhr al-Dīn al-Rāzī used to preach in his palace. He came one day and gave a sermon, at the end of which he said, 'O sultan, neither your power nor al-Rāzī's abstruse notions will endure. We all return to God!' Shihāb al-Dīn wept, so much that the people pitied him for the intensity of his weeping.

He was tender-hearted and a follower of the Shāfi'ī law school, like his brother. However, it is said that he was a Ḥanafī. God knows best!

[217] Account of Bahā' al-Dīn's journey to Ghazna and his death

When Ghiyāth al-Dīn conquered Bāmiyān, he gave it as a fief to his cousin, Shams al-Dīn Muḥammad ibn Mas'ūd, and gave him his sister in marriage. From her he had a son called Sām and he remained there until his death. He was succeeded by his eldest son, whose name was 'Abbās and whose mother was Turkish. Ghiyāth al-Dīn and his brother Shihāb al-Dīn were angry at that and sent men to bring 'Abbās to them. They took his sovereignty from him and set up their sister's son Sām as ruler of Bāmiyān. He took the title Bahā' al-Dīn and his power and position became strong. He gathered money with the aim of ruling the lands after his two maternal uncles. The Ghūrs loved him intensely and revered him.

When his uncle Shihāb al-Dīn was assassinated, one of the Ghūrī emirs went to Bahā' al-Dīn Sām and informed him of this. Hearing of the killing, he wrote to the Ghūrī emirs in Ghazna, ordering them to hold the city and telling them that he was on his way to them. The governor of Ghazna's citadel, known as the justicer, had already sent his son to Bahā' al-Dīn Sām to summon him to Ghazna. He sent back in reply that he had made his preparations, that he would be arriving and that he made him fair and goodly promises.

Bahā' al-Dīn wrote to 'Alā' al-Dīn Muḥammad ibn Abī 'Alī, prince of the Ghūr, to summon him and to Ghiyāth al-Dīn Maḥmūd ibn Ghiyāth al-Dīn and Ibn Kharmīl, governor of Herat, ordering them to institute the khutbah in his name and to hold on to the provinces under their control. He did not think that anyone would oppose him. The people of Ghazna remained in expectation of his arrival or that of Ghiyāth al-Dīn Maḥmūd and the Turks, saying, 'We shall not allow anyone other than our lord's son (meaning Ghiyāth al-Dīn) to enter Ghazna.' The Ghūr meanwhile were manifesting their inclination towards Bahā' al-Dīn and their refusal of anyone else. He travelled from Bāmiyān to [**218**] Ghazna with his troops and accompanied by his two sons, 'Alā' al-Dīn Muḥammad and Jalāl al-Dīn. After he had gone two stages from Bamiyān, he experienced a headache, so halted to rest and wait for relief. His headache increased and he suffered greatly, convinced that he would die. He called his sons, declared 'Alā' al-Dīn his heir and ordered both to make for Ghazna, to look after the elders of the Ghūr, maintain the regime, be kind to the subjects and be generous with money. He also ordered them to come to terms with Ghiyāth al-Dīn on the basis that he should have Khurasan and the lands of the Ghūr, while the two of them should have Ghazna and India.

Account of 'Alā' al-Dīn's taking control of Ghazna and losing it

After Bahā' al-Dīn had completed his last testament, he passed away. His two sons proceeded to Ghazna and the Ghurid emirs and the citizens came out to meet them. The Turks came out too, but unwillingly. They entered the city and took control of it. 'Alā' al-Dīn and Jalāl al-Dīn lodged in the Sultan's Palace on 1 Ramaḍān [11 April 1206], having arrived in a poor state and with few troops. The Turks wished to resist them but Mu'ayyad al-Mulk, Shihāb al-Dīn's vizier, forbade them because of their small numbers and because Ghiyāth al-Dīn was occupied with Ibn Kharmīl, governor of Herat, as we shall recount. However, they did not give up this [course].

When the two were installed in the citadel and lodged in the Sultan's Palace, the Turks made contact with them, saying that they should leave the palace, otherwise they would fight them. [In response] they both distributed large sums among them and asked them to swear an oath [of support], which they duly swore, but excepted Ghiyāth al-Dīn Maḥmūd. The two sons sent robes of honour with an envoy to Tāj al-Dīn Yildiz, who was at his fief, and asked him to declare his allegiance to themselves, promising him money, an increase in his fief, command of the army and authority throughout the kingdom. The envoy came and met him, after he had left [**219**] Kurramān with a large army of Turks, Khalaj, Oghuz and others, making for Ghazna. After the delivery of the message, he paid no attention to the envoy but said, 'Tell them that they should return to Bāmiyān. That is enough [for them]. My lord Ghiyāth al-Dīn has ordered me to march to Ghazna and deny it to them. If they do not return to their lands, I shall do to them and those with them what they will not like.' He returned the gifts and robes of honour that came from them. Yildiz's intention in this was not to preserve his master's house but rather he wished to make this a way to take Ghazna for himself.

The envoy returned and delivered Yildiz's message to 'Alā' al-Dīn, who sent his vizier, previously his father's vizier, to Bāmiyān, Balkh, Tirmidh and other cities to gather troops and then return to him. Yildiz sent to the Turks in Ghazna to inform them that Ghiyāth al-Dīn had ordered him to attack Ghazna and expel 'Alā' al-Dīn and his brother. They came before the son of 'Alā' al-Dīn's vizier[15] and demanded weapons from him. He opened the weapons store, fled to 'Alā' al-Dīn and said, 'Such and such has happened,' and he was unable to do anything. Mu'ayyad al-Mulk, Shihāb al-Dīn's vizier, heard [of this], rode there and reproved the keeper for handing over the keys. On his orders all that the Turks had seized was recovered, because his word was law among them.

Yildiz arrived at Ghazna and to oppose him 'Alā' al-Dīn sent out a detachment of the Ghūr and Turks, among them Savinj, Yildiz's son-in-law. His men advised him not to do this but to wait for the army with his vizier. He did not accept their advice but sent the troops out. They met on 5 Ramaḍān [15 April 1206] and when they confronted Yildiz, the Turks made obeisance to him and turned with him against 'Alā' al-Dīn's army, which they engaged and put to flight, capturing their commander, Muḥammad ibn 'Alī ibn Khardūn(?).[16] Yildiz's troops entered the city and sacked the houses of the Ghūr and the Bāmiyān contingent. When Yildiz besieged the citadel, Jalāl al-Dīn came out [**220**] with twenty horse and left Ghazna. A woman said to him in mockery, 'Where are you going? Take the parasol[17] with you. How wretched it is for sultans to depart like this!' He replied, 'You will see one day. I will treat you people in such a way that will make you acknowledge that I am sultan.' He had previously said to his brother, 'Hold the citadel until I bring you troops.'

Yildiz continued his siege and the men with him wished to sack the city but he forbade that. He sent to 'Alā' al-Dīn, ordering him to leave the citadel and threatening him if he did not. There was an exchange of envoys on this matter and he finally agreed to abandon it and return to his own city, and he sent men to Yildiz to get him to swear that he would subject him to no harm or interference, nor any others included in the oath. He left Ghazna and when Yildiz saw that he had descended from the citadel, he turned aside to the tomb of Shihāb al-Dīn, his lord, and visited it. The Turks plundered what 'Alā' al-Dīn had with him, threw him off his horse, stripped him and left him naked in his drawers. Hearing of this, Yildiz

---

[15] It is not clear who is intended here.

[16] The text has Ḥ.r.d.w.n., which, as the name is possibly Turkish, is not a likely form.

[17] In the text *al-jitr wa'l-shamsa*, although they are normally taken as synonyms.

sent him mounts, clothes and money and made his apologies. 'Alā' al-Dīn accepted the clothes but rejected the rest. When he arrived at Bāmiyān, he put on a countryman's habits and rode a donkey. They supplied him with royal mounts and fine raiment but he neither rode them nor wore them. He said, 'I want people to see what the inhabitants of Ghazna did to me, so that, when I return, destroy and sack it, no one will blame me.' He entered Government House and embarked on the raising of troops.

Account of Yildiz's coming to power at Ghazna

We have already mentioned how Yildiz seized the money, weapons, mounts and other things that had accompanied Shihāb al-Dīn and how he took it all from the vizier, Mu'ayyad al-Mulk. He used it to gather troops [**221**] from all sorts, Turks, Khalaj, Oghuz and others, and marched to Ghazna. What we have just related then took place between him and 'Alā' al-Dīn.

After 'Alā' al-Dīn had left Ghazna, Yildiz remained in his residence for four days, proclaiming allegiance to Ghiyāth al-Dīn, although he did not instruct the preacher to pronounce the khutbah in his name nor in that of anyone else. He merely named the caliph in the khutbah and prayed for mercy for Shihāb al-Dīn, the martyr, and that was all.

On the fourth day he summoned the leaders of the Ghūr and the Turks and criticized those who had written to 'Alā' al-Dīn and his brother. He arrested the justicer, governor of Ghazna. The following day, 16 Ramaḍān [26 April 1206] he called together the cadis, lawyers and commanders, and also summoned the caliph's envoy, namely Shaykh Majd al-Dīn Abū 'Alī [Yaḥyā] ibn al-Rabī', the Shāfi'ī lawyer and professor at the Baghdad Niẓāmiyya. He had come to Ghazna on a mission to Shihāb al-Dīn, but the latter was killed while he was at Ghazna. [Yildiz] sent to him and also to the cadi of Ghazna, saying, 'I wish to transfer to the sultanian palace and to be addressed as ruler. It is essential that you attend. The aim of this is to achieve a settlement of affairs.' The cadi therefore presented himself and Yildiz rode out, wearing mourning garb, with the elite in attendance and installed himself at the palace but not in the seat where Shihāb al-Dīn used to sit. The attitude of many of the Turks was changed by this, because they had followed him in the belief that he was seeking power for Ghiyāth al-Dīn. When they saw him seeking personal power, they changed their obedience; some of them even wept for rage at what he did. He assigned many fiefs and distributed large sums of money.

With Shihāb al-Dīn there had been several sons of princes of Ghūr and Samarqand and others. [**222**] They scorned to attend on Yildiz and demanded that service to Ghiyāth al-Dīn should be the intention. Yildiz gave them leave and many of his men left him to go to Ghiyāth al-Dīn and to 'Alā' al-Dīn and his brother, the two rulers of Bāmiyān. Ghiyāth al-Dīn sent to Yildiz, thanking him and praising him for his expulsion of the sons of Bahā' al-Dīn from Ghazna, and he sent him robes of honour and asked him to acknowledge his name in the khutbah and on coins. Yildiz refused and returned a harsh answer, demanding that he address him as ruler, manumit him, for Ghiyāth al-Dīn was the nephew of his master who had no other heir, and give his son in marriage to Yildiz's daughter. There was no response to this.

It happened that a body of Ghūr from the lord of Bāmiyān's army raided the districts of Kurramān and Sūrān, the former fief of Yildiz. They plundered and killed, so he sent his son-in-law Savinj with an army. They met and overcame the army of Bāmiyān, killing many of them, whose heads were sent to Ghazna and exhibited there.

At Ghazna Yildiz kept the practices of Shihāb al-Dīn in force. He distributed great quantities of money to the inhabitants. He demanded that Mu'ayyad al-Mulk be his vizier, who refused but, after Yildiz insisted, agreed very unwillingly. A friend of his visited Mu'ayyad al-Mulk to congratulate him. He replied, 'On what do you congratulate me? On a donkey after I have ridden a race horse?' And he recited:

> 'Whoever rides an ox after a race horse
> Will disapprove of its hooves and its dewlap.'[18]

'Yildiz used to come to my door a thousand times until I admitted him. I shall now be at his door each morning! Were it not that with these Turks our lives are preserved, I would have another regime.'

Account of Ghiyāth al-Dīn's position after the killing of his uncle

When his uncle Shihāb al-Dīn was killed, Ghiyāth al-Dīn Maḥmūd ibn Ghiyath al-Dīn was at his fief, namely Bust and Isfizār. Prince 'Alā' al-Dīn[19] Muḥammad ibn [**223**] Abī 'Alī had been given control of the lands of Ghūr and other places in Zamīndāwar[20] by Shihāb al-Dīn and when he heard news of his death, he proceeded to Fīrūzkūh, fearing that Ghiyāth al-Dīn would get there before him, secure control of the city and take the treasure it held.

'Alā' al-Dīn was a man of good conduct from one of the great houses of the Ghūr. However, the people did not like him because of their preference for Ghiyāth al-Dīn and the emirs' refusal to serve him while the offspring of their sultan

---

18 Read *aẓlāf* instead of the text's *aṭlāq* in the second line. These verses are by al-Mutanabbī, *Dīwān*, 467. In the complete poem his patron, the Hamdanid Sayf al-Dawla, is compared favourably with other princes.

19 Ignore the 'ibn' that is inserted here in the edition (cf. p. [**217**]).

20 The text has *arḍ Rāwan* (variant: *al-Dāwan*). Arḍ Dāwar (land of Dāwar) is an Arabic rendering of Zamīndāwar, an area south of Ghūr.

Ghiyāth al-Dīn survived, and also because he was a Karrāmī, an extreme member of that sect, while the people of Fīrūzkūh were Shāfi'īs, and he forced them to make the *iqāma*[21] twice. When he came to Fīrūzkūh, he summoned several emirs, including Muḥammad al-Marghanī, his brother and Muḥammad ibn 'Uthmān among the senior emirs and made them swear to aid him in his fight with Khwārazm Shāh and Bahā' al-Dīn, lord of Bāmiyān. He made no mention of Ghiyāth al-Dīn out of contempt for him. They swore oaths to him and his son after him.

Ghiyāth al-Dīn was in the town of Bust, having made no move while waiting to see what the lord of Bāmiyān would do, because they both had made a compact during the days of Shihāb al-Dīn that Ghiyāth al-Dīn should have Khurasan and Bahā' al-Dīn Ghazna and India. After the death of Shihāb al-Dīn, Bahā' al-Dīn, the lord of Bāmiyān, was the stronger and that is why he did nothing. However, when news of Bahā' al-Dīn's death reached Ghiyāth al-Dīn, he mounted the throne and proclaimed himself sultan on 10 Ramaḍān [20 April 1206] and secured oaths from the emirs who came to him, namely Ismā'īl al-Khaljī, Savinj the Emir of the Hunt, Zankī ibn Kharjūm, Ḥusayn al-Ghūrī, lord of Tekīn Ābād,[22] and others. He took the titles of his father Ghiyāth al-Dunyā wa'l-Dīn and wrote to 'Alā' al-Dīn Muḥammad ibn Abī 'Alī, who was at Fīrūzkūh, inviting him to join him and trying to win him over to follow his policy and surrender his kingdom to him. He also wrote to al-Ḥusayn ibn Kharmīl, governor of Herat, in the same vein and promised him an increase in his fief.

[**224**] 'Alā' al-Dīn replied in harsh terms and wrote to the emirs with him to threaten them. Ghiyāth al-Dīn set out for Fīrūzkūh, so 'Alā' al-Dīn dispatched an army with his son, distributed much money among them and awarded them robes of honour with the aim of their stopping Ghiyāth al-Dīn. They met him near Fīrūzkūh and when the two hosts could see one another, Ismā'īl al-Khaljī lifted the visor of his helmet and said, 'Praise be to God when the Turks who do not know their fathers have not overlooked what they owe for their upbringing and have rejected the ruler of Bāmiyān's son.[23] And you, veterans of the Ghūr, who received the bounty of this sultan's father,[24] who raised you up and treated you well, you have denied this kindness and come to fight his son. Is this the action of freeborn men?' Then Muḥammad al-Marghanī, the commander of the army whose counsel they followed, said, 'No, by God!' He dismounted from his horse, cast down his weapons, made straight for Ghiyāth al-Dīn and kissed the earth before him. He

[21] The *iqāma* is the pronouncing in the mosque of the formulae of the call to prayer (*adhān*) before each of the five daily prayers which marks the moment when the *ṣalāt* actually begins. Unlike the other main schools, the Ḥanafīs repeated the formulae and probably influenced the Karrāmiyya in this. See *EI(2)*, iii, 1057.

[22] The text has been emended. See Krawulsky, 59–60: 'a middling-sized town in Nīmrūz, west of Kandahar'.

[23] i.e. 'Alā' al-Dīn Muḥammad ibn Baha' al-Dīn.

[24] i.e. Ghiyāth al-Dīn Muḥammad, father of Ghiyāth al-Dīn Maḥmūd.

broke into loud weeping and all the other emirs did likewise. 'Alā' al-Dīn's men fled along with his son.

When he heard the news, 'Alā' al-Dīn left Fīrūzkūh in flight towards Ghūr, saying, 'I shall go and live in retreat at Mecca.' Ghiyāth al-Dīn sent people in pursuit who brought him back. He was arrested and imprisoned. Ghiyāth al-Dīn took Fīrūzkūh to the joy of the inhabitants and arrested a number of the Karrāmī adherents of 'Alā' al-Dīn, some of whom he put to death. When he entered Fīrūzkūh, he went first to the mosque where he prayed and then he rode to his father's house and made it his residence. He re-established the practices of his father and enlisted members of his retinue. 'Abd al-Jabbār ibn Muḥammad al-Kīrānī,[25] his father's vizier, came to him and was appointed as his vizier. He followed his father's path of generosity and justice.

After he had dealt with 'Alā' al-Dīn, his sole concern was with Ibn Kharmīl in Herat to attract him to his allegiance. He therefore wrote to him and sent a mission, offering to consider him as a father and summoning him to his side. Ibn Kharmīl had heard of Shihāb al-Dīn's death on 8 Ramaḍān [18 April 1206] and gathered the notables, [**225**] including the cadi of Herat, Ṣā'id ibn al-Faḍl al-Sāwī,[26] 'Alī ibn 'Abd al-Khallāq ibn Ziyād, the professor of the Niẓāmiyya at Herat, the Shaykh al-Islam and headman of Herat, the syndic of the Alids and the heads of the quarters. He said to them, 'I have heard of the death of the Sultan Shihāb al-Dīn. I am [an obstacle] in Khwārazm Shāh's throat and fear a siege. I want you to swear to aid me against all who may attack me.' The cadi and Ibn Ziyād replied, 'We swear [to help] against all except the son of Ghiyāth al-Dīn.' He nurtured a grudge against them for this and when Ghiyāth al-Dīn's letter arrived, he feared that the people would incline towards him, so he sent an ambiguous reply.

Ibn Kharmīl had written to Khwārazm Shāh asking him to send him troops so that he could proclaim allegiance to him and use them to resist the Ghurids. Khwārazm Shāh demanded that he send his son as a hostage and then he would send an army. He duly sent his son and so Khwārazm Shāh wrote to his troops in Nishapur and elsewhere in Khurasan, ordering them to proceed to Herat and to act in strict accordance with Ibn Kharmīl's orders. Meanwhile, Ghiyāth al-Dīn was sending a series of envoys to Ibn Kharmīl, who was making one excuse after another in expectation of Khwārazm Shāh's troops, while holding out hopes that he would be loyal to Ghiyāth al-Dīn, although not mentioning him in the khutbah and giving him less than fully committed allegiance.

Emir 'Alī ibn Abī 'Alī, lord of Kālyūn,[27] informed Ghiyāth al-Dīn of Ibn Kharmīl's position, so Ghiyāth al-Dīn determined to go to Herat but some emirs in

---

[25] Perhaps this should be al-Kīdānī. Kīdān is a district of Ghūr.

[26] For his becoming cadi after the death of his father al-Faḍl, see above, p. [**199**].

[27] The text has Kālwīn. Krawulsky, 68–9, places Kalwūn (sic) in the province of Bādghīs and comments on the variety of spellings. Yāqūt, iv, 229, gives Kālwān, 'a strong castle between Bādghīs and Herat in the mountains'. Kālyūn was a 'mountain stronghold … to the north-east of Herat' (Bosworth, 'The Iranian world', 316).

his service discouraged him and advised him to wait and see what Ibn Kharmīl would finally do and to avoid bringing him to account. Ibn Kharmīl consulted people about what to do with Ghiyāth al-Dīn and 'Alī ibn 'Abd al-Khallāq ibn Ziyād, the professor of the Niẓāmiyya at Herat and the administrator of the charitable trusts of Khurasan which were all in the hands of the Ghurids, said to him, 'You ought to make the khutbah for Sultan Ghiyāth al-Dīn and give up your ambiguous policy.' He replied, 'I fear for my life. Do you go and get some guarantees for me from him.' His aim was to remove him far from himself. He set out on a mission to Ghiyāth al-Dīn and informed him [**226**] of the treacherous conduct that Ibn Kharmīl had in mind for him and his inclination to Khwārazm Shāh, whom he was encouraging to attack Herat. He said to him, 'I will surrender it to you the moment you come.' Some of the emirs were in agreement with him and others differed. He said, 'You ought not to leave him any excuse. You should send him a diploma to govern Herat.' He did this and sent it with Ibn Ziyād and one of his men.

Ghiyāth al-Dīn then sent to Amīrān ibn Qayṣar, lord of Ṭāliqān, to summon him but he hesitated [to comply]. Next he sent to the lord of Marv asking him to join him but he also hesitated. The inhabitants said to him, 'If you do not surrender the city to Ghiyāth al-Dīn and go to him, we will give you up, put you in irons and send you to him.' He was therefore obliged to go to Fīrūzkūh, where Ghiyāth al-Dīn gave him a robe of honour and assigned him a fief. Ṭāliqān he assigned to Savinj, his father's mamluke known as Emir of the Hunt.

How Khwārazm Shāh took control of the Ghurid lands in Khurasan

We have already mentioned that al-Ḥusayn ibn Kharmīl, governor of Herat, wrote to Khwārazm Shāh and stated that he would become his ally and offer him obedience and that he rejected allegiance to the Ghurids, deceived Ghiyāth al-Dīn and made a false profession of recognition and loyalty, waiting for the arrival of Khwārazm Shāh's army or the arrival of Ghiyāth al-Dīn's envoy and Ibn Ziyād with robes of honour for himself. When the robes arrived, he and his followers donned them and Ghiyath al-Dīn's envoy demanded that he make the khutbah. He replied, 'On Friday we shall make the khutbah in his name.'

It happened that Khwārazm Shāh's army drew near. When Friday came, he was reminded of the khutbah, but said, 'We are now engaged in a more serious matter by the arrival of this enemy.' There was a long argument between them, while he persisted in his refusal to act. Khwārazm Shāh's troops arrived and were met by Ibn Kharmīl, who let them camp at the city's gate. They said to him, [**227**] 'Khwārazm Shāh has commanded us not to disobey any order of yours.' He thanked them for that and went out to them every day and provided them with abundant supplies.

He received news that Khwārazm Shāh had besieged Balkh and met and fought its ruler outside the city. He did not camp near the city but remained four leagues distant. Ibn Kharmīl then regretted his alliance with Khwārazm Shāh and said to his close followers, 'We have made a mistake in joining with this man, for I see that he is weak.' He began to persuade the army to retire, saying to the emirs, 'Khwārazm Shāh has sent to Ghiyāth al-Dīn to say, "I remain true to the treaty between us. I will not touch what your father had in Khurasan." Your best plan is to retire until we see what happens.' So they retired and he sent them many gifts.

When he received information that Khwārazm Shāh's army had come to Herat, Ghiyāth al-Dīn seized Ibn Kharmīl's fief and sent to Kurzabān and took all his money, children, mounts and other things that were there and put his men in irons. Letters came to Ibn Kharmīl from those Ghūr who favoured him, saying, 'If Ghiyāth al-Dīn sees you, he will kill you.' The people of Herat, having heard what Ghiyāth al-Dīn had done with Ibn Kharmīl's family and possessions, determined to arrest him and write to Ghiyāth al-Dīn to send someone to take over the city. The Cadi Ṣā'id, cadi of Herat, and Ibn Ziyād wrote to Ghiyāth al-Dīn to that effect. When Ibn Kharmīl learnt how Ghiyāth al-Dīn had treated his family and what the people of Herat planned, he feared that they might arrest him before he could do anything. He therefore visited the cadi and summoned the leading citizens. He spoke mildly to them, ingratiated himself and announced his loyalty to Ghiyāth al-Dīn. He said, 'I have sent the troops of Khwārazm Shāh away and I intend to send a messenger to Ghiyāth al-Dīn announcing my obedience. What I would like from you is that **[228]** you write a letter along with me, reporting that I am loyal.' They approved of his words and wrote as he had asked. He, however, sent his messenger towards Fīrūzkūh but gave him orders, when night fell, to return on the Nishapur road to catch up with Khwārazm Shāh's troops and to make all speed and, when he caught up with them, to bring them back.

The messenger did as he was ordered, caught up with the army two days from Herat and commanded them to return, which they did. On the fourth day after the messenger had set out they arrived back at Herat with the messenger in the fore. Ibn Kharmīl met them and let them in to the city with the drums being beaten ahead of them. After their entry they seized Ibn Ziyād and blinded him. The Cadi Ṣā'id they expelled from the city and he made his way to Ghiyāth al-Dīn at Fīrūzkūh. Ibn Kharmīl also expelled the Ghūrīs who were with him and all whom he knew to favour them and handed the city gates over to the Khwārazmians.

Ghiyāth al-Dīn moved out of Fīrūzkūh in the direction of Herat and dispatched a force which seized some mounts at pasture belonging to the people of Herat. The Khwārazmians took the field and carried out raids on Herat al-Rūdh[28] and other places. Ghiyāth al-Dīn ordered his troops to advance to Herat, appointing as their commander 'Alī ibn Abī 'Alī. He himself remained at Fīrūzkūh after he had heard that Khwārazm Shāh was besieging Balkh. The army set out with its advance guard led by Amīrān ibn Qayṣar, the former lord of Ṭāliqān. He was disgruntled

---

[28] See Krawulsky, 92–3, s.v. Harāt Rud: a district of some 50 villages.

with Ghiyāth al-Dīn since he had taken Ṭāliqān from him. He sent to Ibn Kharmīl to tell him that he commanded the advance guard and to bid him come to him, for he would not resist. He swore him an oath on that.

Ibn Kharmīl set out with his troops and made a surprise attack on Ghiyāth al-Dīn's forces. They did not manage to mount their horses before the enemy was amongst them and did much slaughter. Ibn Kharmīl held his men back from the Ghurids for fear that they might be utterly destroyed. He took their belongings as booty and made Ismā'īl al-Khaljī prisoner. While remaining where he was, he sent out raids on Bādghīs territory and elsewhere. [**229**] Ghiyāth al-Dīn was troubled by the situation and he decided to go in person to Herat. He heard a report that 'Alā' al-Dīn, lord of Bāmiyān, had returned to Ghazna, as we shall relate, so he remained there, waiting to see what they and also Yildiz would do.

As for events concerning Balkh, when Khwārazm Shāh was informed of the killing of Shihāb al-Dīn, he released those Ghūr he held whom he had captured at the battle before the gate of Khwārazm, gave them robes of honour and treated them kindly, giving them money. He said, 'Ghiyāth al-Dīn is my brother and there is no division between us. Any of you who wish to remain with me, let him stay, but whoever wishes to go to him, I shall send him on his way. Were he to express a wish for anything he desires from me, I would grant it to him.' He reached an agreement with Muḥammad ibn 'Alī ibn Bashīr, one of the greatest Ghūr emirs, and treated him generously with the assignment of a fief to win over the Ghūr. He made him a go-between in his dealings with the lord of Balkh and sent his brother, 'Alī Shāh, to Balkh ahead of him with his army. When he drew near, the emir there, 'Imād al-Dīn 'Umar ibn al-Ḥusayn al-Ghūrī, came out to meet him and prevented him from descending on the city. He camped four leagues away and sent to his brother Khwārazm Shāh to inform him of their strength. The latter set out for Balkh in Dhū'l-Qa'da this year [9 June–8 July 1206] and when he arrived, its lord came forth to fight them, but was not strong enough to deal with their large numbers. They made camp and he began to harass them by night and his actions put them in a wretched situation. The lord of Balkh continued under siege, while awaiting reinforcements from his comrades, the sons of Bahā' al-Dīn, ruler of Bāmiyān, but they were too engaged at Ghazna to be able to help him, as we shall narrate.

Khwārazm Shāh remained threatening Balkh for forty days, riding out to do battle every day. Many of his men were killed and he was achieving nothing. He made contact with the ruler there, 'Imād al-Dīn, through Muḥammad ibn 'Alī ibn Bashīr al-Ghūrī, about offering him something to persuade him to surrender the city to him. He replied, 'I will not surrender the city except to its [rightful] rulers.' Khwārazm Shāh determined to go to Herat. However, when his superiors, the sons of Bahā' al-Dīn, ruler of Bāmiyān, went to Ghazna for the second time, as we shall narrate, God willing, and Tāj al-Dīn Yildiz took them prisoner, he gave up that [**230**] plan. Muḥammad ibn 'Alī ibn Bashīr sent his deputy to 'Imād al-Dīn to inform him of his superiors' state and their capture, and that he had no recourse left and no excuse to delay a response. He paid him a visit and continued to work on him, now by blandishments and now by threats, until he agreed to submit to Khwārazm Shāh, make the khutbah in his name and name him on the coinage. He stated, 'I know that he will not keep faith with me,' so he sent people to take his oath in the way he desired. Peace was concluded and he went out to Khwārazm Shāh who gave him a robe of honour and restored him to his city. This was on the final day of Rabī' I 603 [4 November 1206].

Then Khwārazm Shāh marched to Kurzabān, where 'Alī ibn Abī 'Alī was, to put it under siege. He sent to Ghiyāth al-Dīn saying, 'This place was assigned by your uncle to Ibn Kharmīl. Will you give it up?' He refused and said, 'Between me and you there is nothing but the sword.' At that Khwārazm Shāh sent to 'Alī by hand of Muḥammad ibn 'Alī ibn Bashīr, offered him inducements and declared he had no hope of aid from Ghiyāth al-Dīn. He persisted with him until he renounced his claim and surrendered the place. He returned to Fīrūzkūh where Ghiyāth al-Dīn ordered him to be put to death, but the emirs interceded for him, so he was left alone. Khwārazm Shāh gave Kurzabān to Ibn Kharmīl. He then sent to 'Imād al-Dīn, ruler of Balkh, demanding his presence, saying, 'An important matter has occurred. It is essential that you attend. You are now one of our closest associates.' He therefore went to him but was arrested and sent to Khwārazm. Khwārazm Shāh proceeded to Balkh and took it, appointing as his deputy there Ja'far[29] al-Turkī.

[231] How Khwārazm Shāh gained Tirmidh and surrendered it to the Qarakhitay

Having taken the city of Balkh, Khwārazm Shāh proceeded to Tirmidh by forced marches. It was held by the son[30] of 'Imād al-Dīn, the former ruler of Balkh. He sent Muḥammad[31] ibn 'Alī ibn Bashīr to him, to say, 'Your father had become one of my closest friends and one of the senior emirs of my state. He surrendered Balkh to me. However, I have become aware of something regarding him that I disapprove of, so I have sent him to Khwārazm in an honoured and respected state. You, however, shall be a brother to me.' He made him promises and offered him a large fief. Thus Muḥammad ibn 'Alī misled him.

The lord of Tirmidh saw that Khwārazm Shāh beleaguered him on one side and the Qarakhitay on the other and that Yildiz had captured his men at Ghazna, so his spirit weakened and he sent to Khwārazm Shāh to seek his sworn word. This he duly gave and accepted the surrender of Tirmidh, which he then handed over to the Qarakhitay. Because of this Khwārazm Shāh gained much reproach and obloquy in the short term, but then it became clear to people later that he surrendered it to

[29] There is an Ms. variant Jaqar, which may be correct.

[30] He is named as Bahrām Shāh (Barthold, *Turkestan*, 352).

[31] Emend the edition to make this Muḥammad the object of the verb.

them merely to be able thereby to take power in Khurasan and then turn against them to take Tirmidh from them and other places too. When he took Khurasan, invaded and seized the lands of the Qarakhitay and destroyed them, people realized that he had done what he did as a trick and a strategem (God show him mercy!).

Account of the return of the sons of the lord of Bāmiyān to Ghazna

We have previously mentioned Yildiz al-Tūrkī's coming to Ghazna and his expulsion of 'Alā' al-Dīn and Jalāl al-Dīn, sons of Bahā' al-Dīn, lord of Bāmiyān, after his capture of it. He remained in Ghazna from 10 Ramaḍān 602 [20 April 1206] until 5 Dhū'l-Qa'da of [**232**] that year [13 June 1206], ruling well and showing justice to the subjects. He assigned fiefs to the soldiers, some of whom stayed, although others went to Ghiyāth al-Dīn at Fīrūzkūh and yet others joined 'Alā' al-Dīn, ruler of Bāmiyān. Yildiz made the khutbah neither in anyone's name nor in his own. He promised the people that his envoy was with his lord Ghiyāth al-Dīn and that on his return he would name him in the khutbah. The people rejoiced to hear his words. However, what he did was a trick to deceive them and Ghiyāth al-Dīn, because, had he not pretended this, most of the Turks and all the subjects would have deserted him. Then he would be too weak to resist the ruler of Bāmiyān. By this statement and similar ones he was able to enlist Turks and others in his service.

After he had overcome the ruler of Bāmiyān, as we shall narrate, he revealed what he was harbouring in his mind. At this juncture news came to him of the approach of 'Alā' al-Dīn and Jalāl al-Dīn, the sons of Bahā' al-Dīn, ruler of Bāmiyān, with large forces and that they planned to sack Ghazna and give property and persons over to destruction. The people were in great fear and Yildiz equipped many of his troops, whom he dispatched to confront them on their route. They met the leading units of the army and several of the Turks were killed. The main army came up and they could not withstand them. They fled, pursued by 'Alā' al-Dīn's army, killing and taking prisoners. The fugitives reached Ghazna but Yildiz left in flight, making for his town of Kurramān. He was overtaken by some of the army of Bāmiyān, about 3,000 horsemen, whom he engaged fiercely and repulsed. From Kurramān he summoned a large sum of money and weapons, which he distributed among his troops.

As for 'Alā' al-Dīn and his brother, they left Ghazna, did not enter but followed Yildiz's tracks. Hearing of this, he deserted Kurramān, whose inhabitants plundered one another. 'Alā' al-Dīn took Kurramān and gave its people guarantees of security. They then determined to return to Ghazna and sack it. The inhabitants there, when they heard of this, sought out Cadi Sa'īd ibn Mas'ūd and complained of their situation. He went to 'Alā' al-Dīn's vizier, known as the Ṣāhib (Master), and told him of the people's plight. He tried to calm their hearts [**233**] but someone else, whom they trusted, told them that a sack was the enemy's agreed intention, so they made their preparations, narrowed the gates of the quarters and the streets and prepared ballistas and stones. Merchants from Iraq, Mosul, Syria and elsewhere came forward and complained to the authorities but nobody listened to their pleas. They sought out the house of Majd al-Dīn [Yaḥyā] ibn al-Rabī', the caliph's envoy, and called upon him for help. He calmed them and promised to intercede for them and the citizens. He sent to a great emir of the Ghūr, called Sulaymān ibn Sīs, who was an important elder, one to whose words they paid attention, to inform him of the situation and to tell him to write to 'Alā' al-Dīn and his brother to intercede for the people. This he did and made his intercession very effective. He warned them what the citizens might do, if they persisted in their intention to sack. They agreed to show mercy to the people after many to-and-fro consultations. They had already promised their troops the sack of Ghazna, so they compensated them from the treasury instead. The people's fears were stilled and the army returned to Ghazna during the last days of Dhū'l-Qa'da [ended 8 July 1206], accompanied by the treasure that Yildiz had taken from Mu'ayyad al-Mulk when he returned in the company of the slain Shihāb al-Dīn. It comprised 900 loads along with the garments and specie that had been added to it. Part of it consisted of 12,000 robes, brocaded with gold thread.

'Alā' al-Dīn decided to appoint Mu'ayyad al-Mulk as his vizier. Jalāl al-Dīn heard this, summoned him, gave him a robe of honour despite his unwillingness to receive it and made him *his* vizier. When 'Alā' al-Dīn learnt of this, he arrested Mu'ayyad al-Mulk, put him in chains and imprisoned him. The mood of people changed and differences appeared. Later 'Alā' al-Dīn and Jalāl al-Dīn divided the treasury and a dispute over the division arose between them, such as does not arise even between merchants. The people deduced from that that nothing would go right for them due to their niggardliness and their disagreements. The emirs regretted having shown support for them and having deserted Ghiyāth al-Dīn with his manifest generosity and liberality.

[**234**] Later Jalāl al-Dīn and his uncle 'Abbās[32] went with part of the army to Bāmiyān, while 'Alā' al-Dīn remained at Ghazna. His vizier 'Imād al-Mulk treated the soldiers and the citizens badly. The wealth of the Turks was plundered, to such an extent that they sold the mothers of their children, who wept and screamed but were disregarded.

Account of Yildiz's return to Ghazna

When Jalāl al-Dīn left Ghazna and his brother 'Alā' al-Dīn remained there, Yildiz and the Turks with him assembled a large force and returned towards Ghazna.

[32] Jalāl al-Dīn's grandmother, the sister of Sultan Shihāb al-Dīn, married the latter's cousin, Shams al-Dīn Muḥammad ibn Mas'ūd. He had a son 'Abbās from a different marriage (cf. p. [**217**]).

They came to Kalū, which they took, killing several of the Ghurid forces. Those that fled came to Kurramān. Yildiz marched against them and put in charge of his advance guard one of Shihāb al-Dīn's senior mamlukes, whose name was Aytakin[33] al-Tatar, leading 2,000 cavalry, Khalaj, Turks, Oghuz, Ghūr and others.

In Kurramān there was a force of 'Alā' al-Dīn's with an emir called Ibn al-Mu'ayyad, accompanied by several emirs, including Abū 'Alī ibn Sulaymān ibn Sīs. He and his father were leading Ghūr but they were distracted by gaming, pleasure-seeking and drinking with never a break from all that. They were told, 'The army of the Turks has come near you,' but they paid no attention and did not give up their pursuits. Aytakin al-Tatar and his Turks attacked and gave them no time to mount their horses. They were slaughtered completely, some killed in the battle and others killed [afterwards] in cold blood. The only survivors were those whom the Turks spared intentionally.

When Yildiz arrived, he saw the Ghūrī emirs all slain and said, 'Did we fight all these?' [**235**] Aytakin al-Tatar replied, 'No, we killed them in cold blood.' He blamed and reprimanded him for that and had the head of Ibn al-Mu'ayyad brought before him. He bowed down in gratitude to God Almighty and gave orders for the dead to be washed and buried. Abū 'Alī ibn Sulaymān ibn Sīs was among the slain.

The news reached Ghazna on 20 Dhū'l-Ḥijja of this year [28 July 1206]. 'Alā' al-Dīn crucified the man who brought the report. The sky clouded over and a violent rainstorm came which destroyed part of Ghazna. After it came large hailstones the size of chickens' eggs. The people clamoured for 'Alā' al-Dīn to take down the crucified man, which he did at the end of the day. The darkness was lifted and the people quietened down.

Yildiz took Kurramān and treated the inhabitants well. They had suffered severely with those others. When 'Alā' al-Dīn had verified the news, he sent his vizier, the Ṣāḥib, to his brother Jalāl al-Dīn at Bāmiyān to tell him of Yildiz's doings and to ask him for aid. Jalāl al-Dīn had already prepared his forces to march to Balkh to drive Khwārazm Shāh away, but when this news came to him, he gave up Balkh and went to Ghazna. Most of the Ghūr in his army had abandoned both him and his brother and sought out Ghiyāth al-Dīn. Towards the end of Dhū'l-Ḥijja [ended 6 August 1206] Yildiz arrived at Ghazna and he and his troops made camp opposite the citadel and put 'Alā' al-Dīn under siege. Fierce fighting followed. Yildiz then ordered a proclamation of protection for the city and that the citizens, the Ghūr and the troops from Bāmiyān would be safe, but he continued to besiege the citadel. Jalāl al-Dīn arrived with 4,000 of the Bāmiyān army and others. Yildiz went to confront them on their way. His siege had lasted forty days before his departure. After he had gone, 'Alā' al-Dīn sent out the troops he had and commanded them to fall upon Yildiz from his rear, while his brother would be facing him, so that none of his army might escape. However, after they had left the citadel, Sulaymān ibn Sīs al-Ghūrī went to Ghiyāth al-Dīn at Fīrūzkūh. On his

---

33 *Kāmil* has Ay D.k.z. Cf. *Ṭabaqāt-i Nāṣirī*, i, 495.

arrival he was received with honour and high favour and appointed justicer of Fīrūzkūh. This was in Ṣafar of the year 603 [7 September–5 October 1206].

[236] Yildiz, meanwhile, advanced on the road Jalāl al-Dīn was taking and they met at the village of Balq.[34] They fought a stubborn battle but Jalāl al-Dīn and his army were defeated. Jalāl al-Dīn himself was taken prisoner and brought to Yildiz, who, when he saw him, dismounted and kissed his hand. He ordered him to be closely guarded and returned to Ghazna, taking Jalāl al-Dīn and one thousand Bāmiyān captives with him. His men plundered their baggage.

After his return to Ghazna, he sent to 'Alā' al-Dīn, telling him to surrender the citadel, otherwise he would kill the prisoners he had. After a refusal to surrender, he put to death four hundred prisoners in front of the citadel. Seeing this, 'Alā' al-Dīn sent Mu'ayyad al-Mulk to ask for terms, which Yildiz granted. However, when he emerged, Yildiz arrested him and set a guard on him and his brother. He also arrested his vizier 'Imād al-Mulk for evil conduct. With 'Alā' al-Dīn in the citadel of Ghazna was Hindūkhān ibn Malikshāh ibn Khwārazm Shāh Tekesh. When he left the citadel, Yildiz arrested him too. He wrote to Ghiyāth al-Dīn to report his victory and sent him the banners and some of the captives.

Account of the lord of Marāgha's and the lord of Irbil's invasion of Azerbayjan

This year the lord of Marāgha, namely 'Alā' al-Dīn,[35] and Muẓaffar al-Dīn Kūkburī, lord of Irbil, agreed to invade Azerbayjan and take it from its ruler, Abū Bakr ibn Pahlawān, because he was occupied day and night with drinking and neglected his watch over his kingdom's affairs and the maintenance of his troops and people. The ruler of Irbil went to Marāgha, where he met with its ruler 'Alā' al-Dīn and the two of them proceeded towards Tabriz. When its ruler Abū Bakr learnt of this, **[237]** he sent to Aydughmish, ruler of the Uplands, Hamadhan, Isfahan, Rayy and the lands between them, who was a vassal of Abū Bakr although he had seized full control and paid no heed to Abū Bakr. Abū Bakr sent to him, asking for support and informing him of the situation. At that time he was in the territory of the Ismā'īlīs and, when this message came to him, he set out to go to him with large forces.

On his arrival he sent to the lord of Irbil to say, 'We used to hear of you that you loved men of religion and virtue and that you were good to them. We believed you had goodness and religion. But now we clearly see you doing the opposite, because you attack Islamic lands, kill Muslims, plunder their goods and stir up dissension. If this is so, you have no intelligence. You come against us, you, the ruler of a

[34] 'A settlement (*nāḥiya*) at Ghazna in Zābulistān' (Yāqūt, i, 729).

[35] A member of the Aḥmadīlī dynasty, his personal name was Qarāsunqur. He died in 604/1207–8. Marāgha is a city east of Lake Urmiya and was the centre of a province of eight districts (Krawulsky, 536–7).

village, while we rule from the gateway to Khurasan to Khilāṭ and Irbil. Assume that you defeat this person, do you not know that he has servants, of whom I am one? Were he to take a prefect from every village or ten men from every town, he would gather together many times more than your army. Your best course is to return home. I say this to you only to save you.' Following on this communication he marched towards him.

When Muẓaffar al-Dīn heard this message and that Aydughmish had set out, he decided to withdraw. The lord of Marāgha strove hard to get him to stay where he was and entrust his troops to him. He said, 'All his emirs have written to me that they would join with me if I march against them,' but Muẓaffar al-Dīn did not accept what he said and returned home. He followed an arduous route, difficult passes and sheer ravines, in fear of pursuit.

Abū Bakr and Aydughmish then marched against Marāgha and put it under siege. Its ruler made peace with them by the surrender of one of his fortresses to Abū Bakr. It had been the cause of the difference. Abū Bakr gave him the two regions of Ustuwā[36] and Urmiya[37] as a fief and withdrew.

[238] How Aydughmish fell upon the Ismā'īlīs

This year Aydughmish marched into Ismā'īlī territory near Qazwin and slaughtered many of them, plundered and took captives and besieged their castles. He conquered five of them. He had planned to besiege Alamut and to extirpate its inhabitants but there occurred what we have mentioned, the expedition of the rulers of Marāgha and Irbil. The Emir Abū Bakr summoned him, so he left their lands and went to Abū Bakr, as we have narrated.

Account of the arrival in the Uplands of an army from Khwārazm Shāh and what they did

This year a large detachment of the Khwārazmian army, about 10,000 horsemen with their wives and children, went to the Uplands. They arrived at Zanjān.[38] Its ruler Aydughmish was occupied with the rulers of Irbil and Marāgha, so they took advantage of the country's being empty. After Muẓaffar al-Dīn had returned to his town and the situation between Aydughmish and the ruler of Marāgha had been settled, Aydughmish moved against the Khwārazmians and met them in battle. The fighting between the two sides was intense but in the end the Khwārazmians gave

---

36 This is an older form for Ostü, a province of Khurasan, whose main town is Khabūshān (Krawulsky, 106; Yāqūt, I, 243–4).

37 Situated west of the lake of the same name in modern Turkey. See Yāqūt, i, 218–19.

38 Krawulsky, 325–6.

way and the sword overwhelmed them. Some were killed and a large number were taken prisoner. Only the odd fugitive escaped. Captives they themselves had taken were seized and their baggage plundered. They had caused much evil in the land with their pillaging and killing. They now met the requital for what they had done.

Account of the raid by the son of Leon on the districts of Aleppo

During this year there was a series of raids by the son of Leon, lord of the Passes, on the region of Aleppo. He plundered, burned, took prisoners and slaves. The ruler of Aleppo, al-Ẓāhir Ghāzī, son of Saladin, assembled his troops and asked for assistance from other [**239**] princes. He gathered many horse and foot and left Aleppo to move against the son of Leon. The latter had camped on the borders of his lands next to Aleppan territory but there was no access to him, because all his lands are without roads, except through arduous mountains and difficult passes. No one else can enter, especially from the Aleppo direction, for the route from there is totally impossible. Al-Ẓāhir camped five leagues from Aleppo and stationed some of his army as an advance guard with a great emir, one of his father's mamlukes, called Maymūn al-Qaṣrī, named after the palace (*qaṣr*) of the Alid caliphs in Cairo, because his father had taken it from them. Al-Ẓāhir sent provisions and weapons to a fortress of his neighbouring Ibn Leon's lands, called Darbsāk. He also sent orders to Maymūn to send a detachment of the troops he had with him to the route these supplies would take to convey them to Darbsāk. He carried this out and dispatched a large body of his force, while he remained with a few. News of this reached Ibn Leon, so he made haste and came upon him when his force was reduced. A fierce battle followed and Maymūn sent to inform al-Ẓāhir but he was far away. The battle lasted long and Maymūn defended himself and his baggage despite the fewness of the Muslims and the large number of Armenians. The Muslims gave way and suffered casualties at the hands of the enemy, being killed or taken. The Muslims likewise inflicted many losses on the Armenians.

The Armenians seized and plundered the Muslims' baggage train and set off with it. However, the Muslims, who had accompanied the supplies to Darbsāk, came upon them by surprise before they realized what was happening. The enemy were not aware of them before they were among their ranks and had put them to the sword. The fighting became very fierce and then the Muslims again gave way. The Armenians returned to their lands with their plunder and sought the protection of their mountains and fortresses.[39]

---

[39] Abū Shāma, *Dhayl*, 53, mentions raids on Aleppo and Ḥārim and that Maymūn was nearly captured through lack of caution. Al-Ẓāhir came to Ḥārim, Leo withdrew and a fort above Darbsāk he had built was demolished by al-Ẓāhir.

[240] How the Georgians plundered Armenia

This year the Georgians in all their hosts invaded the region of Khilāṭ in Armenia. They plundered, killed and enslaved many of the inhabitants and roamed throughout the country unmolested. Nobody came forth from Khilāṭ to stop them, so they were left free to carry on their pillage and seizing of captives, while the country lay devoid of any defender, since its ruler was a boy and the regent had insufficient obedience from the soldiers.

When the suffering of the people increased yet more, they protested and encouraged one another [to act]. The Muslim troops in that region all got together and were joined by many volunteers. All went to meet the Georgians, though in fear. A certain pious Sufi in a dream saw the deceased Shaykh Muḥammad al-Bustī, one of the righteous, and the Sufi said to him, 'Is it you I see here? 'I have come', he replied, 'to aid the Muslims against their enemy.' He awoke, overjoyed at al-Bustī's stance for Islam, and came to the army commander and told him of his dream. Delighted at this, the commander strengthened his determination to attack the Georgians, marched with the troops towards them and took up a position.

News of this came to the Georgians, who planned to surprise the Muslims. They moved from their position in the valley to the heights, where they halted to be able to surprise the Muslims when darkness fell. The Muslims learnt of this, so moved towards the Georgians and held the head of the valley and its lower part against them. It was a valley that had only these two routes. When the Georgians saw this, **[241]** they were convinced they were lost and their spirit was broken. The Muslims, full of confidence, engaged them closely and killed many of them and also took many prisoners. Only a few of the Georgians escaped. God saved the Muslims from their wickedness after having been on the point of destruction.

Miscellaneous events

In Jumādā II this year [13 January–10 February 1206] Emir Mujīr al-Dīn Ṭāshtakīn, emir of the Pilgrimage, died at Tustar. The caliph had made him governor of the whole of Khuzistan and he was emir of the Pilgrimage for many years. He was virtuous and pious, a good governor, constant in his devotions with a tendency towards Shiism. After his death the caliph appointed over Khuzistan his mamluke Sanjar, who was Ṭāshtakīn's son-in-law.

This year Sanjar ibn Muqallad ibn Sulaymān ibn Muhārish, emir of the 'Ubāda,[40] was killed in Iraq. His death came about as follows. He made an accusation about

---

[40] The Banū 'Ubāda were a subdivision of the 'Uqayl tribe, who had returned to desert life after their period of rule in the Jazīra bordering Iraq in the eleventh century (Qalqashandī, *Ansāb al-'arab*, 335).

his father Muqallad to the Caliph al-Nāṣir li-Dīn Allāh, who ordered his father's confinement. He stayed there for a while but then the caliph released him. Later Sanjar killed a brother of his and for these reasons he aroused the rage of his family and his brothers. In Shā'bān of this year [13 March–10 April 1206] he settled in the region of al-Ma'shūq.[41] One day he went riding with his brothers and other companions. When he was separated from his men, his brother 'Alī ibn Muqallad struck him a blow with his sword. He fell to the ground and his brothers dismounted and dispatched him.

[**242**] During this year Ghiyāth al-Dīn Khusroshāh, ruler of Anatolia, prepared for an expedition to Trebizond. He besieged its ruler because he had abandoned his allegiance. He blockaded him closely and for that reason the routes, both by land and by sea, from Anatolia, from the Rūs,[42] the Qipjaq and others were interrupted. None of these came into Ghiyāth al-Dīn's territory and people suffered huge damage on account of that, because they used to carry on commerce with them and enter their lands. Merchants from Syria, Iraq, Mosul, the Jazīra and elsewhere used to visit them. A great host of them now gathered in the city of Sīvās and since the road did not open, they suffered considerable harm. Fortunate indeed were those who retained their initial capital.

This year Abū Bakr ibn Pahlawān, lord of Azerbayjan and Arrān, married the daughter of the king of the Georgians. The reason was that the Georgians carried out a series of raids on his lands, because they saw his incompetence, his addiction to drink, games and such-like, and his neglect of state administration and the defence of the country. When he too became aware of this, but did not possess sufficient pride or shame for these shameful traits to make him give up the course he was wedded to, and saw that he was incapable of protecting his lands with the sword, he turned to protecting them with his penis. He courted their king's daughter and married her, so then the Georgians refrained from pillage, raiding and killing. As it has been said, it was a case of 'He sheathed his hanger and drew his member.'

This year a lamb was brought to Uzbek with a face like a human being's and a body like a lamb's. This was truly a wonder.

The following died this year:

Cadi Abū Ḥāmid Muḥammad ibn Muḥammad al-Mānadā'ī (?) al-Wāsiṭī in Wāsiṭ.

Fakhr al-Dīn Mubārak Shāh ibn al-Ḥasan al-Marwarūdhī in Shawwāl [11 May–8 June 1206]. He wrote excellent poetry in Farsī and Arabic and enjoyed high standing with the elder Ghiyāth al-Dīn, [**243**] lord of Ghazna, Herat and

---

41 Yāqūt, iv, 576: 'a large palace on the west bank of the Tigris opposite Samarra ... one day's journey from Takrit'.

42 The Rūs must be understood to be the early Russians, Norsemen of Swedish origin who in time were absorbed by the Slavs they had conquered. See Minorsky, *Sharvan and Darband*, 108–16; *EI(2)*, viii, 618–29.

elsewhere. He had a guest house provided with books and chess. The scholars perused the books and the fools played chess.

Abū'l-Ḥasan 'Alī ibn 'Alī ibn Sa'āda al-Fāriqī, the Shafi'ī lawyer, in Dhū'l-Ḥijja [9 July–6 August 1206] at Baghdad. For a long time he served as lecturer[43] at the Niẓāmiyya. He became a professor in the madrasa which the mother of Caliph al-Nāṣir li-Dīn Allāh founded. In addition to his learning he was a righteous man. He was asked to be deputy cadi in Baghdad but refused. Compelled to take that position, he held it for a little while and then one day walked to the mosque of Ibn al-Muṭṭalib and resigned. He donned a waist-wrapper of coarse wool and changed his form of dress. He ordered the court officials and others to leave him, and stayed there until the demand for him had quietened down. Then he returned to his house, free of any office.

Shaykh Abū Mūsā al-Makkī, who lived in the *maqṣūra* of the Sultan's Mosque at Baghdad, fell from the roof of the mosque this year. He was a good man, assiduous in his devotions.

'Afīf al-Dīn Abū'l-Makārim 'Arafat ibn 'Alī ibn Biṣallā (?) al-Bandanījī at Baghdad. He was a good man, dedicated to his devotions (God have mercy on him).

---

[43] The Arabic term is *mu'īd* (literally 'repetitor'), a salaried assistant of the *mudarris* (professor) who reinforced and underlined the latter's lectures. See Makdisi, *Colleges*, 193–5, where the career of this al-Fāriqī is discussed.

[244] The Year 603 [1206–1207]

Account of ‘Abbās’s taking of Bāmiyān and its restoration to his nephew

In this year ‘Abbās took Bāmiyān from ‘Alā’ al-Dīn and Jalāl al-Dīn, the sons of his brother Bahā’ al-Dīn.[1] This came about as follows. After the defeat by Yildiz of the army of Bāmiyān and their return to that town, they reported that ‘Alā’ al-Dīn and Jalāl al-Dīn had been taken prisoner and that Yildiz and his men had seized the army’s possessions as booty. Their father’s vizier, known as the Ṣāḥib [the Master], took large sums of money, jewels and other precious items and an elephant and went to Khwārazm Shāh asking him for aid against Yildiz and to send an army with him to rescue his princely lords.

After his departure from Bāmiyān, their uncle ‘Abbās, aware that the city no longer contained the Ṣāḥib or his own nephews, gathered his men and set himself up as ruler. He climbed to the citadel, took it over and expelled the followers of his nephews, ‘Alā’ al-Dīn and Jalāl al-Dīn. Report of this reached the vizier on his way to Khwārazm Shāh. He came back to Bāmiyān, collected large forces and besieged ‘Abbās in the citadel. He was widely obeyed throughout all the realms of Bahā’ al-Dīn and his sons and successors. Although he did not have enough money to meet all his needs, he maintained the siege. All he had with him was what he had got together to take to Khwārazm Shāh.

After Jalāl al-Dīn had escaped from imprisonment by Yildiz, as we shall narrate, he made his way to Bāmiyān. **[245]** He came to Ar.ṣ.f (?), a city of Bāmiyān, and his father’s vizier, the Ṣāḥib, came and joined with him. They proceeded to the fortresses, made contact with ‘Abbās who had seized possession of them, and coaxed him with blandishments. He surrendered all to Jalāl al-Dīn and said, ‘I only held them because I feared that Khwārazm Shāh might take them.’ Jalāl al-Dīn approved of what he had done and he took his place as ruler again.

How Khwārazm Shāh took Ṭāliqān

When Khwārazm Shāh had surrendered Tirmidh to the Qarakhitay, he went to Maymand and Andkhūd and wrote to Savinj, emir of the Hunt, Ghiyāth al-Dīn Maḥmūd’s deputy in Ṭāliqān, to try to win his support. The envoy returned disappointed, as Savinj had not complied with his wishes. Indeed, he gathered his army and marched out to wage war on Khwārazm Shāh. They clashed near Ṭāliqān.

1 ‘Abbās and Bahā’ al-Dīn were half-brothers (see p. [**217**]).

When the two armies were face to face, Savinj made an impetuous charge, alone. However, when he drew near the Khwārazmian army, he threw himself to the ground, cast away his weapons and kissed the earth, asking for forgiveness. Khwārazm Shāh thought that he was drunk but, when he learnt that he was sober, he blamed and reviled him, saying, 'Who would trust this man and any like him!' and he paid no attention to him. He took the money, armaments and mounts in Ṭāliqān and sent all to Ghiyāth al-Dīn with an envoy, whom he charged with a letter expressing his desire for close relations and his benevolence towards him. He left one of his men as his deputy in Ṭāliqān and moved on to the fortresses of Kālyūn and Bīwār. Ḥusām al-Dīn 'Alī ibn Abī 'Alī, lord of Kālyūn, came out against him and fought him on the hill tops. Khwārazm Shāh sent him threats if he did not yield. [**246**] He replied, 'I am a humble servant but these castles I hold on trust and I shall only yield them to their lord.' Khwārazm Shāh approved of this and praised him, though he had blamed Savinj.

When Ghiyāth al-Dīn heard the report about Savinj and his surrender of Ṭāliqān to Khwārazm Shāh, he was outraged and deeply grieved. His followers tried to console him and played down the importance of the matter. Having finished with Ṭāliqān, Khwārazm Shāh proceeded to Herat and camped outside. Ibn Kharmīl did not permit any of the Khwārazmian troops to inflict any harm on the inhabitants, but one group after another would get together and rob travellers, this being the way they normally behave.

Ghiyāth al-Dīn's envoy came to Khwārazm Shāh with gifts and the people were witness to this wonder. The Khwārazmians used to refer to Ghiyāth al-Dīn the elder, father of this present Ghiyāth al-Dīn, as likewise they used to refer to Shihāb al-Dīn his brother, when they were both alive, merely as 'the Ghurid' or 'the ruler of Ghazna'. At this present time, however, Khwārazm Shāh's vizier, despite his powerful position and this Ghiyāth al-Dīn's weakness, only ever referred to him as 'our lord the sultan', although he was weak and feeble and his lands were few.

Ibn Kharmīl left Herat with a detachment of Khwārazm Shāh's army and descended upon Isfizār in Ṣafar [7 September–5 October 1206]. Its ruler had gone to Ghiyāth al-Dīn, so, after he had put it under siege, Ibn Kharmīl sent to those within, swearing by God that, if they surrendered it, he would grant them terms but that, if they resisted, he would remain until he seized them. If he took them forcibly, he would spare neither old nor young. They were frightened and surrendered the place in Rabī' I [6 October–4 November]. He gave them terms and did no harm to the population. Having taken it, he sent to Ḥarb ibn Muḥammad,[2] ruler of Sijistan, to summon him to obey Khwārazm Shāh and make the khutbah for him in his lands. He agreed to do this. Ghiyāth al-Dīn had previously addressed

---

[2] A member of the Nasrid dynasty of Sijistan (or Sistan), initially governors for the Ghaznavids and the Saljuqs, Tāj al-Dīn III Ḥarb b. 'Izz al-Mulūk Muḥammad was ruler by 590/1194. His grandfather Tāj al-Dīn II Abū'l-Faḍl Naṣr ruled 499–559/1106–64 and was an ally and brother-in-law of Sultan Sanjar. See *EI(2)*, ix, 683; Bosworth, *Saffarids of Sistan*, 399–402.

him about making the khutbah and giving him allegiance. He had held out hopes but [finally] did not comply with what was requested.

[**247**] When Khwārazm Shāh was at Herat, Cadi Ṣā'id ibn al-Faḍl returned there. Ibn Kharmīl had expelled him from Herat in the previous year and he had gone to Ghiyāth al-Dīn. He now left him and returned. On his arrival, Ibn Kharmīl said to Khwārazm Shāh, 'This man favours the Ghurids and wants them to rule.' He spoke against him, so Khwārazm Shāh imprisoned him in the citadel of Zūzan and the post of cadi in Herat was filled by Ṣafī al-Dīn Abū Bakr ibn Muḥammad al-Sarakhsī. He had acted as deputy cadi for Ṣā'id and his father.[3]

Account of Ghiyāth al-Dīn's situation regarding Yildiz and Aybak

After Yildiz had returned to Ghazna and taken 'Alā' al-Dīn and his brother Jalāl al-Dīn prisoner, as we have mentioned, Ghiyāth al-Dīn wrote to him with a request that he make the khutbah in his name. Yildiz gave him an evasive answer, although this time his answer was stronger than previously. Ghiyāth al-Dīn sent back a message, 'Either you name us in the khutbah or you inform us of what is in your heart.' When the messenger brought this, Yildiz summoned the preacher of Ghazna and ordered the khutbah to be made in his name after prayers for the soul of Shihāb al-Dīn. Thus at Ghazna the khutbah was made for Tāj al-Dīn Yildiz.

When the people heard that, they were displeased, and their attitudes and those of the Turks with him underwent a change. They no longer saw him fit to be served. They had been obeying him only in their belief that he would support the rule of Ghiyāth al-Dīn. After the khutbah had been made in his name, he sent to Ghiyāth al-Dīn, saying, 'On what basis do you plague me and claim authority over the treasure here? We collected it with our swords. You seized this royal power of yours. Around you have gathered those who are the root of dissension and you have rewarded them with fiefs. You have promised me things that you have not kept to. If you free me, I shall acknowledge you in the khutbah and present myself at your service.'

[**248**] When this messenger arrived, Ghiyāth al-Dīn agreed to manumit Yildiz after he had vigorously refused and expressed his intention of making peace with Khwārazm Shāh on his terms, attacking Ghazna and waging war on Yildiz there. However, having agreed to free him, he was asked to swear to that and he also swore to free Quṭb al-Dīn Aybak, Shihāb al-Dīn's mamluke and his lieutenant in India. To each one he sent 1,000 surcoats, 1,000 caps, gold belts, many swords, two parasols and 100 head of horses. He sent an envoy to each of them. Yildiz accepted the robes of honour but returned the parasol, saying, 'We are slaves and mamlukes. The parasol is for rulers.'

---

3 The text and *Kāmil* (Thornberg), xii, 163, have *ibni-hi* (his son) but *abī-hi* (his father) is an easy and desirable emendation. Only Sa'īd's father al-Faḍl ibn Maḥmūd has been mentioned as cadi of Herat. See above, p. [**199**].

The envoy for Aybak set out to go to him. He was in Peshawar, having brought the kingdom under control, guarded the lands and prevented wrong-doers from causing trouble and damage, so that the people were secure under him. When the envoy had come near, Aybak went some distance to meet him, dismounted, kissed his horse's hoof and donned the robe of honour. He said, 'The parasol is not suitable for mamlukes, but manumission is very acceptable. I shall repay it with everlasting service.'

As for Khwārazm Shāh, he sent to Ghiyāth al-Dīn asking him to make a marriage alliance, to seek to bring Ibn Kharmīl, lord of Herat, to his obedience and to march with him with his armies to Ghazna. If he took it from Yildiz, they would divide the wealth in three, a third for Khwārazm Shāh, a third for Ghiyāth al-Dīn and a third for the army. This was agreed and it only remained to confirm the peace, but news came to Khwārazm Shāh that the ruler of Mazandaran had died. He left Herat to go to Marv. Yildiz heard of this settlement and was greatly upset by it. Its effect on him was manifest. He sent to Ghiyāth al-Dīn: 'What prompted you to do this?' 'I was brought to this by your rebellion and disobedience,' was the reply. Yildiz then went to Tekīn Ābād which he took and then to Bust and its regions and took them. He cancelled the khutbah for Ghiyāth al-Dīn there and sent to the ruler of Sijistan, ordering him to reinstate prayers for the soul of [**249**] Shihāb al-Dīn. He also stopped the khutbah for Khwārazm Shāh and sent similar instructions to Ibn Kharmīl, lord of Herat. He threatened to attack their lands. The people were fearful of him.[4]

Yildiz then brought Jalāl al-Dīn, ruler of Bāmiyān, out of captivity and sent him with 5,000 horse along with Aytakin al-Tatar,[5] Shihāb al-Dīn's mamluke, to Bāmiyān to restore it to his rule and remove his uncle.[6] He was given Yildiz's daughter in marriage and set out with Aytakin, who, when he was alone with him, reprimanded him for donning Yildiz's robe of honour and said, 'You were not content to don Ghiyāth al-Dīn's robe, although he is older than you and of a more noble line, but you put on the robe of this catamite' (meaning Yildiz). He invited him to return with him to Ghazna and informed him that all the Turks were in agreement to oppose Yildiz. This was unacceptable to him, so Aytakin said, 'Then I will not march with you' and returned to Kabul, which was his fief.

When Aytakin arrived at Kabul, he was met by a messenger from Quṭb al-Dīn Aybak to Yildiz with a rebuke to the latter for his actions, ordering him to re-establish Ghiyāth al-Dīn's khutbah and reporting that Quṭb al-Dīn had already made the khutbah for him in his lands. He was also to say that if Yildiz did not also do so in Ghazna and return to obedience, Quṭb al-Dīn would attack and make war on him. When Aytakin learnt this, he was heartened to oppose Yildiz and made up his mind to attack Ghazna. Aybak's envoy also brought Ghiyāth al-Dīn gifts and

---

4 Following the reading *khāfa-hu* in *Kāmil* (Thornberg), xii, 164, rather than the text's *khāfa-humā* ('feared both of them').

5 See note to p. [**234**].

6 Correct text's *ibn 'ammihi*. The reference is to 'Abbās, Jalāl al-Dīn's uncle (*'amm*).

precious objects. He was advising him to agree to Khwārazm Shāh's present demands. When the question of Ghazna was settled, it would be easy to deal with Khwārazm Shāh and others. He also sent him gold coins bearing his name. Aytakin wrote to Aybak to tell him of Yildiz's rebellion against Ghiyāth al-Dīn and what he had done in the lands, and that he himself was determined to break with Yildiz and was awaiting his orders. Aybak replied ordering him to attack Ghazna. If he gained the citadel, he was to stay there until he came. If he did not gain the citadel [**250**] and Yildiz attacked him, he was to withdraw towards him or to Ghiyāth al-Dīn or return to Kabul.

Therefore Aytakin marched towards Ghazna. Jalāl al-Dīn had written to Yildiz to give him the news about Aytakin and what his intentions were. Yildiz wrote to his lieutenants in the citadel of Ghazna ordering them to be on their guard against him. Aytakin arrived there on 1 Rajab this year [1 February 1207]. They were already forewarned about him and did not yield the citadel to him but defended it against him. He then ordered his men to sack the city, which they did in several localities. The cadi tried to moderate the situation by handing over to him 50,000 Ruknī dinars from the Treasury and collecting another sum for him from the merchants. Aytakin made the khutbah for Ghiyāth al-Dīn in Ghazna and put a stop to Yildiz's. The people rejoiced at that. Mu'ayyad al-Mulk was acting as deputy for Yildiz in the citadel.

News came to Yildiz that Aytakin had arrived at Ghazna and that he had received Aybak's messenger. He was deeply discouraged and made the khutbah for Ghiyāth al-Dīn at Tekīn Ābād. He dropped his own name and replaced it with Ghiyāth al-Dīn's, then departed for Ghazna. When he drew near, Aytakin departed for the land of the Ghūr. He stopped at Tamrān and wrote to Ghiyāth al-Dīn with news of his situation. He also sent him the money he took from the Treasury and the citizens. Ghiyāth al-Dīn sent him robes of honour and manumitted him and addressed him with the title 'king of the emirs'. He also returned to him the money he had taken from the Treasury, saying to him, 'The Treasury money I restore to you for your expenditure but the money from the merchants and citizens I send to you to be returned to its owners, so that our rule does not commence with tyranny. I shall give you many times more in recompense.'

He dispatched the people's money to Ghazna to the cadi of Ghazna and ordered him to return the money he sent to its owners. The cadi made Yildiz aware of what was happening and advised him to pronounce the khutbah for Ghiyāth al-Dīn. He added, 'I will attempt to act as a go-between to make a marriage alliance and peace.' He bade him do so but a report of this reached Ghiyāth al-Dīn, who sent to the cadi, forbidding him to come and saying, 'Do not [**251**] petition on behalf of a runaway slave, whose wickedness and contumacy are abundantly clear.' The cadi and Yildiz remained at Ghazna and Ghiyāth al-Dīn sent an army to Aytakin, which stayed with him, while Yildiz sent a force to Rūyīn Kān, a possession of Ghiyāth al-Dīn which he had assigned to one of his emirs. They fell upon its lord, plundered his wealth and seized his children. He escaped, alone, to Ghiyāth al-Dīn.

As the situation demanded, Ghiyāth al-Dīn marched to Bust and that region and regained it. He treated the people well and waived a year's taxes because of the damage they had suffered from Yildiz.

Account of the death of the ruler of Mazandaran and the dispute between his sons

This year Ḥusām al-Dīn Ardashīr, ruler of Mazandaran, died.[7] He left three sons. His eldest son succeeded him and expelled his middle brother, who went to Jurjan, where was Prince 'Alī Shāh, son of Khwārazm Shāh Tekesh and brother of Khwārazm Shāh Muḥammad, who was acting as deputy there for the latter. He complained to 'Alī Shāh about how his brother had banished him and he asked for support to help him take the country so that he could be his loyal adherent. 'Alī Shāh wrote to his brother Khwārazm Shāh about this and the latter ordered him to march with him to Mazandaran, take the country for him and establish the khutbah for Khwārazm Shāh there.

They set out from Jurjan but it fell out that Ḥusām al-Dīn[8] died at this time and the ruler of the land after him became his youngest brother, who took control of the castles and the finances. 'Alī Shāh entered the country, accompanied by the [middle] son of the ruler[9] of Mazandaran, and they pillaged and destroyed it. The youngest brother resisted in the castles, he himself remaining in the fortress of Kūzā,[10] being **[252]** the one in which the money and stores were. They besieged him there after they had set up Usāma[11] as ruler of the lands, such as Sāriya, Āmul and other towns and fortresses. In all of them the khutbah was made for Khwārazm Shāh and they became subject to him. 'Alī Shāh returned to Jurjan and the son of [the late] ruler of Mazandaran remained as ruler of all the country, apart from the fortress in which his younger brother was. He communicated with him, to win him over and conciliate him, but his brother neither made any reply nor gave up his fortress.

---

7 A member (ruled since 576/1171–2) of the Bavandid dynasty, rulers of the southern Caspian littoral. His year of death is often given as 602/1205–6 and his title as Ḥusām al-Dawla (see Borgomale, 'Dynasties du Mâzandarân', 430–32; *EI(2)*, i, 1110, s.v. Bāwand).

8 This only makes sense if Ḥusām al-Dīn was also a title of the oldest son of Ḥusām al-Dīn Ardashīr. The middle son who eventually succeeded with Khwārazmian help was Nāṣir al-Dīn Rustam. Borgomale names the three brothers as Sharaf al-Muluk, Naṣīr al-Dawla (sic) Shams al-Mulūk Shāh Ghāzī Rustam (ruled four years, assassinated 21 Shawwāl 606/1 April 1210), and Rukn al-Dawla Kārin.

9 Following the variant recorded: *walad ṣāḥib*. The text omits *walad*, 'son of'.

10 Correct the text's Kūrā. Kūzā is according to Yāqūt, iv, 320, 'a fortress in Tabaristan.'

11 Who is this unannounced person? One would expect it to be the middle son but he was Nāṣir al-Dīn Rustam. A copyist error?

How Ghiyāth al-Dīn Kaykhusro took the city of Antalya[12]

On 3 Sha'bān [5 March 1207] Ghiyāth al-Dīn Kaykhusro, ruler of Konya and Anatolia, took the city of Antalya on terms. Situated on the coast, it was held by the Greeks.[13] It came about as follows. He had before this present date besieged it, remaining for a long time. He demolished several towers along the city wall and a conquest by force of arms was imminent. The Greeks within sent to the Franks on Cyprus, which is nearby, and asked for their assistance. A number of them arrived and thereupon Ghiyāth al-Dīn despaired of taking it and departed, leaving a detachment of his army nearby in the mountains between Antalya and his own lands. He ordered them to interrupt supplies to the city.

The situation continued like that for a while until the population became hard pressed and their conditions serious. They asked the Franks to sally forth to prevent the Muslims blockading them so tightly. The Franks thought that the Greeks wanted to remove them from the city by these means, so a dispute arose and then they came to blows. The Greeks sent to the Muslims and asked them to come so they could surrender the city to them. They came and agreed together to engage the Franks. The Franks were defeated and retired to the citadel, where they made a last stand. The Muslims sent requesting Ghiyāth al-Dīn, who was in Konya, to come. He set out, making forced marches, with a detachment [**253**] of his army and arrived on 2 Sha'bān [4 March]. An understanding between himself and the Greeks was reached and he took over the city on the following day. He laid siege to the citadel where the Franks were and captured it, killing all the Franks within.

Account of the deposition of the son of Baktimur, lord of Khilāṭ, the rule of Balabān, and the lord of Mardin's expedition to Khilāṭ and his return home

This year the standing troops of Khilāṭ arrested the son of Baktimur[14] and the city was taken over by Balabān, a mamluke of Shāh Arman ibn Sukmān. The people of Khilāṭ wrote to Nāṣir al-Dīn Artuq ibn Īlghāzī ibn Alpī ibn Timurtāsh ibn Īlghāzī ibn Artuq, inviting him to come.

This was because Baktimur's son was a foolish boy who arrested his atabeg and regent, Emir Shujā' al-Dīn Qutlugh, a mamluke of Shāh Arman, a man who dealt

---

[12] Throughout this section, the text reads Antioch (Anṭākiyya) instead of Antalya (Anṭāliyya). *Kāmil* (Thornberg), xii, 167, has Antalya.

[13] In fact, Antalya was held by a Tuscan adventurer in Byzantine employ, called Aldobrandini.

[14] After the death of Sukman II in 581/1185, the Shāh Arman regime was maintained by a series of mamluke commanders, the first being Sayf al-Dīn Baktimur. After a tenure of two others, al-Manṣūr Muḥammad, Baktimur's son took power in 593/ 1197 (*New Islamic Dynasties*, 197).

well with the army and the subjects in general. After he had killed him, the army and the common people spoke out in opposition to him, while he was occupied with pleasure-seeking, gaming and constant drinking. A group of the commons of Khilāṭ and a group of the army[15] wrote to Nāṣir al-Dīn, ruler of Mardin, inviting him to come to them. They wrote to him rather than any other prince because his father Quṭb al-Dīn Īlghāzī was the nephew[16] of Shāh Arman ibn Sukmān and the latter during his lifetime had got the people to swear an oath to him [as successor] since he himself had no son. When, after his death, this new crisis arose, they were mindful of those oaths and said, 'We shall call upon him and make him ruler, for he is of the house of Shāh Arman.' So they wrote to him and asked him to come.

[254] One of Shāh Arman's mamlukes, named Balabān, who had already openly declared his enmity and rebellion against Baktimur's son, marched from Khilāṭ to Malāzgird and took it. Troops flocked to him and his following became numerous. He then marched to Khilāṭ and put it under siege. This coincided with the arrival of the ruler of Mardin, who was imagining that nobody would oppose him and that they would surrender the city to him. He camped near Khilāṭ for several days and Balabān sent to him to say, 'The people of Khilāṭ suspect me of favouring you and they are averse to the Arabs.[17] Your best course is to withdraw one day's distance and wait there. If I take over the city, I will surrender it to you, because it is impossible for me to rule it.' The ruler of Mardin did this and then, when he was at some distance from Khilāt, Balabān sent to say to him, 'You should go home, otherwise I shall move against you and destroy you and those with you.' He only had a few troops, so he returned to Mardin.

Al-Ashraf Mūsā ibn al-'Ādil Abī Bakr ibn Ayyūb, lord of Ḥarrān and the Jazīra regions, had previously written to the ruler of Mardin when he heard that he had his eye on Khilāṭ, saying, 'If you march to Khilāṭ, I shall attack your city.' He feared that he might take Khilāṭ and become too powerful for them. When he did march to Khilāṭ, al-Ashraf gathered his forces and proceeded to the principality of Mardin, whose revenues he seized. He then stopped at Dunaysir and collected its taxes. Having completed this, he returned to Ḥarrān. The ruler of Mardin's position was as in the saying, 'The ostrich went forth seeking horns and returned with no ears.'

Balabān gathered and enlisted troops and besieged Khilāṭ, closely blockading its inhabitants. Baktimur's son was there and he gathered together the soldiers and common people available in the city and made a sally. In the fight that followed Balabān and his followers were routed. He returned to the lands he already held, namely Malāzgird, Arjīsh and other fortresses, collected troops in very large numbers and repeated his siege of Khilāṭ and his blockade of the population. He

[15] Adopting the variant in the note: *al-jund*, which is also the reading of *Kāmil* (Thornberg), xii, 168.

[16] Literally 'son of the sister'.

[17] It is not clear why the attitude to the Arabs is in question. Nāṣir al-Dīn Artuq was of Turkoman origin.

forced them to abandon [**255**] Baktimur's son because of his youth, his ignorance of how to rule and his preoccupation with pleasure-seeking and pastimes. They arrested him in the citadel, made contact with Balabān, secured his oath to observe their wishes and then handed over to him the city and Baktimur's son. He took control of all the dependencies of Khilāṭ and imprisoned Baktimur's son in a castle there. His rule became firmly established. Glory be to Him who, when He wills a matter, prepares its means. Only yesterday Shams al-Dīn Muḥammad Pahlawān and Saladin were seeking to take it but neither was able to do so. Now this weak mamluke appears, short of men, lands and money, and captures it as easy as pie.

Subsequently Najm al-Dīn Ayyūb ibn al-'Ādil, lord of Mayyāfāriqīn, marched towards the region of Khilāt, having taken control of several castles among its dependencies, including the fortress of Mūsh[18] and its adjoining settlement. When he drew near Khilāṭ, Balabān made a show of being too weak to face him. Spurred on by this, Najm al-Dīn committed himself to a complete advance, whereupon Balabān cut his communications, brought him to battle and defeated him. Only a few of his men escaped and those were wounded. He himself returned to Mayyāfāriqīn.

Account of the Georgian capture of Kars and the death of the Georgian queen[19]

This year the Georgians captured the fortress of Kars, one of the dependencies of Khilāṭ. They had besieged it for a long time and pressed hard on those within. They collected the revenue of this region for several years. None of those who ruled Khilāṭ were giving the defenders any assistance or making any effort to get relief to them. Its governor sent a stream of messengers asking for assistance and for the Georgians besieging them to be driven away. His pleas were not answered. When this situation had lasted a long time and he saw no help coming, he made terms with the Georgians for the surrender of the fortress in return for a large sum of money and a fief he would receive from them. Thus it became a home of [**256**] polytheism after it had been a home of unitarian belief. 'Verily we are God's and verily to Him do we return.' We beseech God to provide for Islam and its adherents some aid from Himself, for the princes of our age have occupied themselves with their pleasures, their pastimes and their tyrannies to the dereliction of the guarding of frontiers and maintenance of the lands.

In the end God Almighty saw how few were those who aided Islam and He

[18] Following the Ms. variant rather than the edition's Ḥisn Mūsā. Mūsh, about 50 miles west of Lake Van, 'has a ruined fortress and buildings of the Saljuq period' (Krawulsky, 447–8). See also Yāqūt, iv, 682.

[19] Presumably *malik* (king) is an error. The reading of *Kāmil* (Thornberg), xii, 169, is *malika*, which is also found below in this present section.

showed himself its friend. He brought about the death of the queen[20] of the Georgians and then they fell into internal disputes. God dealt with their evil until the end of the year.

Account of the hostilities between the caliph's army and the ruler of Luristan

In Ramaḍān this year [April 1207] the caliph's army, led by his mamluke Sanjar, marched from Khuzistan to the mountains of Luristan. He was the governor of those regions, which he had taken over after the death of Ṭāshtakīn, emir of the Pilgrimage, because he was Ṭāshtakīn's son-in-law. The ruler of the mountains, which are difficult of access, lying between Fars, Isfahan and Khuzistan, was known as Abū Ṭāhir. The army engaged the inhabitants but withdrew defeated.

This came about as follows. A mamluke of the Caliph al-Nāṣir li-Dīn Allāh, called Qashtimur, one of his greatest mamlukes, had left his service owing to a lack of consideration he experienced from Vizier Naṣīr al-Dīn al-'Alawī al-Rāzī. He passed through Khuzistan, taking what he could, and joined Abū Ṭāhir, ruler of Luristan, who received him with honour and respect and gave him his daughter in marriage. Later Abū Ṭāhir died and Qashtimur's position grew powerful and he was obeyed by the people of that region.

Sanjar was commanded to gather troops and to attack and fight him. He did as he was ordered, gathered a force and set out. Qashtimur then sent his excuses, asking not to be attacked and in return he would not cast off his obedience. His excuses were not accepted. He therefore assembled the inhabitants of this region and descended to face [**257**] the [caliphal] army, which he engaged and routed. He made contact with the ruler of Fars, Ibn Dakalā,[21] and Shams al-Dīn Aydughmish, ruler of Isfahan, Hamadhan and Rayy, to inform them of the situation and to say, 'I am not strong enough to deal with the caliph's army. Perhaps other armies from Baghdad will be added to these and they will wage war on me again. Then I will not be equal to them.' He asked for assistance and warned them of the caliph's army if they took those regions. They agreed to his request, so his heart was strengthened and he continued to maintain his position.

Miscellaneous events

This year in Baghdad a young man killed another young man. They had been close friends and both were about twenty years old. One said to the other, 'Now I am

[20] This was Queen Tamar or Tamara, who ruled from 1184 to her death in 1213.

[21] This member of the Salghurid dynasty, Turkoman atabegs of Fars, was in fact 'Izz al-Dīn Sa'd ibn Zankī (ruled 594–623(?)/1198-1226). Dakalā (or Degele) was his brother. His father was Muẓaffar al-Dīn Zankī. See *EI(2)*, viii, 978–9.

going to strike you with this dagger,' making a joke of it. He lunged towards him with the dagger but it pierced his belly and he died. The culprit fled but was caught and ordered to be killed. When they were about to put him to death, he asked for a pen-box and some paper and wrote the following:

> I approach the Generous One without a supply of good works but with a pure heart.
> It is a bad idea to prepare provisions when your journey is to a Generous One.

This year Burhān al-Dīn Ṣadr Jihān[22] Muḥammad ibn Aḥmad ibn 'Abd al-'Azīz ibn Māra al-Bukhārī went on pilgrimage. He was the head of the Ḥanafīs in Bukhara, effectively its ruler, who delivered the tribute to the Qarakhitay and acted as their deputy in the city. When he went on pilgrimage, his behaviour on the way was not found praiseworthy [**258**] and he did no good works. On his arrival from Bukhara he had been honoured in Baghdad but when he returned, he was disregarded because of his bad treatment of the pilgrims, who dubbed him Ṣadr Jahannam.[23]

In Shawwāl [May 1207] our teacher Abū'l-Ḥaram Makkī ibn Rayyān ibn Shabba, the grammarian and Koran reader at Mosul, died. He was learned in grammar, lexicography and the Koran readings. In his age there was no one to match him. He was blind from birth but apart from the sciences mentioned he knew canon law, mathematics and others very well. He was one of the virtuous and pious servants of God, very humble, under whom people studied from morning to night.

The Emir of the Pilgrimage Muẓaffar al-Dīn Sunqur, the caliph's mamluke known as Lion-Face, abandoned the pilgrim caravan at a place called al-Marjūm and proceeded to Syria with a group of his followers. The caravan continued as they had troops with them and they arrived safely. He came to al-'Ādil Abū Bakr ibn Ayyūb, who assigned him a large fief in Egypt, and remained with him until he returned to Baghdad in Jumādā I of the year 608 [12 October–10 November 1211]. After the vizier's arrest he felt his life was safe and sent asking to return. This was allowed and when he arrived, the caliph honoured him and assigned him Kufa.

In Jumāda II [January 1207] Abū'l-Faḍl 'Abd al-Mun'im ibn 'Abd al-'Azīz al-Iskandarānī, known as Ibn al-Naṭrūnī, died in the Hospital of Baghdad. He had gone on a mission to 'the Majorcan'[24] in Ifrīqiya and acquired from him 10,000 Maghribī dinars, which he distributed in his home town among his acquaintances and friends. He was learned and virtuous, an excellent man (God have mercy on

---

22 'The leader of the World'.

23 'The leader of Hell'.

24 i.e. al-Māyūrqī. This refers to 'Alī ibn Isḥāq of the Banū Ghāniya, the branch of the Almoravids who continued to resist the Almohads from their base in the Balearics.

him). He was the author of some good poetry and upheld the discipline of belles-lettres. He resided in Mosul for a while and studied with Shaykh Abū'l-Ḥaram.[25] I met him often at his house.

[25] See the notice of his death just above.

The Year 604 [1207–1208]

Account of Khwārazm Shāh's conquest of Transoxania and the discords that occurred in Khurasan and their settlement

During this year 'Alā' al-Dīn Muḥammad, the son of Khwārazm Shāh [Tekesh], crossed the Oxus to fight the Qarakhitay. The reason for this was that the Qarakhitay had ruled for a long time in Turkestan and Transoxania, and the inhabitants had suffered under their burdensome oppression. They had a deputy in every town to collect taxes for them, while they lived in tents as was their custom before they came to rule. They dwelt in the regions of Uzkand, Balāsāghūn, Kashgar and those parts. It happened that the sultan of Samarqand and Bukhara, who was entitled Khān Khānān (which means sultan of sultans), a member of the Qarakhānid house, a noble lineage as regards Islam and kingship, became recalcitrant and tired of infidels wielding authority over Muslims.[1] He sent to Khwārazm Shāh to say, 'God (great and glorious is He), because of the extensive kingdom and numerous troops He has given you, has made it your duty to deliver the Muslims and their lands from infidel hands and to rescue them from the tyranny over their possessions and persons that they endure. We will cooperate with you to fight the Qarakhitay and will bring to you what we now bring to them. We shall mention your name in the khutbah and on our coinage.' He agreed with this but said, 'I fear that you will not keep faith with me.' The ruler of Samarqand sent him the leading citizens of Bukhara and Samarqand, after they had taken their ruler's oath to be true to his proposals, and on his behalf they guaranteed that he spoke the truth and would remain firm on what [**260**] he offered. They were kept with Khwārazm Shāh as hostages.

Khwārazm Shāh embarked on the settlement of Khurasan and the setting-up of its basic pattern of government. He put his brother 'Alī Shāh in control of Tabaristan in addition to Jurjan and ordered him to hold it with care. Emir Kuzlik Khan, one of his mother's relations and a leading magnate of the state, he put in charge of Nishapur and stationed an army with him. The city of Jām[2] he entrusted to Emir Jaldik and put Emir Amīn al-Dīn Abū Bakr in charge of the city of Zūzan. This Amīn al-Dīn had been a porter, who became a very great emir, one who conquered Kurramān, as we shall relate, God willing. He appointed Emir al-Ḥusayn [ibn Kharmīl] to Herat and stationed with him there 1,000

[1] For an account of the growth of opposition to the Qarakhitay and the alliance of Khwārazm Shāh and Sultan 'Uthmān of Samarqand, see Juvainī, *History*, i, 358–9.

[2] The text has al-Khām. Jām (modern Turbat-i Jam) is south-east of Mashhad. See Krawulsky, 86.

Khwārazmian cavalry. With Ghiyāth al-Dīn Maḥmūd he made peace on the basis that he hold on to the Ghūr lands and Garmsīr that he had. He appointed deputies in Marv, Sarakhs and other parts of Khurasan and commanded them to rule well and be watchful and careful. He gathered all his troops, proceeded to Khwārazm and, setting out from there, crossed the Oxus and joined with the sultan of Samarqand. The Qarakhitay heard of this, so they mustered their troops and moved against him. Many battles and skirmishes ensued between them, some of them Khwārazm Shāh won and some he lost.

Account of the killing of Ibn Kharmīl and the siege of Herat

Ibn Kharmīl, lord of Herat, saw how the troops of Khwārazm Shāh treated the population badly and laid violent hands on their property, so he seized and imprisoned them. He sent a messenger to Khwārazm Shāh to explain himself and tell him what they had done. Khwārazm Shāh was very displeased but was unable to bring him to account because he was busy [**261**] fighting the Qarakhitay. He wrote to approve of his actions and to order him to send the troops he had arrested because he needed them. He said, 'I have commanded 'Izz al-Dīn Jaldik ibn Ṭughril, lord of Jām, to be with you because I know him to be wise and a good administrator.' He therefore sent to Jaldik, ordering him to proceed to Herat and secretly instructing him to find a means of arresting al-Ḥusayn ibn Kharmīl, even the first moment he met him.

Jaldik set out with 2,000 horse. His father Ṭughril had been governor of Herat in the days of Sanjar, so he longed for it, preferring it to all of Khurasan. On his approach to Herat, Ibn Kharmīl ordered men to go out to meet him. He had a vizier called Khwāja al-Ṣāḥib, an old man, made wise by his experiences of the world. To Ibn Kharmīl he said, 'Do not go out to meet him. Let him come to you by himself, for I fear that he will prove a traitor to you and that Khwārazm Shāh will have so instructed him.' His reply was, 'Such a great emir as this may not be allowed to arrive without my meeting him. I fear that Khwārazm Shāh would hold that as a grudge against me. I do not think that Jaldik will dare to attack me.'

So al-Ḥusayn ibn Kharmīl rode out to him. When they both caught sight of one another, they dismounted to meet. Jaldik had given orders to his men to arrest him, so they mingled with them both and got between Ibn Kharmīl and his followers. They then seized him and his own men fled back into the city, where they told the vizier what had happened. He ordered the gate to be closed and the walls to be manned, preparing for a siege. Jaldik camped around the city and sent threats to the vizier that, if he did not surrender, [**262**] he would kill Ibn Kharmīl. At that the vizier proclaimed the watchword of Ghiyāth al-Dīn Maḥmūd al-Ghūrī and said to Jaldik, 'I shall surrender the city neither to you nor to the traitor Ibn Kharmīl. It belongs only to Ghiyāth al-Dīn and to his father before him.' They brought Ibn Kharmīl forward to the wall, where he addressed the vizier, ordering him to surrender. He refused, so Ibn Kharmīl was put to death. This is the reward of treachery. His previously told history with Shihāb al-Dīn al-Ghūrī demonstrates his treachery and his ingratitude for the benevolence of those who were kind to him.[3]

After Ibn Kharmīl was killed, Jaldik wrote to Khwārazm Shāh with a full account of the matter. Khwārazm Shāh sent to Kuzlik Khān, governor of Nishapur, and Amīn al-Dīn Abū Bakr,[4] lord of Zūzan, to order them to go to Herat, besiege and take it. They set out with 10,000 horse, put Herat under siege and communicated with the vizier about a surrender. He paid them no attention and said, 'You do not have sufficient status for the likes of Herat to be surrendered to you, but, if Khwārazm Shāh comes, I will surrender it to him.' They then attacked him and strove manfully in their fight with him but were unable to overcome him.

Ibn Kharmīl had fortified Herat, constructed four strongly built towers, deepened its ditch and stocked it with provisions. Having completed all he wished, he had said, 'I still fear one thing for this city, that is that its water courses might be dammed for many days, released all at once and break down the walls.' After these men had begun the siege, they heard of what Ibn Kharmīl had said, so they dammed the waters until large amounts had collected, then they released them against Herat. They encompassed the city but did not reach the wall because the level of the city was raised up. The ditch was filled with water and all around became mud. The army retired and were not able to fight because of their distance from the city. This had been Ibn Kharmīl's plan, that the ditch should be filled with water and the mud prevent any approach to the city. The besiegers waited some time until the water had dried up. What Ibn Kharmīl said was [**263**] an excellent stratagem.

Let us return to Khwārazm Shāh's war with the Qarakhitay and his capture. The fighting between Khwārazm Shāh and the Qarakhitay continued a long time. One day they had a battle, which was very fierce and lengthy. The Muslims suffered a dreadful defeat and many of them were taken prisoner. Khwārazm Shāh himself was among the prisoners and a great emir was taken with him, called (first name unknown[5]) Ibn Shihāb al-Dīn Mas'ūd. The same man captured both of them.

The Muslim armies arrived at Khwārazm and the sultan was not to be seen among them. Kuzlik Khān, ruler of Nishapur, had a message from his sister, while he was besieging Herat, to tell him of the situation. When he received the news, he left Herat by night for Nishapur. Emir Amīn al-Dīn Abū Bakr, lord of Zūzan, became aware of this and he and the emirs with him wanted to stop him, fearing that there might be hostilities between them and that this would encourage the people of Herat to make a sortie and gain some desired success. In the end they refrained from opposing him.

Khwārazm Shāh had demolished the wall of Nishapur when he took it from the

[3] The reference is not obvious. Perhaps see p. [**187**] above.

[4] For this emir, see below s.a.611, p. [**303**].

[5] In Arabic *fūlān*, that is 'so-and-so'.

Ghurids. Now Kuzlik Khān began to repair it, brought in provisions and increased the number of his troops. His purpose was to take control of Khurasan, if the demise of the sultan was confirmed. News that the sultan was missing came to his brother 'Alī Shāh in Tabaristan. He proclaimed himself ruler, dropped his brother's name from the khutbah and prepared to make a bid for the sultanate. Khurasan fell into great confusion.

Meanwhile, after Khwārazm Shāh had been captured, Ibn Shihāb al-Dīn Mas'ūd said to him, 'You must give up being sultan at this time and become a servant in the hope that I can find some way of rescuing you.' He started to act as servant to Ibn Mas'ūd, offer him food, take off his clothes and boots and pay him respect. [**264**] The man who had captured them both said to Ibn Mas'ūd, 'I see this man respects you. Who are you?' He replied, 'I am so-and-so and this is my page.' At that the man rose and honoured him. He said, 'If my people did not know that you are here with me, I would release you.' He left him alone for a few days and then Ibn Mas'ūd said to him, 'I fear that my defeated colleagues will return home and my family will not see me among them. They will think that I have been killed and will hold a gathering of condolence and a funeral. They will grieve and then divide my property. I shall be lost. I want you to name a sum of money I can pay you.' He named a ransom price. Then he said, 'I would like you to instruct an intelligent man to take a letter to my family to tell them that I am well. He can bring the ransom back with him.' He continued, 'However, your men do not know my family. This servant of mine is a man I trust and my family will believe him.' The Khitan gave him permission for this mission. He was sent on his way and the Khitan provided a horse and a number of horsemen to protect him. They finally arrived near Khwārazm. The horsemen returned, leaving Khwārazm Shāh to enter Khwārazm. The people rejoiced, beat the celebratory drums and decked out the city. He then heard the news of what Kuzlik had done in Nishapur and what his brother 'Alī Shāh had done in Tabaristan.

What Khwārazm Shāh did in Khurasan

When Khwārazm Shāh reached Khwārazm, he received news of what Kuzlik Khān and his own brother 'Alī Shāh and others had done. He therefore set out for Khurasan, followed by his troops. They became scattered and so he himself arrived six days later with only six mounted men. Kuzlik Khan heard of his arrival, [**265**] took his property and his troops and fled to Iraq. It also came to the knowledge of his brother 'Alī Shāh, who feared him and set off on the road to Quhistan to seek refuge with Ghiyāth al-Dīn Maḥmūd al-Ghūrī, lord of Fīrūzkūh. The latter welcomed him with honour and gave him a place with him.

Meanwhile Khwārazm Shāh entered Nishapur, organised its affairs, appointed a lieutenant there and then left for Herat, where he joined his army that was already besieging it. He showed his gratitude to the emirs of that force and trusted them because they had persisted in obeying his orders during recent circumstances and had not wavered. They had not been able to achieve any success at Herat due to the excellent precautions of the vizier there. Khwārazm Shāh sent to the vizier to say, 'You promised my troops that you would surrender the city when I arrived. I have now arrived, so give it up.' The vizier replied, 'I shall not because I know that you are all treacherous. You will not spare anyone. I shall surrender the city only to Ghiyāth al-Dīn Maḥmūd.'

At this Khwārazm Shāh was furious and made an assault with his troops but no approach brought success. Then a group of citizens of Herat gathered together and said, 'The people have perished from hunger and shortages. Our livelihoods have been ruined. A year and a month have now gone by. The vizier promised us to surrender the city to Khwārazm Shāh if he came. Khwārazm Shāh is here but he has not surrendered. We must devise a way of yielding the city and escaping from this hardship we are suffering.' This was reported to the vizier, who sent a detachment of his soldiers to them and ordered their arrest. The troops set out but a riot flared up in the city and became very serious. The vizier needed to handle it in person and he proceeded to do so. Information of this had been sent from the city by letter to Khwārazm Shāh. He carried out an assault while the people were in confusion. His men demolished two wall towers, effected an entry and took the city. They seized the vizier and Khwārazm Shāh put him to death. He took the city in the year 605 [1208–9], reorganized it and entrusted it to his maternal uncle Amīr Malik, who was one of [**266**] his leading emirs. It remained in his hands until the downfall of Khwārazm Shāh.

As for Ibn Shihāb al-Dīn Mas'ūd, he remained with the Qarakhitay for a little while and one day the man who had taken him prisoner said to him, 'Khwārazm Shāh is missing. What news do you have of him?' 'Do you not know him?' he replied. 'No,' said the man. 'He is the prisoner you had.' 'Why did you not tell me, so that I could have served him and taken him to his kingdom?' he asked. 'I feared what you might do to him,' was the reply. The Khitan said, 'Take us to him,' so they went and Khwārazm Shāh was generous and liberal towards them to the utmost degree.

Account of the killing of Ghiyāth al-Dīn Maḥmūd

When Khwārazm Shāh had entrusted Herat to his maternal uncle Amīr Malik and left for Khwārazm, he ordered him to attack Ghiyāth al-Dīn Maḥmūd ibn Ghiyāth al-Dīn Muḥammad ibn Sām al-Ghūrī, lord of the Ghūr and Fīrūzkūh, to arrest him and his own brother 'Alī Shāh and to take Fīrūzkūh from Ghiyāth al-Dīn. He therefore marched towards Fīrūzkūh. Maḥmūd heard of this, so sent an offer of allegiance and a request for guarantees of security. When this was granted, Maḥmūd yielded to Amīr Malik but was arrested, as also was 'Alī Shāh, Khwārazm Shāh's brother. They both asked him to convey them to Khwārazm

Shāh for him to decide what to do with them. He sent to Khwārazm Shāh to tell him the news and his order was that they should be killed. They were put to death on [**267**] the same day and all of Khurasan became firmly under the control of Khwārazm Shāh. This was also in the year 605 [1208–9].

This Ghiyāth al-Dīn was the last of the Ghurid princes,[6] whose rule was one of the best administered, the most just and the most dedicated to the Jihad. He was just, mild and generous, one of the best princes for the manner of his rule and the noblest in character (God Almighty have mercy upon him).

Account of Khwārazm Shāh's return to the Qarakhitay

After Khurasan had come firmly under the control of Khwārazm Shāh and he crossed the Oxus, the Qarakhitay gathered a great host and marched against him, led by an elder of their state, who took the role of ruler among them, known as Ṭāyankū. He was at the time more than one hundred years old. He had experienced many wars and had been victorious, a good and wise general. Khwārazm Shāh and the ruler of Samarqand joined forces and they and the Qarakhitay faced one another in battle lines during the year 606 [1209–10]. Battles took place the like of which there had never been for severity and endurance. The Qarakhitay suffered a terrible defeat and unknown numbers of them were killed or taken prisoner. Among the captives was their commander Ṭāyankū. He was brought before Khwārazm Shāh, who honoured him, gave him a seat on his throne and then sent him to Khwārazm. Khwārazm Shāh moved against Transoxania and conquered it, city by city and region by region, until he came to the city of Uzkand. He placed his deputies there and returned to Khwārazm, accompanied by the ruler of Samarqand. The latter was one of the most handsome of men and the people of Khwārazm used to gather to look at him. He was married [**268**] by Khwārazm Shāh to his daughter[7] and sent back to Samarqand. A prefect was sent to be with him in Samarqand according to what had been the practice of the Qarakhitay.[8]

How the ruler of Samarqand behaved treacherously towards the Khwārazmians

When the ruler of Samarqand returned there, along with a prefect of Khwārazm

6 Ghiyāth al-Dīn Maḥmūd, who, in fact, died in Ṣafar 607/July 1210, was not the last of the Ghurids. The dynasty maintained a tenuous existence at Fīrūzkūh until 612/1215–16 (Jackson, 'Fall of the Ghurid dynasty', 226-9).

7 Her name was Khan-Sultan (Juvainī, *History*, ii, 395).

8 The battle in which Tayangu (sic), the Qarakhitan commander of Talas, was defeated, is described and dated to August–September 1210 in Biran, *Empire of the Qara Khitai*, 77–8, on the authority of Juvainī, *History*, i, 344.

Shāh's, he remained with him about a year and witnessed such bad government by the Khwārazmians and despicable behaviour as made him repent of breaking with the Qarakhitay. He sent to the ruler of the Qarakhitay summoning him to Samarqand to surrender it to him and return to his allegiance. He ordered the killing of all the Khwārazmians in Samarqand, both old and new residents, and seized Khwārazm Shāh's men and would cut individuals into two pieces and hang them up in the markets just as a butcher hangs his meat. He behaved with this extreme wickedness. He went to the citadel to kill his wife, Khwārazm Shāh's daughter, but she shut the gates and stood with her women to resist him. Her message to him was 'I am a woman. To kill such as me is wicked. I have done nothing to you that merits your acting so. Perhaps if you leave me alone, that will be better for you in the end. Fear God in what you do to me!' He therefore let her be but put guards on her to stop her having any personal freedom of action.

News of this reached Khwārazm Shāh and all Hell broke loose. He was furiously angry and ordered all strangers in Khwārazm to be killed but his mother stopped that, saying, 'People have come here from all regions of the earth. None of them has approved of what this man has done.' He then ordered the people from Samarqand to be killed but his mother forbade him that too, so he refrained. He gave orders for his troops to prepare for an expedition to Transoxania and sent them off in batches. As soon as a detachment was ready, it crossed the Oxus. A huge number beyond counting crossed over. He himself crossed among the last and descended on Samarqand. He despatched a messenger to its ruler to say, 'You have done what no Muslim has ever done. You have sanctioned [**269**] the shedding of Muslim blood that no man of sense, either Muslim or infidel, would permit. God has forgiven what is over and done. Leave your lands and depart wherever you wish.' He replied, 'I shall not leave and I shall do what I like.'

Khwārazm Shāh ordered an assault by his troops. A man in his service advised him to order some of the emirs, if they captured the city, to make for the quarter where the merchants live and to prevent plunder and their ill-treatment, for they were foreigners and all disapproved of what he had done. He gave this order to some emirs and then made the assault. Ladders were set up against the wall and in no time at all they had taken the city. He allowed his troops to pillage and to kill any inhabitants of Samarqand they found. For three days the city was sacked and the people massacred. It is said that they killed 200,000 of them. The quarter where the foreigners were was kept safe. Not a single one, not one man among them was lost.

Then he ordered the pillage and killing to be stopped and next made an assault on the citadel. Its ruler saw what filled his heart with awe and dread, so he sent asking for terms but Khwārazm Shāh said, 'For you there are no terms from me.' They attacked and took the citadel, taking its ruler prisoner. Brought before Khwārazm Shāh, he kissed the earth and begged for forgiveness but no pardon was given. He ordered his death and he was summarily executed. Several of his relatives were also killed and he spared no one related to the Qarakhanids. In

Samarqand and the rest of the country he appointed his lieutenants and nobody but he was left with any authority in the land.[9]

Account of the battle which destroyed the Qarakhitay

After Khwārazm Shāh had treated the Khitay as we have described, those of them that survived went to their ruler, for he had not been present at the battle, and they gathered around him. A large group of Tatars[10] had erupted **[270]** from their homeland, the borders of China, in the past, and settled beyond Turkestan. There were enmity and hostilities between them and the Qarakhitay, so when they heard what Khwārazm Shāh had done to the Khitay, they attacked them, led by their ruler Kuchlug Khan.[11] The ruler of the Khitay, having become aware of this, sent to Khwārazm Shāh to say to him, 'What you have done, taking our lands and killing our men, is pardoned, for in this enemy who has now come, we have someone too strong for us. If they are victorious over us and become our rulers, there will be no protection from them for you. Your best course is to come to us with your armies and help us to fight them. We swear to you that, if we overcome them, we will not dispute the lands you have taken, but will be content with what we have.' Then Kuchlug Khan, the Tatar ruler, sent him a message. 'These Qarakhitay are your enemies, your ancestors' enemies and they are our enemies. Aid us against them. We swear that, if we defeat them, we will not approach your lands. We will be content with the places we now inhabit.' Khwārazm Shāh replied to each of them, saying 'I am with you and shall support you against your rival.'

He marched with his troops until he camped near the place where they had drawn up their lines but without mingling with them in a manner that would allow it to be known that he was with either one of them. Each side thought that he was with them. The Qarakhitay and the Tatars clashed and the Qarakhitay were disastrously defeated. Then did Khwārazm Shāh take sides and began killing, making prisoners and plundering. He allowed not one of them to escape. Only a small group of them survived with their ruler in a place in the districts of the Turks, surrounded by a mountain with access from only one direction. They fortified themselves there. A detachment of them joined Khwārazm Shāh and

---

9 Cf. Juvainī, *History*, ii, 394–5: Khan-Sultan, 'Uthmān's wife, whom he had humiliated, insisted on his death, which is dated to 609/1212–13.

10 In this section Ibn al-Athīr uses the term 'Tatars' to denote various Turko-Mongolian tribes (e.g. the Tatars, Keraits, Naimans and Merkits) which, defeated in their rivalry with Chingiz Khan, fled westwards and were subsequently either eliminated or incorporated in Chingiz Khan's Mongol confederation.

11 In the text called Kushlī Khān. He was the leader of the Naimans, who were defeated in 1208 by their rival Chingiz Khan. For his career and relations with Khwārazm Shāh Muḥammad, see Biran, *Empire of the Qara Khitai*, 78–84 (there called Güchülüg). For another account, see Juvainī, *History*, 61–8.

formed part of his army. Khwārazm Shāh sent to Kuchlug Khan, the Tatar ruler, [**271**] congratulating him that he had come to his help, claiming that, were it not for him, Kuchlug would not have dealt with the Qarakhitay. For a while Kuchlug Khan acknowledged that but then Khwārazm Shāh sent to him, demanding division of the Qarakhitay's lands and saying, 'As we agreed to destroy them, so it is fitting that we divide their territory.' His reply was 'You have nothing from me but the sword. You are not a stronger threat than the Khitans nor a more powerful kingdom. If you are not content to keep silent, I will march against you and treat you worse than I treated them.' He made his preparations and marched to a camp near them.

Khwārazm Shāh realized that he did not have the strength to deal with him, so he tried to outdo him in cunning. Whenever he went anywhere, Khwārazm Shāh would attack his people and their baggage to plunder it. If he heard that a detachment had travelled from their home base, he would follow and fall upon them. Kuchlug Khan sent to him to say, 'This is not how princes behave. This is to act like thieves. However, if you are a sultan, as you say, we ought to meet. Either you defeat me and take the lands I hold, or I do that to you.'

Khwārazm Shāh would give him deceptive replies but not agree to what he asked. However, he ordered the populations of Shāsh, Ferghana, Isfījāb, Kāsān and other cities around about, than which there were none more attractive or better developed, to abandon them and to move into Islamic territory. He then demolished them all out of fear that the Tatars might conquer them.

Subsequently there occurred the irruption of those other Tatars who destroyed the whole world, whose ruler was Chingiz Khan, [called] Temujin,[12] and their attack on Kuchlug Khan, the ruler of these first Tatars. Kuchlug Khan was distracted by them from Khwārazm Shāh, for whom the field was left, so he crossed the river back into Khurasan.

[272] Account of Najm al-Dīn ibn al-'Ādil's taking power in Khilāṭ

This year al-Awḥad Najm al-Dīn Ayyūb ibn al-'Ādil Abī Bakr ibn Ayyūb took power in the city of Khilāṭ. This came about as follows. He was in Mayyāfāriqīn, on behalf of his father, and when Balabān took power in Khilāṭ, as we have related,[13] he attacked the town of Mūsh,[14] put it under siege and took it along with the surrounding places. Balabān's position had not become established enough to allow him to prevent this. After his success, Najm al-Dīn was eager for Khilāṭ and he marched there, but was defeated by Balabān, as we have also mentioned.[15] He returned to his lands and gathered and enlisted men. His father also sent him some

12 The text has al-N.h.r.jī. Cf. the comparable passage later in *Kāmil*, p. [**361**].

13 See above, pp. [**253–5**].

14 South of River Arsanas in the plain west of Lake Van (Le Strange, *Caliphate*, 116).

15 See above, p. [**255**].

troops, so he marched to Khilāṭ. Balabān moved against him and they both drew up their forces and fought. Balabān was defeated and Najm al-Dīn seized the lands and drew added strength from them.

Balabān entered Khilāṭ, fortified himself within and sent a messenger to Mughīth al-Dīn Ṭughril Shāh ibn Qilij Arslān, the lord of Erzurum,[16] seeking his aid against Najm al-Dīn. He came in person with his troops. They united, defeated Najm al-Dīn and besieged Mūsh. The fortress was on the point of being taken when Ibn Qilij Arslān betrayed the ruler of Khilāṭ and killed him out of a desire for his lands. Having killed him, he proceeded to Khilāṭ but the inhabitants resisted him, so he went to Malāzgird, where the people also rejected him and held out against him. When he found no chance of success in any part of the land, he returned to his own.

The inhabitants of Khilāṭ sent to Najm al-Dīn to invite him to rule over them. He came and took power in Khilāt and its dependencies, except for a few. The neighbouring princes disliked his coming to power there, because they feared his father. The Georgians similarly feared and disapproved of him. They carried out a series of raids on its dependencies [**273**] and its territory, while Najm al-Dīn remained in Khilāṭ, unable to leave it, which exposed the Muslims to severe hardship.

A group of the army of Khilāṭ withdrew and seized control of the fortress of Van, one of the largest and most impregnable of fortresses. They declared their rebellion against Najm al-Dīn and were joined by a large number. They took the town of Arjīsh. Najm al-Dīn sent to his father al-ʻĀdil to inform him of the situation and ask him to supply him with an army. He sent him his brother al-Ashraf Mūsā ibn al-ʻĀdil with an army. The two of them got together with a large force and besieged the fortress of Van,[17] where the rebels from Khilāt were, and engaged them energetically. These men were too weak to resist them, so they surrendered it on terms and left. Najm al-Dīn took it over and his rule in Khilāṭ and its dependencies became firmly established. His brother al-Ashraf returned to his lands, Ḥarrān and Edessa.[18]

Account of Frankish raids in Syria

During this year the Franks gathered in large numbers at Tripoli and Ḥiṣn

---

[16] One of the many sons of Qilij Arslān, the Anatolian Saljuq sultan. On his father's death he was assigned Albistan (see *Chronicle of Ibn al-Athīr (2)*, p. [**88**], s.a. 588/1192). Soon after 1201 he exchanged Albistan for Erzurum with his brother Rukn al-Dīn (Cahen, *Pre-Ottoman Turkey*, 111 and 115).

[17] Situated between Khilāṭ and the region of Tabriz, part of the district of Qālīqālā (Yāqūt, iv, 895).

[18] For the taking of Khilāṭ and Ayyubid 'eastern' involvements in the following years, see Minorsky, *Studies*, 148–56.

al-Akrād, and carried out many raids on Homs and its territories. They descended on the town of Homs and their numbers were so great that its ruler, Asad al-Dīn Shīrkūh ibn Muḥammad ibn Shīrkūh, was not powerful enough for them and could not resist and repel them. He sought reinforcements from al-Ẓāhir Ghāzī, lord of Aleppo, and other Syrian princes, but only al-Ẓāhir supplied them, for he sent him some troops that stayed with him and defended his territory from the Franks.

Later al-'Ādil left Egypt with numerous forces and attacked the city of Acre. The Frankish ruler made a truce with him on the basis that Muslim prisoners should be released and other terms. He proceeded to Homs and made camp at Lake Qadas. He was joined by the troops of the East and the Jazīra, and invaded the lands of Tripoli. He blockaded a place [**274**] called al-Qulay'āt, which he then took on terms, allowing its ruler to go free but taking as booty the mounts and weaponry it contained. He then razed it and advanced to Tripoli, where he pillaged, burned, took captives and booty, before returning. The length of his stay in Frankish lands was twelve days. He returned to Lake Qadas.

There was an exchange of envoys between him and the Franks to discuss peace but no terms were settled. Winter arrived and the eastern armies asked to return home before the severe cold. A detachment of the troops stayed at Homs with its lord and al-'Ādil returned to Damascus, where he wintered. The troops of the Jazīra returned to their own towns.

Al-'Ādil's expedition from Egypt with the troops came about as follows. The Frankish inhabitants of Cyprus had taken several ships of the Egyptian fleet and made their crews prisoner. Al-'Ādil sent to the ruler of Acre about restoring what had been taken, saying, 'We are at truce.[19] Why have you acted treacherously towards our men?' His excuse was that he had no jurisdiction over the people of Cyprus and that they only deferred to the Franks in Constantinople. The Cypriots later went to Constantinople because of a famine they had but they were unable to procure provisions. Rule over Cyprus reverted to the lord of Acre. Al-'Ādil repeated his diplomatic mission but nothing was settled, so he marched out with his troops and treated Acre as we have mentioned.[20] Its ruler then agreed to what was demanded and set the captives free.

Account of dissension in Khilāṭ and the killing of many of its inhabitants

After al-Awḥad ibn al-'Ādil had completed his take-over of Khilāṭ and its dependencies, he left to go to Malāzgird to arrange its administration too and to do what ought to be done there. When he departed from Khilāṭ, the inhabitants made a surprise attack on the troops there and drove them out. They declared rebellion

---

[19] A truce had been signed in September 1204 to last until the summer of 1210 (Stevenson, *Crusaders*, 297).

[20] However, no details of operations against Acre are given.

and put the citadel, where al-Awḥad's men were, under siege and proclaimed the slogan of Shāh Arman, although he was dead, meaning thereby to restore power to his associates and mamlukes.

[**275**] The news reached al-Awḥad, so he went back to deal with them, having been joined by troops from the Jazīra and strengthened by them. He put Khilāṭ under siege. The population were at odds and some of them inclined towards him out of their grudge against the others. He gained control of the city, slew large numbers of the people and took several notables prisoner, whom he sent to Mayyāfariqīn. Every day he would send for a group of them to be killed. Only a few survived. After this event the men of Khilāṭ were humbled and the unity of the 'young men'[21] was destroyed. They had exercised authority but the people were now saved from their evil. They had begun to set up and slay one ruler after another. In their eyes the designated ruler had no authority. Authority was merely for their interest and in their hands.

Account of Abū Bakr ibn Pahlawān's taking power in Marāgha

During this year Emir Nuṣrat al-Dīn Abū Bakr ibn Pahlawān, lord of Azerbayjan, took power in Marāgha. This came about as follows. The ruler there, 'Alā' al-Dīn Qarāsunqur, died this year and was succeeded by a young son of his.[22] The regency and his upbringing were undertaken by a eunuch of his father's. However, an emir, who had served his father, rebelled against him and raised a large following. The eunuch sent the troops he had to confront them but this emir fought and defeated them. The rule of 'Alā' al-Dīn's son remained firm but his reign did not last long before he died at the beginning of the year 605 [began 16 June 1208]. This was the end of his house and none of them was left.

After his death Nuṣrat al-Dīn Abū Bakr marched from Tabriz to Marāgha and took it. He seized control of all the realm of the house of Qarāsunqur, except for the castle of Rūyīndiz,[23] for the eunuch held out there in possession of the treasure chests and stores. He continued to resist Emir Abū Bakr there.

---

21 Arabic *fityān*, plural of *fatā*. In many urban centres their social organization, called *futuwwa*, frequently challenged regular authority and was closely related to the *'ayyārūn* (urban gangs). In the early thirteenth century the Caliph al-Nāṣir tried to institutionalize the *futuwwa* and 'tame' it (Cahen, *Pre-Ottoman Turkey*, 195–200).

22 'Alā' al-Dīn is called Körp Arslan in *New Islamic Dynasties*, 198 or Karpā in *EIr*, ii, 898-900, s.v. Atabakān-e Marāgha. The son who succeeded him remains unnamed. He may have had two other sons who died before their father. It is possible that by 618/1221 a daughter (or granddaughter) of Qarāsunqur (Sulāfa Khātūn) was ruling Marāgha from Rūyandiz, *EI(2)*, vi, 500, and see below, p. [**377**].

23 See *EI(2)*, vi, 501, s.v. Marāgha.

[276] Account of the dismissal of Naṣīr al-Dīn, the caliph's vizier

This Naṣīr al-Dīn Nāṣir ibn Mahdī al-'Alawī was a citizen of Rayy, a member of a great family. He came to Baghdad when Mu'ayyad al-Dīn ibn al-Qaṣṣāb, the caliph's vizier, took control of Rayy and he received a good reception from the caliph, who appointed him deputy vizier. Later he made him vizier, giving him full authority, and made his son[24] master of the Storeroom.

On the 22 Jumādā II this year [13 January 1208] he was dismissed and put under house arrest.[25] The reason for his dismissal was that he had treated the senior mamlukes of the caliph very badly,[26] including the Emir of the Pilgrimage Muẓaffar al-Dīn Sunqur, known as Lion Face. The latter fled from his control to Syria in the year 603 [1206–7] and abandoned the pilgrims at al-Markhūm.[27] He sent to explain his flight, saying, 'I fled from the hands of the vizier.' Then the Emir Jamāl al-Dīn Qashtimur, one of the elite mamlukes and the caliph's favourite, followed him. He went to Luristan and sent to excuse his actions, saying, 'The vizier desires to leave not one of the caliph's mamlukes in the caliph's service. There is no doubt that he wishes to lay claim to the caliphate.' The people spoke of this frequently and made verses about it. An example of what someone[28] said is:

Is there nobody to tell the Caliph Aḥmad for me:
Take care (may you be protected against evil) in what you are doing.
This vizier of yours is engaged in double-dealing, in which
Your cause, O best of men, is lost.
If he is truly from the lineage of Aḥmad,[29]
This is a vizier ambitious for the caliphate.
[277] If he is not truthful in what he claims,
His deeds will harm all the more what he has.

The caliph therefore dismissed him, although a different explanation is mentioned. After his dismissal he sent to the caliph as follows: 'I came here without a dinar or a dirham. I have gained in cash and precious objects and such-like what is worth

---

[24] He is called Qiwām al-Dīn Naṣr in Sibṭ ibn al-Jawzī, 533. It appears that his death is recorded under the year 605/1208–9. See p. [**283**], although his grandfather is there named as Makkī rather than Mahdī.

[25] In the Arabic 'his door was locked'.

[26] See for example his having 'Alā' al-Dīn Tunāmish poisoned because he was too close to the Caliph al-Nāṣir (Sibṭ ibn al-Jawzī, 535–6).

[27] See above, p. [**258**].

[28] The poet is Abū Yūsuf Ya'qūb ibn Ṣābir al-Manjanīqī (born Monday 4 Muḥarram 554/26 January 1159; died 28 Ṣafar 626/26 January 1229). His career at Baghdad began in the military as a specialist in siege engines (hence his *nisba* al-Manjanīqī, the mangonel specialist). See *Wafāyāt*, vii, 35–46.

[29] i.e. of the Prophet Muḥammad.

more than 5,000 dinars,' asking that everything be taken from him and he be freed and allowed to dwell in the Shrine in the fashion of certain Alids. The reply was, 'We did not bestow anything upon you with the intention of getting it back from you, even were it the world's fill of gold. You are safe in God's hands and ours. We have heard nothing of you that requires such action. However, your enemies have spoken much against you. Choose a place for yourself you can move to, well supplied and respected.' He preferred to remain under surveillance by the caliph, to avoid falling into his enemy's hands and losing his life. This was what was done.

He was a man of excellent conduct, close to the people, able to meet them on good terms and relax with them. He kept his hands off their wealth and did not act the tyrant over them. On his arrest the Emir of the Pilgrimage returned from Egypt, where he had been in the service of al-'Ādil. Qashtimur also returned. Fakhr al-Dīn Abū'l-Badr Muḥammad ibn Aḥmad ibn Amsīnā al-Wāsiṭī was appointed as deputy vizier, although he was not given full powers.

Miscellaneous events

This year on the eve of Wednesday 5 days from the end of Rajab [= 13 February 1208] there was an earthquake at dawn. At the time I was in Mosul, where it was not very severe. News came from many parts that there had been an earthquake but it had not been powerful.

[**278**] This year the Caliph al-Nāṣir li-Dīn Allāh waived all the sales tax and the non-canonical taxes that were taken from traders on all items sold. This was a great sum. The reason was that a daughter of 'Izz al-Dīn Najāḥ, the caliph's butler, died. A cow had been purchased for her, to be slaughtered and its flesh given as alms on her behalf. When the cost was calculated they included the tax for the cow, which was considerable. The caliph became aware of this and ordered the cancellation of all these taxes.

In the month of Ramaḍān [20 March–18 April 1208] the caliph ordered the construction of houses in the quarters at Baghdad for the poor to break their fast in them. They were called 'hospitality houses' where lamb was cooked and good bread baked. He did this on both sides of Baghdad and in every house he appointed men, whose probity could be trusted, to give each person a full *qadaḥ* of stew and meat and a *mann* of bread.[30] Every night a multitude too numerous to count broke their fast with his food.

This year the Tigris rose greatly and water entered the Baghdad moat from the direction of the Kalwādhā[31] Gate. It was feared that the city would be inundated. The caliph was concerned to block the moat. The deputy vizier Fakhr al-Dīn and

---

[30] A *qadaḥ* was between 1 and 1.9 litres, and a *mann* more or less 816 gm or 2 lb, a modern loaf. See Hinz, 16–17 and 48.

[31] Kalwādhā, chief town of a district of the same name, a little south of Baghdad, see *EI(2)*, iv, 513.

'Izz al-Dīn the Butler rode out to a position outside the city and did not leave until the moat was dammed.

This year Shaykh Ḥanbal ibn 'Abd Allāh ibn al-Faraj, the crier[32] of the Ruṣāfa mosque, died. His transmission of Ḥadīth was of high authority. From Ibn al-Ḥaṣīn he transmitted the *Musnad* of Ibn Ḥanbal with an excellent chain of authorities. He came to Mosul and taught Ḥadīth there and elsewhere.[33]

[32] In Arabic *al-mukabbir*, i.e. the mosque functionary who repeats in a loud voice the words of the imam or preacher.

[33] He died at 90 years of age on 14 Muḥarram/10 August 1207 (Sibṭ ibn al-Jawzī, 536–7).

The Year 605 [1208–1209]

Account of the Georgians' taking of Arjīsh and then their withdrawal

During this year the Georgians with all their hosts marched to the province of Khilāṭ and attacked the city of Arjīsh, which they took by force after a siege. They plundered all the money, goods and other things that it contained, and took captives and enslaved the population. They torched the city and destroyed it utterly. Not one of its citizens survived there. It became 'collapsed on its timbers',[1] as though it had not recently been thronged with people.

The lord of Armenia, Najm al-Dīn Ayyūb, was in the city of Khilāṭ with a large number of troops but he made no move against the Georgians for several reasons. Among them was the fact that they were very numerous and that he was fearful of the people of Khilāṭ on account of the killing and damage he had previously inflicted on them. He feared that, if he left the city, he would be unable to return to it. After he had failed to move out to engage the Georgians, they returned safe and sound to their own lands, undisturbed by any threat. All this, although it was very distressing for Islam and the Muslims, was insignificant in comparison with the events we shall mention in the period 614 to 617 [1217–1221].

The killing of Sanjar Shāh and the accession of his son Maḥmūd

Sanjar Shāh ibn Ghāzī ibn Mawdūd ibn Zankī ibn Āqsunqur, the lord of Jazīrat Ibn 'Umar and the cousin of Nūr al-Dīn, lord of Mosul, was killed this year, slain by his son [**280**] Ghāzī. In killling him he followed a surprising method that indicated cunning and resourcefulness. This came about because Sanjar was a wicked ruler towards all his people, the citizens, the soldiery, his womenfolk and children. In his wicked behaviour to his children he went so far as to send his two sons, Maḥmūd and Mawdūd, to the castle of Faraḥ in Zūzan and to expel this other son of his to a house in the town which he made his residence, putting him under guard to prevent his going out.

The house was next to an orchard belonging to a certain citizen, from which snakes, scorpions and other noxious creatures would find their way in. One day he caught a snake and sent it to his father in a kerchief in the hope that he would be sympathetic to him, but he showed no feeling for him. He therefore contrived to leave the house and hid himself. He made an arrangement with a man in his service to leave Jazīrat [Ibn 'Umar] and go to Mosul, where he claimed that he was

---

[1] A Koranic expression (see Koran, ii, 259; xviii, 42; xxii, 45).

Ghāzī ibn Sanjar. When Nūr al-Dīn heard that he was near, he sent expenses, clothes and mounts, and ordered him to go back. He said, 'Your father blames us for crimes we have not committed and blackens our good name. If you come to me, he will make that a pretext for his slanders and calumnies and we shall become involved in a struggle with him that will demand all our attention.'[2] He therefore went to Syria.

Ghāzī ibn Sanjar, meanwhile, climbed into his father's residence and hid with one of his concubines. Most of the women in the residence knew he was there but kept his secret out of hatred for his father and in the hope of getting free of him because he was so cruel to them. Ghāzī remained in this situation and his father abandoned the search for him, thinking that he was in Syria. It happened one day that his father drank wine outside the town with his boon companions. He proposed to his singers that they sing about parting and similar themes, while he wept and referred explicitly to his imminent end, the approach of death and the collapse of his position. He continued [**281**] in this fashion until the end of the day, when he returned to his palace and got drunk with one of his concubines. During the night he went to the privy. His son was with that concubine and, coming into his presence, struck him fourteen blows with a dagger, before cutting his throat and leaving him lying on the ground. He then entered the bathhouse and sat idly, sporting with the servant girls. If he had opened the palace gate, summoned the soldiery and asked for their oath of loyalty, he would have gained the kingdom, but he felt secure and confident and had no doubts that he would become ruler.

It chanced that one of the young pages went out to the gate and told Sanjar's major-domo what had happened. He summoned the notables of the state and informed them. Then he locked the doors on Ghāzī and secured the people's oaths in favour of Maḥmūd ibn Sanjar Shāh, before sending for him and bringing him from Faraḥ along with his brother Mawdūd. After the people had sworn their oath and settled down, they opened the palace gate to Ghāzī and entered to lay hands on him. He resisted them, so they killed him and threw him down at the palace gate, where the dogs ate part of his flesh before his remains were buried.

Maḥmūd came to the town and took control there, taking the title of Mu'izz al-Dīn, the same as his father's. When he was firmly in position, he arrested many of the slave girls his father had had and drowned them in the Tigris.

A friend of ours told me that he saw seven drowned slave girls in the Tigris over the distance of about a bowshot, three of whom had had their faces burnt. I did not know how this burning came about until a slave girl, one of his girls, whom I bought in Mosul, told me that Maḥmūd took girls, put their faces in the fire and, after they had been burnt, threw them into the Tigris. Those he did not drown he sold. Thus the inhabitants of that palace were scattered to the four winds.

---

2 This last phrase defeats the translator. Literally it is 'whose child will not be chided'. It is explained by al-Fayrūzabādī, s.v. *w.l.d.*, as follows: a matter 'with which they are so preoccupied that, if a child stretched his hand towards a very precious object, he would not be addressed with any rebuke'.

Sanjar Shāh was a wicked ruler, tyrannical, brutal and much given to duplicity and hypocrisy [**282**] and to investigating affairs, both minor and major. He did not refrain from any wickedness towards his subjects and others, such as taking their money and properties, killing and humiliating them. He followed a harsh practice towards them, cutting tongues out and noses and ears off. He also shaved off innumerable beards. Most of his thoughts concerned what injustice he could commit. His tyranny reached such a pitch that, if ever he summoned a person to do him a favour, he would come only after having been at death's door from the intensity of his fear. He gave high positions to fools during his days and the market for evil men and informers was brisk. He ruined the country and dispersed its people. It is no wonder that God gave him into the power of his closest relative who killed him. Then his son Ghāzī was killed and after a little his son Maḥmūd killed his brother Mawdūd. In his house there were incidents of burning, drowning and banishing, some of which we have mentioned. If we wished to detail the wickedness of his conduct, it would take a long time, but God Almighty lies in wait for every tyrant.

Miscellaneous events

This year on 2 Muḥarram [17 July 1208] Abū'l-Ḥasan Warrām ibn Abī Firās, the ascetic, died at the Sayfī settlement (al-Ḥilla), where he came from.[3] He was a righteous man.

In Ṣafar [15 August–12 September 1208] Shaykh Muṣaddiq ibn Shabīb, the grammarian, died. He was a citizen of Wāsiṭ.

The Cadi Muḥammad ibn Aḥmad ibn al-Manadā'ī al-Wāsiṭī died in Sha'bān [8 February–8 March 1209] at Wāsiṭ. He transmitted much Ḥadīth and his authority was high. He was the last person to transmit the *Musnad* [**283**] of Aḥmad ibn Ḥanbal on the authority of Ibn al-Ḥaṣīn.

In the same month there was the death of Qiwām al-Dīn Abū'l-Fawāris Naṣr ibn Nāṣir ibn Makkī al-Madā'inī, the master of the Storeroom at Baghdad.[4] He was a cultured man of letters, perfect in virtue. He loved prose literature and its practitioners and also poetry, which he would reward with excellent purses. After his death he was succeeded in post by Abū'l-Futūḥ al-Mubārak, son of Vizier 'Aḍud al-Dīn Abū'l-Faraj ibn Ra'īs al-Ru'asā'. He was honoured and given a high status and remained in post until 7 Dhū'l-Qa'da [13 May 1209], when he was dismissed because of old age.

---

[3] *Al-Ḥilla al-Sayfiyya* denotes the town of Ḥilla (mid-way between Kufa and Baghdad), whose name is associated with its founder, the Emir Sayf al-Dīn Ṣadaqa ibn Manṣūr, the 'Prince of the Arabs' and with the sedentarization of the Banū Asad, the power base of the Mazyadid dynasty. See *EI(2)*, iii, 389–90.

[4] This is the son of Vizier Naṣīr al-Dīn Nāṣir, who died in 617/1220–21 (see pp. [**276**] and [**400**]), but his grandfather is there called Mahdī. It is not known which is correct.

This year there was a serious earthquake in Nishapur and Khurasan, the worst effects being in Nishapur. The citizens went out into open country for several days until it stopped and then they returned to their homes.

[**284**] The Year 606 [1209–1210]

Account of al-ʻĀdil's taking Khābūr and Nisibis, his siege of Sinjār, followed by his withdrawal, and the alliance of Nūr al-Dīn Arslān Shāh and Muẓaffar al-Dīn

In this year al-ʻĀdil Abū Bakr ibn Ayyūb took control of Khābūr and Nisibis and besieged the town of Sinjār and all the districts of al-Jazīra, which were in the hands of Quṭb al-Dīn Muḥammad ibn Zankī ibn Mawdūd. This came about as follows. Between this Quṭb al-Dīn and his cousin Nūr al-Dīn Arslān Shāh ibn Masʻūd ibn Mawdūd, lord of Mosul, there was an entrenched enmity, which has already been mentioned.[1] When the year 605 [1208–9] came, a marriage connection was established between Nūr al-Dīn and al-ʻĀdil, for a son of al-ʻĀdil's married a daughter of Nūr al-Dīn. There were some ministers of Nūr al-Dīn who wanted him to be distracted from what they were doing, so they recommended him to make contact with al-ʻĀdil and make an agreement with him to divide between them the lands that were Quṭb al-Dīn's and the principality that the son[2] of Sanjar Shāh ibn Ghāzī ibn Mawdūd held, namely Jazīrat Ibn ʻUmar and its districts. Quṭb al-Dīn's possessions would pass to al-ʻĀdil and Jazīrat Ibn ʻUmar would be Nūr al-Dīn's.

Since this suggestion was in tune with Nūr al-Dīn's inclination, he sent to al-ʻĀdil to discuss the matter. The latter agreed with delight, having received what he had never hoped for, as he was aware that, when he controlled these lands, [**285**] he could take Mosul and other places. He also encouraged Nūr al-Dīn to hope that he would give these lands, if he took them, to his son, who was the son-in-law of Nūr al-Dīn and who would reside at the latter's service in Mosul. They arrived at an agreement on this and both swore oaths to keep to it. Al-ʻĀdil hastened to march from Damascus to the Euphrates with his troops, attacked Khābūr and took it.

When Nūr al-Dīn heard of his arrival, it seems that he was fearful and apprehensive. He summoned men whose opinions and words he used to take note of, told them of al-ʻĀdil's arrival and asked for their advice about what to do. Those who had advised his former course held their peace. There was among them one who did not know of the state of affairs[3] and he was horrified and advised him to prepare for a siege, gather men and acquire stores and whatever was needed.

---

1 See above, p. [**192**].

2 i.e. Muʻizz al-Dīn Maḥmūd.

3 It is possible that Ibn al-Athīr is here indirectly referring to his brother Majd al-Dīn, who was a close adviser of Nūr al-Dīn and died at the end of this present year (see below). It must be said, however, that Ibn Wāṣil, iii, 191–2, did not understand one person to be involved but several, against the obvious sense of his source.

Nūr al-Dīn said, 'We have done that,' and told him the situation. He replied, 'What was the idea in going to an enemy of yours, who is more powerful and has more men, yet is far off? If he makes a move to attack you, you would learn of it and he would only arrive after you have completed all [the preparations] you want. [Why] are you doing all you can to make him a neighbour of yours and add strength to his strength? Moreover, what has been agreed between you means that he can take it first without effort or difficulty and you will be left unable to leave Mosul to go to Jazīrat Ibn 'Umar and besiege it, while al-'Ādil is here. If he is faithful to the arrangement that has been made, it will not be possible for you to leave Mosul, even if he returns to Syria, because he now has control of Khilāṭ, part of Diyār Bakr and all the regions of al-Jazīra. Everything is in the hands of his sons. When you march from Mosul, they will be able to cut you off from it. You have done no more than harm yourself and your cousin and strengthen your enemy and make [his name] your watchword. The situation is lost. All you can do is stand by what you two have agreed, lest he makes it a justification and takes the initiative against you.'

Meanwhile, al-'Ādil had taken Khābūr and Nisibis and had marched to Sinjār and put it under siege. [**286**] It was its ruler Quṭb al-Dīn's intention to surrender it to al-'Ādil in exchange for some other place but an emir who was with him, named Aḥmad ibn Yarunqush, the mamluke of his father Ghāzī, prevented that. He undertook to hold and defend the town. Nūr al-Dīn equipped an army under his son al-Qāhir to move against al-'Ādil.

When affairs were in this state, something happened that they had not taken into calculation, namely that Muẓaffar al-Dīn Kūkbūrī, lord of Irbil, sent his vizier to Nūr al-Dīn to offer his help to deny Sinjār to al-'Ādil and that his alliance with him would be on whatever terms he wanted. The envoy arrived at night and stood opposite Nūr al-Dīn's palace and shouted. Then a boat crossed over to ferry him across. He met with Nūr al-Dīn during the night and delivered his message. Nūr al-Dīn agreed to the alliance he asked for and gave his oath on that. That very night the vizier returned. Muẓaffar al-Dīn set out and, after he had joined up with Nūr al-Dīn, both of them made camp with their forces outside Mosul.

The reason why Muẓaffar al-Dīn did this was that the lord of Sinjār sent his son to Muẓaffar al-Dīn to ask him to intercede with al-'Ādil to allow him to keep Sinjār. Muẓaffar al-Dīn thought that, if he interceded concerning half of al-'Ādil's realm, he would take notice of that because of his excellent record in his service and his efforts to defend his realm on more than one occasion, as has been previously mentioned. He therefore interceded with him but al-'Ādil did not accept his intercession, being of the opinion that after his agreement with Nūr al-Dīn he had no need to worry about Muẓaffar al-Dīn. However, when al-'Ādil rejected his intercession, he made contact with Nūr al-Dīn about forming an alliance against al-'Ādil.

After Muẓaffar al-Dīn had come to Mosul and joined forces with Nūr al-Dīn, they both sent to al-Ẓāhir Ghāzī, son of Saladin, who was lord of Aleppo, and

Kaykhusro ibn Qilij [**287**] Arslān, lord of Anatolia, about coming to an agreement with them. These two both responded positively and they all promised to make hostile moves against al-'Ādil's lands if he refused to make peace and allow the ruler of Sinjār to remain. In addition the [first] two sent to the Caliph al-Nāṣir li-Dīn Allāh to persuade him also to send an envoy to al-'Ādil about making peace. Thereupon the lord of Sinjār's spirit was strengthened to hold out. The caliph's envoys then arrived, that is to say, Hibat Allāh ibn al-Mubārak ibn al-Ḍaḥḥāk, the major-domo, and Emir Āq-Bāsh, one of the closest and greatest of the caliph's mamlukes. They came to Mosul and from there proceeded to al-'Ādil, who was besieging Sinjār. The men around him were not giving him their whole-hearted support in the struggle, especially Asad al-Dīn Shīrkūh, lord of Homs and Raḥba, for he was sending sheep and other foodstuffs into the town quite openly and not attacking it, and others were acting likewise.

When the caliph's envoys came to al-'Ādil, he initially agreed to withdraw but then he declined and made specious proposals. He spun the business out, in the hope of achieving something, but in the end gained nothing of what he had hoped from Sinjār. He agreed to peace on condition that he would hold what he had taken, while Sinjār would remain in the hands of its lord. Agreement was established on this basis. All gave their oaths to this and that all would unite against whoever broke the terms. Al-'Ādil withdrew from Sinjār to Ḥarrān and Muẓaffar al-Dīn returned to Irbil. Each one of the princes remained in his own lands. During his stay at Mosul Muẓaffar al-Dīn had married two of his daughters to the two sons of Nūr al-Dīn, namely 'Izz al-Dīn Mas'ūd and 'Imād al-Dīn Zankī.

Miscellaneous events

This year in Rabī' I [September 1209] Fakhr al-Dīn ibn Amsīnā (?) was dismissed from the post of deputy vizier for the caliph and was confined to his house. Later he was moved to the Storeroom by way of keeping him under surveillance and he was succeeded [**288**] as deputy vizier by Makīn al-Dīn Muḥammad ibn Muḥammad ibn Baraz[4] al-Qummī, the Chancellery secretary, who was given the title Mu'ayyad al-Dīn. He moved to the residence of the vizier opposite the Nubian Gate.

In Shawwāl [29 March–26 April 1210] Fakhr al-Dīn Abū'l-Faḍl Muḥammad ibn 'Umar, son of the preacher of Rayy, a Shafi'ī lawyer, died. He was the author of celebrated works on jurisprudence, Koran and Ḥadīth and other disciplines and was the leading authority of his age. I have heard that he was born in the year 543 [1148–9].[5]

---

4 Instead of Baraz, Ibn al-Sā'ī, 181, 193, 286, has 'Abd al-Karīm.

5 Fakhr al-Dīn al-Rāzī was a celebrated theologian and exegete, sometimes suspect for his philosophical studies. See *EI(2)*, ii, 751–5. He is generally said to have been born in 543,

On the last day of Dhū'l-Ḥijja [24 June 1210] my brother died, Majd al-Dīn Abū'l-Sa'ādāt al-Mubārak ibn Muḥammad ibn 'Abd al-Karīm, the secretary.[6] He was born in either Rabī' I or II of the year 544 [July or August 1149]. He was learned, and outstandingly so, in several branches of learning, such as canon law, the 'Two Fundamentals',[7] grammar, Ḥadīth and lexicography, and he wrote celebrated works on Koranic exegesis, Ḥadīth, grammar, mathematics and rare [words and expressions in] Ḥadīth, and his letters have been collected. He was an accomplished government secretary, whose career became a byword, a man of solid religion, who clung to the straight path (may God have mercy on him and be pleased with him). He was one of the best ornaments of the age. Possibly anyone who reads what I have set down will be suspicious of my words, but his contemporaries who knew him know that my words are inadequate.

This year Majd al-Dīn al-Muṭarrizī, the grammarian from Khwārazm, died. He was a leading scholar in grammar and the author of excellent works on the subject.[8]

There also died this year al-Mu'ayyad ibn 'Abd al-Raḥīm ibn al-Ikhwa at Isfahan. He was a student of Ḥadīth (God have mercy on him).

---

but *Wāfī*, iv, 248–57, gives 544/1149–50. According to Sibṭ ibn al-Jawzī, 542–3, he died in Dhū'l-Ḥijja/June 1210.

[6] *EI(2)*, iii, 723–4; *Wafayāt*, iv, 141–3. He was a frequent source for his brother in *Bāhir*.

[7] In Arabic *al-usūlān*, 'an aberrant dual form, ... denoting equal competence in *fiqh* [jurisprudence] and *kalām* [theology]'. See *EI(2)*, x, 930.

[8] This was almost certainly Abū'l-Fatḥ Nāṣir ibn 'Abd al-Sayyid al-Muṭarrizī, born Rajab 538/January 1144 and died 21 Jumādā I 610 (sic)/9 October 1213, according to *Wafayāt*, v, 369–71. See also *GAL*, i, 293–4, for a list of his works that include a commentary on Ḥarīrī's *Maqāmāt*.

The Year 607 [1210–1211]

Account of the rebellion of Sanjar, the caliph's mamluke, and the army's march against him

Quṭb al-Dīn Sanjar, the mamluke of the Caliph al-Nāṣir li-Dīn Allāh, had been appointed governor of Khuzistan by the caliph after Ṭashtakīn, Emir of the Pilgrimage, as we have related. When the year 606 [1209–10] came, it was clear that there had been a change in his loyalty. He was ordered by messenger to come to Baghdad but he temporized and did not present himself. He made a show of obedience but was nurturing a secret desire to seize power. This remained the situation until Rabī' I of the present year [began 23 August 1210]. The caliph commanded Mu'ayyad al-Dīn, the deputy vizier, and 'Izz al-Dīn[1] Najāh the butler and an intimate of the caliph, to march against him in Khuzistan with the troops. They duly set out with large forces towards Khuzistan. When Sanjar ascertained that they were coming to him, he abandoned his lands and joined the ruler of Shiraz, the Atabeg 'Izz al-Dīn Sa'd ibn Dakalā, seeking protection with him. The latter received him with honour and took his side.

The caliph's army arrived at Khuzistan in Rabī' II [22 September–20 October 1210], meeting no resistance. When their position was secure, they wrote to Sanjar, calling him to obedience, but he did not respond, so they proceeded to Arrajān with the intention of attacking the ruler of Shiraz. Winter overtook them and they stayed for several months, while envoys went to and fro between them and the ruler of Shiraz. However, he did not agree [**290**] to surrender Sanjar. When Shawwāl arrived [began 18 March 1211], they set out for Shiraz and at that time its ruler sent to the vizier and the butler, interceding for Sanjar and asking for an undertaking for him, that he would not be harmed. This was granted, so he handed him over, his person, his property and his family. They then returned to Baghdad, taking Sanjar with them under guard. The caliph appointed his mamluke, Yāqūt, Emir of the Pilgrimage, to Khuzistan.

The vizier came to Baghdad in Muḥarram 608 [15 June–15 July 1211] along with the butler and the troops. The citizens went out to greet them. They entered the city accompanied by Sanjar riding a mule with a pack-saddle. Attached to his leg were two chains, each one held by a soldier. He stayed in prison until Ṣafar began [16 July]. A great gathering of emirs and notables was brought together at the residence of Mu'ayyad al-Dīn, the deputy vizier, and Sanjar was summoned. He was charged with various reprehensible matters that were attributed to him and he confessed to them. Mu'ayyad al-Dīn said, 'You all know this man's punishment that state policy demands but the caliph has pardoned him.' He ordered him to be given robes of honour, which he donned and then returned to his house. The people

[1] The edition adds an erroneous *ibn* here.

were amazed at this.

It is said that Atabeg Sa‘d plundered the money, treasure and mounts of Sanjar, everything that he and his followers had, and he allowed the latter to go. When Sanjar came to the vizier and the butler and they demanded the money from Sa‘d, he sent an insignificant amount. God knows best.

[291] Account of the death of Nūr al-Dīn Arslān Shāh and a little about his rule

This year towards the end of Rajab [ended 26 January 1211] Nūr al-Dīn Arslān Shāh ibn Mas‘ūd ibn Mawdūd ibn Zankī ibn Āqsunqur, lord of Mosul, died.[2] He had been ill for a long time and his physical state had become bad. His rule lasted for seventeen years and eleven months. He was resolute and brave, a strong ruler of his people and severe on his followers, who feared him greatly. This prevented them from transgressing against one another. He had high aspirations and restored the reputation and influence of, and respect for, the Atabeg house, which had dwindled away. Princes feared him. He was quick to take action in pursuit of kingly power, although he had no patience, and that is why his kingdom did not become extensive. Although he may not have had the highest virtue, nevertheless, when al-Kāmil ibn al-‘Ādil withdrew from Mardīn, as we have related under the year 595 [1198–9], he kept his hands off it and preserved it for its lord. Had he attacked and besieged it, it would have had no capacity to resist, because the men there were exhausted and tired with hardly any spark of life left in them, but he preserved it for its lord.

When he became ruler, a merchant appealed to him for help. He enquired about his case and was told that he had brought textiles to the town for sale but no sale was concluded, so he wanted to export them and had been prevented from doing so. He asked, ‘Who prevented him?’ and was told, ‘The tax farmer for textiles wants the customary duty.’ The state’s regent Mujāhid al-Dīn Qāymāz was by his side, so he asked him what the custom was. He replied, ‘If the owner has stipulated the export of his goods, he is able to take them away, but if he has not made that condition, he may not take them out until there has been levied what it is customary [**292**] to levy.’ Nūr al-Dīn said, ‘By God, this custom is well devised![3] A man sells none of his goods, why should his money be taken from him?’ ‘There is no doubt’, Mujāhid al-Dīn said, ‘that this is a bad custom.’ ‘If you and I say that it is a bad custom, what is to stop our giving it up?’ said Nūr al-Dīn. He then ordered the man’s money to be reimbursed and that duty should only be taken from those who make a sale.

---

[2] Ibn Wāṣil, iii, 202, agrees the date of his death, but Sibṭ ibn al-Jawzī, 546, writes ‘died in Ṣafar’/25 July–22 August 1210.

[3] The text has *mudabbara* and the sense is unclear. Is irony the explanation?

I heard my brother, Majd al-Dīn Abū'l-Sa'ādāt (God have mercy on him), one of the people closest to him, say, 'On no single day did I propose doing some good deed which he refused; on the contrary he hastened to do it with joy and delight.' My brother was summoned one day. He rode to the palace and when he was at the palace entrance, a woman met him with a petition in her hand. She was complaining and eager to present it to Nūr al-Dīn, so my brother took it. When he came into Nūr al-Dīn's presence, he tackled him on some important matter. My brother said, 'Before anything else would you read this petition and settle the petitioner's business?' 'There is no need to read it,' he replied, 'tell us what is in it.' 'By God,' said my brother, 'I only know that I saw a woman at the palace gate, complaining of some wrong.' Nūr al-Dīn said, 'Yes, I know her case,' and then he became disturbed and was visibly vexed and angry. There were two men with him who carried out his state business. To my brother he continued, 'Consider to what I have been brought with these two. This woman had a son, who died a while ago in Mosul. He was a foreigner and left some textiles and two mamlukes. The agents of the treasury sequestered the textiles and they brought the two mamlukes to us. They remained with us awaiting the arrival of someone with a proper claim to take the estate. This woman arrived with a document from a cadi's court to the effect that the property of her son was now hers, so we ordered the property to be handed over to her and I said to these two, 'Buy the two mamlukes from her and give her a fair price.' They came back, saying, 'We have not concluded any sale because she has demanded a high price.' I ordered the two mamlukes to be given back to her two months or more ago. Until now I have heard nothing more from her. [**293**] I thought that she had got her property. But there is no doubt that they have not given the two mamlukes back to her. She pleaded for their help but they did not act fairly with her. So she has come to you. Everyone who sees this woman complaining and pleading for help thinks that I have kept her property from her, so they blame me and call me a tyrant, but I know nothing about it. All this is the doing of these two. I wish you to take charge of the two mamlukes and hand them over to her.' And so the woman got her property and became grateful and blessed his name. There are many instances of this sort associated with him which we will not take the time to mention.

Account of the accession of his son al-Qāhir

When Nūr al-Dīn's death was imminent, he ordered his son, al-Qāhir 'Izz al-Dīn Mas'ūd, to be installed in power as his successor and took oaths of loyalty to him from the army and the notables. He had declared him his heir a while before his death and he now renewed his will when close to death. To his younger son 'Imād al-Dīn Zankī he gave the castle of 'Aqr al-Ḥumaydiyya and the castle of Shūsh[4]

---

[4] Yāqūt, iii, 334–5: 'Shūsh is a very high, strong castle near 'Aqr al-Ḥumaydiyya in the

with their dependent territory. He sent him to 'Aqr and ordered the administration of the two possessions, their defence and their development to be undertaken by his mamluke, Emir Badr al-Dīn Lu'lu',[5] because of his intelligence, uprightness, the excellence of his political and administrative skills and the perfection of the leadership qualities that he saw in him. At this time al-Qāhir was ten years old.

When Nūr al-Dīn's illness worsened and he despaired of life, his doctors ordered him to go down the river to the hot spring known as the Spring of al-Qayyāra,[6] which is near Mosul. He did so but found there no alleviation and became weaker. Badr al-Dīn took him in a barge (*shabbāra*) upstream towards Mosul, but he died at night on the journey in the company of sailors and doctors, separated from them by a curtain.

[294] With Badr al-Dīn, serving Nūr al-Dīn, were two mamlukes. When Nūr al-Dīn died, Badr al-Dīn said to them, 'Let nobody hear of his death,' and he said to the doctors and the sailors, 'Let no one talk. The sultan is asleep.' They all kept silent. When they reached Mosul at night, he ordered the doctors and the sailors to leave the barge so that they would not see him dead. They went some distance away and then he and the two mamlukes carried him into the palace and left him in his former quarters,[7] accompanied by the mamlukes. A trusted person took post at his door, not allowing anyone to go in or out. Meanwhile Badr al-Dīn sat with the elite, carrying out business that needed to be dealt with.[8]

When he had completed all he wanted, he made the death public at the time of the afternoon prayer. He was buried at night in the madrasah he had erected facing his palace. Order was preserved in the city that night in an excellent manner, so that people continued to circulate during the night and nobody lost as much as a grain of wheat. The rule of his son was firmly established and Badr al-Dīn undertook the administration of the state and the overseeing of its interests.

Miscellaneous events

In the month of Rabī' II [22 September–20 October 1210] Cadi Abū Zakariyā' Yaḥyā ibn al-Qāsim ibn al-Mufarrij, the cadi of Takrit, gave lectures in the

---

district of Mosul. It is said to be higher and larger than 'Aqr, but it is below it in prestige.' See also Krawulsky, 355: it is 18 km south-west of Dezful.

[5] The regent and from 629/1232 the independent ruler of Mosul and also a patron of Ibn al-Athīr; see *EI(2)*, v, 821.

[6] According to Yāqūt, iv, 211, it was a source of pitch and the hot spring was used by the people of Mosul for curative bathing. *Ta'rīkh Irbil*, i, 136, places it 'below Mosul on the Tigris' and says that there were various springs, both hot and cold.

[7] *Bāhir*, 198: 'and left him in the place where he had been ill'.

[8] *Bāhir*, 198: 'during that day he carried out what instructions [Nūr al-Dīn] had given on his journey before he died'.

Niẓāmiyya Madrasah at Baghdad. He had been summoned there from Takrit.[9]

This year the Tigris in Iraq became very low, with the result that the water at Baghdad was flowing about five cubits deep. The caliph ordered the dredging of the Tigris and brought together a great multitude of people. [**295**] As often as they dug something, the silt returned and covered it. Above Baghdad people were wading across the Tigris. This was quite without parallel.

This year the Pilgrimage was led by 'Alā' al-Dīn Muḥammad, son of Emir Mujāhid al-Dīn Yāqūt, the Emir of the Pilgrimage. His father had been appointed governor of Khuzistan by the caliph and *he* made him Emir of the Pilgrimage and placed men alongside him to manage the pilgrims, because he was still a youth.

On 20 Rabī' II [11 October 1210] Ḍiyā' al-Dīn Abū Aḥmad 'Abd al-Wahhāb ibn 'Alī ibn 'Abd Allāh, the Baghdādī emir, who was the grandson of Ṣadr al-Dīn Ismā'īl the Chief Shaykh, died in Baghdad at the age of eighty-seven years and a few months. He was a sufi, a lawyer and a Ḥadīth scholar, from whom I heard much (God have mercy on him). He was one of the pious servants of God, much given to devotional exercises and righteousness.

Our teacher died this year, Abū Ḥafṣ 'Umar ibn Muḥammad ibn al-Mu'ammar ibn Ṭabarzad al-Baghdādī, whose transmission of Ḥadīth was of high authority.

---

9 According to *Wāfī*, xxviii, 273–5, he initially studied with his father in Takrit and then studied variously in Haditha, Mosul, Aleppo and Baghdad, before returning to be cadi in Takrit. He died in Baghdad in 616/1219–20 (sic).

[296]

The Year 608 [1211–1212]

Account of Manklī's taking control of the Uplands and Isfahan and the flight of Aydughmish

In Sha'bān of this year [9 January–6 February 1212] Aydughmish, lord of Hamadhan, Isfahan, Rayy and the lands between them, came to Baghdad in flight from Manklī. This came about in the following way. Aydughmish had become powerful in the lands and of great importance. His fame had spread and his army grown numerous, so that he limited the power of his master, Abū Bakr ibn Pahlawān, lord of these lands, Azerbayjan and Arran, as we have mentioned.[1] In the present year a mamluke, called Manklī, rebelled against him and became his rival for the country. His following increased and the mamlukes of Pahlawān gave him their obedience, so he gained control of the lands and Shams al-Dīn Aydughmish fled from him to Baghdad. When he arrived there, the caliph ordered that he be received with all consideration. All the important persons went out and the day of his arrival was a notable one. Later, in Ramaḍān [7 February–7 March 1212], his wife came in a litter, was received with honour and lodged with her husband, who remained in Baghdad until the year 610 [1215–16], when he left. What happened to him we shall relate later.

[297] Account of the pillaging of the pilgrim caravan at Mina

This year the pilgrim caravan was pillaged at Mina. This came about because a Bāṭinī attacked one of the family of Emir Qatāda, ruler of Mecca, and killed him at Mina, in the belief that he was Qatāda. When Qatāda heard this, he gathered the Sherifs,[2] the Bedouin, the slave troops and the inhabitants of Mecca and moved against the pilgrims. They came down upon them from the mountain and attacked them with stones, arrows and other missiles. The Emir of the Pilgrimage, the son of Emir Yāqūt whom we have mentioned before, was a youth who did not know how to react. He was fearful and at a loss. The ruler of Mecca was able to plunder the pilgrims. Those on the fringes were despoiled but the pilgrims remained as they were until nightfall.

The caravan then fell into confusion and the pilgrims spent the night in a wretched state in fear of death and pillage. Somebody suggested to the Emir of the

---

[1] See above, p. [**195**].

[2] Arabic: *al-Ashrāf*, i.e. members of the nobility of Islam, the descendants of the Prophet through his daughter Fatima.

Pilgrimage that he shift the caravan to the camp of the Syrian caravan. He accordingly ordered the move and they lifted their baggage onto the camels. The people were fully occupied with this, so the enemy, their greed aroused, were able to plunder them at will and camels were seized along with their loads. Those that escaped reached the pilgrims from Syria and joined with them. They then moved off to al-Zāhir,[3] but were [at first] prevented from entering Mecca. Later they were allowed to do so, so they entered, completed their pilgrimage and returned home.[4]

Subsequently Qatāda sent his son and several of his men to Baghdad. They entered the city with drawn swords and winding-sheets, kissed the threshold and apologized for what had happened to the pilgrims.

[298] Miscellaneous events

This year the Ismāʿīlīs, whose leader was Jalāl al-Dīn ibn al-Ṣabbāḥ, announced that they had moved away from their perpetrating and allowing of things that are forbidden.[5] Jalāl al-Dīn ordered the establishment of the public prayers and ordinances of Islam in his lands, Khurasan and Syria. He sent envoys to the caliph and other princes of Islam to inform them of this and sent his mother to perform the Pilgrimage. She was received with great honour in Baghdad and likewise on the route to Mecca.

At the end of Jumādā II [9 December 1211] Abū Ḥāmid Muḥammad ibn Yūnus ibn Mīʿa, the Shāfiʿī lawyer, died in Mosul. He was a leading scholar, who attained the headship of the Shāfiʿīs. There was nobody to match him in his times, a man of excellent character, who was often indulgent towards students of the Law and did them kindnesses (God have mercy on him).[6]

In the month of Rabīʿ I [14 August–12 September 1211] there died Cadi Abū'l-Faḍā'il ʿAlī ibn Yūsuf ibn Aḥmad ibn al-Āmidī al-Wāsiṭī. He was cadi of Wāsiṭ and an excellent man.

In Shaʿbān [9 January–6 February 1212] Muʿīn al-Dīn Abū'l-Futūḥ ʿAbd al-Wāḥid ibn Abī Aḥmad ibn ʿAlī al-Amīn, the chief shaykh in Baghdad, died. His death occurred on the island of Kīsh, where he had gone on a mission from the

---

3 A district in the north-west of Mecca, to the west of the road to Medina.

4 A pilgrim in the Syrian caravan was Rabīʿa Khātūn, daughter of al-ʿĀdil. She protected the Iraqi pilgrims and also persuaded the emir to allow them into Mecca (Ibn Wāṣil, iii, 210–11).

5 The restoration of the Shariah was carried out by Jalāl al-Dīn Ḥasan III (1210–21), the son of Muḥammad II ibn Ḥasan II ibn Muḥammad ibn Ḥasan al-Ṣabbāḥ (see Hodgson, *Order of Assassins*, 217–25). This change is reported under the year 609/1212–13 in Abū Shāma, *Dhayl*, 81.

6 Born in 535/1140–41 and, according to Sibṭ ibn al-Jawzī, 558–9, died in Rajab/10 December 1211–8 January 1212.

caliph.[7] He was a friend of ours. Between us there was a strong affection and great companionship. He was one of God's pious servants (God have mercy on him and be pleased with him). He had an excellent hand and was the author of some good poetry and a scholar of jurisprudence and other things. When he died, his brother Zayn al-Dīn ʻAbd al-Razzāq ibn Abī Aḥmad was installed. He had been overseer of the ʻAḍudī Hospital but he gave this up and confined himself to the sufi hospice.

In Dhū'l-Ḥijja [6 May–3 June 1212] Muḥammad ibn Yūsuf ibn Muḥammad ibn ʻUbayd Allāh al-Naysabūrī died, the secretary who had an excellent hand. He used to follow the method of Ibn al-Bawwāb.[8] He was a lawyer, mathematician and theologian.

ʻUmar ibn Abī'l-ʻIzz Masʻūd, Abū'l-Qāsim, the Baghdad textile merchant, died this year. He was a righteous man who would often host gatherings of sufis and be generous to them.

There also died Abū Saʻīd al-Ḥasan ibn Muḥammad ibn al-Ḥasan ibn Ḥamdūn al-Thaʻlabī al-ʻAdawī, the son of the author of *The Notebook* (*al-Tadhkira*).[9] He was a man of religious learning.

---

[7] ʻAbd al-Wāḥid ibn ʻAbd al-Wahhāb, known as Ibn Sakīna, was born in 552/1157, travelled widely, headed Sufi establishments in Jerusalem and Damascus, before returning to Baghdad as head of the Hospice of the Chief Shaykh. He died on a mission to Kīsh, an island in the Gulf (although the text of *Kāmil* has Kās). See *Wāfī*, xix, 260.

[8] ʻAlī ibn Hilāl ibn al-Bawwāb, a famous calligrapher of the Buyid period, died in Baghdad in 413/1022; see *EI(2)*, iii, 736–7.

[9] For his father, see *Chronicle of Ibn al-Athīr (2)*, p. [**330**], s.a. 562/1166–7.

The Year 609 [1212–1213]

Account of Ibn Manklī's coming to Baghdad

In Muḥarram of this year [3 June–2 July 1212] Muḥammad, son of the Manklī who had seized control of the Uplands, came to Baghdad. The reason for this was that his father Manklī, after he had taken control of the Uplands and after their ruler Aydughmish fled away to Baghdad, feared that the caliph might give him aid and send an army with him, which would make his own position parlous, because he had not yet fully mastered the lands. He therefore sent his son Muḥammad with a detachment of his army. The leading people of Baghdad went out according to their various degrees to meet him. He was given lodgings and treated with honour, and remained at Baghdad until Aydughmish was killed.[1] He and those with him were then given robes of honour, nobly treated and sent back to his father.

Miscellaneous events

During this year al-ʿĀdil Abū Bakr ibn Ayyūb, ruler of Egypt and Syria, arrested an emir whose name was Usāma. He possessed a large fief that contained the castle of Kawkab in the district of the Jordan in Syria. Al-ʿĀdil took the castle of Kawkab from him, destroyed it and razed it to the ground.[2] Afterwards he built a fort near Acre on a hill called Ṭūr, which is well-known there, and fully manned it and supplied it with stores and armaments.[3]

This year the lawyer Muḥammad ibn Ismāʿīl ibn Abī'l-Ṣayf al-Yamanī died, the lawyer of the Sacred Precinct at Mecca.

---

1 See p. [**301**].

2 In 607/1210–11 Emir ʿIzz al-Dīn Usāma went to Egypt to have a rest from the hostility of al-ʿĀdil's son, al-Muʿaẓẓam. There were accusations of plotting with al-Ẓāhir of Aleppo and al-Muʿaẓẓam told Sibṭ ibn al-Jawzī, 560–61, that items of correspondence had been found. The following year he was being urged to surrender Kawkab and ʿAjlūn and take Fayyūm instead. He refused and slipped away from Egypt but was taken near Darum and imprisoned, with his son, in Kerak, where he later died. His castles were besieged and captured. Usāma's fall is part of the passing of the old guard of Saladin's emirs. See al-Ḥamawī, fols. 130a and 131a; Ibn Wāṣil, iii, 208–10. On Kawkab or Belvoir, see Pringle, *Churches*, i, 120–22; Pringle, *Secular buildings*, 32–3.

3 The monastery on Mt. Tabor was immeasurably strengthened as a fortress by al-ʿĀdil. The Franks saw it as a special threat to their position and made great efforts to recover it, which led al-Muʿaẓẓam to destroy it by the summer of 1218. See below, p. [**322–3**] and al-Ḥamawī, fols. 130a and 135a; Ibn Wāṣil, iii, 215–16; Pringle, *Churches*, ii, 63–85, especially 66–7.

[301] The Year 610 [1213–1214]

Account of the killing of Aydughmish

In Muḥarram of this year [23 May–21 June 1213] Aydughmish, who was the ruler of Hamadhan, was killed. We have mentioned under the year 608 [1211–12] that he came to Baghdad and took up residence there. The caliph was gracious to him and honoured him with robes of honour, gave him ceremonial drums and whatever he needed. He then sent him back to Hamadhan. He left Baghdad with Hamadhan as his destination in Jumādā II [18 October–15 November 1213]. He reached the lands of Ibn Barjam[1] and the two of them met together. Aydughmish waited there in expectation of the arrival of Baghdad troops to march together according to the agreement between them.

The caliph had previously dismissed Sulaymān ibn Barjam from the leadership of his clan of the Īwā'ī Turkomans and appointed his younger brother. Sulaymān sent to Manklī to tell him what Aydughmish was doing. He continued on his way and then they seized and slew him, sending his head to Manklī. His followers with him scattered throughout the lands with each looking out for himself.

News of his death came to Baghdad and upset the caliph, who sent to Manklī, finding fault with what he had done. The latter gave a robust reply and seized the lands, his position being now strong and his army's numbers having increased greatly. What happened to him later we shall relate, if God wills.

[302] Miscellaneous events

This year the people were led on pilgrimage by Abū Firās ibn Ja'far ibn Firās al-Ḥillī, acting as deputy for Emir of the Pilgrimage Yāqūt. Yāqūt's son was forbidden to take part in the Pilgrimage because of what had happened to the pilgrims when he was in charge.

In Muḥarram [23 May–21 June 1213] the doctor Muhadhdhab al-Dīn 'Alī ibn Aḥmad ibn Habal, the celebrated physician, died. He was the most learned of his contemporaries in medicine and also transmitted Ḥadīth. He dwelt in Mosul and there he died. He was devoted to almsgiving, of excellent character and the author of a good work on medicine.

In the same month Ḍiyā' al-Dīn Aḥmad ibn 'Alī al-Baghdādī, the Ḥanbalī lawyer and student of Ibn al-Mannī, died.

---

[1] For the father Barjam al-Īwā'ī in the Uplands, see *Chronicle of Ibn al-Athīr (2)*, pp. **[239]**, **[394]**.

The same month Aḥmad ibn Mas'ūd al-Turkistānī, the Ḥanafī lawyer, died in Baghdad. He was the professor at the Shrine of Abū Ḥanīfa.[2]

In Jumādā I [18 September–17 October 1213] Mu'izz al-Dīn Abū'l-Ma'ālī Sa'īd ibn 'Alī, known as Ibn Ḥadīda, a former vizier of the Caliph al-Nāṣir li-Dīn Allāh, died.[3] He had been confined to his house and when he died, his bier was carried to the Shrine of the Commander of the Faithful 'Alī (peace be on him) at Kufa. His conduct was excellent during his time as vizier and he did much good and much that was useful for the people.

---

[2] He was also in charge of the Court of Complaints (*maẓālim*); see Abū Shāma, *Dhayl*, 84.

[3] He was born at Samarra in 536/1141–2, moved to Baghdad and was made vizier for Caliph al-Nāṣir in 584/ 1188–9. He was confined by his rival, the Vizier Ibn Mahdī, escaped in disguise and only returned to Baghdad after this rival's death. See Sibṭ ibn al-Jawzī, 567, and Abū Shāma, *Dhayl*, 85. The printed text gives his name as Sa'd and Ibn Ḥadīd.

The Year 611 [1214–1215]

How Khwārazm Shāh 'Alā' al-Dīn [Muḥammad] took Kirman, Makrān and Sind

I do not know for sure in which year this happened. It was either this present year or a little before or a little afterwards, because the person who told me about it was a soldier of Mosul who travelled to those regions and remained there for several years. He went with Emir Abū Bakr, the conqueror of Kirman, and later came home. He told me about it with some doubt about its dating, although he had been present. He said:

> One of the emirs of Tekesh, the father of Khwārazm Shāh Muḥammad, was an emir whose name was Abū Bakr and his title Tāj al-Dīn.[1] At the beginning of his career he was a cameleer who hired out camels for journeys. Good fortune came to him and he joined Khwārazm Shāh's service, becoming head of his camel train. Khwārazm Shāh saw him to be steadfast and trustworthy, so advanced him until he became one of the leading emirs of his army and was made governor of the town of Zūzan. He was intelligent, sensible, determined and brave, so he prospered greatly in Khwarazm Shāh's service. He trusted him more than all the emirs of his state.
>
> Abū Bakr said to Khwārazm Shāh, 'The territory of Kirman is next to my lands. If the sultan assigned an army to me, I would conquer it in the quickest possible time.' So he sent a large army with him to Kirman, whose ruler was called Ḥarb ibn Muḥammad ibn Abī'l-Faḍl,[2] this last named having ruled Sijistan in the days of Sultan Sanjar. He brought Abū Bakr to battle but had no strength to oppose him, for he was weak, so Abū Bakr conquered Kirman in very quick time. From there he proceeded to the regions of Makrān, all of which he took as far as Sind on the borders of Kabul. He marched to Hormuz, a town on the Makrān coast, and received the submission of its ruler, called Malank, who made the khutbah in Khwārazm Shāh's name. He carried away [**304**] money from there. The khutbah was made in his name at Qalhāt[3] and in part of Oman, because the rulers there were subordinate to the ruler of Hormuz.

[1] This 'lord of Zūzan' was Abū Bakr ibn 'Alī (called Amīn al-Dīn on p. [**262**] above), who died in 614/1218. For his origins and career, see Adle, 'Le pays du Zuzan', 24–31.

[2] See note to p. [**246**] above.

[3] A town on the coast of Oman populated by members of the Ibāḍī sect (Yāqūt, iv, 168).

The reason why they submitted to him despite the great distance (separated as they were by the sea) was that they sought his favour by offering allegiance in order that the masters of the ships that travel there might have nothing to fear from him, for Hormuz is a great harbour and a meeting place for merchants from the furthest parts of India, China, Yemen and other countries. There were battles and raids between the lord of Hormuz and the lord of Kīsh, and each forbade the ship captains to anchor in the territory of his rival. They continue in the same way until now.

Khwārazm Shāh was spending the summer in the regions of Samarqand on account of the Tatars, the followers of Kuchlug Khan, to prevent them attacking his lands. Kuchlug could move very quickly and when he attacked an area, he always outstripped the news of his coming.

Miscellaneous events

This year Mu'ayyad al-Mulk al-Sijzī was killed.[4] He had been vizier for Shihāb al-Dīn al-Ghūrī and for Tāj al-Dīn Yildiz after him. His conduct in office was excellent and his faith exemplary. He was generous to the ulema, men of virtue and others, paying them visits and supporting them. He used to attend Friday prayers on foot and alone.

He was killed because some of the troops of Yildiz hated him. Every year at the beginning of winter he used to go to the 'hot lands' in the service of Yildiz. This year he set out as usual and forty Turks came to him and said, 'The sultan says that you should present yourself with ten persons, leaving your effects behind, for some important business that has arisen.' He went with them without baggage and with ten mamlukes. When they reached Nihawand [**305**] near the Indus,[5] they killed him and fled. Subsequently Khwārazm Shāh captured them and put them to death.

In Rajab [6 November–5 December 1214] Rukn al-Dīn Abū Manṣūr 'Abd al-Salām ibn 'Abd al-Wahhāb ibn 'Abd al-Qādir al-Jīlī al-Baghdādī died in Baghdad. He had held a number of official positions and was suspected of following the philosophers. One day his father saw him wearing a Bukhārī shirt and said, 'What is this shirt?' He replied, 'A Bukhārī,' at which his father said, 'That

---

[4] The conspiracy to murder the former vizier is mentioned in *Ṭabaqāt-i Nāṣirī*, 504–5, where he is called Muḥammad ibn 'Abd Allāh Sanjarī (sic). The edition has al-Sh.ḥ.rī. For the emendation, see above, p. [**213**].

[5] The text has *mā' al-Sind* (the Water of Sind), which is one of several terms for the Indus River (see *EI(2)*, vii, 20–21, s.v. Mihrān). Nahāvand is south of Hamadhan and there is a Nehavand south-west of Qazwin, neither 'near the Indus'. I wonder whether one should read *mā' al-Baṣra*, a difficult but not impossible emendation. See Cornu, 41: Māh al-Baṣra denotes the territory of Nihawand and sometimes the main town itself, Nihawand. See also Yāqūt, iv, 405–6.

is a surprise! We have always heard "Muslim and Bukhārī", but as for "infidel and Bukhārī", that we have never heard."[6]

A few years before his death his books were seized and exposed to public scrutiny. They were seen to deal with the offering of incense to the stars, the addressing of Jupiter as divine and other such infidelities.[7] They were burnt at the Commoners' Gate and he was put in prison. He was then released on the intercession of his father and later on was employed again.[8]

This year too Abū'l-'Abbās Aḥmad ibn Hibat Allāh ibn al-'Alā', known as Ibn al-Zāhid, died at Baghdad. He was learned in grammar and lexicography.

In Sha'bān [6 December 1214–3 January 1215] Abū'l-Muẓaffar Muḥammad ibn 'Alī ibn al-Bull al-Lūrī, the preacher, died. He was buried in a hospice on the 'Īsā Canal. His year of birth was 511 [1117–18].

In Shawwāl [3 February–7 March 1215] 'Abd al-'Azīz ibn Maḥmūd ibn al-Akhḍar died, aged eighty-seven years. He was an outstanding scholar of Ḥadīth.[9]

---

6 A play on the names of the authors of the *Ṣaḥīḥān*, the two most influential collections of Sunni Ḥadīth.

7 The belief persisted that the planets could control a person's fate and that they could be profitably approached with prayer and suffumigants. For instance, Fakhr al-Dīn al-Rāzī wrote a treatise called *al-Sirr al-maktūm fī mukhāṭabat al-nujūm* (The hidden secret concerning addressing the stars). See Pingree, 'Al-Ṭabarī'. For Ibn Taymiyya's generally hostile view, see Michot, 'Ibn Taymiyya on Astrology'. 296–7.

8 He was in fact made 'agent' (*wakīl*) for Emir 'Alī, the caliph's young son (Sibṭ ibn al-Jawzī, 571). For an account of his career, see *Wāfī*, xviii, 429–31.

9 He was born in 526/1131–2 and used to hold a Ḥadīth study circle *(ḥalqa)* in the Palace Mosque at Baghdad (Abū Shāma, *Dhayl*, 88).

[306] The Year 612 [1215–1216]

Account of the killing of Manklī and how Ighlamish took possession of the lands that he held

In Jumādā I of this year [28 August–26 September 1215] Manklī, lord of Hamadhan and Isfahan, was defeated, ran away and was killed. This came about as follows. He had made his territorial gains, as we have related, and he slew Aydughmish. To express disapproval of this act an envoy was sent to him from the caliphal Diwan. He had also caused a rift with Emir Uzbek ibn Pahlawān, lord of Azerbayjan, his lord and master. The caliph sent to the latter to urge him to act against Manklī, promising him aid for this, and he also contacted the Ismā'īlī Jalāl al-Dīn, lord of the Ismā'īlī castles in Persian lands, Alamut and others, ordering him to support Uzbek in the fight against Manklī. They reached an understanding among them that the caliph should receive some of his lands, as should Uzbek, and that Jalāl al-Dīn should be given some. When these terms had been settled, the caliph equipped a large army and appointed as its commander his mamluke Muẓaffar al-Dīn Sunqur, who was called Lion Face. He sent to Muẓaffar al-Dīn Kūkbūrī ibn Zayn al-Dīn 'Alī Kūchuk, who was at that time lord of Irbil, Shahrazūr and their dependencies, ordering him to present himself with his troops to be overall commander of the armies and the ultimate authority in military matters.

He duly came and with him came the troops of Mosul, the Jazīra districts and Aleppo. Large forces gathered together and set out for Hamadhan. When all the forces had gathered, Manklī retired [**307**] before their advance and took refuge in the mountains. They followed him and camped at the foot of a mountain while he was at the top, near the town of Karaj. All the caliphal army and those accompanying it became short of fodder and provisions. Had Manklī remained in his position, they would not have been able to maintain theirs for more than ten days. However, in his eagerness, he descended the mountain with part of his army opposite Emir Uzbek. He, when they charged him, did not stand firm but fled in disarray. Manklī's men returned and went back up the mountain. Uzbek also returned to his tents. Then on the next day Manklī, full of confidence, came down from the mountain with all his troops and the lines were drawn for a pitched battle, which became as fierce as could be. Manklī gave way and ascended the mountain. Had he stayed where he was, nobody would have been able to climb up to him. All they could have done was to withdraw and leave him. However, he slipped away under cover of darkness, abandoned his position and fled. A small contingent of his troops followed him. The rest abandoned him and scattered to the four winds.

The army of the caliph and Uzbek took control of the land and Jalāl al-Dīn, the ruler of the Ismā'īlīs, was given the territory that had been agreed. Uzbek took the rest and handed it to Ighlamish, his father's mamluke, who had gone to Khwārazm Shāh 'Alā' al-Dīn Muḥammad and remained with him [a while] but then returned and took part in the battle and performed admirably in it. Uzbek put him in charge of the lands and each part of the army returned home.

Manklī, after his defeat, went to Saveh, where the prefect in charge was a friend of his. He made contact with him, asking for permission to enter the town, which was granted. The prefect lodged him in his residence but later took away his weapons[1] and intended to put him in irons and send him to Ighlamish. Manklī asked him to kill him himself and not send him back, so he put him to death and sent his head to Uzbek, who then sent it to Baghdad. The day it entered was a day of celebration but that did not bring complete joy for the caliph, for it arrived just when his son died. The head was returned and buried.

[308] Account of the death of the caliph's son

On 20 Dhū'l-Qa'da [11 March 1216] the caliph's son died, his youngest. He was entitled al-Mu'aẓẓam and his name was Abū'l-Ḥasan 'Alī. He was the caliph's best beloved son and he had nominated him as his heir-apparent, having removed his eldest son from that position and put him aside for the sake of this son.

He was (God have mercy on him) generous, active in almsgiving and good works, and of excellent conduct, beloved by the elite and commons alike. His death was caused by a bout of dysentery. At his death the caliph was afflicted with a grief, the like of which had never been heard of. He even sent to the rulers of provinces forbidding them to send him any message of condolence for his son. He neither read any letter nor heard any missive. He withdrew from public view and was alone with his cares and his sorrows. Unheard-of sadness and grief were evident on his person.

When he died, his body was carried out during the daytime and all the men of note walked before his bier to his grandmother's mausoleum near the tomb of Ma'rūf al-Karkhī, where he was laid to rest. After the bier was taken in, the doors were closed and a terrible crying could be heard from within the mausoleum. It was said to be the voice of the caliph.

The common people of Baghdad also grieved for him greatly and the mourning continued throughout the quarters of Baghdad night and day. There was not one district of Baghdad that did not have its hired mourners and no woman who did not proclaim her grief.[2] Neither in former nor recent days had anything like this been heard of in Baghdad.

---

1 This may refer to the detail in Sibṭ ibn al-Jawzī, 573–4, that the friend, who took him in, coveted Manklī's horse and arms.

2 As in the parallel passage in Sibṭ ibn al-Jawzī, 523: 'women came forth, loosed their hair and beat [their breasts]'.

His death occurred at the time when Manklī's head arrived at Baghdad. The procession had been ordered to go out to meet the head. Everyone had left and when they came back with the head to the top of Habīb Street, [**309**] the cry went up that the caliph's son had died. The head was then returned. This is the way of the world. Its joy is never free from grief, although its misfortunes are often free of the admixture of joy.[3]

How Khwārazm Shāh took Ghazna and its dependencies

In Sha'bān of this year [25 November–23 December 1215] Khwārazm Shāh Muḥammad ibn Tekesh took the city of Ghazna and its dependencies. The reason for this was that, after Khwārazm Shāh had gained control of all Khurasan and conquered Bāmiyān and elsewhere, he sent to Tāj al-Dīn [Yildiz], the ruler of Ghazna, whose history up to his taking control there has already been given, requesting him to make the khutbah for him, strike coins in his name and send him an elephant, so that he could come to terms with him, confirm his possession of Ghazna and not be his rival for it. Yildiz summoned his emirs and the notables of his state and consulted them.

There was among them a senior emir, called Qutlugh Takīn, another of the mamlukes of Shihāb al-Dīn al-Ghūrī, who wielded authority in Yildiz's state and was his deputy in Ghazna. He said, 'I think that you should make the khutbah for him, give him what he has asked for and save yourself war and fighting. We do not have strength to resist this sultan.' They all said the same, so Yildiz agreed to the demands, made the khutbah for Khwārazm Shāh, struck the coins in his name, sent him an elephant and returned his envoy to him, then went hunting.

Qutlugh Takīn, the governor of Ghazna, sent to Khwārazm Shāh, asking him to come, that he might surrender Ghazna to him. [**310**] Khwārazm Shāh made forced marches and arrived before any news of his move. Qutlugh Takīn surrendered Ghazna and its citadel to him. When he made his entry, he killed the members of the Ghurid army there, especially the Turks. The report of this reached Yildiz and he said, 'What has Qutlugh Takīn done? How could the citadel be taken when he was there?' He was told, 'He is the one who summoned him and surrendered to him.' Yildiz himself and his followers fled to Lahore. Khwārazm Shāh stayed at Ghazna and when he was in charge there, he summoned Qutlugh Takīn and asked him, 'How are you with Yildiz?' although he knew it. His only wish was to have some pretext against him. He replied, 'Both of us are mamlukes of Shihāb al-Dīn. Yildiz only remained in Ghazna four months in the summer. I had authority there. I was the person referred to in all matters.' Khwārazm Shāh continued, 'If you did

---

3 *Kāmil* (Thornberg), xii, 202, repeats 'grief' (*taraḥ*) here. For similar expression of irony and pessimism, also antithetical in content and chiastic in form, see *Chronicle of Ibn al-Athīr (2)*, p. [**371**].

not look after the interests of your comrade and the person who was a good friend to you and treated you with kindness, how will my position be with you and what would you do with my son, if I left him with you?'

He arrested him and took large sums of money from him, loading thirty beasts with all sorts of belongings and goods. He also had four hundred mamlukes brought to him. After he had taken his wealth, he put him to death. He then left his son, Jalāl al-Dīn, in Ghazna with a number of his troops and his emirs. It is reported that Khwārazm Shāh's taking of Ghazna happened in the year 613 [1216–17].

[311] How Yildiz took control of Lahore and then was killed

When Yildiz fled from Ghazna to Lahore, the latter's ruler, Nāṣir al-Dīn Qubāja, also one of Shihāb al-Dīn al-Ghūrī's mamlukes, faced him. His lands included Lahore, Multan, Uchch, Daybul and other places as far as the coast and he had about 15,000 mounted men. About 1,500 horse remained with Yildiz. Battle lines were drawn up between them and they fought. Both Yildiz's right and left wings were routed and the elephants he had were taken. He was left with only two elephants in his centre.

The mahout said, 'In that case I shall risk your good fortune,' and he ordered one of the two elephants to charge and seize the banner that Qubāja had and he ordered the other elephant which he also had to take the parasol that Qubāja had. This he also seized. A trained elephant understands what is said to it. I have seen this myself. Both elephants charged and Yildiz charged with them along with his remaining troops. He uncovered his head and said in Persian the equivalent of 'Either victory or destruction!' Both sides became intermingled. However, the two elephants did what their mahout ordered them, seizing the banner and the parasol, so Qubāja and his troops fled the field and Yildiz took the city of Lahore.

He then proceeded into Indian lands to take the city of Delhi and others that were held by Muslims. The ruler of Delhi was an emir called Iltutmish,[4] who bore the title Shams al-Dīn, a mamluke of Quṭb al-Dīn Aybak, who was himself another mamluke of Shihab al-Dīn and had become ruler of India after his master. [**312**] When Iltutmish heard this, he marched against him with all his troops and met him in battle near the town of Sāmāna.[5] Yildiz and his army were defeated and he was taken and put to death.

During his time as ruler Yildiz was praised for his conduct. He was very just and kind to his subjects, especially to merchants and foreigners. As an illustration of

---

4 For an account of his career, see *EI(2)*, iii, 1155–6. His name is given incorrectly in the text.

5 Correct the text's Samātā. Perhaps Sāmāna is intended, a place in the eastern Panjab (Jackson, *Delhi Sultanate*, see index and Map 3a on p. 131, where Sāmāna is encircled by Kuhrām, Sunnām and Sirhind).

his good practice, he had a tutor to instruct his sons. The tutor beat one of them [so hard] that he died. Yildiz summoned him and said, 'You wretch! What brought you to do this?' He replied, 'By God, my intention was only to chastise him. His death was an accident.' Yildiz said, 'You are right,' and he gave him money. 'Go abroad, for his mother will not be able to bear this. She will perhaps destroy you and I shall be unable to defend you.' When the child's mother heard of his death, she sought for the tutor to kill him but could not find him, and so he escaped. This is one of the best things to be related about anyone.

Miscellaneous events

During this year Wajīh al-Dīn al-Mubārak ibn Abī'l-Azhar Sa'īd ibn al-Dahhān al-Wāsiṭī, the blind grammarian, died. He was a clever and educated man, who studied with Kamāl al-Dīn ['Abd al-Raḥmān ibn Muḥammad][6] ibn al-Anbārī and others. He was a Ḥanbalī, who became a Ḥanafī and then a Shāfi'ī. Abū'l-Barakāt [Muḥammad][7] ibn Zayd al-Takrītī said of him:

> Is there anyone to convey a message to al-Wajīh for me,
> Although messages used not to be of much use with him?
> You adopted the school of al-Nu'mān[8] after Ḥanbal,
> Then abandoned him when you lacked things to eat.
> You did not choose Shāfi'ī's view for religious reasons,
> But you were grasping what was to hand.
> Soon, no doubt, you will be going
> To Mālik.[9] Understand well what I am saying.[10]

---

6 Supplied from *Wāfī*, xviii, 247.

7 His name is taken from Yāqūt, *Irshād*, vi, 236.

8 The personal name of Abū Ḥanīfa, after whom the Ḥanafī school of law is named.

9 A play on the name of the founder of the Mālikī school of law and that of the guardian of Hell.

10 The subject of the verses was in fact al-Mubārak ibn al-Mubārak ibn Sa'īd, Abū Bakr, born in 532 or 34/1137–38 or 1139–40 and died at Baghdad in Sha'bān (Abū Shāma, *Dhayl*, 90–91; *Wāfī*, xxv, 91–5, Sibṭ ibn al-Jawzī, 573). Yāqūt, *Irshād*, vi, 231–8, gives his death date as 16 Sha'bān/10 December 1215, although he also gives his year of birth as 502/1108–9 (!). Yāqūt also mentions the linguistic abilities of the man who was his teacher, a knowledge of Farsi, Turkish, 'Ḥabashī', Greek, Armenian and 'Zanjī'. The verses quoted here have been partially emended according to the text in *Wāfī*.

[313] The Year 613 [1216–1217]

Account of the death of al-Ẓāhir, lord of Aleppo

In Jumādā II this year [October 1216] al-Ẓāhir Ghāzī, son of Saladin and ruler of Aleppo, Manbij and other Syrian territories, died.[1] He had been ill with dysentery. He was a strong ruler who kept control of all his affairs and collected large sums of money from the customary sources. He was severe in punishing faults, giving no consideration to pardon. He was a cynosure for many, sought out by many members of great families from distant lands, poets, men of religion and others, whom he received with generosity and supplied with handsome pensions.

When his sickness worsened, he named as the ruler to follow him a young son of his, called Muḥammad. He was titled al-'Azīz Ghiyāth al-Dīn and was three years old. He turned his back on an older son, because the young one's mother was the daughter of his uncle, al-'Ādil Abū Bakr ibn Ayyūb, lord of Egypt, Damascus and other lands. He named him as his successor so that his uncle would keep the lands for him and not dispute them with him.

A surprising story that is told is that before his death al-Ẓāhir sent an envoy to his uncle al-'Ādil in Egypt, asking him to swear an oath to his young son. Al-'Ādil said, 'Heavens above! What need is there for this oath? Al-Ẓāhir is like one of my sons.' The envoy said, [**314**] 'He has requested this and chosen it as the best course. You must grant him this.' Al-'Ādil then said, 'How many a ram is in the field and how many a lamb at the butcher's!' He gave his oath.

At that time it came about that al-Ẓāhir died, while the envoy was on his travels. When al-Ẓāhir named his son as his successor, he appointed as his atabeg and his guardian a Rūmī[2] eunuch, called Ṭughril, who bore the title Shihāb al-Dīn, one of the virtuous servants of God and a man of much almsgiving and good works.

After al-Ẓāhir passed away, Shihāb al-Dīn ruled well over the people and exercised justice among them. He removed many current practices and gave back properties that had been taken from their owners. The education of the child he undertook in the best possible manner. He guarded his lands, and affairs proceeded well with his excellent rule and his justice. He gained control of what it had been impossible for al-Ẓāhir to take, for example, Tell Bāshir. Al-Ẓāhir was incapable of making hostile moves against it and after his death Kaykā'ūs, the ruler of Anatolia, took it, as we shall relate, God willing. It then changed hands and came

[1] He died on the eve of Tuesday 20 Jumādā II/4 October 1216 (Abū Shāma, *Dhayl*, 94).

[2] Rūmī could mean 'Greek' or generally denote an Anatolian connection. However, according to *Wafayāt*, vii, 100, Shihāb al-Dīn Abū Sa'īd Ṭughril was of Armenian race. He died at Aleppo on the eve of Monday 11 Muḥarram 631/17 October 1233.

to Shihāb al-Dīn. How ignominious for princes and the sons of princes that this lone foreigner should be a better ruler, more respectful of the property of the subjects and closer to virtue than they! Today among those that rule the affairs of the Muslims I do not know a better ruler than him. May God preserve and defend him. What I have heard about him is everything that is good and fine.

Miscellaneous events

This year in Muḥarram [20 April–19 May 1216] much hail fell at Basra. In addition to quantity, it was of great size. The smallest piece was like a large orange. People described the larger pieces in a way that one is ashamed [**315**] to mention. It broke many of the tops of palm trees.

Also in Muḥarram the Caliph al-Nāṣir li-Dīn Allāh sent the two sons of his son al-Mu'aẓẓam 'Alī, namely al-Mu'ayyad and al-Muwaffaq, to Tustar. With them went Mu'ayyad al-Dīn, the deputy vizier, and 'Izz al-Dīn the butler. They both remained there a while and then al-Muwaffaq returned with the vizier and the Butler to Baghdad towards the end of Rabī' II [ended 15 August 1216].

At Baghdad in Ṣafar [20 May–1216] a violent black wind blew with much dust and gloom, dropped a lot of sand and uprooted many trees. The people were fearful and implored God's help. It continued from the final evening prayer for a third of the night and then ceased.

This year Tāj al-Dīn Zayd ibn al-Ḥasan ibn Zayd al-Kindī, Abū'l-Yumn, died. He was born and raised in Baghdad, but moved to Syria and resided in Damascus. He was a leading scholar of grammar and lexicography. His transmission of Ḥadīth was of high authority. He possessed skill in many branches of various disciplines (God have mercy on him).[3]

---

[3] Born 25 Sha'bān 520/15 September 1126, died Monday 6 Shawwāl/16 January 1217. His personal library, which was made a *waqf* and stored in the Umayyad Mosque, consisted of 761 volumes, broken down as follows: Koran studies 140; Ḥadīth 19; law 39, language/lexicography 143; poetry 122; grammar/syntax 175; 'studies of the ancients', e.g. medicine, 123. They were later taken out, lost or sold, secretly and openly (Abū Shāma, *Dhayl*, 95–9). Yāqūt, *Irshād*, iv, 222–3, attributes less longevity, giving the year of his death as 597/1200–1201.

[316] The Year 614 [1217–1218]

How Khwārazm Shāh took the Uplands

This year Khwārazm Shāh 'Alā' al-Dīn Muḥammad ibn Tekesh marched to the Uplands and conquered them. Various things were behind his expedition at this time. One was that he had taken control of Transoxania and defeated the Qarakhitay, so that his status and power were great and people near and far gave him allegiance. Another was that he was eager to have the khutbah in his name at Baghdad and to be entitled sultan. The actual situation was the opposite since he found no acceptance from the Caliphal Diwan. The likelihood was that, if he came to Baghdad, another would be given precedence over him. In his army there were possibly a hundred fit to be the one granted access before him. When he heard that, it made him angry.

Another reason was that, when Ighlamish took the Uplands, he had made the khutbah in Khwārazm Shāh's name in all the towns, as we have mentioned. When Ighlamish was slain by the Ismā'īlīs, Khwārazm Shāh was outraged for him and took the field so that the lands would not leave his allegiance. He set out on forced marches with an army that filled the earth and came to Rayy, which he conquered.

When Atabeg Sa'd ibn Dakalā, lord of Fars, heard of the killing of Ighlamish, he gathered his troops and marched to the Uplands, eager to take them because they were devoid of any protector or defender. He arrived at Isfahan and the population submitted to him. From there he set out towards Rayy but he did not know that Khwārazm Shāh had arrived. He was met by Khwārazm Shāh's advance guard and thought that they were the troops of that region that had assembled [**317**] to fight him and drive him away. He engaged them and fought them stoutly until he almost put them to flight.

While this was the state of affairs, he suddenly caught sight of Khwārazm Shāh's parasol. He enquired about it, was told the truth, so gave up. His troops fled and he was taken prisoner. Taken before Khwārazm Shāh, he was received with honour and promised fair and handsome treatment. His personal security was guaranteed and an oath of allegiance was taken from him. Agreement was reached between them that he should surrender some of his lands to Khwārazm Shāh and retain part of them. Khwārazm Shāh then released him and sent an army with him to Fars for him to surrender to them what had been agreed upon. When he came to his eldest son, he saw that he had seized power in Fars and refused to give it up to his father. Subsequently he became ruler over the lands, as we shall narrate, and he made the khutbah there for Khwārazm Shāh.

Khwārazm Shāh went to Saveh, took it and then assigned it as a fief to 'Imād al-Dīn, the inspector of his army, who was a local inhabitant. Next he went to

Qazwin, Zanjan and Abhar, all of which he took with no resistance or opposition, and then to Hamadhan, which he also took. He assigned these lands to his followers. He took Isfahan and also Qumm and Qashan. He achieved power throughout all the lands and he and Uzbek ibn Pahlawan, lord of Azerbayjan and Arran, came to an agreement that Uzbek should name him in the khutbah in his lands and submit to him.

He then resolved to march to Baghdad and sent in advance a great emir with 15,000 horse. He gave him Ḥulwan as a fief, to which he eventually came, and then Khwārazm Shāh dispatched another emir to follow him. When he had gone two or three days' journey from Hamadhan, he was caught by an unheard-of snowfall. Their mounts perished and many of the men died. The Turkish Banū Barjam and the Kurdish Banū Hakkār were tempted to attack them. They harrassed them and those that returned to Khwārazm **[318]** Shāh were only very few.[1] Khwārazm Shāh drew a bad omen from this expedition and, fearful of the Tatars,[2] decided to return to Khurasan, because he had thought that he would complete his business and achieve his plans in a short period of time, but his expectation was disappointed and he saw a long campaign before him. He therefore decided to return. As governor of Hamadhan he left an emir, a relative of his on his mother's side, called Ṭā'īsī.[3] In charge of all the lands he put his son Rukn al-Dīn[4] and he placed with him as effective ruler 'Imād al-Dīn from Saveh, who was highly regarded by him and eager to attack Iraq.

Khwārazm Shāh returned to Khurasan, arriving at Marv in Muḥarram of the year 615 [April 1218]. Some men he directed to proceed to Transoxania and they set out on their way. When he had come to Nishapur, he sat one Friday at the minbar and ordered the preacher to drop the khutbah for the Caliph al-Nāṣir li-Dīn Allāh, saying, 'He is dead.' That was in Dhū'l-Qa'da 614 [February 1218]. When he came to Marv, he discontinued the khutbah there and likewise in Balkh, Bukhara and Sarakhs. In Khwārazm, Samarqand and Herat the khutbah was still not discontinued, unless by a deliberate decision to drop it, because these cities did not avoid such matters as this; if they wanted to, they made the khutbah, and if they wished, they dropped it. The towns continued as they were until his eventual fate.[5]

This is counted among the blessings of this noble Abbasid house; nobody has intended to do it harm without himself suffering from his actions and his plan going awry. No wonder that it was not long before this Khwārazm Shāh was

---

1 For this disastrous attempt to march on Baghdad with 400,000 or 600,000 men (sic), see Abū Shāma, *Dhayl*, 100–101.

2 According to Juvainī, *History*, ii, 367, it was at this time that Khwārazm Shāh heard about the incident at Utrar (see below, pp. [**361–2**]).

3 Cf. the Mongol commander Taisi (Ṭaysy), a name meaning 'prince' from Chinese via Uighur (Juvainī, *History*, i, 144, note 4).

4 His name was Ghūr-Sanji. He was later killed by the Mongols after having been besieged in Fīrūzkūh (Juvainī, *History*, ii, 368, 474–6).

5 The Caliph al-Nāṣir died in 622/1225.

overwhelmed by what we shall relate, the like of which this world has never heard tell of in either former or recent times.

[319] Account of what happened to Atabeg Sa'd with his children

After the killing of Ighlamish, lord of the Uplands, Hamadhan and Isfahan and the territory between them, Atabeg Sa'd ibn Dakalā, lord of Fars, gathered his troops and set out from his lands to Isfahan. He took it and received the submission of its population. He then had ambitions for all these lands, so marched from Isfahan to Rayy. When he reached it, he met the troops of Khwārazm Shāh, who had just arrived, as we have related. He decided to engage the advance guard of this army and fought them until he almost defeated them, but the full forces of Khwārazm Shāh appeared. Sa'd saw the parasol and despaired. He cast himself down, his and his army's strength being too weak. They turned their backs in flight and Atabeg Sa'd was taken prisoner. He was brought before Khwārazm Shāh, who received him with honour and bade him be of good heart, promising him kind treatment. He took him with him to Isfahan and from there sent him to his lands, which were adjacent, accompanied by an army and a great emir who was to take over what had been agreed between them, for they had agreed that Khwārazm Shāh should have some of the lands and Atabeg Sa'd some also but that the khutbah should be in Khwārazm Shāh's name throughout all the lands.

Atabeg Sa'd had left a son of his as deputy in the country. When the son heard of his father's captivity, he proclaimed himself ruler in the khutbah and discontinued that of his father. After his father's arrival in the company of Khwārazm Shāh's army, the son refused to give up the lands to his father, gathered troops and moved out to fight him. When the two forces came in sight of one another, the troops of Fars sided with their lord, Atabeg Sa'd, and left his son with his personal guard. He charged his father and the latter, when he saw him, thought that he had not recognized him. He said to him, 'I **[320]** am Sa'd,'[6] but his son replied, 'It is you I seek!' At this, he fought back and put his son to flight.

Sa'd arrived and made his victorious entry. He took his son prisoner and has kept him in prison until now. However, I have heard at the present time, namely the year 620 [1223], that he has mitigated his imprisonment and made him comfortable.

After Khwārazm Shāh had returned to Khurasan, Sa'd was false to the emir who was left with him. He killed him and renounced his allegiance to Khwārazm Shāh, who was preoccupied with the great crisis which took his attention away from Sa'd and everything else. Nevertheless, God revenged him through his son Ghiyāth al-Dīn, as we have mentioned under the year 620 [1223], because Sa'd rejected

---

6 The text has 'I am so-and-so (*fūlān*)', referring to the name known and understood, but a literal translation is unacceptable in English.

Khwārazm Shāh's kindness and the rejection of kindness brings great punishment.[7]

Account of the arrival of Franks in Syria, their journey to Egypt, their conquest of[8] the city of Damietta and its return to the Muslims

This crisis from its beginning until its end lasted four years, less one month. We have mentioned it here because this was the year they made their appearance and we have made an unbroken narrative of it so that its various parts can follow one another.

This year Frankish reinforcements arrived by sea from Rome and other places in Frankish lands, east and west. The organizer of them was the Pope of Rome,[9] because he holds a high status in Franks' eyes. They hold that his orders should not be disobeyed nor his ordinances diverged from whether in weal or woe. He equipped armies of his own, led by several Frankish commanders, and ordered other Frankish princes either to go in person or to send an army. They did [**321**] what he ordered and assembled at Acre on the Syrian coast.

Al-'Ādil Abū Bakr ibn Ayyūb was in Egypt. He set out for Syria and came to Ramla, and from there to Lydda. The Franks moved out of Acre to attack him and al-'Ādil also marched towards them. He arrived at Nablus, intending to get to the frontiers of his lands near Acre before them, to defend them against them. The Franks, however, set out and arrived before them. Al-'Ādil made camp at Baysan in the Jordan Valley. The Franks advanced towards him during Sha'bān [November 1217] with the intention of bringing him to battle as they knew that he had few troops because they were scattered throughout his lands.

When al-'Ādil saw that they were near, he thought that he would not face them with the detachment he had for fear that he would meet with a defeat. He was prudent and very cautious, so he left Baysan to move towards Damascus to wait nearby and send to his lands to gather troops. He then came to Marj al-Ṣuffar and camped there.

When the people of Baysan and those regions saw al-'Ādil with them, they felt confident, so did not leave their lands, thinking that the Franks would not come against them. When they did advance, al-'Ādil left, taking the locals by surprise, only a few of whom were able to seek safety. The Franks took all the supplies that had been collected in Baysan and they were substantial. They seized a good deal of booty and plundered the area from Baysan to Nablus. They sent out raiding parties to the villages, which reached as far as Khisfīn, Nawā and the border areas. They descended upon Banyās, remained for three days and then retired to the Acre

[7] The repetition in this section of much that is found in the preceding section may well indicate lack of a final revision.

[8] The rubric up to this point is missing in the edition. A whole line of the text has been omitted. Cf. *Kāmil* (Thornberg), xii, 208.

[9] i.e. Pope Innocent III (1198–1216), who revitalized the Crusading movement.

plain with their booty, captives and prisoners of war beyond numbering. This is apart from those they killed and what they burned and destroyed. They remained for several days taking their rest.

Then they came to Tyre with Beaufort as their objective. They made camp about two leagues distant from Banyās [**322**] and plundered the area, Sidon and Beaufort, before returning to Acre. All this occurred between the middle of Ramaḍān and the Feast[10] [16–31 December 1217]. Any survivor from those lands had to be nimble and unencumbered to be able to escape.

I have heard that, when al-'Ādil went to Marj al-Ṣuffar, on the way he saw a man carrying a load, who was walking for a while and then sitting down to rest. Al-'Ādil, by himself, turned aside to him and said, 'Old man, do not hurry. Take care of yourself.' The man recognized him and replied, 'O sultan of the Muslims, you may not hurry yourself! But when we see you have set out for your lands and left us to the enemy, why should we not be in a hurry!'

Taken altogether, what al-'Ādil did was prudent and for the best, in order not to risk an encounter when his troops were scattered. After al-'Ādil had camped at Marj al-Ṣuffar, he sent his son al-Mu'aẓẓam 'Īsā, lord of Damascus, with a good-sized detachment of the army to Nablus to protect Jerusalem from the Franks.

Account of the Franks' siege and destruction of Ṭūr castle

After the Franks had camped in the plain of Acre, they made their preparations, took with them siege equipment, such as trebuchets and the like, and marched to Ṭūr castle, which was a strong fortress, constructed recently by al-'Ādil, on the summit of a hill near Acre. Having made their way to it and put it under siege, they carried out an assault and climbed the hill until they reached its wall. They almost took it, but then it chanced that one of the Muslim defenders killed a certain prince of the Franks, so they retired from the castle, left it alone and set out towards Acre. Their stay there had lasted seventeen days.[11] [**323**] After their departure from Ṭūr, they remained a short while and then travelled by sea to Egypt, as we shall narrate, if God Almighty wills. Al-Mu'aẓẓam proceeded to Ṭūr and razed it to the ground because it was in the vicinity of Acre and difficult to hold.

How the Franks besieged Damietta and eventually took it

After the Franks had returned from the siege of Ṭūr, they remained at Acre until

---

[10] i.e. the *'īd al-fiṭr* on 1 Shawwāl, the celebration to mark the end of the Ramaḍān fast.

[11] This agrees with the dates given by Sibṭ ibn al-Jawzī, as quoted by Abū Shāma, *Dhayl*, 102–3; arrival on Wednesday 18 Sha'bān/22 November 1217 (although Sibṭ ibn al-Jawzī, 584–5, probably in error, gives 28 Sha'bān); departure on Thursday 6 Ramaḍān/ 8 December. Cf. other sources in Stevenson, *Crusaders*, 302, note 2.

the beginning of the year 615 [began 30 March 1218] and then they travelled to Damietta by sea, arriving in Ṣafar [29 April–27 May 1218]. They made anchor on the peninsula's bank,[12] separated from Damietta by the Nile, for a branch of the Nile flows into the sea[13] at Damietta. A large strong tower had been built in the Nile, in which they had installed strong iron chains and stretched them across the Nile to the walls of Damietta to prevent any ships that arrived by sea from proceeding up the Nile into Egypt. Had it not been for this tower and these chains nobody would have been able to keep the enemy's ships out of any part of Egypt, near or far.

After the Franks had disembarked on the peninsula, separated by the Nile from Damietta, they built a defensive wall and made a ditch to guard them from attacks. They began to engage the garrison in Damietta and they made siege equipment, *maramma*s[14] and towers to use them on their ships for attacks on that [Chain] tower with the aim of taking it by assault. The tower was well garrisoned with men. Al-Kāmil ibn al-'Ādil, [**324**] who was the ruler in Egypt,[15] had made camp at a place known as al-'Ādiliyya in the vicinity of Damietta, while sending a series of reinforcements to Damietta to prevent the enemy crossing over to its side.

The Franks persevered with successive attacks on the tower but achieved nothing. Their *maramma*s and siege engines were smashed[16] and yet, nevertheless, they kept up their assaults. They continued thus for four months but were unable to take it. When they did finally overcome it, they cut the chains to allow their vessels to enter the Nile from the open sea and for them to gain control of the land [outside the city]. To replace the chains al-Kāmil prepared a large pontoon bridge which stopped their access to the Nile, so then they fought over that too, an intense, hard fight without respite, until they eventually cut it. After it had been cut, al-Kāmil took a number of large ships, filled them up, holed them and sank them in the Nile. The Frankish ships were thus prevented from entering the river.

Seeing this, the Franks turned their attention to a channel there, known as the Blue [Channel], where the main Nile had flowed in olden times. They dug and deepened that channel upstream of the ships that had been scuttled in the Nile and

---

[12] Arabic: *barr al-jīza*. *Jīza* refers to the point of land, having the Nile on one side and the sea on the other, opposite Damietta, sometimes called *jīzat Dimyāṭ*. I translate it as 'peninsula', following Gottschalk, *al-Malik al-Kāmil*, 60.

[13] The text here and elsewhere has *al-baḥr al-māliḥ*, 'the salt sea', to differentiate it from the Nile, which is commonly known as *al-baḥr*, 'the sea'.

[14] Arabic plural: *marammāt*. The Franks put together six *maramma*s, each described as a composite vessel formed by linking two ships together. Attacking towers, with drop-down gangways, were built around the masts (see Blochet, 'Patriarches', 242; Gottschalk, *al-Malik al-Kāmil*, 77).

[15] Initially he was al-'Ādil's deputy. For the fullest account of his career, see Gottschalk, *al-Malik al-Kāmil*.

[16] According to other accounts, winds blew some ships to the east bank and they were burnt by the Muslims.

they got water to flow in it to the open sea. They brought their vessels up to a place called Būra,[17] also on the peninsula side, opposite the position where al-Kāmil was, so that they could engage him from there. This was because they had no route by which they could come to grips with him, as Damietta was a barrier separating them from him. When they established themselves at Būra, they came opposite him and fought him on water. They attacked more than once but gained no advantage.

Meanwhile, nothing had changed for the population of Damietta, because supplies and reinforcements reached them uninterruptedly and the Nile was a barrier between them and the Franks. They remained defiant, untouched by any harm. The gates of the city were still open and it was suffering no hardship or damage from the siege.

It then happened, as God (mighty and glorious is He) willed, that al-ʻĀdil died in Jumādā II in the year 615 [August 1218], as we shall relate, God willing.[18] The spirits of the people weakened, because he was the sultan in fact and his sons, although they were princes, were under his authority and he controlled affairs. He was the one who had made them princes in the lands. His death occurred just when the state of affairs in the fight against the enemy was as it has been described.

[**325**] Among the emirs in Egypt was one called ʻImād al-Dīn Aḥmad ibn ʻAlī, known as Ibn al-Mashṭūb,[19] a Hakkārī Kurd, who was the greatest emir in Egypt and had a numerous following. All the emirs followed his lead and obeyed him, particularly the Kurds. He reached an agreement with other emirs, in a plan to depose al-Kāmil from power and to set up his brother al-Fa'iz ibn al-ʻĀdil, so that they might gain authority over him and the country. Al-Kāmil heard of this, so abandoned his camp at night, leaving his baggage train. He went to a village called Ashmūm Ṭannāḥ and camped there. In the morning the army found their sultan gone. Each person followed his own inclination and nobody concerned himself with anyone else.[20] They were only able to take a little of their tents, stores, property and weapons, that which was light to carry. They left the rest, provisions, weapons, mounts, tents and such-like, just as it was and caught up with al-Kāmil.

As for the Franks, when the next day dawned, they saw none of the Muslims on the Nile bank, as they normally were, and they were left not knowing what had happened. Then there came to them people who told them the true state of affairs. Thereupon they crossed the Nile to the Damietta side, safely and without any opposition or resistance. Their crossing was on 20 Dhū'l-Qaʻda 615 [7 February 1219]. They seized as booty what was in the Muslims' camp. It was a great amount, beyond the powers of those who tried to quantify it.

---

[17] Yāqūt, i, 755. Būra was clearly on the west or left bank of this branch of the Nile.

[18] See below, p. [**350**], where 7 Jumādā II/31 August is the date given.

[19] His father, a great emir under Saladin, was Sayf al-Dīn ʻAlī, known as al-Mashṭūb (Scarface or, as in the western sources, Le Balafré). For a survey of the lives of both his father and ʻImād al-Dīn himself, see Minorsky, *Studies*, 144–6.

[20] Literally 'no brother stopped for his brother'.

Al-Kāmil was about to abandon Egypt because he did not trust any of his troops and the Franks had all but taken everything without any trouble or difficulty, when it chanced by the favour of God Almighty to the Muslims that al-Mu'aẓẓam 'Īsā ibn al-'Ādil came to his brother al-Kāmil two days after this development, when the people were in a state of disorder. His heart was strengthened by his coming, his back stiffened and his spirit made steady, so he remained in his position. They expelled Ibn al-Mashṭūb to Syria. He then joined with al-Ashraf and became part of his army.

[**326**] After the Franks had crossed to the Damietta bank, the Bedouin gathered in all their various tribes and plundered the area in the neighbourhood of Damietta, cut the road and caused mayhem to an exceptional degree. They were worse for the Muslims than the Franks were, and the most damaging thing for the inhabitants of Damietta was that none of the army was there, because the sultan and the troops with him had been nearby, defending it from the enemy, then this commotion came upon them unexpectedly and no troops had gone into the city. This was all the doing of Ibn al-Mashṭūb. No wonder God did not give him much more time but 'punished him with a punishment exceeding [others]'[21] as we shall narrate, God willing.

The Franks surrounded Damietta and engaged it by land and by sea. They dug a ditch to guard themselves against any Muslims who might attack them. This was their normal practice. They kept up their assaults and the situation became serious for the inhabitants. Food and other things became difficult to find and they were tired of the constant fighting, because the Franks were able to fight them in shifts on account of their large numbers, while in Damietta there were not enough men to be able to organize the fighting by rota. Nevetheless, they persevered in a way that was unheard of. Many of them were killed and wounded or passed away or fell ill. They endured the siege until 27 Sha'bān of the year 616 [7 November 1219][22] but then the surviving inhabitants were unable to hold out because they were so few and food was impossible to obtain. On that date they surrendered the city to the Franks on terms. Some people left, while others remained because they were too weak to move. Thus were they scattered to the four winds.

How the Muslims took Damietta from the Franks

After the Franks had captured Damietta, they remained there but sent out their squadrons throughout all the regions near them to plunder and kill. Their populations abandoned them. The Franks embarked on repairing and fortifying Damietta and went so far in this that it was left unassailable.

---

[21] Koran, lxix, 10.

[22] The fall of the city is dated to Tuesday 5 November in Stevenson, *Crusaders*, 304 and see the listing of variant dates in note 4. See also below, p. [**357**].

[**327**] Al-Kāmil remained close to them on the confines of his territory to defend it. When the Franks in their homelands heard of the conquest of Damietta at the hands of their fellows, they hurried to join them 'from every deep valley'.[23] It became the goal of their emigration. Al-Malik al-Mu'aẓẓam returned to Syria and demolished [the walls of] Jerusalem. He did this because people without exception were fearful of the Franks. Islam and all its people and its lands were on the point of foundering both in the east and the west. The Tatars had come from the eastern lands and reached districts of Iraq, Azerbayjan, Arran and elsewhere, as we shall narrate, God willing. The Franks came from the west and had conquered a city the like of Damietta in Egypt, not to mention the fact that there were no fortresses to defend the country from its enemies. Thus all the lands in Egypt and Syria were on the point of being overcome and all the people were fearful of them and had come to expect disaster at any time.[24] The population of Egypt wanted to evacuate their land for fear of the enemy, 'but it was not a time to escape',[25] for the enemy had encompassed them on every side. Had al-Kāmil allowed them to do this, they would have left the land [in ruins], 'collapsed on its roof timbers', but they were prevented from doing this and stood firm.

Al-Kāmil sent letter after letter to his brothers, al-Mu'aẓẓam, lord of Damascus, and al-Ashraf Mūsā ibn al-'Ādil, lord of Mesopotamia, Armenia and elsewhere, asking them for reinforcements and urging them to come in person. If that was not possible, they should sent troops to him. The lord of Damascus went in person to al-Ashraf at Ḥarrān and saw that he was too preoccupied by opposing interests that threatened him to be able to give them any assistance and also by the loss of the loyalty of many who had been loyal to him. We shall give an account of this under the year 615 [1218–19], God willing, in connection with the death of al-Qāhir, lord of Mosul. The reader will find it there. Al-Mu'aẓẓam accepted his excuse and returned. Meanwhile the situation with the Franks remained unchanged. [**328**] In fact, the dissensions disappeared from the lands of al-Ashraf and the princes who were in rebellion against him returned to his allegiance. By the year 618 [1221–2] his position was firmly re-established, while al-Kāmil was still facing the Franks.

At the beginning of 618 [began 25 February 1221] al-Kāmil heard that the obstacles to al-Ashraf's assisting him had been removed, so he sent asking for reinforcements from him and his brother, the lord of Damascus. The latter, al-Mu'aẓẓam, went to al-Ashraf to urge him to set out, which he did and marched to Damascus with the troops he had with him. He ordered the remainder to join him at Damascus, where he remained for a while to wait for them. Some of his emirs and close advisers suggested to him that he should send the troops but himself return to his lands for fear of any dispute that might occur in his absence,

---

[23] Koran, xxii, 27. The original context is that of pilgrims flocking to Mecca.

[24] Literally 'any morning or evening'.

[25] Koran, xxxviii, 2.

but he did not accept what they said. 'I have set out on the Jihad,' he said, 'and it is essential to fulfil this intention.' He proceeded to Egypt.

The Franks had marched out of Damietta with their horse and foot and moved against al-Kāmil, taking up camp opposite him with a channel of the Nile, called the Ashmūm branch, separating them. They were shooting with trebuchets and crossbows into the Muslim army and they and everyone were convinced that they were going to conquer Egypt.

Al-Ashraf completed his march to Egypt and when his brother al-Kāmil heard that he was near, he went to meet him and he and all other Muslims rejoiced that they had joined forces in the hope that God would bring about a victory and some success thereby. As for al-Mu'aẓẓam, he also marched to Egypt and he made for Damietta, thinking that his two brothers and their armies had already invested it. A different version says that he was informed on his way that the Franks had set out [back] to Damietta and he tried to get there before them to meet them from the front while his two brothers were in their rear, but God knows best!

[**329**] After al-Ashraf had joined al-Kāmil, it was agreed between them that they should advance to the channel of the Nile, known as the al-Maḥalla branch. They did so and battled with the Franks, as they had now become closer. The Muslim galleys moved up on the Nile and, having clashed with the Franks' galleys, took three of their vessels along with the men on board and the money and armaments they contained. The Muslims rejoiced at this and were delighted, taking it as a good omen. Their spirits rose and they gained the upper hand over their enemy.

While this was taking place, envoys were going to and fro between them to establish the basis of peace. The Muslims offered them the surrender of Jerusalem, Ascalon, Tiberias, Sidon, Jabala, Lattakia and all that Saladin had conquered from the Franks on the coast, which has been recorded previously, not including Kerak, if they would give up Damietta. They did not agree and asked for 300,000 dinars in recompense for the destruction of Jerusalem so that they could use that sum to rebuild it. Nothing was settled between them. The Franks also said, 'We must have Kerak.'

While this was the situation, with the Franks holding out, the Muslims were forced to fight them. The Franks, because of their overconfidence, had not brought with them sufficient food for a number of days, imagining that the Muslim armies would not stand against them and that the settlements and the hinterland would all be left in their hands, so that they could take from them all the provisions they wanted, all this because of a plan that God Almighty had in mind for them. A detachment of Muslims crossed to the terrain the Franks were on. They opened the Nile sluices and the water inundated most of that land. The Franks were left with nowhere to go except one direction, which was confined. At that time al-Kāmil put in place the pontoon bridge on the Nile at Ashmūm and the troops crossed over it. Thus he took control of the route the Franks would follow, if they wished to return to Damietta, and there was no way of escape left to them.

At this juncture it happened that a large vessel of the Franks, one of the largest ships, called a *maramma*, came to them, escorted by a number of *ḥarrāqas*.[26] All of them were loaded with provisions and armaments [**330**] and things they needed. The Muslims' galleys fell upon them and brought them to battle. They overcame the *maramma* and its accompanying *ḥarrāqa*s and seized them. Seeing this, the Franks despaired and realized that they had been misguided to leave Damietta in country they were ignorant of.

Meanwhile, the Muslim troops were surrounding them, shooting arrows at them and charging their flanks. When the situation became serious for the Franks, they burnt their tents, trebuchets and baggage, and intended to advance against the Muslims and engage them, in the hope that they would be able to get back to Damietta. However, they saw that what they hoped for was a remote chance. They were prevented from gaining what they desired because of the mud and waters around them. The way they were able to march was already held by the Muslims.

When they became convinced that they were surrounded on all sides and supplies were unable to get to them and that fate had bared its fangs at them, their morale collapsed, their crosses were broken and their Satan deserted them. They contacted al-Kāmil and al-Ashraf asking for terms to surrender Damietta with nothing in return. While the negotiations were taking place, a large host approached with much dust and great tumult from the direction of Damietta. The Muslims thought that reinforcements for the Franks had arrived, so they were apprehensive. Suddenly it was seen to be al-Mu'aẓẓam, lord of Damascus, who had arrived. He had taken a route via Damietta, because of what we have mentioned. The dominance of the Muslims grew while the Franks became more defeatist and exhausted. They concluded peace in return for the surrender of Damietta. The agreement and the swearing of oaths were completed on 7 Rajab 618 [27 August 1221]. The princes of the Franks, their counts and nobles went to al-Kāmil and al-Ashraf as hostages for the surrender of Damietta, namely the ruler of Acre,[27] the representative of the Pope of Rome,[28] Count Rīsh (?) and others, twenty princes in all. They wrote to their priests and monks at Damietta to effect the surrender, and the men there did not refuse but surrendered it to the Muslims on 9 Rajab [29 August 1221].[29] It was a day to remember!

[**331**] A wondrous thing is that, when the Muslims took over the city, reinforcements for the Franks arrived by sea. Had they preceded the Muslims, they would have refused to surrender it, but the Muslims arrived first in order that God might fulfil a matter that was destined to be done. Only odd individuals remained there of its population. They had been scattered to the four winds; some had left by choice, some had died and some had been taken by the Franks.

---

26 The etymology would suggest that *ḥarrāqa* meant 'a fire ship'. However, in general use it denoted a small, swift vessel.

27 The titular king of Jerusalem, John of Brienne.

28 This was the papal legate, Cardinal Pelagius of Albano.

29 Ibn al-Athīr's dating is questionable. The agreement was signed on Monday 30 August and Damietta surrendered on Wednesday 8 September; see Stevenson, *Crusaders*, 306–7.

When the Muslims entered the city, they saw that the Franks had mightily fortified it, so that it was left unassailable and unreachable. However, God (glorious and mighty is He) restored the Truth to its proper place and gave it back to its rightful owners. He gave the Muslims a victory that they had not reckoned on, for all they had hoped for had been to yield the lands that had been taken from the Franks in Syria to recover Damietta. God, however, granted them the recovery of Damietta while those lands remained in their hands as they were. God is to be praised and thanked for his grace towards Islam and the Muslims in frustrating this enemy's aggression. He also saved them from the evil of the Tatars, as we shall record, God willing.[30]

Miscellaneous events

In Muḥarram [10 April–9 May] of this year [614/1217] there was dissension at Baghdad between the inhabitants of al-Ma'mūniyya and those of Azaj Gate because of the killing of a lion.[31] The trouble between them grew and they fought, leading to the wounding of many. The deputy officer of the [Palace] Gate came and restrained them but they would not accept that and used some disagreeable language towards him. An emir, one of the caliph's mamlukes, was sent from the Diwan, who made the inhabitants of each quarter return to their quarter and so the disturbance quietened down.

This year there were many rats in the town of Dujayl in the district of Baghdad. A man was not able [**332**] to sit down without having a stick to keep the rats away. Great numbers of them were clearly to be seen, following one another.

This year the Tigris rose greatly in a way that had never been witnessed in olden days. Baghdad was on the brink of inundation. The vizier, the emirs and all the notables rode out and gathered a great crowd of the common people and others to work on the dykes around the city. The people were anxious and very disturbed, looking destruction in the face. They made ready boats to save themselves. The caliph made a public appearance and urged on the work. One of the things he said to them was, 'If what I see could be bought off with money or anything else, I would do it. If it could be repelled by arms, I would do it, but God's decree is not to be averted.'

The water rose up from the drains and wells on the East Side and much of it was flooded. The shrine of Abū Ḥanīfa, part of Ruṣāfa, the mosque of al-Mahdī, the village of al-Malakiyya and the Kiosk were all flooded and prayers were discontinued in the Sultan's mosque. As for the West Side, most of al-Qurayya, 'Īsā

30 On the face of it this is an unexpected comment but it reflects Ibn al-Athīr's belief that, except for the far Islamic east, the Mongol incursion was a passing phenomenon. Cf. below, p. [**399**].

31 This is another inexplicable incident.

Canal and al-Shaṭiyyāt were destroyed and the orchards, the shrine of the Straw Gate, the cemetery of Aḥmad ibn Ḥanbal, the Ṭāhirī Harem, part of Basra Gate, the houses on the ʿĪsā Canal and most of the quarter of Quṭuftā were ruined.

This year Aḥmad ibn Abī'l-Faḍā'il ʿAbd al-Munʿim ibn Abī'l-Barakāt Muḥammad ibn Ṭāhir ibn Saʿīd ibn Faḍl Allāh ibn Saʿīd ibn Abī'l-Khayr al-Mayhanī, Abū'l-Faḍl, the Sufi, shaykh of the caliph's hospice at Baghdad, died. He was a pious man from a family of Sufis and pious men.[32]

[32] Bahā' al-Dīn Aḥmad's father was Chief Shaykh and head of the Sufis at Baghdad. Aḥmad was shaykh of the Khilāṭiyya hospice and administered its endowments. He ended his life in disgrace due to his slave embezzling some money and the involvement of his own sister. He died on 8 Rajab/11 October 1217 (Sibṭ ibn al-Jawzī, 586, and Abū Shāma, *Dhayl*, 103).

[333] The Year 615 [1218–1219]

Account of the death of al-Qāhir, the accession of his son Nūr al-Dīn and the dissensions that occurred because of his death until affairs became settled

This year al-Qāhir 'Izz al-Dīn Mas'ūd ibn Arslān Shāh ibn Mas'ūd ibn Mawdūd ibn Zankī ibn Āqsunqur, lord of Mosul, died on the eve of Monday 3 days from the end of Rabī' I [= 25 June 1218]. His rule had lasted seven years and nine months.

The cause of his death was that he was seized by a fever, which left him on the next day. He remained weakened for two days and then the fever returned, accompanied by much vomiting, great distress and continuous anxiety. His body then became cold and he sweated. This continued to be his condition until the middle of the night and then he passed away.

He was generous and mild with little desire for the wealth of his subjects, and he avoided causing them any harm. He used to indulge in his pleasures as though he was snatching them and hurrying to enjoy them before he died. He was a man of intense sensitivity and was often talking of death.

A person who was close to him told me the following: 'One night two weeks before his death we were with him and he said to me, "I feel bored with sitting here. Get up and let us stroll to the 'Imādī Gate." We got up and he left his palace in the direction of the 'Imādī Gate. He came to the mausoleum he had built for himself near his palace. He halted near it, lost in thought and not speaking. Then he said to me, [**334**] "By God, we are nothing! Do we not all end up here, buried under the ground?" He spoke for a long time about this and similar matters, then returned to his palace. I said to him, "Shall we not walk to the 'Imādī Gate?" He replied, "I have no energy left for this or anything else." He entered his palace and died a few days later.'

The people of his lands were dismayed by his death and they felt his loss keenly, for he was beloved by them and close to their hearts. There was wailing and lamentation in every household for his sake. When his demise was imminent, he bequeathed kingly power to his eldest son, Nūr al-Dīn Arslān Shāh [II], who was about ten years old at that time. He appointed as his guardian and regent Badr al-Dīn Lu'lu', who was the person who was in charge during the reign of al-Qāhir and that of his father Nūr al-Dīn before him. Some account of him has preceded, enough for his standing to be known, and more will be given that will increase the reader's insight into him.

After he passed away Badr al-Dīn undertook Nūr al-Dīn [Arslān Shāh's] affairs and seated him on the throne of his father. He sent to the caliph asking for a diploma and mark of investiture for him and sent to the princes, the rulers of the neighbouring provinces, requesting them to renew their recognition of Nūr al-Dīn on the same basis that had been between them and his father. Before the dawning of the day he had completed all that was necessary. He then held a session of condolence and took the oaths of the army and the subjects. He secured the kingdom from disturbance and upheaval, despite the youth of the sultan and the great number of aspirants for kingship, for with him in the city were his father's uncles and his uncle 'Imād al-Dīn Zankī ibn Arslān Shāh was in his seat of power, namely the castle of 'Aqr al-Ḥumaydiyya, persuading himself that he could be ruler and not doubting that the position of ruler should come to him after his brother. Badr al-Dīn patched up that hole and repaired that crack. He showered bounty and gifts of robes of honour on all, and got them to put aside their robes of mourning. In this he did not single out any noble before any commoner, nor any great man rather than any small. He ruled well and held sessions to uncover people's misdeeds and to achieve justice for some from others.

After some days the diploma that recognized his rule arrived for Nūr al-Dīn from the caliph and for Badr al-Dīn as overseer [**335**] of the affairs of state. Robes of honour for both also arrived. Envoys from the princes came to them both with messages of condolence and offering the recognition that was asked for. The two of them became firmly established.

How 'Imād al-Dīn took the Hakkārī castles and Zūzan

In connection with the death of Nūr al-Dīn [Arslān Shāh I] in the year 607 [1211] we mentioned that he gave his youngest son Zankī the two castles of 'Aqr and Shūsh, both of them close to Mosul. One moment he was in Mosul and the next in his own domain, finding fault because of his frequent changes of mood.[1] In the castle of al-'Imādiyya there was a governor, one of the mamlukes of his grandfather 'Izz al-Dīn Mas'ūd ibn Mawdūd. It is said that he held some discussions with Zankī about surrendering al-'Imādiyya to him. Intelligence of this was passed to Badr al-Dīn, who hastened to dismiss him with the help of a great emir and a body of soldiers that he could not resist. He surrendered the castle to Badr al-Dīn's deputy and Badr al-Dīn placed deputies of his own in castles other than al-'Imadiyya.

Nūr al-Dīn [Arslān Shāh II], al-Qāhir's son, had long been ill from wounds[2] he had and from other diseases. For a long time he remained unable to ride or appear in public. Zankī sent to the troops in al-'Imādiyya, saying, 'My nephew has died[3]

---

[1] *Recueil*, ii, 128–9, translates: 'cherchant de vains prétextes, à cause de son extrême mobilité d'esprit'.

[2] *Jurūḥ* is the reading of the edition, although 'wounds' is perhaps not to be expected for someone who died when not much more than ten years old (Ibn Wāṣil, iii, 262). A footnote and *Kāmil* (Thornberg), xii, 219, have *khurūj* 'abscesses, boils' or as *Recueil*, ii, 129, has it 'hémorrhoïdes externes'.

[3] For the subsequent account of his death, see below, p. [**338**].

and Badr al-Dīn wants to rule the land. I have a better right to succeed my fathers and grandfathers as ruler.' He did not stop until the troops there invited him to come and they yielded it to him on 18 Ramaḍān 615 [8 December 1218], arresting Badr al-Dīn's deputy and the men with him.

[**336**] The news reached Badr al-Dīn at night but he acted energetically in the matter. He called upon the troops to depart immediately. They set out with all haste to al-'Imādiyya, where Zankī was, to besiege him there. Before dawn had come he had completed the dispatch of the troops, who marched to al-'Imādiyya and put it under siege. It was wintertime; the cold was intense and the snow was deep there, so they were not able to engage the defenders but they remained to prosecute the siege. Muẓaffar al-Dīn Kūkbūrī ibn Zayn al-Dīn, lord of Irbil, rose in support of 'Imād al-Dīn [Zankī] and undertook to aid him. Badr al-Dīn wrote to him to remind him of his oaths and undertakings, which included that he would not interfere in any of the districts of Mosul, including the castles of the Hakkārīs and Zūzan, named explicitly, and that if anyone, whoever he might be, interfered in them, he himself and his troops would stop him and help Nūr al-Dīn and Badr al-Dīn to stop him. [Badr al-Dīn wrote] demanding that he fulfil his undertakings.

Later he waived this and was satisfied that he should stay quiet, neither being for them nor against them, but Kūkbūrī did not comply and made his support for 'Imād al-Dīn Zankī quite open. At this time it was impossible to overwhelm Zankī with men and troops because of the nearness of this opponent to Mosul and its dependencies, although Badr al-Dīn's army was still besieging al-'Imādiyya and Zankī within.

One of the emirs in the Mosul army, one who had no knowledge of war but was brave and, being new to his position as emir, wished to demonstrate his bravery to gain further advancement, then suggested to some of the troops there that they advance against the castle and directly engage it in battle. They had retired a little from the castle because of the intense cold and the snow. They did not agree with him and thought his plan a bad one. He left them and moved forward at night, so that they were forced to follow him for fear that some harm might befall him and those with him. They set out after him not in good order because of the narrowness of the route, because he had not given them enough time and also because the snow hampered them.

Zankī and his men heard of this, came down [from the castle] and confronted the first units. 'The people of Mecca know its valleys best!'[4] The troops did not stay firm to meet them but returned in rout to their camp. The [main] army did not stand [**337**] against them but was compelled to withdraw. When they had withdrawn, Zankī made contact with the remaining Hakkārī castles and Zūzan and summoned their men to his allegiance. They responded and surrendered to him. He appointed governors, took them over and established his rule in them.

---

4 For this proverb, see al-Yūsī, i, 139.

Account of Badr al-Dīn's alliance with al-Ashraf

When Badr al-Dīn saw that the fortresses had passed out of his hands, that Muẓaffar al-Dīn and 'Imād al-Dīn had formed an alliance against him, that neither gentleness nor harshness was any use with them and that they continued to strive to take his lands and to interfere on the borders, plundering and causing damage, he sent to al-Ashraf Mūsā ibn al-'Ādil, lord of all of Mesopotamia but for a small part and lord of Khilāṭ and its region, asking for his alliance and support. He offered to be his vassal and obedient to him, linked into his chain of allies. Al-Ashraf responded with willing acceptance, joy and delight, and offered him help and support, military action to protect him and the recovery of his former fortresses that had been captured.

At this time al-Ashraf was in Aleppo at camp outside the city because of what we have mentioned,[5] the interference of Kaykā'ūs, the ruler of the land of Anatolia that was in Muslim hands, Konya and other places, in the region of Aleppo and his taking some of its castles. Al-Ashraf sent to Muẓaffar al-Dīn to find fault with this state of affairs and to say, 'The treaty was agreed between all of us in the presence of [caliphal] envoys. We should all be against whoever breaks it until the right is re-established. It is imperative that the territory of Mosul that was taken be restored so that we may remain true to the oath we all agreed to. If you refuse and persist in supporting Zankī and giving him help, I will come in person with my troops and attack your lands and others and I shall recover what you two have taken and restore it to its owners. Your best course is to agree and return to what is right, in order that our concern might be to gather troops, march to Egypt and expel the Franks [**338**] before the danger from them grows great and their sparks fly.'

His agreement to none of that was secured. Nāṣir al-Dīn Maḥmūd, lord of Ḥiṣn [Kayfā] and Āmid, had already refused to cooperate with al-Ashraf. He attacked and ravaged some of al-Ashraf's lands and so did the lord of Mardin. The two of them allied with Muẓaffar al-Dīn. Having become aware of this, al-Ashraf equipped an army and sent it to Nisibis to reinforce Badr al-Dīn, if he needed them.

Account of the defeat of 'Imād al-Dīn Zankī by Badr al-Dīn's army

When Badr al-Dīn's army retired from the siege of al-'Imādiyya, where Zankī was, as we have related, the latter's morale strengthened. He also left and went back to the castle of al-'Aqr, which was his, to gain control of the Mosul region in the open country, for he had already finished with the mountainous country. Muẓaffar al-Dīn reinforced him with a large contingent of troops.

When this information reached Badr al-Dīn, he dispatched a contingent of his

[5] In fact this matter is dealt with below, p. [**347**].

army to the borders of Mosul territory to protect them. They remained four leagues from Mosul. Then they agreed among themselves to march against Zankī, who was at al-'Aqr with his troops, and bring him to battle. This they did and they did not take instructions from Badr al-Dīn but they informed him of their making this march without any baggage train, having with them only their weapons and the mounts on which they fight. They marched overnight and came upon Zankī the next day, on the morning of Sunday four days from the end of Muḥarram 616 [14 April 1219]. They met and fought beneath al-'Aqr and the conflict was fierce between them. God sent down victory on the army of Badr al-Dīn. 'Imād al-Dīn and his army fled and went to Irbil in rout. Badr al-Dīn's troops returned to their former camp. Envoys from the Caliph al-Nāṣir li-Dīn Allāh and from al-Ashraf came to renew the peace. The parties came to terms and swore mutual oaths in the presence of the envoys.

[339] Account of the death of Nūr al-Dīn, lord of Mosul, and the accession of his brother

After peace was established Nūr al-Dīn Arslān Shāh ibn al-Qāhir, lord of Mosul, passed away. He had continued to be ill with several illnesses. Badr al-Dīn set up as his successor on the throne his brother Nāṣir al-Dīn Maḥmūd, who was about three years old. He was the only remaining son of al-Qāhir. The army gave him their oath and paraded him in public. The people were pleased because Nūr al-Dīn had not been able to process on horseback because of his illness. When they now processed with this [prince], the people understood that they had a sultan of the Atabeg house, so they settled down and were calm. Much of the disorder was stilled by this means.

How Badr al-Dīn suffered a defeat at the hands of Muẓaffar al-Dīn

After the death of Nūr al-Dīn and the accession of his brother Nāṣir al-Dīn, there was a renewal of the ambitions of Muẓaffar al-Dīn and 'Imād al-Dīn [Zankī] because of the young age of Nāṣir al-Dīn. They both gathered men and made preparations for a campaign. This became widely known and some of their followers attacked the outlying parts of the principality of Mosul, plundering and doing wicked acts.

Badr al-Dīn had sent his eldest son with a sizeable part of his army to al-Ashraf at Aleppo as reinforcements for him because of the gathering of the Franks in Egypt. Al-Ashraf was hoping to enter Frankish territory on the Syrian littoral to pillage and cause havoc there, to make some of the men at Damietta return to their lands and thus lighten the burden for al-Kāmil, lord of Egypt. When Badr al-Dīn became aware of the activity of Muẓaffar al-Dīn and 'Imād al-Dīn and saw that part of his army was in Syria, he sent to al-Ashraf's troops at Nisibis, inviting them to come and give him support. Their commander was a mamluke of al-Ashraf, named ['Izz al-Dīn] Aybak. They set out for Mosul on 4 Rajab 616 [15 September 1219].

When Badr al-Dīn saw them, he thought them insufficient because they were fewer than the army he had [**340**] in Syria or about the same. Aybak urged that they cross the Tigris and attack the territory of Irbil, but Badr al-Dīn prevented him from doing that and ordered him to rest. Aybak made camp for some days outside Mosul and then insisted on crossing the Tigris, so Badr al-Dīn did so, falling in with his wishes. He camped one league from Mosul, east of the Tigris. When Muẓaffar al-Dīn heard of this, he assembled his troops and moved to meet the enemy, accompanied by Zankī. He crossed the Zāb and outstripped the report of his coming. When Badr al-Dīn did hear of him, he drew up his men for battle and placed Aybak in the vanguard (*jālishiyya*) with his bravest men, providing him with many of them, with the result that only a few remained with himself. On his left he stationed a great emir, who requested to be moved from there to the right wing. This was done.

When the time for the last evening prayer came, that emir asked to be transferred again from the right to the left wing, while the enemy was close at hand. Badr al-Dīn refused him and said, 'If you and your men move during this night, perhaps our people with think it is a rout and no one will hold his position.' He therefore remained where he was, having a large part of the army. When the night was half over, Aybak made a move. Badr al-Dīn ordered him to stay put until the morning because of the proximity of the enemy, but he did not accept this because of his ignorance of warfare. The men were forced to follow him and in the darkness of the night they became disorganized. They met with the enemy on 20 Rajab [1 October 1219], three leagues from Mosul. As for 'Izz al-Dīn [Aybak], he moved off in a right-hand direction and joined up with the right wing, then charged with his own squadrons and the right wing against the left wing of Muẓaffar al-Dīn, putting it to flight along with Zankī.

The emir who moved to the right wing had become some way distant from it and took no part in the action. When Aybak saw the flight of the left wing, he followed it and caught up with it. Badr al-Dīn's left wing was then defeated and he himself left with a small body of men. Muẓaffar al-Dīn advanced on him with the men who were with him in the centre and had not scattered. Badr al-Dīn was unable to stand firm, so retired towards Mosul and crossed the Tigris to the citadel. From there he went down into the city and when the people saw him, they rejoiced and joined with him. He made for the Bridge Gate, with the enemy opposite it and the Tigris separating them. Muẓaffar al-Dīn made camp with those of his troops who were still with him [**341**] beyond the hill of the Nineveh fort, where he remained for several days.

When he saw the gathering of Badr al-Dīn's troops in Mosul and that only a small number of them had been lost, and when the news reached him that Badr al-Dīn was intending to cross on pontoons and boats at night to engage him with his horse and foot in a surprise attack, he departed at night without sounding a drum or a trumpet. They set out back to Irbil and when they had crossed the Zāb, they made camp. Then envoys came and strove to make a peace. Agreement was reached on the understanding that whatever anybody held he should keep. Treaties and oaths formalized that.

How 'Imād al-Dīn took the castle of Kawāshī, Badr al-Dīn Tell A'far and al-Ashraf Sinjār

This Kawāshī[6] was one of the strongest, highest and most formidable of the castles of Mosul. When the garrison there saw what the men of al-'Imādiyya and other places had done in surrendering to Zankī and that they had [in reality] become rulers of the castles, nobody being able to exercise authority over them, they wanted to do the same. They expelled the lieutenants of Badr al-Dīn and prepared to defend themselves. Their hostages were at Mosul, making a show of loyalty to Badr al-Dīn but harbouring sedition. There was an exchange of envoys about their return to loyalty, but this they did not do. They made contact with Zankī about his coming to them. He did so, took over the castle and remained with them. Messages were sent to Muẓaffar al-Dīn to remind him of the treaties recently sworn and to demand his restoration of Kawāshī. No agreement on this was forthcoming. Badr al-Dīn then sent to al-Ashraf, who was at Aleppo, asking him for aid. He set out and crossed the Euphrates to Ḥarrān. He was faced with troubled affairs from a number of directions which prevented him from coming quickly.

[**342**] The cause of his trouble was that Muẓaffar al-Dīn was in correspondence with the princes who ruled the outlying provinces to win them over and to persuade them of the need to act against al-Ashraf and to warn them of what he might do, if he had no concerns. He had a positive response from 'Izz al-Dīn Kaykā'ūs ibn Kaykhusro ibn Qilij Arslān, the lord of Anatolia, and from the lord of Āmid and Ḥiṣn Kayfā and the lord of Mardin. All agreed to submit to Kaykā'ūs and made the khutbah in his name in their lands. We shall relate what happened between him and al-Ashraf at Manbij, when he invaded Aleppan territory, for he was full of bitter anger against him. It came about that Kaykā'ūs died at this time and al-Ashraf and Badr al-Dīn were saved from his wickedness. 'The only good fortune is one which removes men from you.'[7] Muẓaffar al-Dīn had written to several of the emirs with al-Ashraf and offered them inducements. They accepted, including Aḥmad ibn 'Alī, [that is] Ibn al-Mashṭūb, whom we have mentioned as

---

6 A castle east of Mosul, formerly called Ardumusht; see Yāqūt, iv, 315, where it is spelt Kawāshā.

7 Cf. al-Maydānī, *Amthāl al-'arab*, ii, 489, where 'men' is replaced by 'what you dislike' and the whole translated as 'Non est fortuna nisi quod a te res tibi ingratas repellit.' It is said to have been uttered by the Umayyad caliph Mu'āwiya on hearing of the demise of a rival.

doing what he did at Damietta. He was al-Ashraf's greatest emir. Others acted in concert with him, including 'Izz al-Dīn Muḥammad ibn Badr al-Ḥumaydī and others. They parted from al-Ashraf and came to Dunaysir below Mardin, with the aim of joining up with the lord of Āmid and preventing al-Ashraf from crossing to Mosul to aid Badr al-Dīn.

After they had met together there, the lord of Āmid returned to his alliance with al-Ashraf and abandoned the others. The two now made peace and al-Ashraf handed the city of Ḥānī and Jabal Jūr to him and promised to take Dārā and give it to him. When the lord of Āmid left them, their project unravelled and some of those emirs were forced to return to al-Ashraf's allegiance. Ibn al-Mashṭūb remained alone and he made his way to Nisibis to go on to Irbil. The prefect of Nisibis opposed him with the troops he had. They fought and Ibn al-Mashṭūb was defeated, and the following he had with him scattered. He left in flight and passed through an outlying part of Sinjār's lands. The ruler there, Farrūkh Shāh ibn Zankī ibn Mawdūd ibn Zankī, sent a force against him, which defeated and took him prisoner. They brought him to Sinjār, whose ruler was in alliance with al-Ashraf and Badr al-Dīn.

[**343**] When Ibn al-Mashṭūb was in his hands, the former encouraged him to break with al-Ashraf. Farrūkh Shāh agreed to do so and set him free. Men who had evil in mind flocked to him and they attacked al-Buq'ā, a dependent district of Mosul, plundering several villages there. They returned to Sinjār and then he and they proceeded to Tell A'far, a possession of the lord of Sinjār,[8] to raid Mosul territory and pillage that region. Having heard of this, Badr al-Dīn sent an army which brought them to battle and put Ibn al-Mashṭūb to flight. He went up into Tell A'far and made it his refuge. After he had been blockaded and put under siege, Badr al-Dīn came from Mosul on Tuesday nine days from the end of Rabī' I in the year 617 [= 26 May 1220]. He pressed the siege hard, made assaults time after time and captured it on 17 Rabī' II of the same year [21 June 1220]. He took Ibn al-Mashṭūb with him to Mosul, where he put him in prison. Subsequently, al-Ashraf took him and imprisoned him at Ḥarrān until his death in Rabī' II of the year 619 [15 May–12 June 1222]. May God make him meet the punishment for what he did at Damietta.[9]

As for al-Ashraf, when the lord of Ḥiṣn [Kayfā] and Āmid declared his allegiance and the emirs broke up, as we have related, he left Ḥarrān for Dunaysir and made it his base. He seized the territory of Mardin, appointed prefects there and assigned it in fiefs and blocked supplies reaching [the city of] Mardin. The lord of Āmid was present with him. Envoys went to and fro between al-Ashraf and the lord of Mardin about peace. They came to terms on condition that al-Ashraf would take Ra's 'Ayn, which he had formerly given as a fief to the lord of Mardin,

---

8 i.e. 'Umar ibn Muḥammad ibn Zankī. See below, p. [**355**].

9 Ibn al-Mashṭūb led a plot to depose al-Kāmil which resulted in the flight of the army from Damietta. See above, p. [**325**].

and also receive from him 30,000 dinars, and that the lord of Āmid should take from him al-Muwazzar, part of Shabakhtan. When peace was concluded, al-Ashraf left Dunaysir for Nisibis on the way to Mosul. While he was on the road, envoys from the lord of Sinjār met him with an offer to surrender that city to him and asking for the city of Raqqa in exchange.

[**344**] The reason for this was his loss of Tell A'far, which wounded his heart. To add to that his trusty advisers betrayed him and caused him excessive fear and fright because he threatened them but they ate him for lunch before he could sup on them, and also because he had severed the ties of kinship and killed his brother who had ruled Sinjār after his father. He killed him, as we shall relate, and became ruler. God made him meet [the consequences of] his wicked deed and did not allow him to enjoy its benefit. When he was certain that al-Ashraf had departed, he was at a loss what to do, so he sent suggesting that he surrender it to him. Al-Ashraf agreed to an exchange and gave him Raqqa, which he took over on 1 Jumādā I 617 [4 July 1220]. The lord with his brothers, their families and their property departed from Sinjār. This was the last of the princes of the Atabeg house at Sinjār. Praise be to the Eternal Living God whose kingdom has no end. The period of their rule there was ninety-four years. This is the way of the world with its children. What a wretched home it is, how it betrays those who dwell in it!

Account of al-Ashraf's arrival at Mosul and peace with Muẓaffar al-Dīn

After al-Ashraf had taken Sinjār, he set out for Mosul to pass by it on his route. He sent his troops on in front of him. Every day a large group of them was arriving and then last of all he himself arrived on Tuesday 19 Jumādā I of the above-mentioned year[10] [= 21 July 1220]. The day he arrived was a noteworthy occasion. The envoys of the caliph and of Muẓaffar al-Dīn came to him on the subject of peace and to offer to Badr al-Dīn all the castles that had been taken, except for the castle of al-'Imādiyya, for that should remain in the hands of Zankī. The right course of action was to accept this to bring an end to discords and to concentrate efforts on Jihad against the Franks.

Talks concerning this lasted about two months and then al-Ashraf set out to visit Muẓaffar al-Dīn, [**345**] lord of Irbil, and came to the village of Salāmiyya, near the River Zāb. Muẓaffar al-Dīn was camping there on the Irbil side. He now returned the envoys. The army's campaign had been long and the men were discontented. Nāṣir al-Dīn, lord of Āmid, was sympathetic towards Muẓaffar al-Dīn but he advised him to accept what was offered and others added their support to him. Agreement was then reached and they made peace on those terms. A time-limit was set for the surrender of the castles and Zankī was brought to al-Ashraf to be a hostage with him until the castles were surrendered. The castles of al-'Aqr and

[10] i.e. 617.

Shūsh, which were Zankī's, were handed over to al-Ashraf's lieutenants as surety for the surrender of the castles mentioned in the terms. When they were given up, Zankī would be freed and the castles of al-'Aqr and Shūsh restored to him. They swore oaths on that. [Subsequently] al-Ashraf yielded the two castles to Zankī and returned to Sinjār. He departed from Mosul on 2 Ramaḍān 617 [31 October 1220] and sent to the castles for them to be surrendered to the lieutenants of Badr al-Dīn. However, only the castle of Jallaṣawrā[11] was handed over to him, part of the Hakkārī region. As for the other castles, the troops in them openly refused. The time-limit passed when only Jallaṣawrā had been surrendered.

'Imād al-Dīn Zankī attached himself to Shihāb al-Dīn Ghāzī, son of al-'Ādil, served and courted him, so Ghāzī gained the favour of his brother al-Ashraf for him. Al-Ashraf inclined to him and released him, then removed his deputies from the castle of al-'Aqr and that of Shūsh and gave both of them to him. Meanwhile, Badr al-Dīn heard that al-Ashraf had a hankering for the castle of Tell A'far, for it had belonged to Sinjār in ancient and modern times. Talks about this went on for a long time and eventually Badr al-Dīn gave it up to him.

[346] Account of the return of the Hakkārī fortresses and al-Zūzan to Badr al-Dīn

After Zankī had taken control of the Hakkārī fortresses and al-Zūzan, he did not treat the inhabitants with the kindness and benevolence that they expected, but rather he did the opposite and pressed hard upon them. They were hearing how Badr al-Dīn treated his soldiers and his subjects, his kindness towards them and his bestowing money upon them, and so they wished to return to him but fear held them back because of what they had done to him in the past. At this present time they spoke openly[12] of how Zankī treated them and they sent to Badr al-Dīn during Muḥarram 618 [25 February–26 March 1221] about surrendering to him. They asked him to swear an oath and to forgive them, and they mentioned some fief that might be theirs. He granted them this and sent to al-Ashraf asking for permission so to act, but no permission was given.

Zankī returned from being with al-Ashraf, gathered bodies of men and put al-'Imādiyya Castle under siege but achieved nothing against them. They repeated their missive to Badr al-Dīn, proposing surrender to him, so he wrote to al-Ashraf on the subject and offered him the castle of Judayda and[13] Nisibis and a region between the two rivers if he would allow him to take the fortresses. He gave him permission so he sent lieutenants to all of them and they took them over. He treated the inhabitants with kindness. Zankī departed and Badr al-Dīn fulfilled on his behalf what he had offered them.

---

[11] Yāqūt, ii, 103.

[12] Reading the verb in the active, not the passive, voice.

[13] The 'and', absent in the text, is present in *Kāmil* (Thornberg), xii, 226.

When the troops of the remaining fortresses heard what they had done and the kindness and extra grants they had received, all of them desired to surrender to him, so he sent his lieutenants to them and all their people agreed to obey him and be commanded by him. It is a wondrous thing that armies had gathered from Syria, al-Jazīra, Diyār Bakr, Khilāṭ and elsewhere to recover these fortresses and were incapable of [**347**] that. When they broke up, the inhabitants presented themselves and asked that the fortresses be taken from them, so they were recovered as easy as pie without use of force. How well someone expressed it:

> Nothing is easy except what you make easy.
> If you wish, you can make a quagmire out of hard ground.

Blessed be God who effects what He wills. No one can withhold what he bestows and no one can bestow what He withholds. He is powerful over everything.[14]

Account of Kaykā'ūs's attack on the territory of Aleppo, its ruler's submission to al-Ashraf and the defeat of Kaykā'ūs

This year 'Izz al-Dīn Kaykā'ūs ibn Kaykhusro, the ruler of Anatolia, marched to the territory of Aleppo with the intention of conquering it. He was accompanied by al-Afḍal, son of Saladin. This came about because there were in Aleppo two men of great wickedness and troublemaking among the people. They used to report to the ruler, al-Ẓāhir, son of Saladin, about his subjects and stir up bitterness in his heart. The people suffered much at their hands. After the death of al-Ẓāhir and Shihāb al-Dīn Ṭughril's taking over the administration, the latter cast them off and also others who were doing the same sort of thing. He closed the door on those who would act in this way and allowed none of his people any access to it. When these two men saw that their wares were no longer in demand, they remained closely confined at home. The people rose against them, molested and threatened them because of the evil they had done them in the past. In fear they abandoned Aleppo, sought out Kaykā'ūs and encouraged his designs on the city. They established in his mind the idea that, when he attacked it, it would collapse before him, he would take it and it would be easy for him to conquer what lay beyond it.

[**348**] When he determined on this, men of good sense among his courtiers gave him advice and said, 'You will not achieve this except by having with you someone of the Ayyubid house, so that it will be easy for the people and soldiers of those lands to obey him. Such a one is al-Afḍal, Saladin's son, who gives you his allegiance. Your best course is to take him with you and to reach some understanding between you about the lands you may conquer. If he is with you, the people will obey you and what you desire will come easily for you.'

---

[14] This last phrase is common in the Koran.

He summoned al-Afḍal to him from Sumaysāṭ, honoured him and conveyed to him a large quantity of horses, tents, weapons and other things. It was agreed between them that the lands of Aleppo and its dependencies that he conquered should be al-Afḍal's, while being subordinate to Kaykā'ūs, for whom the khutbah would be made in all of them. Subsequently they would attack the Jazīra regions and whatever they took of what was held by al-Ashraf, such as Ḥarrān, Edessa, in the Jazīra would be for Kaykā'ūs. Oaths were sworn to that and they gathered armies and set out. The castle of Ra'bān was taken and handed over to al-Afḍal. Thereupon people's support switched to these two.

They then went to the castle of Tell Bāshir, where was its lord, the son of Badr al-Dīn Dildirim al-Yārūqī. They put him under siege, pressed him hard and took it from him. Kaykā'ūs took it for himself and did not surrender it to al-Afḍal. This made al-Afḍal apprehensive and he said, 'This is the start of treachery.' He feared that, if he took Aleppo, he would treat him in the same way and all that he would achieve would be to dispossess his family in favour of others. His intentions faltered and he turned away from his course of action. It was the same with the inhabitants of the area. They were expecting that al-Afḍal would rule it and this was something they could stomach. When they saw the opposite case, they paused.

As for Shihāb al-Dīn, the atabeg of al-Ẓāhir's son,[15] the lord of Aleppo, he stayed fast in the citadel of Aleppo, not coming down nor leaving it at all. This was his custom since the death of al-Ẓāhir, for fear that someone might rise up against him. When this crisis arose, he feared that they would come to him and perhaps [**349**] the citizens and the soldiers would surrender the city to al-Afḍal because they inclined to him. He therefore sent to al-Ashraf ibn al-'Ādil, lord of the Jazīra regions, Khilāṭ and elsewhere, inviting him to come to him, so that they might declare allegiance to him, make the khutbah for him and strike the coinage in his name and so that he might take whatever he chose of the dependencies of Aleppo and also because the son of al-Ẓāhir was his nephew.[16] He responded to this and set out towards them with the troops that he had with him and sent for the rest, asking them to join him. He was pleased with this because of the common advantage for all. He summoned the Arabs of Ṭayy and other tribes to him and made camp outside Aleppo.

When Kaykā'ūs took Tell Bāshir, al-Afḍal was advising that Aleppo should be tackled quickly before troops could be gathered there and before they could take precautions and get prepared. He now retreated from that and took to saying, 'Our best plan is to attack Manbij and other places so that they retain nothing behind our backs,' with the aim of temporizing and wasting time. They marched from Tell Bāshir in the direction of Manbij and al-Ashraf advanced towards them with the Arabs in his van. A detachment of Kaykā'ūs's army had gone ahead as his advance

---

[15] i.e. al-'Azīz Muḥammad, who was a two-year-old child at this time (Eddé, *Principauté ayyoubide*, 84–5).

[16] Literally 'his sister's son'.

guard. They and the Arabs together with those of al-Ashraf's army with them met and fought. Kaykā'ūs's troops were defeated and returned to him in rout. The Arabs took many prisoners and much booty because of the excellence of their horses and the poor state[17] of the Anatolians' horses. When his men came to him in flight, he did not stand firm but turned on his heels, rolling up the stages to his lands, fearful and watchful. When he arrived at the frontier, he halted. He acted thus merely because he was an inexperienced youth with no knowledge of warfare, otherwise the advance guards of the armies would not have continuously come into contact with one another.

At that time al-Ashraf proceeded to seize Ra'bān and he besieged Tell Bāshir, where was a body of Kaykā'ūs's troops who resisted him until they were overcome. The citadel was taken from them and they were allowed to go free by al-Ashraf. On their coming to Kaykā'ūs he put them in a building and set fire to it, so they perished. This outraged [**350**] everyone and they condemned him and lost respect for him. It is no wonder that God Almighty did not give him a long respite because of the lack of mercy in his heart. He died a little after this incident.

Al-Ashraf handed Tell Bāshir and other places in Aleppan territory to Shihāb al-Dīn the Atabeg, ruler of Aleppo. He planned to pursue Kaykā'ūs and enter his lands but he received news of his father al-'Ādil's death. The general good necessitated his return to Aleppo, because the Franks were in Egypt. When such a great sultan as this passes away, there often occurs some disturbance in the lands, the outcome of which cannot be known, so he returned to Aleppo and thus each of them was spared any damage from the other.

Account of the death of al-'Ādil and how his sons became rulers after him

Al-'Ādil Abū Bakr ibn Ayyūb died on 7 Jumādā II in the year 615 [31 August 1218]. We have already mentioned the beginning of the Ayyubid regime when his uncle Asad al-Dīn Shīrkūh became ruler of Egypt in the year 564 [1168]. When his brother Saladin (Yūsuf ibn Ayyūb) became ruler of Egypt after his uncle and went to Syria, he left him as his deputy in Egypt because he trusted him, relied on him and knew his ample intelligence and the excellence of his administration.

After the death of his brother Saladin he became ruler of Damascus and Egypt, as we have related, and remained sovereign over the lands until this present time. When the Franks appeared, as we have told, in the year 614 [1217] he made for Marj al-Ṣuffar. When the Franks went to Egypt, he moved [**351**] to 'Āliqīn and camped there, but he fell ill and died and was carried to Damascus, where he was buried in his mausoleum.

He was wise, a man of good sense, great cunning and trickery, patient, mild,

[17] The root *dabara* means for a camel or beast of burden 'to have sores on the back'. Cf. Dozy, *Supplément*, i, 422.

long-suffering, willing to hear what displeased him and overlook it, even as though he had never heard it, very quick to anger when the moment needed it, not stopping at anything, but not if there was no need.

He was seventy-five years and a few months old, since he was born in Muḥarram 540 [24 June–23 July 1145]. He took power in Damascus in Sha'bān 592 [28 August–25 September 1196] from al-Afḍal, his nephew, and took Egypt from him too in Rabī' II 596 [20 January–17 February 1200].

It's the most surprising case of the adversity of the stars I have seen. Every realm that al-Afḍal became ruler of, his uncle al-'Ādil took from him. That began with the fact that Saladin gave his son al-Afḍal Ḥarrān, Edessa and Mayyāfāriqīn as a fief in the year 586 [1190] after the death of Taqī al-Dīn. He set out towards them but when he arrived at Aleppo, his father dispatched al-'Ādil after him, who sent him back from Aleppo and took these lands from him.

Later, after the death of his father, al-Afḍal became ruler of Damascus and al-'Ādil took it from him. After the death of his brother al-'Azīz ['Uthmān] he became ruler of Egypt and again he took it from him. Then he ruled Ṣarkhad and he took it from him.

More surprising than this is that I saw in Jerusalem a unique marble column lying in the church of Zion. The priest in the church said, 'This is what al-Afḍal had taken to transport to Damascus. Subsequently al-'Ādil seized it. He asked him for it and took it.' This is too much and is one on the most extraordinary things to be told.

During his lifetime al-'Ādil divided his lands among his sons. In Egypt he placed al-Kāmil [**352**] Muḥammad and in Damascus, Jerusalem, Tiberias, Jordan, Kerak and other fortresses near them his son al-Mu'aẓẓam 'Īsā. Part of the Jazīra regions, Mayyāfāriqīn, Khilāṭ and its dependencies he assigned to his son al-Ashraf Mūsā and he gave Edessa to his son Shihāb al-Dīn Ghāzī and Qal'at Ja'bar to his son al-Ḥāfiẓ Arslān Shāh. When he died, each of them became established in the realm his father had given him. They agreed well together and the sort of dissension that normally occurs between the sons of princes after their fathers did not occur between them. On the contrary they were like one soul, each one trusting the other, so much so that one would visit another alone without troops and not be fearful. No wonder that their dominion prospered and they experienced effective rule and authority that their father did not.[18]

By my life, what excellent princes they were, exponents of clemency, Jihad and the defence of Islam. The Damietta affair gives enough proof. As for al-Ashraf, money in his eyes had no significance, while he dispensed it in abundant showers, because he kept his hands off his subjects' wealth. His liberality was constant and he never listened to the reports of informers.

---

[18] This last comment is rather unexpected and the cooperation of al-'Ādil's sons had its limits, as subsequent events showed.

Miscellaneous events

This year, in Dhū'l-Qa'da [August 1218], al-Kāmil ibn al-'Ādil left the territory of Damietta, because he heard that a group of emirs had agreed to put his brother al-Fā'iz on the throne in his place. He feared them, abandoned his position and the Franks moved into it. They then besieged Damietta [**353**] by land and by sea and gained the upper hand. This has already been mentioned in more detail under the year 614 [1217–18].

In Muḥarram [30 March–28 April 1218] Sharaf al-Dīn Muḥammad ibn 'Ulwān ibn Muhājir, the Shāfi'ī jurist, died. He was a professor in several of Mosul's madrasahs. He was a righteous man of much virtue and religion, sound of heart (God have mercy on him).

This year 'Izz al-Dīn Najāḥ the butler, the caliph's intimate and the man closest to him, died. He held authority in his state and was very just and liberal, a man who did much good in solidarity with the people. His intelligence and his administrative skills reached the ultimate degree and became a by-word.[19]

There also died this year 'Alī ibn Naṣr ibn Harūn, Abū'l-Ḥasan al-Ḥillī, the grammarian, nicknamed 'the Proof'. He studied under Ibn al-Khashshāb and others.

---

[19] A notice in Abū Shāma, *Dhayl*, 113–14, calls him Najm al-Dawla Najāḥ ibn 'Abd Allāh, a mamluke of Caliph al-Nāṣir. The caliph gave as alms large sums of money from Najāḥ's estate 'on his behalf' and made his library of 500 volumes a waqf. The notice also quotes the *Kāmil* for an incident in 569 ('567' is an error) in which the future caliph had an accident that could have been fatal and Najāḥ showed no inclination to survive him. Cf. *Chronicle of Ibn al-Athīr (2)*, p. [**410**].

The Year 616 [1219–1220]

Account of the death of Kaykā'ūs and the accession of his brother Kayqubād

In this year there died the victorious prince, 'Izz al-Dīn Kaykā'ūs ibn Kaykhusro ibn Qilij Arslān, lord of Konya, Aqsaray, Malaṭya and the territory of Anatolia between the latter two. He had gathered and mobilized his forces and marched to Malaṭya to attack the lands of al-Ashraf because of the arrangement agreed between him and Nāṣir al-Dīn, lord of Āmid, and Muẓaffar al-Dīn, lord of Irbil. They had made the khutbah for him, struck his name on the coinage in their lands and formed an alliance against al-Ashraf and Badr al-Dīn in Mosul.

Kaykā'ūs marched to Malaṭya to prevent al-Ashraf who was there from going to Mosul to aid his ally Badr al-Dīn, in the hope that Muẓaffar al-Dīn would achieve some success at Mosul. He was already in the grip of consumption and when his illness worsened, he withdrew. His death occurred and his brother Kayqubād succeeded him. The latter was in prison, having been seized by his brother Kaykā'ūs when he took the country from him. Some of his men had advised him to put him to death but he had not done so. On his death he left no son fit for rule because of their young age, so the army released Kayqubād and made him ruler. 'Whoever ... has been treated unjustly, God shall surely aid him.'[1]

It has been said, however, that, when his illness worsened, Kaykā'ūs sent and summoned him from prison [**355**] and designated him as successor, having made people swear oaths to him. When he became ruler, his uncle,[2] the lord of Erzurum, declared opposition to him. He also feared the Byzantines who were the neighbours of his lands, so he sent to al-Ashraf and made peace with him. They undertook to be sincere partners and to cooperate, and they made marriage alliances. Thus al-Ashraf was spared trouble from that direction and his mind was eased because of the improvement in their relations. How truly it has been said, 'The only good fortune is one which removes men from you.'[3] It is as though the meaning of this saying is 'Your good fortune pierces without a spear point.' This is the fruit of good will, for he showed good will towards his subjects and his followers, refraining from harm that he might cause them and not intending to harm or dominate lands that are adjacent to his, despite the weakness of their rulers and his own strength. It is no wonder that territories came to him easily with no effort.

---

1 Koran, xxii, 59.

2 i.e. Mughīth al-Dīn Ṭughrilshāh.

3 See above, p. [**342**].

Account of the death of the lord of Sinjar, the accession of his son, his son's murder and the rule of his brother

This year on 8 Ṣafar [25 April 1219] Quṭb al-Dīn Muḥammad ibn Zankī ibn Mawdūd ibn Zankī, lord of Sinjar, died. He was a distinguished man who ruled his subjects well and treated the merchants well, showing them much kindness. His followers lived a life of ease with him, for his liberality covered them all and they feared no wrong from him. He was, however, incapable of defending his land, entrusting its affairs to his deputies.

After his death he was succeeded by his son, 'Imād al-Dīn Shāhinshāh. He made a royal progress with the leading men and continued as ruler for several months. He went to Tell A'far which was his possession and there his brother 'Umar ibn Muḥammad ibn Zankī came into his presence with a body of men and they slew him. His brother 'Umar then became ruler and remained thus until he surrendered Sinjār to al-Ashraf, as we shall relate,[4] God willing. [**356**] No long enjoyment of his rule was allowed to the one who betrayed the ties of kinship and shed unlawful blood for the sake of it.

When he surrendered Sinjar, he took al-Raqqa in exchange. It was then taken from him shortly afterwards and he died soon after it was taken from him. He was deprived of his soul and his youth. This is the result of betraying kinship ties. To maintain them adds to one's life but to betray them destroys it.

Account of the expulsion of the Banū Ma'rūf from the Marshes and their slaughter

During Dhū'l-Qa'da of this year [8 January–6 February 1220] the Caliph al-Nāṣir li-Dīn Allāh ordered the Sharīf Mu'add, the administrator of the territory of Wāsiṭ, to go to fight the Banū Ma'rūf. He made his preparations and assembled a large host of infantry from Takrīt, Hīt, al-Ḥadītha, al-Anbār, al-Ḥilla, Kufa, Wāsiṭ, Basra and elsewhere. He marched against them, whose leader at this time was Mu'allā ibn Ma'rūf. They were a tribe of Rabī'a.

Their tents were west of the Euphrates below Sūrā' and the adjacent Marshes. Their depredations and damage were serious for the villages in their vicinity. They cut communications and caused trouble in the regions near to the marsh of al-'Arrāq. The inhabitants of these areas complained of them to the Diwan, so Mu'add was ordered to march against them in force. When he set out, the Banū Ma'rūf prepared to give him battle. They fought at a place known as al-Maqbar, which is a large eminence in the marsh near al-'Arrāq. Between them many were killed before the Banū Ma'rūf fled, having had many killed, [**357**] captured or

---

[4] In fact these events have already been mentioned above, pp. [**343–4**].

drowned. Their possessions were seized and many heads of the slain were taken to Baghdad in Dhū'l-Ḥijja [7 February–6 March 1220].

Miscellaneous events

In Muḥarram this year [April 1219] 'Imād al-Dīn Zankī was defeated by the troops of Badr al-Dīn.[5]

On 20 Rajab [1 October 1219] Badr al-Dīn was defeated by Muẓaffar al-Dīn, lord of Irbil, and Muẓaffar al-Dīn retired to his own land. This has already been mentioned in detail under the year 615 [1218–19].[6]

On 8 Ṣafar [25 April 1219] Quṭb al-Dīn Muḥammad ibn Zankī ibn Mawdūd ibn Zankī, lord of Sinjar, died and was succeeded by his son Shāhinshāh.[7]

This year on 27 Sha'bān[8] [7 November 1219] the Franks conquered the city of Damietta. This has already been fully dealt with under the year 614 [1217–18].[9]

This year Iftikhār al-Dīn 'Abd al-Muṭṭalib ibn al-Faḍl al-Hāshimī al-'Abbāsī, the Ḥanafī lawyer and head of the Ḥanafīs at Aleppo, died. He transmitted Ḥadīth from 'Umar al-Bisṭāmī, who settled in Balkh, from Abū Sa'd al-Sam'ānī and others.

There also died this year Abū'l-Baqā' 'Abd Allāh ibn al-Ḥusayn ibn 'Abd Allāh al-'Ukbarī, the blind grammarian, and others.

In this year died Abū'l-Ḥasan 'Alī ibn Abī Muḥammad al-Qāsim ibn 'Alī ibn al-Ḥasan ibn 'Abd Allāh al-Dimashqī, the *ḥāfiẓ* and son of the *ḥāfiẓ* known as Ibn 'Asākir.[10] He had made Khurasan his destination and heard much Ḥadīth there. He then set out back to Baghdad. His caravan was attacked by brigands and he was wounded. He remained in Baghdad and died in Jumādā I [15 July–13 August 1219] (God have mercy on him).

---

5 See above, p. [**338**].

6 See above, pp. [**339–41**].

7 See above, p. [**355**].

8 The text reads 29 Sha'bān, although at this point *Kāmil* (Thornberg), xii, 233, has 27 Sha'bān and also cf. p. [**326**].

9 See above, pp. [**323–6**].

10 The celebrated scholar and historian of Damascus (499–571/1105–76).

The Year 617 [1220–1221]

Account of the irruption of the Tatars[1] into the lands of Islam

For several years I continued to avoid mention of this disaster as it horrified me and I was unwilling to recount it. I was taking one step towards it and then another back. Who is there who would find it easy to write the obituary of Islam and the Muslims? For whom would it be a trifling matter to give an account of this? Oh, would that my mother had not given me birth! Oh, would that I had died before it occurred and been a thing forgotten, quite forgotten![2] However, a group of friends urged me to record it, although I was hesitant. I saw then that to leave it undone was of no benefit, but we state that to do it involves recounting the most terrible disaster and the greatest misfortune, one the like of which the passage of days and nights cannot reproduce. It comprised all mankind but particularly affected the Muslims. If anyone were to say that since God (glory and power be His) created Adam until this present time mankind has not had a comparable affliction, he would be speaking the truth. History books do not contain anything similar or anything that comes close to it.

One of the greatest disasters they mention is what Nebuchadnezzar did to the Israelites, slaughtering them and destroying Jerusalem. What is Jerusalem in relation to the lands that these cursed ones destroyed, where each city is many times larger than Jerusalem? And what are the Israelites compared with those they killed? Amongst those they killed the inhabitants of a single city are more numerous **[359]** than were the Israelites. Perhaps humanity will not see such a calamity, apart from Gog and Magog, until the world comes to an end and this life ceases to be.

As for the Antichrist, he will spare those who follow him and destroy those who oppose him, but these did not spare anyone. On the contrary, they slew women, men and children. They split open the bellies of pregnant women and killed the foetuses. To God do we belong and to Him do we return. There is no power nor strength except in God the High, the Mighty.

This is the calamity whose sparks flew far and wide and whose damage was all-embracing. It spread through the lands like a cloud driven on by the wind, for a people emerged from the confines of China and made for the cities of

---

1 The term 'Mongol' is generally used for the confederation of tribes, both Turkish- and Mongol-speaking, and the war machine created by Chingiz Khan, but the Mongols (Chingiz Khan's own people) were but one element. Before the 'Mongols' the Tatars had been predominant in the inner steppes and Ibn al-Athīr now uses 'Tatars', a part to signify the whole, and his usage has been retained.

2 This is a reference, only slightly modified, to Koran, xix, 23.

Transoxania, such as Samarqand, Bukhara and others. They took them and treated their inhabitants as we shall recount. A group of them then crossed into Khurasan and thoroughly dealt with it, conquering, destroying, slaughtering and plundering. Then they passed on to Rayy and Hamadhan, the Uplands and cities up to the boundary of Iraq. Subsequently they attacked Azerbayjan and Arran, which they ruined and most of whose people they killed. Only the rare fugitive survived. [All this was] in less than a year. Nothing like this had ever been heard of.

When they had finished with Azerbayjan and Arran, they proceeded to Darband,[3] Shirwān[4] and took the cities there. Only the citadel, where their king was, remained safe. From there they crossed into the lands of the Alān[5] and the Lakz[6] and the various peoples of that region. They dealt them widespread slaughter, plunder and destruction. Then they attacked the land of the Qipjaqs, some of the most numerous of the Turks, and killed **[360]** all who resisted them. The rest fled to the woods and the mountain tops, abandoning their lands, which these Tatars seized. They achieved this in the quickest possible time and only lingered according to the [daily] amount they could travel, nothing more.

Another group, different from this group [just mentioned], went to Ghazna and its dependencies and to the neighbouring lands of India, Sijistan and Kirman. There they perpetrated the same deeds as the others, or worse.

Nothing like this has ever been heard of before. Alexander, who is agreed by historians to have conquered the world, did not conquer it with this rapidity. He only conquered it in about ten years and did not kill anyone. He merely accepted the allegiance of people. In about a year these men conquered most of the known earth, its fairest part and the most civilized and populated and of its inhabitants the most equitable in manners and conduct. In the lands they did not reach there was nobody who was not in fearful expectation of them, watching for their arrival.

The Tatars do not need a supply of provisions and foodstuffs, for their sheep, cattle, horses and other pack animals accompany them and they consume their flesh and nothing else. The animals they ride dig the earth with their hooves and eat the roots of plants, knowing nothing of barley. Thus, when they make a camp, they require nothing from without.

---

3 Darband (modern Derbent) is the name of a settlement on a narrow strip of land on the western coast of the Caspian Sea, fortified by two parallel walls, running east-west from the shore to inland crags and ravines, dominated by a citadel. For a description, map and photographs, see Minorsky, *Sharvān and Darband*, 86–9.

4 Shirwān (or Shirvān) is a Caspian province lying north of the River Kur, west of Baku (Minorsky, *Sharvān and Darband*, 75–6). See also Krawulsky, 566–7; *EI(2)*, ix, 487–8. Darband Shirwān (meaning 'the gate, pass of Shirwān') appears to denote a more extensive coastal area than Darband itself.

5 An Iranian people of the Caucasus, also called the Ās. At the time of the Mongolian invasion they were Greek Orthodox Christians. See *EI(2)*, i, 354.

6 A Muslim (Shāfi'ī sunnī) people of the Caucasus, inhabitants of central Daghistan. See *EI(2)*, v, 617–18, s.v. Laḳ.

As for their religion, they bow down to the sun when it rises and hold nothing ritually forbidden, for they eat all animals, even dogs and pigs and others. They have no concept of marriage. Any woman is visited by more than one man. Any child that is born does not know his father.

During this period Islam and the Muslims were tried by misfortunes that no community had ever been afflicted with. For example, these Tatars (God damn them) appeared from the east and did the deeds that horrified all who heard of them. You will see them consecutively set forth, God willing. Then there was the coming of the Franks (God curse them) from the west to Syria, their attack on [**361**] Egypt and their taking of the port of Damietta. Egypt, Syria and other places were on the point of falling to them, had it not been for the grace of God Almighty and His helping hand against them. We have mentioned this under the year 614 [1217–18].

Another misfortune was that those who escaped these two hordes were at daggers drawn between themselves and dissension was raging. We have mentioned this too. Verily we belong to God and to Him do we return. We pray to God to supply Islam and the Muslims with help from Himself, for there is nobody to help, aid and defend Islam. 'When God wills evil to a people, there is no averting it and they have no protector other than Him.'[7] The cause of these Tatars only prospered because of the lack of a strong defender.

The reason why such a one was lacking is that Khwārazm Shāh Muḥammad had taken power over the lands and killed and eliminated their princes. He alone was left, sultan of all the lands. When he was defeated by the Tatars, nobody was left in the lands who could resist them or defend the lands 'in order that God might complete a thing destined to be done.'[8] This is the time for us to mention the beginning of their irruption into the lands.

Account of the Tatars' irruption into Turkestan and Transoxania and what they did

This year the Tatars appeared in the lands of Islam. They are a numerous variety of the Turks,[9] who dwell in the mountains of Ṭamghāj[10] in the direction of China, which are separated from Islamic lands by more than six months' [journey]. Their

7 Koran xiii, 11.

8 Koran, viii, 42 and 44. For the parallel notion that Khwārazm Shāh had, as it were, dug his own grave by removing all who might have been allies against the Mongols, see Juvainī, *History*, i, 70.

9 Ibn al-Athīr is here following a common usage by which 'Turks' denotes steppe nomads in general.

10 'The Tamghach ... a Turkish or proto-Mongol people who founded the Chinese dynasty of the Wei (436–557) and whose name became synonymous with Northern China' (Juvainī, *History*, i, 279, note 12).

appearance came about because their ruler, named Chingiz Khan and known as Temujin,[11] had left his lands and gone to the regions of Turkestan. He dispatched a company of merchants and Turks, accompanied by a large quantity of bullion, beaver [skins] and other items, [**362**] to the cities of Transoxania, Samarqand and Bukhara, to purchase for him textiles for wearing apparel. They arrived at a city in the lands of the Turks called Utrar, the frontier of the realm of Khwārazm Shāh, where he had a governor. When this group of Tatars came to him, he sent to Khwārazm Shāh to inform him of their arrival and to tell him of the goods they had with them. Khwārazm Shāh sent to him, ordering them to be killed and their goods to be seized and conveyed to him. He therefore put them to death and dispatched what they had, which was a considerable amount. When it reached Khwārazm Shāh, he distributed it among the merchants of Bukhara and Samarqand and took from them the price he set.

After Khwārazm Shāh had conquered Transoxania from the Qarakhitay, he closed the routes from Turkestan and the lands beyond it. Another group of Tatars had previously emerged when the country belonged to the Qarakhitay. When Khwārazm Shāh conquered the lands in Transoxania from the Qarakhitay and killed them, these Tatars took control of Turkestan, Kashghar, Balāsāghūn and elsewhere, and began to make war on the troops of Khwārazm Shāh. For this reason he withheld goods from them, textiles and such-like. There is another report concerning the reason for their irruption into the lands of Islam, such as is not to be mentioned within the covers of books.[12]

What happened happened, something I shall not mention.
Think the best and do not ask about the facts.

After Khwārazm Shāh's governor killed Chingiz Khan's followers, he sent spies to Chingiz Khan to see what sort of man he was, how many Turks he had with him and what were his intentions. The spies set out and crossed the desert and the mountains on their route until they reached him. After a long time they returned

---

[11] In fact his personal name was Temujin and his title was Chingiz Khan, long understood to mean something like 'Oceanic Ruler'. Rachewiltz, 'The title of Činggis Qan', 282–3, has argued for a new etymology and interpretation, 'Fierce Ruler'. For an account of Chingiz Khan's rise to power, see Morgan, *Mongols*, 55–61, also *EI(2)*, ii, 41–4.

[12] This refers to the accusation that the Abbasid caliph invited the Mongols to start a 'second front' against his rival Khwārazm Shāh. The accusation is explicit and given credence on p. [**440**] below. Ibn Wāṣil, iv, 170–71, refers to this accusation and adds that, if it is true, the later fall of the Abbasid dynasty was God's punishment. Al-Mu'aẓẓam 'Īsā told Sibṭ ibn al-Jawzī that, when Jalāl al-Dīn was campaigning near Baghdad in 622/1225 (see below, p. **426**), he wrote to al-Mu'aẓẓam asking for aid against the caliph 'for he was the reason for the death of my father and the infidels' coming to the lands and we have found his letters to the Khitay [sic] and orders to reward them with lands, horses and robes of honour' (Sibṭ ibn al-Jawzī, 634). For the background to the Mongol attack on Khwārazm Shāh, see Juvainī, *History*, i, 77–81.

and told him of their vast numbers, that they were beyond counting, that they were the most steadfast of God's creatures in battle, knowing nothing of flight, and that they make what weapons they need with their own hands. Khwārazm Shāh regretted having killed their men and taken their goods. He became increasingly occupied in reflection and summoned Shihāb al-Dīn al-Khīwaqī,[13] who was a lawyer, [**363**] a man of learning, held in great esteem by him and one whose advice he did not contradict. He came before the sultan who said, 'A serious matter has occurred. It is essential to ponder it and consult your ideas about what we should do. The fact is that an adversary has moved against us from the region of the Turks in numbers vast beyond counting.' Shihāb al-Dīn replied, 'Your armies are numerous. We should write to the provinces and gather the troops. Let the call to arms be general, for it is the duty of all Muslims to aid you with money and with their persons. Then let us go with all the troops to the bank of the Jaxartes' (a great river, dividing the lands of the Turks from the lands of Islam). 'We shall be there and when the enemy comes, having travelled a long distance, we shall meet him, having rested, while he and his troops will have been affected by exhaustion and fatigue.'

Khwārazm Shāh assembled his emirs and the councillors at his court and consulted them. They did not agree with his plan but said, 'The best plan is to allow them to cross the Jaxartes to us and to journey through these mountains and narrow passes, for they are ignorant of their routes, while we know them. Then we shall overwhelm them and destroy them. Not one of them shall escape.'

While they were thus engaged, an envoy arrived from this accursed one, Chingiz Khan, accompanied by several others, to threaten Khwārazm Shāh and to say, 'You kill my men and my merchants and you take from them my property! Prepare for war, for I am coming against you with a host you cannot withstand.'

Chingiz Khan had gone to Turkestan and taken Kashghar, Balasaghun and all those lands. He eliminated the initial Tatars there and nothing more was known of them and no trace of them remained, but they were destroyed like the fate of the Qarakhitay. He sent the message that has been mentioned to Khwārazm Shāh, who, when he heard it, ordered the execution of his envoy. He was duly killed and the order was given to shave the beards of the group with him. They were then sent back to their master, Chingiz Khan, to tell him what had been done [**364**] to his envoy and to say, 'Khwārazm Shāh says to you, "I am coming to you, though you were at the end of the earth, to deliver punishment and to treat you as I treated your followers."'

Khwārazm Shāh made ready and set out after the embassy to hurry to arrive before news of his coming and to take them by surprise. He made forced marches and covered the distance of four months' [journey]. Arriving at their tents, he saw only women, children and the baggage train there. He fell upon them, took

---

[13] He was Abū Sa'd ibn 'Imrān. After the Khwārazmian debacle, he fled to Nasā and after it had succumbed to a siege, he and his son were killed (Nasawī, 109–14).

everything as booty and enslaved the women and their offspring. The infidels were absent from their tents because they had gone to wage war on a prince of the Turks, called Kuchlug Khan. Having fought and defeated him and seized his property as booty, they returned and on the way were met by the news of what Khwārazm Shāh had done to those they had left behind. They pressed on with all speed and came up with him before he had left their tents. They formed their lines for battle and fought a fight such as had never been heard of. They continued in battle for three days and nights and on both sides the dead were beyond counting. Nobody gave way in flight. The Muslims held firm out of zeal for religion and because they knew that, if they fled, there would be no survival for the Muslims and they would be taken because they were far from their homelands. The infidels on the other hand held firm to rescue their families and their property. The situation became critical. Some even dismounted from their horses and fought their opponents on foot, exchanging blows with daggers. Blood ran on the ground, so that the horses began to slip because there was so much of it. Both side exhausted their capacity to endure and fight. The whole of this engagement was with the son of Chingiz Khan. His father was not present at the battle and was unaware of it. The Muslims killed in this battle were counted and were twenty thousand in number. There was no counting the infidels who were killed.[14]

On the fourth night they separated and camped opposite one another. When it was dark, [**365**] the infidels lit their camp fires, left them burning and departed. The Muslims did likewise. Each side had wearied of the fighting. The infidels returned to their ruler Chingiz Khan and the Muslims retired to Bukhara, where Khwārazm Shāh prepared for a siege because he realized his weakness since he had been unable to win a victory over a part of Chingiz Khan's army. How would it be if they all came with their ruler? He ordered the people of Bukhara and Samarqand to made ready for a siege and to collect stores to prepare to resist. He placed in Bukhara 20,000 horse from his army to defend it and 50,000 in Samarqand. He said to them, 'Hold the city to enable me to return to Khwārazm and Khurasan and gather troops, call on the aid of Muslims and return to you.' When he had finished there, he set out back to Khurasan, crossed the Oxus, stopped in the vicinity of Balkh and set up camp.

As for the infidels, after they had made their preparations, they set out for Transoxania, arrived at Bukhara five months after Khwārazm Shāh had come there and invested the city and assaulted it for three days with intense, continuous fighting. The Khwārazmian army was not strong enough to face them and abandoned the city, returning to Khurasan. When the citizens woke up and found none of the army with them, their spirits weakened. They sent the cadi, who was Badr al-Dīn Qāḍī Khān, to seek terms for the populace. The Tatars granted them terms.

---

[14] There had perhaps been an earlier Khwārazmian–Mongol clash in the spring of 1209; see Buell, 'Early Mongol expansion', 9–16.

A detachment of the army, which had been unable to flee with their comrades, had remained behind and fortified themselves in the citadel. When Chingiz Khan agreed to grant terms, the gates of the city were opened on Tuesday 4 Dhū'l-Ḥijja 616 [= 11 February 1220].[15] The infidels entered Bukhara and did not harm anyone. However, they said to the people, 'Everything that you have that belongs to the sultan, [**366**] treasure and other things, bring out to us and help us to fight those in the citadel.' They made a show of justice and good conduct towards them. Chingiz Khan himself entered and surrounded the citadel. He made a proclamation in the city that nobody should hang back and that anyone who did would be killed.[16] All presented themselves and were ordered to fill in the moat. They filled it with timbers and earth and other things. The infidels were even taking the minbars and the Koran containers and throwing them into the moat. Verily we belong to God and to Him do we return. In truth did God call Himself patient and forebearing, otherwise the earth would have swallowed them up when they did such a thing.

They kept up their assaults on the citadel, where were about four hundred Muslim warriors, who did their best and defended the citadel for twelve days, fighting the host of infidels and the city's inhabitants. Some of them were killed but they continued as they were until the Tatars made an assault and the sappers reached the citadel wall and mined it. The fighting then became intense. The Muslims within were shooting whatever stones, fire or arrows they could find. The accursed one became angry and withdrew his men for that day, but they began again early on the following day and fought with all their strength. The defenders in the citadel had become tired and exhausted. They were now overcome by overwhelming forces. The infidels subdued them and entered the citadel, where the Muslims fought them until they were slain to the last man.

Having finished with the citadel, Chingiz Khan proclaimed that a list of the notables and headmen should be made for him. This was done and when it was handed to him, he ordered that they be summoned. They came and he said, 'I want from you the bullion that Khwārazm Shāh sold you, for it is mine; it was taken from my followers and you have it.' Anyone who had any of it brought it before him. Then he ordered them to leave the city, so they left, stripped of their possessions. None of them had anything with him but the clothes he was wearing. The infidels entered the city, plundered it and killed anyone they found there. He had the Muslims surrounded and ordered his men to divide them among themselves, which was done. It was a dreadful day from the amount of weeping by the men, women and children. They were scattered [**367**] to the four winds and completely torn apart. They divided the women among themselves too. Bukhara became [a waste land], 'collapsed on its roof timbers', as though it had not been

[15] Cf. the account of the fall of Bukhara in Juvainī, *History*, i, 102–7. According to this, Chingiz Khan arrived only in Muḥarram 617/March 1220.

[16] A short but vivid picture of this Mongol practice, the use of captives to move siege engines up to walls and the killing of any who retreated, is in Nasawī, 114.

thronging with people just the day before. They committed horrid acts with women, while people looked on and wept, unable to defend themselves from any part of what befell them. There were some who did not accept this and, choosing death instead, fought until they were killed. Among those who did this and chose to be killed rather than see what befell the Muslims were the lawyer and imam, Rukn al-Dīn Imāmzāde, and his son, for, when they saw what was being done to the womenfolk, they fought until they were slain. The Cadi Ṣadr al-Dīn Khān acted in the same way. Those that gave up the infidels took prisoner and then they set fire to the city, the madrasahs and the mosques. They tortured the inhabitants in various ways in search of money.[17]

They departed in the direction of Samarqand, having ascertained that Khwārazm Shāh, who was[18] still in his position between Tirmidh and Balkh, was powerless against them. They took with them as prisoners the survivors of the Bukhara population. They made them travel on foot in the most wretched fashion. All who became exhausted and unable to walk they killed. When they approached Samarqand, they sent the cavalry on before and left the infantry, the prisoners and the baggage behind them, until they advanced little by little, to be more terrifying to the hearts of the Muslims. When the people of the city saw the dense mass of them, they were horrified.

On the next day the prisoners, infantry and baggage arrived. With every ten prisoners there was a banner, so the city's inhabitants thought that all were fighting troops. The city, in which were 50,000 warriors of the Khwārazmian army and, as far as the common people were concerned, an innumerable multitude, was fully surrounded. Some brave locals, men of steadfast strength, sallied forth on foot. None of the Khwārazmian troops went out with them because of the fear of these accursed ones in their hearts. The men on foot engaged the enemy outside the city. The Tatars continued to withdraw and the citizens to follow them with eager confidence. The infidels had positioned an ambush for them and, when they had passed beyond the ambushers, they emerged and cut them off from the city. The others who had initially engaged them turned back and [the local volunteers], caught in the middle, were cut down by the sword on every side. Not one of them survived. [**368**] They were killed to the last man as martyrs (may God be pleased with them). According to reports, they numbered 70,000.

When the remaining troops and commons saw this, their morale collapsed and they were certain they were doomed. The soldiers, who were Turks, said, 'We are of their race. They will not kill us,' so they asked for terms, which were granted. The city gates were then opened, as the common people were unable to stop them, and they went out to the infidels with their families and property. The infidels said to them, 'Hand over to us your weapons, goods and mounts. We shall convey you to a place where you will be safe.' They complied but, after taking their weapons

[17] The capture of Bukhara was completed on 10 Dhū'l-Ḥijja 616/18 February 1220 (*Ṭabaqāt-i Nāṣirī*, 274).

[18] Reading *wa-huwa* rather than *wa-hum*.

and mounts, the infidels put them to the sword, killed them to the last man and seized their property, mounts and womenfolk.

On the fourth day there was a proclamation in the city that all the population should leave. Anyone who stayed behind would be killed. All the men, women and children left and then they treated the people of Samarqand as they had treated the people of Bukhara, despoiling, killing, enslaving them and committing outrages. They entered the city and plundered what it contained. They set fire to the main mosque but left the rest of the city as it was. They deflowered virgins and tortured people with varieties of torture in search of money. Those not fit to be enslaved they slew. This took place in Muḥarram 617 [March 1220].[19]

Khwārazm Shāh was still at his camp. Every time a body of troops came and joined him he sent it to Samarqand, but they would return, being unable to reach it. We seek refuge in God from being so abandoned by Him. On one occasion he sent 10,000 cavalry and they returned like defeated men, without having fought a battle. He sent 20,000 and they also came back.

[369] Account of the Tatars' expedition against Khwārazm Shāh, his flight and death

After the infidels had taken Samarqand, Chingiz Khan decided to despatch 20,000 horse, saying to them, 'Pursue Khwārazm Shāh, wherever he may be, even if he has climbed to the sky, until you catch up with him and seize him.' This group the Tatars call 'the westward', because they travelled west of Khurasan, to make the distinction between them and the rest, since they are the ones who penetrated deep into our lands.[20] When Chingiz Khan ordered them to set out, they set out in the direction of a place named Panj Āb, which means 'Five Waters'.[21] Having arrived, they found not a single boat there, so they made what resembled large troughs out of wood and covered them with cattle skins so that they would be impermeable to water. They placed their weapons and belongings in them and then urged their horses into the water and held on to their tails with those wooden troughs tied to their own bodies. Thus each horse dragged a man and each man dragged the trough that was full of his weapons and other things. All of them crossed over at one time and the first thing Khwārazm Shāh knew of them they were with him on the same ground.

---

[19] According to *Ṭabaqāt-i Nāṣirī*, 274, Samarqand fell on 10 Muḥarram/19 March 1220. Cf. the account of the conquest of Samarqand in Juvainī, *History*, i, 115–23, where the date is given (p. 122) as Rabīʿ I 618 (an error for 617, i.e. May–June 1220).

[20] For another account of this expedition, whose members eventually crossed the Caucasus and returned north of the Caspian, see Juvainī, *History*, i, 142–9.

[21] 'Near the mouth of the Wakhsh, the well-known crossing place of Mela, three days' journey from Balkh, and two farsakhs [leagues] from Tirmidh' was known as Panj Āb in the thirteenth century (see Barthold, *Turkestan*, 72).

The Muslims were full of fear and terror of them and they were at odds amongst themselves, although they were holding together on the basis that the River Oxus separated them [from the Tatars]. Once they had crossed, they were unable to stand firm or to manoeuvre collectively. On the contrary they scattered to the four winds, **[370]** and each detachment went its own way. Khwārazm Shāh departed with a small group of his special guard, with no regard for anything else, and made for Nishapur. After he had entered it, some of his army gathered around him but he had not established himself before these same Tatars arrived. They were not indulging in any plunder or killing on their journey but pressing on in pursuit of him, not allowing him any respite to organize resistance to them. When he heard of their approach, he set off to Mazandaran, also one of his possessions. The 'westward' Tatars set off on his tracks, did not turn aside to Nishapur but followed him. Whenever he left a stopping place, they descended on it. He came to a harbour on the Caspian Sea, known as Ābaskūn, where he had an off-shore castle. When he and his men embarked on the boats, the Tatars arrived and, seeing that Khwārazm Shāh had put to sea, they halted at the water's edge. Despairing of catching up with him, they withdrew. These are the ones that attacked Rayy and places beyond, as we shall relate, God willing.

This is what I was told by a certain lawyer who was at Bukhara and was taken as a captive to Samarqand, but later escaped and came to us. Others, who were merchants, told that Khwārazm Shāh left Mazandaran, eventually came to Rayy and then from there to Hamadhan with the Tatars on his tracks. He left Hamadhan with a small band and no baggage train to conceal his identity and hide information about himself. He returned to Mazandaran and then put to sea to this castle.

This latter version is the true one, for the lawyer was in captivity at this time, whereas these merchants told that they were in Hamadhan. Khwārazm Shāh arrived and he was followed by people who informed him that the Tatars were coming, so he abandoned Hamadhan. Similarly, these merchants abandoned it too. The Tatars arrived there less than a day later. They, therefore, were reporting as eye-witnesses. After Khwārazm Shāh had come to this same castle, he passed away there.[22]

[371] A description of Khwārazm Shāh and something about his life

He was 'Alā' al-Dīn Muḥammad ibn 'Alā' al-Dīn Tekesh and his reign lasted for

---

22 Nasawī, 107–8, describes his dramatic escape by boat, pursued by arrows from the shore. For a different version of the sultan's flight and death, which has him leave the island and die on his way to Khwārazm, where he was buried by his son Jalāl al-Dīn; see *Ṭabaqāt-i Nāṣirī*, 277–9. In yet another version the sultan was buried at Ardahn Castle in the region of Rayy (Juvainī, *History*, ii, 386–7).

roughly twenty-one years and a few months. His realm was extensive and his prestige high. He enjoyed universal obedience. Since the Saljuqs no one had ruled a kingdom such as his, for he ruled from the frontier of Iraq as far as Turkestan; he ruled the territory of Ghazna, part of India, Sijistan, Kirman, Tabaristan, Jurjan, the Uplands, Khurasan and part of Fars. He also did great deeds against the Qarakhitay and took their lands.

He was an educated man, knowledgeable in law, the fundamentals of religion and other subjects. He was respectful towards the ulema, deeply fond of them and generous to them, often joining their sessions and having them dispute in his presence. He could endure fatigue and hard riding, not at all given to luxury and not given to pleasures. His only care was his kingdom, its administration and maintenance, and the protection of his subjects. He revered the men of religion, favoured them and sought the blessing of associating with them.

One of the servitors of the Prophet's tomb chamber (God bless him and give him peace), who returned from Khurasan, told me the following. He said, 'I arrived at Khwārazm, found lodgings and went to the bathhouse. Then I sought out the court of Sultan 'Alā' al-Dīn. When I came there, I was met by a man, who said, "What is your business?" I replied, "I am one of the servitors of the Prophet's chamber (God bless him and give him peace)." He ordered me to take a seat and left me for a while. Then he came back and escorted me into the sultan's residence. One of the sultan's chamberlains received me and said, "I have informed the sultan [**372**] about you and he has commanded your presence." I entered. He was seated at the centre of the back wall of a large vaulted hall. When I got to the middle of the courtyard, he rose to his feet and walked towards me, so I hastened my progress and met him in the centre of the vaulted hall. I went to kiss his hand but he stopped me, embraced me and sat down, giving me a seat beside him. He said, "So you serve the Prophet's chamber (God bless him and give him peace)," to which I replied, "Yes." He took my hand and passed it over his face, before questioning me about our circumstances, our life, the description of Medina and how big it was. He held a long conversation with me and when I left, he said, "Were it not that I am planning a campaign at this time, I would not take leave of you. We are intending to cross the Oxus to meet the Qarakhitay. This is now a blessed journey since we have seen one who serves at the Prophet's chamber (God bless him and give him peace)." He then bade me farewell, sent me a large amount for expenses and went on his way.'

What happened to him and the Qarakhitay we have already narrated. To sum up, there was united in him what other rulers of this world only share, distributed among them (God have mercy on him). If we had a mind to list his virtues, that would be a long task.

How the 'westward' Tatars overwhelmed Mazandaran

When the 'westward' Tatars despaired of catching Khwārazm Shāh, they returned and made for the land of Mazandaran, which they took in the quickest possible time despite its defensibility and difficulty of access and the strength of its castles, for it had continued to resist attacks in ancient and modern times, so much so that when the Muslims took all the lands of the Persian emperors, from Iraq to the furthest parts of Khurasan, the districts of Mazandaran survived as tribute-paying and the Muslims were unable to enter them until they were taken [**373**] in the reign of Sulaymān ibn ʻAbd al-Malik in the year 90 [709]. These accursed ones took them with no trouble for a purpose that God Almighty willed.

When they took Mazandaran, they murdered, enslaved, plundered and burned. Having finished with it, they proceeded in the direction of Rayy. On their way they saw the mother of Khwārazm Shāh, his womenfolk, property and treasures, such precious objects as had never been heard of. The reason for this was that, when Khwārazm Shāh's mother heard what had happened to her son, she was fearful and left Khwārazm, meaning to go towards Rayy, to reach Isfahan, Hamadhan and the Uplands to hold out there. The Tatars encountered her on the road and seized her and what she had with her before they reached Rayy. The contents filled their eyes and hearts, every rare object, precious gem and so forth, the like of which had never been seen. They sent all of it to Chingiz Khan at Samarqand.[23]

Account of the Tatars' arrival at Rayy and Hamadhan

In the year 617 [1220–21] the Tatars (God curse them) came to Rayy in pursuit of Khwārazm Shāh Muḥammad, because they had heard that he had fled from them in the direction of Rayy. They travelled with all speed on his tracks. Many troops, Muslims and infidels, had attached themselves to them, as also did those trouble-makers who wanted to plunder and do mischief. They arrived at Rayy, taking the inhabitants by surprise. They had no inkling of them until they arrived. They took and sacked the city, captured the women and enslaved the children. They perpetrated acts unheard of, but did not stay and hurried away in the hunt for Khwārazm Shāh. On the road they plundered every town and village they passed and in all of them did things much worse than what they had done at Rayy. They burned, destroyed and put men, women and children to the sword. They spared nothing.

[**374**] They continued in the same fashion as far as Hamadhan. Khwārazm Shāh had arrived there with a small body of followers and then left. This was the last information concerning him for it was not known what happened to him, according to some persons' report. However, there was a different account and we have mentioned it.

---

[23] According to Nasawī, 95–6, the sultan's mother, Terken Khātūn, having fled Khwārazm, was besieged in a castle of Mazandaran, surrendered and was taken to Chingiz Khan and after that there was no news of her. Juvainī, *History*, ii, 466–8, tells that she was sent to Qaraqorum, where she lived wretchedly until 630/1232–3.

When the Tatars drew near Hamadhan, the headman went out with a load of money and clothes and with horses and other items to seek terms for the population. They gave them terms, then left and went to Zanjan, where they did much more of the same. They travelled on and came to Qazwin, whose population resisted them in their city. The Tatars engaged them fiercely and entered by force of arms. They and the citizens fought within the city, even fighting with daggers. On both sides untold numbers were slain. Eventually they left Qazwin. The dead from the people of Qazwin were counted and came to more than forty thousand.

Account of the Tatars' arrival at Azerbayjan

When winter came upon the Tatars in Hamadhan and the Uplands, they experienced intense cold and snow in drifts, so they travelled to Azerbayjan and in the villages and small towns on their way they engaged in killing and plundering, similar to what they had previously done, destroying and burning. They came to Tabriz, where its lord, Uzbek ibn Pahlawan, was. He did not move to confront them nor did he resolve to fight them, because he was busy with the constant drinking that he indulged in night and day, never being sober. He just sent to them and bought them off with money, clothes and horses, all of which he conveyed to them. So they left him, making for the coast of the [Caspian] Sea, because it could be less cold, to winter there, and because there were many pasturages for their animals. They came to Mūqān.[24] [**375**] On their way they entered the lands of the Georgians. They were met by the Georgians with a large number of troops, about 10,000 fighting men. A battle was fought and the Georgians were defeated, most of them being killed.

The Georgians sent to Uzbek, asking him to make peace and form an alliance to resist the Tatars. They made an agreement to unite their forces when the winter was over. The Georgians also sent to al-Ashraf ibn al-ʿĀdil, lord of Khilāṭ and the Jazīra, asking him to reach an agreement with them. They all thought that the Tatars would wait out the winter until the coming of spring, but they did not do so. They moved on, going towards the Georgians' lands, joined by a Turkish mamluke of Uzbek's, whose name was Aqūsh. He had gathered the inhabitants of those mountains and plains, Turkomans, Kurds and others, until a large host assembled around him, and made contact with the Tatars about joining them. They agreed to this and inclined towards him on the basis of [common] ethnicity. Having come together, they marched in the van of the Tatars against the Georgians. They took one of their forts and razed it, plundered and ruined the lands. They killed the inhabitants and plundered their possessions. Eventually they arrived near Tiflis.

The Georgians concentrated their men and took the field in all their force.

---

24 Also spelt Mughān, this steppe area is south of the River Aras on the western coast of the Caspian.

Initially they were met by Aqūsh leading his followers. A fierce battle was fought in which all held firm. A large number of Aqūsh's men were slain. The Tatars came up with them when the Georgians had tired of the fight and many of them had been killed. They did not withstand the Tatars but gave way in a most dreadful rout. They fell to the sword on every side. Untold numbers of them met their death. This battle took place in Dhū'l-Qa'da of this year [January 1221]. The Tatars then despoiled the lands that had previously escaped their attentions.

Indeed, these Tatars had done something unheard of in ancient or modern times. A people emerges from the borders of China and before a year passes some of them reach the lands of Armenia in this direction and go beyond Iraq in the direction of Hamadhan. By God, there is no doubt that anyone who comes after us, when a long time has passed, and sees the record of this event will refuse to accept it [**376**] and think it most unlikely, although the truth is in his hands. When he deems it unlikely, let him consider that we and all who write history in these times have made our record at the time when everybody living knew of this disaster, both the learned and the ignorant, all equal in their understanding of it because of its notoriety. May God provide for the Muslims and Islam someone to preserve and guard them, for they have been forced to meet a terrible enemy and reduced, as for Muslim princes, to those whose aspirations do not go beyond their bellies and their private parts. Since the coming of the Prophet (God bless him and give him peace) until this present time the Muslims have not suffered such hardship and misery as afflict them now.

This enemy, the infidel Tatars, trampled over the lands of Transoxania, seized and ruined them. That is an extensive enough territory for you! But this particular group crossed the river into Khurasan, took it and did the same sort of thing. They next came to Rayy, the Uplands and Azerbayjan, and then they came into contact with the Georgians and overwhelmed their country.

The other enemy, the Franks, came forth from their lands in the furthest reaches of the lands of the Rūm, in the north-west, and coming to Egypt, conquered a city like Damietta. They remained there and the Muslims were unable to dislodge them or drive them out. The rest of Egypt was in danger. Verily we belong to God and to Him do we return. There is no power nor strength except in God the High, the Mighty.

One of the greatest misfortunes of the Muslims was that their sultan, Khwārazm Shāh Muḥammad, was missing and the truth of what had happened to him was unknown. At one moment it was said that he had died at Hamadhan and his death was concealed; at another that he had entered the confines of Fars, where he died and his death was kept secret so that the Tatars in pursuit of him would not come there. At yet another time it was said that he returned to Tabaristan, put to sea and passed away on an island there. In short, he was missing. Subsequently it was verified that he had died at the Caspian Sea. This is truly dreadful, that the like of Khurasan and eastern Iraq have become 'a loose beast' with no defender and no sultan to protect them, while the enemy prowls the country, taking or leaving what he wishes. However, they did not spare a single city, [**377**] but destroyed, burned and sacked everything they passed by. Whatever was no good for them they burned. They gathered silk in heaps and set fire to it. They did the same with other items.

Account of the Tatars' conquest of Marāgha

In Ṣafar 618 [March 1221] the Tatars conquered Marāgha in Azerbayjan. This came about as follows. We have mentioned under [this present year] 617 [1220–21] what the Tatars did to the Georgians. The year came to an end while they were still in the lands of the Georgians but when the year 618 began, they left Georgian territory because they saw that they were faced by a powerful force and narrow passes that required to be fought and overcome. They therefore turned aside. This was their normal practice. If they attacked a city and saw that it was strongly defended, they veered around it. They came to Tabriz and its lord bought them off with money, clothes and horses, so they went on to the city of Marāgha, which they put under siege. It had no ruler who could defend it, because its ruler was a woman,[25] who resided in the castle of Rūyīndiz. The Prophet (God bless him and give him peace) said, 'No people will prosper who appoint a woman to rule over them.'[26]

When they besieged it, the inhabitants resisted them, so they erected trebuchets to attack it and made assaults. It was their custom, when they attacked a city, to send the Muslim prisoners they held forward in front of them to carry out the assault and do the fighting. If they fell back, they would kill them, so, wretched as they were, they used to fight unwillingly. It was like the saying: 'the sorrel horse, if he advances, will be slaughtered and if he hangs back, will be hamstrung'.[27] The Tatars themselves fought behind the Muslims, so the losses were among their Muslim prisoners, while they were safe.

They maintained the siege for a few days and eventually took the city by force of arms on 4 Ṣafar [30 March 1221]. They put the inhabitants to the sword, killing more than it was possible to count, and they plundered all [**378**] that was useful for them and whatever was not they burned. Some people hid from them, so they took their prisoners and said to them, 'Call out in the districts that the Tatars have departed.' When they did so, those that had hid emerged and so were seized and put to death.

I was told that a Tatar woman entered a house and killed several of its inhabitants, who thought that she was a man. She put down her arms and armour

---

25 Possibly Sulāfa Khātūn, the daughter or granddaughter of 'Alā' al-Dīn Qarāsunqur of the Aḥmadīlī dynasty of Atabegs (see the note to p. [**275**]).

26 This *ḥadīth* is found, for example, in Bukhārī, *Ṣaḥīḥ*, iii, 184 (*Maghāzī, bāb* 82).

27 This proverb will be found in *Mustaqṣā*, ii, 203–4, with the comment: 'they [the Arabs] look upon a sorrel (*al-faras al-ashqar*) as ill omened in warfare'.

and – there was a woman! A man whom she had taken prisoner killed her. I also heard from someone who lived there that a Tatar man entered a district that contained a hundred men. He continued to kill them one by one until he eliminated them all. Nobody raised a finger to try to harm him. People were totally submissive and could not defend themselves to any extent whatever. We take refuge in God from such abasement.

They then departed in the direction of Irbil. News of this reached us in Mosul and we were fearful, so that some people planned to become refugees for fear of violence. Letters from Muẓaffar al-Dīn, lord of Irbil, came to Badr al-Dīn, ruler of Mosul, asking for reinforcements of troops. He duly sent him a sizeable detachment of his army and planned to move to the frontier of his lands in the direction of the Tatars and guard the passes, to stop anyone passing through them. Those areas are all rugged mountains and narrows that cannot be passed except by horsemen proceeding one behind another. Thus he would prevent them reaching himself.

The caliph's letters and envoys came to Mosul and to Muẓaffar al-Dīn, ordering all to gather with their troops at the city of Daqūqā to resist the Tatars, for there was the possibility that they might turn aside from the mountains of Irbil, because of their difficulty, into this region and penetrate Iraq. Muẓaffar al-Dīn set out from Irbil in Ṣafar [27 March–24 April 1221]. They were joined by a detachment of the Mosul army, which was followed by many civilian volunteers.

The caliph also sent to al-Ashraf, ordering him to attend in person with his troops in order that all might unite to move against and fight the Tatars. It happened that al-Mu'aẓẓam ibn al-'Ādil came from Damascus to his brother al-Ashraf, who was in Ḥarrān, to seek his aid against the Franks [**379**] in Egypt. He asked him to come in person, so that all might march to Egypt to recover Damietta from the Franks. Al-Ashraf made his excuses to the caliph, pleading his brother['s situation] and the strength of the Franks. If he did not take steps to deal with it, Damietta and other places would be lost. He therefore embarked on preparations to march to Syria to enter Egypt. The sequel, which we have recounted, was the recovery of Damietta.

When Muẓaffar al-Dīn and the troops had assembled at Daqūqā, the caliph sent them his mamluke Qashtimur, the senior emir in Iraq, accompanied by other emirs, at the head of about 800 cavalry. They gathered there to allow the rest of the caliph's army to link up with them.

Muẓaffar al-Dīn related the following: 'When the caliph sent to me on the subject of tackling the Tatars, I said to him, "The enemy is a powerful one. I do not have sufficient troops to meet them with. If I was joined by 10,000 cavalry, I could recover the lands they have taken." He ordered me to set out and promised that troops would arrive. When I [was about to] march, only a number fewer than 800 *ṭawāshīs*[28] had presented themselves to me. So I stayed, not thinking it a good idea to imperil myself and the Muslims.'

---

[28] In addition to the separate sense of 'eunuch', *ṭawāshī* signified a fully equipped, heavy

When the Tatars heard that troops had gathered to meet them, they withdrew under the impression that the army would follow them, but when they saw that nobody was pursuing them, they stopped where they were. The Muslim force remained at Daqūqā and, when they saw that the enemy did not move against them and that they were receiving no reinforcements, they disbanded and returned to their own lands.

[380] How the Tatars took Hamadhan and massacred the inhabitants

When the Muslim force disbanded, the Tatars returned to Hamadhan and camped nearby. They had a prefect there who was governing the city, to whom they sent, for him to demand money and clothing from the inhabitants. They had exhausted[29] their resources over a lengthy period. The headman of Hamadhan was an Alid *sharīf*, a member of a family that had long held the headship of this city. He was managing the citizens' affairs in relation to the Tatars and conveying to them the money he collected. When they now demanded money from them, the people of Hamadhan could not find anything to bring them. The people came before the headman, alongside whom was a lawyer who had undertaken in a praiseworthy fashion to unite sentiment against the infidels. To these two they said, 'These infidels have consumed our resources. We have nothing left to give them. We have been ruined by their taking our property and by the disgraceful treatment their deputy gives us.' The Tatars had appointed a prefect in Hamadhan to govern the population as he chose. The *sharīf* said, 'If we are powerless against them, what is to be done? We can only buy them off with money.' They then said, 'You are harder on us than the infidels,' and they abused him. 'I am one of you,' he continued, 'do what you will.' The lawyer then suggested that they expel the Tatars' prefect, fortify themselves in the city and fight the Tatars. Thereupon the common people attacked and killed the prefect and prepared to resist in the city. The Tatars advanced and put them under siege. Provisions were difficult to come by in all those regions because of their ruinous state, the killing of the inhabitants and flight of the survivors. Only a little food could be found by anyone. On the other hand, the Tatars were not troubled by the lack of foodstuffs because they ate only the flesh [of their mounts] and their mounts ate only plants; they dig the ground with their hooves to uncover the plant roots which they eat.

When they besieged Hamadhan, the inhabitants fought them hard, with the headman and the lawyer among the foremost. [**381**] A great many of the Tatars were slain. The lawyer received several wounds before both sides separated. On the following day the people made a sally and fought more fiercely than in the

---

cavalryman. See Gibb, 'Armies of Saladin', 87, note 31. According to Minorsky, *Studies*, 140–41, the term 'represents Turkish *tavachı*, a high staff officer'.

[29] Emending the text to read *istanfadhū*.

initial encounter. Furthermore, more Tatars were killed than on the first day and the lawyer was again wounded several times but he remained resolute. On the third day they again wanted to move out to fight but the lawyer was unable to mount his horse. People looked for the Alid *sharīf* but could not find him. He and his family had fled by a tunnel he had made leading to outside the city, to a castle there on a high hill, in which he took refuge. When the people found him missing, they were left at a loss, not knowing what to do, except that they were of one mind to fight to the death. They remained within the city and did not make any sally.

The Tatars had decided to raise the siege because of their heavy losses, but when they saw that nobody came out of the city to engage them, their eagerness grew and they inferred that the population had weakened. They continued their attacks during Rajab 618 [21 August–19 September 1221], broke into the city by the sword and fought the people in the various quarters. [Large] weapons were useless because of the dense crowd. They fought with knives. On both sides numbers known only to God Almighty were slain. The Tatars overwhelmed the Muslims and annihilated them. The only survivors were those who had made a cellar to hide in. The slaughter of the Muslims continued for several days. Then the Tatars set fire to the city and burned it down. They departed towards the city of Ardabil.

The reason for the taking [of Hamadhan] was that, when the citizens complained to the headman, the *sharīf*, of their treatment by the infidels, he advised them to write to the caliph to ask him to send them some troops with an emir who would unite them. They agreed to that and wrote to the caliph, telling him of their fear and humiliation, the shame and ignominy the enemy was subjecting them to and requesting help, if only a thousand cavalry led by an emir with whom they could fight and behind whom they could rally. When the messengers set out with the letters, someone who knew what was happening sent to inform the Tatars. They intercepted, seized them and took the letters from them. They then sent to the headman, blaming him for the situation. He denied it all, [**382**] so they sent him his letters and those of the others. This made them totally disheartened. The Tatars then came against them and engaged them in battle, which resulted in what we have already described.

Account of the Tatars' proceeding to Azerbayjan and their conquest of Ardabil and elsewhere

When the Tatars had finished with Hamadhan, they proceeded to Azerbayjan. They came to Ardabil and conquered it with very great slaughter, ruining most of it. From there they went to Tabriz, where matters had been taken in hand by Shams al-Dīn al-Ṭughrā'ī.[30] He united its population after the city had been abandoned by

[30] His nephew Niẓām al-Dīn was headman of Tabriz. He himself exercised great influence without any formal position (Nasawī, 196). See below, p. [**436**].

its ruler, Uzbek ibn Pahlawān, an idle emir, who was lost night and day in wine-drinking, not appearing in public for a month or two at a time. Whenever he heard of any alarm, he would take flight in panic. He possessed all of Azerbayjan and Arrān, although he was of all God's creatures the least capable of defending the lands from any enemy who made them the object of his attack.

When he heard that the Tatars had marched from Hamadhan, he abandoned Tabriz, made for Nakhchevan and sent his family and womenfolk to Khoy to be distant from the Tatars. Al-Ṭughrā'ī took charge of the city's affairs, created a united spirit and encouraged people to resist, warning them of the results of defeatism and dilatoriness. He fortified the city to the extent of his ability and power. When the Tatars approached, they heard of the united decision of the inhabitants to fight them, that they had fortified the city and repaired its walls and moat, so they sent asking them for money and clothing. A decision was reached between them on a fixed amount, which was sent to them. Having received it, they left for Sarāv,[31] which they sacked, killing all within.

From there they travelled to Baylaqān,[32] part of the land of Arrān. They sacked all the towns they passed [**383**] and all the villages. They caused devastation and slew all the inhabitants they laid hands on. When they reached Baylaqān, they besieged it. The populace called for them to send an envoy with whom they could settle peace terms. When they sent as envoy one of their chiefs and leaders, the citizens killed him, so the Tatars made some assaults and eventually took the place by force in the month of Ramaḍān 618 [19 October–17 November 1221] and put them to the sword, not sparing young or old, or any female. They even split open the bellies of pregnant women and killed the foetuses. They also raped women and then killed them. One of them would enter a quarter that contained a number of persons and kill them one by one until he had dealt with them all, while not one of them raised a finger against him.

When they had finished with the town, they thoroughly sacked and destroyed the surroundings. Then they travelled to Ganja, the chief city of Arrān. They had learnt of its large population and their bravery, [the latter] resulting from their frequent practice[33] of warfare against the Georgians, and of the strength of its position. They therefore made no move against it but sent to its people, asking them for money and clothing. When what they asked for had been brought to them, they went away.

---

[31] A middle-sized town (modern Sarāb), situated halfway between Ardabil and Tabriz, it was the centre of a district of the same name. See Yāqūt, iii, 64; Krawulsky, 554.
[32] Situated near modern Shusha in Nagorno-Karabakh; see Yāqūt, i, 797–8; *EI(2)*, i, 1134.
[33] That the text's meaningless *dhurriyya*, 'offspring' is a mistake for *durba* is confirmed by the reading of *Kāmil* (Thornberg), xii, 251.

Account of the Tatars' invasion of Georgian lands

Having finished with the Muslim lands in Azerbayjan and Arrān, in part by conquest and in part by coming to terms, they marched to the Georgian territory that was also in these regions. The Georgians had prepared for them and made ready, sending a large force to the frontier of their land to keep the Tatars out. The Tatars came against them and in the resulting encounter, the Georgians did not stand firm but turned their backs in flight. They became prey to the sword and only the odd fugitive survived.

I have heard that about 30,000 of them were slain. The Tatars sacked whatever part they came to [**384**] of their lands and laid waste to them, behaving in their customary fashion. When the fugitives came to Tiflis, where their ruler was, they raised other bodies of men and sent these too against the Tatars to prevent their penetration into the middle of their territory. However, they saw that the Tatars had already entered the land, held back by no mountain, no pass, nor anything else. Seeing what had been done, they withdrew back to Tiflis and emptied the country [of troops]. The Tatars did whatever they wished, plundering, slaughtering and destroying. Nevertheless they saw that the country had many narrow roads and passes, so they did not risk penetrating deeply into it but withdrew.

A great dread of them overcame the Georgians, so that I have heard the following from one of the Georgian nobles who came as an envoy: 'If anyone tells you that the Tatars have been defeated and taken prisoner, do not believe him, but if he tells you that they have been killed, then believe it, for they are a people who never run away. We once took a prisoner. He threw himself down from his mount and beat his head with a rock until he died. He refused to allow himself to be taken.'

Account of their arrival at Darband Shirwān and what they did there

When the Tatars left the Georgian lands, they made for Darband Shirwān and gave siege to the town of Shamākhī,[34] engaging the inhabitants who stoutly resisted the siege. Then the Tatars scaled the wall with ladders. It is reported otherwise, that they gathered together some [dead] camels, cattle, sheep and other animals and the corpses of some local victims and of others, threw them on top of one another until they made a sort of hill, which they climbed and so dominated the town. The fighting continued and the inhabitants still resisted. For three days the fighting raged. When they were on the point of being overwhelmed, they said, 'There is nothing for us but the sword. To fight on is best for us. Let us die with honour!' [**385**] They held on for the following night and then those corpses rotted and disintegrated, so the Tatars no longer commanded the city wall or had the upper

---

34 i.e. modern Shemakha, a former capital of Shirwān. See Yāqūt, iii, 317; *EI(2)*, ix, 289.

hand in the battle. However, they repeated their assaults and constant attacks. The inhabitants lost heart, overcome by fatigue, tiredness and exhaustion. When they became too weak, the Tatars took the town, did much slaughter there and plundered property, which they carried away with them.

When they had finished there, they wished to pass by Darband but were unable to do so, so they sent an envoy to Shirwān Shāh,[35] the ruler of Darband Shirwān, to speak to him about sending them a envoy who could arrange some peace terms between them. He sent ten of his leading men but the Tatars seized one of them and put him to death, then said to the rest, 'If you inform us of a route we can follow, we will guarantee your lives, but if not, we shall kill you as we have killed this man.' They replied, 'This Darband has no route through it at all, but there is one place which offers the easiest way there is.' They then led them to that route, so they took it and left Darband behind their backs.[36]

Account of what they did to the Alān and the Qipjaq

Having gone through Darband Shirwān, the Tatars travelled onwards in those further lands in which are many peoples, such as the Alān and the Lakz and tribes of Turks. They despoiled and killed many of the Lakz, who were mixed Muslims and infidels. They dealt harshly with other inhabitants of those parts and then came to the Alān, who form many communities. They had already received information of the Tatars and taken precautions. They had gathered with them a body of Qipjaqs. They fought the Tatars and neither side gained any advantage over the other. The Tatars sent to the Qipjaqs to say, 'We and you are of one race. These Alān are not the same as you that you should aid them, nor is their religion the same as yours. We will promise you **[386]** that we will not trouble you and we will bring you whatever money and clothing you want, if you leave us to deal with them.'

An agreement was reached between them in return for the supply of money, clothing and other things. What was stipulated was provided and the Qipjaq abandoned their allies, the Alān, whom the Tatars then fell upon. They slaughtered many of them, plundered and made captives and then moved against the Qipjaq, who were feeling secure and had disbanded because of the peace that had been agreed. They heard no word of the Tatars, not until they had come upon them and entered their lands, where they destroyed them one by one and seized back many times more than they had provided.

Those Qipjaq that dwelt far away heard the news and fled a long distance without putting up any fight, some taking refuge in the forests and some in the

---

35 For the title and dynasties that used it, see *EI(2)*, ix, 488–9.

36 Juvainī, *History*, i, 149, merely refers to an unspecified 'strategem' to traverse Darband. Rashīd al-Dīn has the same story as Ibn al-Athīr (see op. cit., note 33).

mountains, while some even sought the lands of the Rūs. The Tatars remained in the Qipjaq lands, which are plentiful in pasturages summer and winter. There are places that are cool in summer with plentiful pasturage and others warm in winter, also with plentiful pasturage, the latter being wooded areas on the sea coast. They came to the town of Sūdāq, which is the Qipjaq's city from which they trade. It is on the Black Sea and ships come there, bearing textiles. The Qipjaq buy them and sell female slaves and mamlukes, fox,[37] beaver and grey squirrel furs and other items found in their lands. This Black Sea is a sea that connects with the Bosphorus.

When the Tatars came to Sūdāq, they took it and the population fled. Some of them climbed the mountains with their families and possessions, while some went to sea and travelled to Anatolia which was in the hands of Muslims, the sons of Qilij Arslān.

[387] Account of what the Tatars did to the Qipjaq and the Rūs

When the Tatars had taken control of the land of the Qipjaq and the latter had scattered, as we have related, a large group of them went to the territory of the Rūs, a large neighbouring country, extensive and broad, whose inhabitants professed the Christian religion. After their arrival, all the Rūs gathered and agreed to fight the Tatars, if they were attacked. The Tatars remained in the Qipjaq lands for a while and subsequently came to the land of the Rūs in the year 620 [1223–4]. The Rūs and the Qipjaq heard news of them and they were prepared to give battle. They proceeded towards the route the Tatars were taking to confront them before they reached their territory and to keep them out. News of their march came to the Tatars, so they retraced their steps. The Rūs and the Qipjaq were eager to be at them, thinking that they had withdrawn out of fear of them and from being too weak to fight them. They were energetic in their pursuit and the Tatars continued to retreat and these others to follow in their tracks for twelve days.

The Tatars then turned on the Rūs and the Qipjaq, who, before they realized it, were confronted by them in an unready state, because they had come to feel safe from the Tatars and sense that they had the upper hand over them. Their preparations for battle were not completed before the Tatars had already won a considerable advantage. However, both sides held firm in a way that was unheard of. The battle lasted for several days but in the end the Tatars were victorious. The Qipjaq and the Rūs suffered a terrible defeat after much slaughter had been done among them. Many of those who fled were killed and only a few escaped. All the baggage with them was plundered. The survivors reached their lands in a dreadful

---

[37] In Arabic *burṭāsī*, named after a Turkish tribe from whose country pelts of black and red foxes were exported. See Minorsky, *Sharvān and Darband*, 149. For details on the fur trade, see Serjeant, 'Islamic Textiles', xv–xvi (1951), 73–5.

state because of the long journey and flight. The Tatars pursued them, killing, plundering [**388**] and destroying the country, so that most of it became uninhabited.

Many of the leading Rūs merchants and wealthy men gathered together, loaded up what they held precious and set out to cross the sea to the lands of Islam in several ships. When they drew near the harbour they were making for, one of their ships foundered and sank, although those on board were saved. The custom in force was that every ship that foundered belonged to the sultan, who gained a great deal from that. The rest of the ships arrived safely and their passengers told of this circumstance.

Account of the Tatars' return from the lands of the Rūs and the Qipjaq to their ruler

After the Tatars had treated the Rūs as we have described and plundered their country, they withdrew and went to the Bulghars in the year 620 [1223–4]. When the Bulghars heard of their approach, they laid ambushes for them in several places. They then marched out to engage them and drew them on until they had passed the ambush site. They emerged behind their backs, so that they were caught in the middle. They fell to the sword on every side. Most of them were killed and only a few escaped.

There is another version, however. They numbered about four thousand and they set out for Saqsīn[38] on the way back to their ruler, Chingiz Khan. The lands of the Qipjaq became free of them and the survivors returned home. [**389**] Their trade route had been interrupted since the entry of the Tatars. No sable, squirrel or beaver furs or other items that were exported from those lands were sent out by them. After the Tatars left and returned to their lands, the route opened up and goods were exported as before.

This is the account of the 'westward' Tatars, which we have related as a single narrative to avoid its being interrupted.

Account of what the Tatars did in Transoxania after Bukhara and Samarqand

We have already recounted the acts of the 'westward' Tatars, whom their ruler Chingiz Khan (God curse him) sent against Khwārazm Shāh. After he had dispatched this group against Khwārazm Shāh and he had heard of the latter's flight from Khurasan, he divided his followers into several bands. One he sent to

[38] Its location is uncertain. It was 'the name of one or more cities in West Eurasia'. Modern scholarship places it either on the Yayik/Ural river or on the Volga. See *EI(2)*, viii, 895–8.

Ferghana with the object of conquering it, another he sent to Tirmidh and yet another to Kalāna (?), a strong fortress on the banks of the Oxus, one of the strongest and most defensible. Each band marched to the place it had been ordered to attack, descended upon it and took control there, perpetrating the same sort of killing, enslaving, plundering, destroying and all sort of wickedness as their comrades did.

When that was done, they returned to their ruler Chingiz Khan at Samarqand. He then prepared a large force with one of his sons and sent them off to Khwārazm. He also sent a second army which crossed the Oxus into Khurasan.

[390] Account of the Tatars' conquest of Khurasan

When the army sent to Khurasan departed, they crossed the Oxus and made for the city of Balkh. The population asked for terms which were granted and the city was surrendered in the year 617 [1220–21]. The Tatars subjected it to no plunder or slaughter but appointed a prefect there and then set out for Zūzan, Maymand, Andkhūd and Qāriyāt. They took all of them and appointed governors in each, not exposing their populations to any bad or harmful treatment, apart from the fact that they were taking the men to use them to fight whoever offered resistance. They came eventually to Ṭāliqān, which is a region comprising several towns and has a strong fortress called Manṣūrkūh.[39] It was beyond reach of missiles because of its great height and tall walls, and it was garrisoned by brave fighting men. The Tatars besieged it for six months, engaging the defenders night and day but without achieving anything.

They sent to Chingiz Khan to inform him of their inability to take this fortress because of the great number of its defenders and its strong position that made it so impregnable. He therefore came in person with the forces he had and joined the siege. He had with him a large host of Muslim prisoners whom he ordered to engage in the attack, otherwise he would kill them. They therefore fought alongside him. He remained there for four more months and a large number of Tatars were killed in their assaults. Seeing this, their ruler ordered the collection of whatever kindling and timber could be collected. This was done and they began making a layer of timber and a layer of earth above it and kept on doing this until it made a high mound, **[391]** the same height as the fortress. Soldiers climbed onto it and erected a trebuchet which began to shoot into the middle of the fortress. The [defenders] then made a single charge against the Tatars. Their cavalry escaped and survived, traversing those mountains and woods. The infantry, however, were slain. The Tatars then entered the fortress, enslaved the women and children and plundered the money and chattels.

---

39 According to *Ṭabaqāt-i Nāṣirī*, ii, 1003–13, this fortress was called Naṣīrkūh or possibly Naṣrkūh.

Later Chingiz Khan gathered the people, to whom he had granted safe conduct at Balkh and elsewhere, and sent them with one of his sons to the city of Marv. When they arrived there, more than 200,000 Arabs, Turks and other Muslims who had survived had already assembled there and were camped outside Marv, determined to confront the Tatars, convincing themselves that they could defeat and beat them. When the Tatars arrived, a battle ensued in which the Muslims held firm. The Tatars, however, do not understand what flight is. Indeed, one of their number was taken prisoner and while he was in Muslim hands, he said, 'If it is said that Tatars have been killed, believe it, but if it is said that they have fled, do not believe it.'[40]

When the Muslims saw the Tatars' perseverance and fearlessness, they turned their backs in flight. Many of them were killed or captured and only a few escaped. Their baggage, weapons and mounts were seized. The Tatars then sent to the towns that were around and about to collect men for the siege of Marv. When they had collected what they wanted, they advanced to Marv and put it under siege, making every exertion and keeping up constant attacks.

[**392**] The inhabitants were weakened by the flight of those troops and by the large number of their own killed or taken. On the fifth day of the siege the Tatars sent to the emir who was there in command of the garrison to say, 'Do not destroy yourself or the inhabitants. Come out to us and we will make you emir of this city and then leave you.' He sent requesting guarantees for himself and the inhabitants, and they were granted, so he went out to them. The son of Chingiz Khan gave him a robe of honour and treated him with respect. He also said to him, 'I want you to review your men for me, so that we may see who is fit to serve us and we will enrol them, give them a fief and have them join us.' When they presented themselves and he had them under his control, he seized them and tied their hands. When this had been done, he said to them, 'Write me a list of the merchants and headmen of the city and the men of wealth and write down the artisans and craftsmen in another list and present that to us.' They did as they were ordered. When he had read the lists, he ordered the inhabitants to leave the city with their families, so everyone did and nobody was left behind. He took a seat on a golden chair and ordered the soldiers who had been arrested to be brought before him. This was done and their heads were struck off in cold blood, while people looked on and wept.

As for the common people, the Tatars divided up the men, women, children and their property. It was a dreadful day with so much shrieking, weeping and wailing. They took the men of substance and beat and tortured them with various methods in the search for money. Some of them died from the severity of the beating, as they had nothing left to ransom their lives with. Then the Tatars set fire to the city and burned down the mausoleum of Sultan Sanjar, having dug up his grave in search of precious objects. They continued in this way for three days. On the

---

40 A similar passage will be found at p. [**384**]. However, the sentiment expressed here is somewhat weakened by the fact that the Tatar had himself been taken prisoner!

fourth day he commanded the entire population to be killed, saying, 'These people rebelled [**393**] against us,' so they were all massacred. He ordered the slain to be counted and they were about 700,000. Verily we belong to God and to Him do we return – to be spared what befell the Muslims on that day.

The Tatars then proceeded to Nishapur and besieged it for five days. It held a sizeable contingent of Muslim troops but they were not strong enough for the Tatars, who seized the city and drove the population into the open country where they killed them, enslaved their women and tortured those they suspected of being wealthy, as they had done at Marv. They stayed for five days, causing destruction and searching the dwellings for money.

After their massacre of the people of Marv, the Tatars were told that many of their victims survived and escaped to Islamic territory, so they ordered that the people of Nishapur should have their heads cut off, so that nobody would survive the massacre. When they had completed this, they sent a group of their men to Ṭūs, where they acted in a similar manner, causing destruction. They ruined the shrine where 'Alī ibn Mūsā al-Riḍā and al-Rashīd[41] are buried. Indeed, they razed it to the ground.

They then went to Herat, one of the best defended cities, and besieged it for ten days before they took it. They granted terms to its population but killed some of them. They placed a prefect over those that survived. Ghazna was their next destination, where they were met by Jalāl al-Dīn ibn Khwārazm Shāh who fought and defeated them, as we shall relate, God willing.[42] The people of Herat then attacked and killed the prefect, but when those who had been defeated came back, they entered the city by force and killed all there, plundered property, enslaved the womenfolk, ravaged the surrounding countryside and destroyed and burned all the city. They then returned to their ruler Chingiz Khan, who was in Ṭāliqān, despatching squadrons throughout all Khurasan, [**394**] where they acted similarly.

Account of their conquest and destruction of Khwārazm

The detachment of the army which Chingiz Khan sent to Khwārazm was the largest of all the squadrons because of the size of the country. They travelled until they came to Khwārazm, where there was a large army and whose inhabitants were known to be brave and numerous. They gave the invaders the fiercest fight that people had heard of. The siege lasted for five months and on both sides a great host of men were killed, although the dead among the Tatars were more numerous because the Muslims were protected by the city wall.

---

41 'Alī (died 203/818) was the eighth of the Twelver Shiite Imams, who was at one stage promoted by the Abbasid caliph al-Ma'mūn as his successor. The celebrated caliph Hārūn al-Rashīd, father of al-Ma'mūn, ruled 786–809.

42 See below, p. [**395**].

The Tatars sent to their ruler Chingiz Khan to ask for reinforcements which he supplied to them in great quantity. When they had reached the city, they made a series of assaults, eventually taking a part of it. The inhabitants gathered to oppose them at the place which they had taken but were unable to expel them. They kept up the fight, although the Tatars were seizing district after district from them. Every time they took a district, the Muslims fought them in the next one. Men, women and children fought and continued to do so until the whole city had fallen with everyone in it killed and all it contained plundered. They opened the dam which kept the waters of the Oxus away from the city, so it was completely inundated and the buildings collapsed. The site was left an expanse of water. Not one of the populace survived, although in other cities some of the people had survived; some hid, some fled, some got out and escaped and yet others threw themselves down among the corpses [**395**] and so were saved. However, from among the people of Khwārazm those who hid from the Tatars were either drowned or died under the rubble. The city became a deserted ruin.

> It's as though no person had lived between al-Ḥajūn and al-Ṣafā
> And no reveller had whiled away the evening in Mecca.[43]

Nothing like this had ever been heard of in ancient or modern times. We seek refuge in God from decline after power and from defeat after victory. This disaster touched all Islam and all Muslims. How many of the people of Khurasan and elsewhere were slain, because the visiting merchants and others were very many and all passed under the sword!

When the Tatars had finished with Khurasan and Khwārazm, they returned to their ruler in al-Ṭāliqān

Account of the Tatars' conquest of Ghazna and the land of the Ghūr

After the Tatars had finished with Khurasan and returned to their ruler, he equipped a large army and sent it to Ghazna, where the ruling prince was Jalāl al-Dīn ibn Khwārazm Shāh. The surviving men of his father's army had rallied to him there and, according to one report, were 60,000 strong. When the Tatars arrived at the dependencies of Ghazna, the Muslims went forth to meet them with the son of Khwārazm Shāh to a place called Balq.[44] There they met and fought a fierce fight, which was kept up for three days. Eventually God sent down victory upon the Muslims. The Tatars fled and the Muslims killed them at will. Those that escaped went back to their ruler at al-Ṭāliqān.

---

[43] The poet is Muḍāḍ ibn 'Amr ibn al-Ḥārith al-Jurhumī (*al-Aghānı*, xv, 11, 18, 20, 22, 25). The two places named in the first line are hills near Mecca.

[44] See note to p. [**236**].

When the citizens of Herat heard of this, they rose against the governor [**396**] whom the Tatars had placed among them and put him to death. Chingiz Khan sent them an army which took the city and demolished it, as we have related.[45]

After the Tatars' defeat, Jalāl al-Dīn sent an envoy to Chingiz Khan to say to him, 'In which locality do you want the battle to be, so that we may make our way to it?' Chingiz Khan prepared a large army, larger than the first one, with one of his sons and dispatched him towards Jalāl al-Dīn. He came to Kabul and the Islamic forces set out to meet them. They lined up against each other there and a great battle followed. The infidels were defeated a second time and many of them slain. The Muslims took as booty what the Tatars had with them, which was considerable. They also had with them a great host of Muslim captives, who were rescued and set free.

Then discord broke out among the Muslims over the booty. The reason was that an emir, called Sayf al-Dīn Bughrāq, one of the Khalaj Turks in origin, who was brave and bold, a wise and cunning man in war, and himself engaged in warfare with the Tatars, said to the troops of Jalāl al-Dīn, 'Stay back, for you are full of fear of them.' He is the one who truly broke the Tatars. There was also among the Muslims a great emir called Malik Khan, who was a relative of Khwārazm Shāh and the lord of Herat. These two emirs disagreed over the booty. Their followers clashed and a brother of Bughrāq was killed. Bughrāq said, 'I put the infidels to flight and my brother is slain for the sake of this ill-gotten gain!' Angry, he left the army and went to India. He was followed by 30,000 men, all of whom favoured him. Jalāl al-Dīn tried every way to win him back. He visited him in person, reminded him of the duty of Jihad and warned him of God's displeasure. He wept in his presence but he did not come back. He travelled on, [**397**] taking his leave. The Muslims were broken and weakened because of this.

Meanwhile, news came that Chingiz Khan had arrived with his hordes and armies. When Jalāl al-Dīn saw how weak the Muslims were on account of those who had deserted the army so that he was unable to maintain his position, he set out towards India. He reached the Indus, a great river, but found no boats there to take him over. Chingiz Khan was hastening to follow his tracks and Jalāl al-Dīn was unable to cross before Chingiz Khan and the Tatars caught up with him. The Muslims were then forced to fight and stand firm because crossing the river was not an option for them. At that moment they were like 'the sorrel horse, if he hangs back, he will be killed and if he advances, he will be hamstrung.'[46] They drew up their battle lines and fought a very fierce fight. All recognized that the battles that had preceded were child's play in comparison with this battle. They kept it up for three days. The emir Malik Khān, whom we have mentioned before, and a vast number were slain, but the losses were greater among the infidels, and also the number of wounded. The infidels withdrew to some distance and camped far off.

---

45 See above, p. [**393**], although the narrative differs a little.

46 See the footnote to p. [**377**].

When the Muslims saw that they had no reinforcements and that they had been weakened because of their comrades killed or wounded, although they did not know the similar misfortunes of the infidels, they sent people to look for boats. Some came, so the Muslims crossed 'in order that God might complete a thing destined to be done.'[47]

On the following day the infidels returned to Ghazna with their hearts strengthened because the Muslims had crossed the river towards India and were far away. When they arrived there, they took the city immediately because it was devoid of troops and defenders. They killed the inhabitants, plundered their property and enslaved the womenfolk. Nobody was left. They destroyed and burned the city. They acted likewise in the countryside, plundering, killing and burning. [**398**] Those regions all became empty of people, totally devastated, as though they had not been but yesterday thronging with life.

How al-Ashraf surrendered Khilāṭ to his brother Shihāb al-Dīn Ghāzī

Towards the end of this year al-Ashraf Mūsā ibn al-'Ādil assigned the city of Khilāṭ and all its dependencies, Armenia, the city of Mayyāfāriqīn in Diyār Bakr and the city of Ḥānī to his brother Shihāb al-Dīn Ghāzī ibn al-'Ādil and took from him the cities of Edessa and Sarūj in the Jazīra. He sent him to Khilāṭ at the beginning of the year 618 [began 25 February 1221].

The reason for this was that, when the Tatars attacked the lands of the Georgians, defeated them, plundered them and killed many of their people, the Georgians sent to Uzbek, lord of Azerbayjan and Arran, asking him to make peace and form an alliance to repel the Tatars. They also sent to al-Ashraf in the same sense. They said to all, 'If you do not agree with us to fight these people, drive them from our lands and come in person and with your troops for this crucial task, then we shall make a treaty with them against you.'

Their envoys came to al-Ashraf, when he was preparing an expedition to Egypt on account of the Franks, who were in his eyes of more significance: this for various reasons, firstly that the Franks had conquered Damietta and thus Egypt was on the point of being taken. If they took that, [**399**] they would leave no dominion in Syria or elsewhere for anyone; secondly that the Franks were more determined, seeking [permanent] rule. If they took a town, they would not for a single day abandon it except after they were [completely] unable to defend it; thirdly that the Franks were eager for the seat of power of al-'Ādil's house, namely Cairo, whereas the Tatars had not reached it, nor had they trespassed on any part of their lands,[48] nor were they people who desired to be rivals for dominion. Their

[47] Koran, viii, 42 and 44.

[48] Here Ibn Wāṣil, iv, 90, who mostly repeats Ibn al-Athīr's text, has 'had not gone beyond Persian lands (*bilād al-'Ajam*)', which gives a clearer sense.

only aim was to plunder, kill, destroy the lands and pass on from one town to another.

When the Georgian envoys came to him with the message we have mentioned, he answered with the excuse that he was marching to Egypt to repel the Franks. He said to them, 'I have assigned the province of Khilāṭ to my brother and have sent him there to be near you. I have left troops with him. When you need his assistance, he will come to repel the Tatars.' He himself then went to Egypt, as we have mentioned.

Miscellaneous events

In Rabīʻ II of this year [5 June–3 July 1220] Badr al-Dīn took the fortress of Tell Aʻfar.

In Jumādā I [4 July–2 August 1220] al-Ashraf took the city of Sinjar.

Also this year he came to Mosul and camped outside before setting out for Irbil to attack its ruler. There was an exchange of envoys to discuss peace and peace terms were agreed in Shaʻbān [October 1220]. All this has already been dealt with in detail under the year 615 [1218–19].

This year the Tatars came to Rayy, which they took, and killed everyone there and sacked it. [**400**] They then left and arrived at Hamadhan, where the headman met them with an offer of submission and tribute. They spared the inhabitants and went on to Azerbayjan, which land they ruined and burned, slaughtering and enslaving. They perpetrated unheard-of acts, but this has already been fully detailed.

Naṣīr al-Dīn Nāṣir ibn Mahdī al-ʻAlawī, who was the caliph's vizier, died this year and prayers were said over him at the Palace Mosque.[49] The magnates of state attended and he was buried in the Shrine.[50]

There also died this year Ṣadr al-Dīn Abū'l-Ḥasan Muḥammad ibn Ḥamawayh al-Juwāynī, the Chief Shaykh in Egypt and Syria.[51] He died in Mosul, to which he had come on a mission. He was a lawyer, a man of letters and a pious sufi, a member of a great family from Khurasan (may God have mercy on him). He was an excellent man.

This year a group of the Banū Maʻrūf returned to their tribal areas in the Marsh.

---

[49] The Jāmiʻ al-Qaṣr in East Baghdad was built in the tenth century by Caliph al-Muktafī (see Le Strange, *Baghdad*, 252).

[50] This is most likely to be the cemetery in north-west Baghdad attached to the burial place of the seventh Imam, Mūsā al-Kāẓim.

[51] His name was Muḥammad ibn ʻUmar (Ibn Wāṣil, iv, 91). Born in 543/ 1148 in Khurasan, he came to Damascus with his father, whom he succeeded as Chief Shaykh. He married a daughter of Saladin's associate Ibn Abī ʻAṣrūn and had four sons who played prominent roles in late Ayyubid history. See *EI(2)*, i, 765–5, s.v. Awlād al-Shaykh.

They had previously gone to al-Aḥsā and al-Qaṭīf[52] but had been unable to settle there because of their numerous enemies. They approached the prefect of Basra and requested him to write to the Diwan at Baghdad to gain a pardon for them. He gave them a letter to that effect and sent them with his own men to Baghdad. When they drew near Wāsiṭ, they were met by a messenger from the Diwan with instructions for them to be killed, so they were put to death.[53]

---

52 See Yāqūt, i, 148. Aḥsā (modern al-Hasā) is a coastal area south of Dhahran in Saudi Arabia. The text reads al-Ajnā but the variant reading has been preferred. Qaṭīf is also in Saudi Arabia, south of Ra's Tannūrah on the west coast of the Gulf.
53 For previous troubles, see above, p. [**356**].

[**401**] The Year 618 [1221–1222]

Account of the death of Qatāda, Emir of Mecca, the accession of his son al-Ḥasan and the killing of the Emir of the Pilgrimage

In Jumadā II of this year [23 July–20 August 1221] Qatāda ibn Idrīs al-'Alawī al-Ḥasanī, emir of Mecca, died at Mecca (may God protect it).[1] He was about ninety years old and his realm stretched from the borders of Yemen to [Medina,] the city of the Prophet (God bless him and give him peace). He possessed the castle of Yanbu' in the district of Medina. His army was numerous and he had enlisted many mamlukes. The Bedouin in those lands feared him greatly.

At the beginning of his reign in Mecca (God protect it) he was a good ruler. He removed the evil-doing black slaves, protected the settlements and favoured and respected the pilgrims. He continued thus for a while but then later he ruled badly, renewed the non-canonical taxes at Mecca and did some shameful things. In some years he plundered the Pilgrim caravan, as we have related.

When he died, he was succeeded by his son al-Ḥasan. He had another son, named Rājiḥ, who dwelt among the Bedouin outside Mecca, causing trouble and offering himself as a rival to his brother as ruler of Mecca. When the Pilgrim caravan from Iraq came, their commander was a mamluke of the Caliph al-Nāṣir li-Dīn Allāh, named Aqbāsh, who had behaved well toward the pilgrims on the way and gave excellent protection. Rājiḥ ibn Qatāda sought him out and offered him and the caliph money to help him become ruler of Mecca. Aqbāsh agreed to this [**402**] and together they came to Mecca, and camped at al-Zāhir. He then advanced on Mecca to fight its ruler, Ḥasan.

Ḥasan, who had gathered large groups of Bedouin and others, moved out of Mecca to offer him battle. The Emir of the Pilgrimage advanced alone before his troops and ascended the mountain full of self-confidence and sure that nobody would move against him, but Ḥasan's men surrounded him and killed him, then suspended his head [from a spear]. The forces of the Commander of the Faithful fled and Ḥasan's men surrounded the pilgrims to plunder them. However, Ḥasan sent them his turban as a guarantee of security for the pilgrims, so his men retired and did not despoil them of anything. Calm spread and Ḥasan allowed them to enter Mecca and do whatever they wanted, perform their pilgrimage, buy and sell and other such things. They remained at Mecca for ten days, then set out home and arrived in Iraq safely. The caliph was outraged by this incident. Envoys arrived from Ḥasan, making excuses and requesting pardon, which was granted.

---

1 According to Sibṭ ibn al-Jawzī, 617–18, who saw Qatāda on a pilgrimage and appreciated his good qualities, he died in Jumādā I 617/ 4 July–2 August 1220.

There is a different version of Qatāda's death, namely that his son Ḥasan throttled him to death. This came about as follows. Qatāda assembled many bodies of men and marched from Mecca towards Medina. He camped at the valley of al-Fur'[2] in a state of sickness. He sent his brother in command of the army, accompanied by his son, al-Ḥasan ibn Qatāda. When they had gone some distance, al-Ḥasan heard that his uncle said to some of the troops, 'My brother is ill. He is going to die, for sure,' and he asked them to swear to him that he would be the emir after his brother Qatāda. Al-Ḥasan came into his uncle's presence and he was joined by many of his father's troops and mamlukes. Al-Ḥasan said to his uncle, 'You have done such and such.' He insisted that he had not, but nevertheless al-Ḥasan ordered those present to put him to death. They refused and said, 'You are an emir and he is an emir. We will not raise our hands against either of you.' Two mamlukes of Qatāda then said to him, 'We are your slaves. Order us to do whatever you want,' so he ordered them to put his uncle's turban [**403**] around his neck, which they did and killed him.

News of this reached Qatāda. His anger knew no bounds and he swore that he would kill his son. He was ill, as we have mentioned. One of his men wrote to al-Ḥasan to inform him of the situation, saying, 'Deal with him first before he kills you.' Al-Ḥasan therefore returned to Mecca and when he arrived, he made for his father's residence with a small band. He found a large gathering at the door of the residence and ordered them to depart to their homes, so they left and went away to their dwellings. Al-Ḥasan went in to his father, who, when he saw him, upbraided him and blamed and threatened him at great length. Al-Ḥasan turned on him and throttled him on the spot. After going out to the Sacred Enclosure, he summoned the *sharīf*s and said, 'My father has become seriously ill. He has ordered you to swear to me that I should be your emir.' They gave their oath. Subsequently he brought out a coffin and buried it so that people would think that he had died [naturally]. In fact, he had already buried him in secret.

When he had become established as emir in Mecca, he sent to his brother, who was in the castle of Yanbu', as though there was a message from his father to summon him. He concealed the death of his father and when his brother arrived, he killed him too. His position became firmly established. He dealt with the Emir of the Pilgrimage as we have already described. He commited a great sin, killing his father, his uncle and his brother within a few days. No wonder that God (glorious and mighty is He) did not grant him a long respite but deprived him of his power and made him an outcast and fugitive, fearful and wary.

It is said that Qatāda used to produce poetry. For example, he was asked to attend upon the Emir of the Pilgrimage, as was customary for the emirs of Mecca, but he refused. He was reprimanded for that from Baghdad but replied with some verses of poetry which contained:

---

2 A settlement between Medina and Mecca (Yāqūt, iii, 877–8).

I have the paw of a lion in the power of which I take pride.
With it I buy and sell amongst mankind.
The princes of the earth continue to kiss its back
While in its palm is spring verdure for the parched.
[**404**] Shall I put it beneath the millstone and then desire
To save it? I would then be foolish indeed!
I am but the musk which in every land
Is wafted abroad, although with you it is wasted.[3]

Miscellaneous events

In this year the Muslims recovered the city of Damietta in Egypt from the Franks. A fully detailed account of this has already been given.[4]

In Ṣafar of this year [27 March–24 April 1221] the Tatars took Marāgha, ruined and burned it, killed most of its people, plundered their wealth and enslaved their womenfolk. From there the Tatars went to Hamadhan, which they put under siege. The population resisted but the Tatars overcame them, killed them in numbers beyond counting and sacked the town. They then went to Azerbayjan, where they repeated their pillage and plundered what was left of the land that they had not plundered initially. They arrived at Baylaqān in Arrān and took it after a siege. They killed [many of] the inhabitants, almost to the point of exterminating them, and plundered their wealth.

From Azerbayjan and Arrān they went to the land of the Georgians, a large host of whom met and fought them. The Georgians were defeated with heavy losses and most of their land was ravaged and its population killed. From there the Tatars went to Darband Shirwān, where they besieged and took the town of Shamākhī and slew many of its inhabitants.

They proceeded to the land of the Alān and the Lakz and the neighbouring peoples. They did much damage, [**405**] then moved away from the Qipjaq, having driven them out of the land and taken control of it. They roamed in that part of the world until they reached the land of the Rūs. All this has been previously related in detail. We have only given it here in summary fashion to make clear which events occurred in this year.

This year our friend died, Amīn al-Dīn Yāqūt, the Mosul secretary. In his lifetime there was no secretary to rival him nor anyone who practised the method of Ibn al-Bawwāb[5] as he did. He was a man of comprehensive merits in the literary field and others, a man of great virtue and a fine fellow of wide repute. People were all united in singing his fair praises and lauding him. They have many sayings

---

3 See *Wāfī*, xxiv, 193.
4 See above, pp. [**326–31**].
5 See the footnote to p. [**299**].

about him, in poetry and prose. An example is the ode in which he is praised by Najīb al-Dīn al-Ḥusayn ibn 'Alī al-Wāsiṭī:

> Gatherer of the fleeting branches of learning, without whom the mother of merits (knowledge) would be bereaved,
> Possessor of a reed pen, whose might the lion fears and to which squadrons humbly submit.
> When its mouth reveals black [ink] on white [paper], then swords and spears are abashed.
> You are a full moon and Secretary Ibn Hilāl is like his father.[6] There is no pride in those who take over the lead.

Another line is as follows:

> If he was first, you are more fit to be preferred, for you outstripped him and he came second.

It is a long ode. The 'Secretary Ibn Hilāl' is Ibn al-Bawwāb, who is too famous to require identification.

Also this year there died Jalāl al-Dīn al-Ḥasan, one of the descendants of al-Ḥasan ibn al-Ṣabbāḥ, who has been mentioned before, the lord of Alamut and Girdkūh, the leader of the Ismā'īlīs. We have mentioned that he had proclaimed the Shariah of Islam, that is, the call to prayer and the ritual of prayer. He was succeeded by his son, 'Alā' al-Dīn Muḥammad.[7]

---

6 i.e. 'Alī ibn Hilāl (lit. son of crescent moon) ibn al-Bawwāb, the famous calligrapher, is merely a crescent moon compared with the full moon of Yāqūt.

7 For Jalāl al-Dīn's return to orthodoxy, see above, p. [**298**]. His son Muḥammad III ruled 1221–55.

The Year 619 [1222–1223]

Account of the irruption of a group of Qipjaq into Azerbayjan, what they did to the Georgians and what happened to them

This year a large group of Qipjaq gathered together, left their lands after the Tatars had overrun them and travelled to Darband Shirwān. They sent to the ruler there, whose name was Rashīd, and said to him, 'The Tatars have seized our lands and plundered our possessions, so we have come to you to dwell in your land. We will be your mamlukes, conquer lands for you and you shall be our sultan.' He rejected that offer and was afraid of them. They renewed their communication, saying, 'We will make our children and wives your surety for our allegiance and service to you and our obedience to your rule.' Again he did not grant their request. They then asked him to allow them to provision themselves from his town, entering ten at a time. When they had purchased what they needed, they would depart from his land. This he agreed to, so they began to enter in separate groups, buy what they wanted and leave.

One of their chiefs and commanders came to Rashīd and said, 'I was in the service of Sultan Khwārazm Shāh and I am a Muslim. My religion urges me to give you advice. Know that the Qipjaq are your enemies. They purpose treachery towards you. Do not permit them to dwell in your lands. [**407**] Give me an army, so that I can fight them and drive them out of your lands.' He complied and entrusted him with a detachment of his army, giving them the weapons and other things that they needed. They marched with this chief and fell upon a body of the Qipjaq, killing a number of them and taking plunder. The Qipjaq made no move to fight but said, 'We are the mamlukes of the prince Shirwān Shāh Rashīd. Were that not so, we would have fought his troops.' When this Qipjaq commander along with Rashīd's troops returned safe and sound, the latter was delighted with them.

Later the Qipjaq left the place where they had been and travelled for three days. This Qipjaq [commander] said to Rashīd, 'I would like a force that I can pursue them with and take what they have as booty.' He ordered that he should have the forces that he wanted and then he set out to follow the Qipjaq's trail. He fell upon the stragglers and took booty from them.

A large number of the Qipjaq, men and women, came to him, weeping and having cut their hair. With them was a coffin, which they clustered around, weeping. They said to him, 'Your friend so-and-so has died. His wish was that we should bring him to you to bury him in whatever place you wished. We shall attend you.' So he and those who were weeping for the deceased bore him away back to Shirwān Shāh Rashīd. He told him that the deceased was a friend of his. He had brought him with him and his family requested that they should be at his court in his service. Rashīd ordered them to enter the town and he gave them lodgings there.

This company used to travel with the chief and ride when he rode, and go up with him into the castle that belonged to Rashīd and sit and drink with him, they and their womenfolk. Rashīd fell in love with the wife of the man who was said to have died. In fact he had not died and they had merely done this to enter the town. The man who they claimed was dead was with them in the chamber, unknown to Rashīd, one of the greatest chiefs of the Qipjaq. They kept this up for several days. Several Qipjaq would come each day in different groups and many gathered in the castle. Their plan was to seize Rashīd and take his lands but he got wind of this and left the castle by the postern gate. He fled away to Shirwān and the Qipjaq took the castle. They said to the inhabitants [**408**] of the town, 'We are better for you than Rashīd' and they brought back the rest of their comrades to join them. They took all the armaments that were in the town and appropriated the money and possessions that Rashīd had in the castle. They then left the castle and made for Qabala,[1] which belonged to the Georgians, descended upon it and put it under siege.

When Rashīd heard that they had left the castle, he returned and recovered it, killing the Qipjaq who were there. The Qipjaq who were at Qabala were unaware of this and sent a detachment of their number to the castle and these also were killed by Rashīd. News of this came to the Qipjaq, so they returned to Darband and had no further ambition for the castle.

The lord of Qabala, when the Qipjaq were besieging him, had sent to them to say, 'I shall send to the king of the Georgians to get him to send you robes of honour and money. We and you will unite and rule the country.' For several days they refrained from plundering his territory but then they turned their hands to plunder and evil-doing and pillaged all the land of Qabala. They travelled on to near Ganja in Arrān, which was held by Muslims. They made camp there and the emir in Ganja, a mamluke of Uzbek, lord of Azerbayjan, whose name was Kūshkhara, sent an army against them to deny them access to his territory.[2] He dispatched an envoy to them, to say, 'You have acted treacherously towards the ruler of Shirwān and taken his castle. You have acted treacherously towards the ruler of Qabala and pillaged his land. Nobody trusts you.' They replied, 'We came only with the intention of serving your sultan. Shirwān Shāh kept us from you and therefore we attacked his lands and took his castle. We then left it, but not because we were afraid. The ruler of Qabala is your enemy and our enemy. Had we wanted to be with the Georgians, we would not have taken our route by Darband Shirwān, for it is very difficult, troublesome and distant, and we would have come to their lands [**409**] in our normal way, while sending hostages to you.'

1 An ancient city near Darband, whose name is spelt thus in Yāqūt, iv, 32. It was situated on the upper course of one of the rivers of Shirwān, the Tūriyān (Minorsky, *Sharvān and Darband*, 75).

2 This last phrase translates the variant reading given in the text's notes.

When Kūshkhara heard this, he set out towards them. The Qipjaq heard of his coming and two of their emirs, commanders among them, rode in a small band to meet and salute him. They said, 'We have come without equipment and in small numbers to show you that our only aim is to be faithful and serve your sultan.' Kūshkhara ordered them to transfer to a camp at Ganja and he married the daughter of one of them. He sent to his master Uzbek to inform him of their situation and the latter ordered robes of honour for them and that they should settle at Mt. Kīlakūn, which they did.

The Georgians were fearful of them and gathered troops for a surprise attack. Word of this reached Kūshkhara, the emir of Ganja, so he told the Qipjaq and ordered them to return to camp at Ganja. This they did. An emir of the Qipjaq led a body of them against the Georgians and fell upon them by surprise. He killed many, put them to flight and seized what they had as booty. Great were their losses, killed or captured. Their defeat was complete and the Qipjaq returned to Mt. Kīlakūn and settled there as before.

After their return another Qipjaq emir wished to make the same mark on the Georgians as his comrade had done. Kūshkhara heard of this and sent, forbidding him to make a move until he collected intelligence on the Georgians. However, he did not wait and set out for their lands with his following. He pillaged, destroyed and seized booty but the Georgians came by a route they knew and cut him off. When he came upon them, a battle was fought. They charged him and the men with him when he was unprepared and taken by surprise. They were put to the sword and great was the slaughter among them. The Georgians recovered the booty, while he and his men returned in a very wretched state and made for Bardha'a.[3]

[**410**] They sent to Kūshkhara to ask him to come, in person with his army, to attack the Georgians and to take revenge on them. He refused and warned them, saying, 'You disobeyed me and acted on your own opinion. I shall not reinforce you with a single horseman.' They sent asking for their hostages but he did not give them back. They banded together and took many Muslims, in numbers equal to the hostages. The local Muslims then rose up against them and fought them, killing many. The Qipjaq were fearful, moved towards Shirwān and crossed into Lakz lands. The inhabitants, Muslims, Georgians, Lakz and others, were eager to deal with them and destroyed them utterly through killing, plundering, capturing [the men] and enslaving [the women], so that a mamluke from among them could be bought in Darband Shirwān for a paltry price.

[3] Modern Barda, south of the Caucasus and north of River Kur, one-time capital of Arrān. See *EI(2)*, i, 1040–41.

How the Georgians plundered Baylaqān

In the month of Ramaḍān this year [9 October–7 November 1222] the Georgians marched from their territory into that of Arrān and attacked the town of Baylaqān. The Tatars had already ruined and pillaged it, as we have mentioned before. When the Tatars went to the land of the Qipjaq, the surviving population returned to the town and repaired what they were able to repair of its wall.

While they were so engaged, the Georgians came upon them, entered the town and took it. The Muslims in this area had become familiar with the Georgians, the way in which, when they took control of a town, they would negotiate its fate for some money and then withdraw. They were the best of enemies when they had the upper hand.[4] On this present occasion the Muslims thought that they would act as they had before, so they did not make great efforts to defend themselves, **[411]** nor did they flee from them. After the Georgians had taken the town, they put the inhabitants to the sword and subjected them to slaughter and pillage worse than the Tatars had done.

While all this was taking place, the lord of Azerbayjan, Uzbek ibn Pahlawān, was in Tabriz, not stirring himself to any advantage nor moving to any good purpose. On the contrary, he was content with eating, drinking bouts and depravity. May God damn him and provide the Muslims with someone to come to their aid and preserve their lands through Muḥammad and his family!

Account of Badr al-Dīn's taking of the castle of Shūsh

This year Badr al-Dīn, lord of Mosul, took the castle of Shūsh in the district of al-Ḥumaydiyya. It is situated twelve leagues from Mosul. This came about as follows. This castle and the castle of al-ʻAqr were neighbours of ʻImād al-Dīn Zankī ibn Arslān Shāh. Between the two there was a dispute, as has already been mentioned. During this year Zankī went to Azerbayjan to make obeisance to its ruler Uzbek ibn Pahlawān. He joined his service, received some fiefs and stayed at his court. Badr al-Dīn marched to the castle of Shūsh and put it under a close siege. It is situated on the top of a high mountain, so his stay there was a long one because of its impregnability. He himself returned to Mosul but left a force to continue the siege. **[412]** When the siege had dragged on for the defenders and they saw nobody able to raise it or send them aid, they surrendered the castle on terms that were agreed, namely an [alternative] fief and robes of honour and such-like. Badr al-Dīn's deputies took it over at that time, organized its affairs and returned to Mosul.

---

4 The translation of the phrase *aḥsan al-aʻdāʼ maqdara* is speculative.

Miscellaneous events

This year on 20 Sha'bān [29 September 1222] a large comet with a long thick tail appeared in the sky in the east. It rose at daybreak and continued so for ten days. Then it appeared at the beginning of the night in the north-west. Each night it moved southwards by about ten cubits, as it appeared to the eye. It continued to move more to the south until it became pure west. Then it became south-west, having been north-west. It remained thus until the end of Ramaḍan [7 November 1222] and then disappeared.

This year Nāṣir al-Dīn Maḥmūd ibn Muḥammad [ibn] Qarā Arslān, ruler of Ḥiṣn Kayfā and Āmid, died. He was a tyrant who ruled his subjects badly. It is said that he used to profess the beliefs of the philosophers, that bodies will not be raised from the dead. They lied (God curse them). After his death he was succeeded by his son al-Mas'ūd.[5]

[5] Al-Mas'ūd Rukn al-Dīn Mawdūd ibn Maḥmūd died 629/1232, the last ruler of the branch that ruled in Ḥiṣn Kayfā and Āmid (see Bosworth, *New Islamic Dynasties*, 194).

The Year 620 [1223–1224]

How the ruler of Yemen took Mecca (may God Almighty protect it)

This year al-Mas'ūd Atsiz, son of al-Kāmil Muḥammad, lord of Egypt, went to Mecca, whose ruler at that time was Ḥasan bin Qatāda ibn Idrīs al-'Alawī al-Ḥusaynī, who had come to power there after his father, as we have related.[1] Ḥasan had badly treated the *Sharīf*s and the mamlukes that his father had had, and they had abandoned him. None but his maternal uncles remained with him. When the lord of Yemen reached Mecca, his troops sacked it until early evening.[2]

A certain worthy person who was in pious retreat at Mecca told me that their pillaging was such that they took the clothes from the people's backs and reduced them to penury. The ruler of Yemen ordered that Qatāda's corpse should be exhumed and burnt, so they dug up the grave. The coffin, in which his son Ḥasan had buried him in sight of the people, appeared but nothing was to be seen inside it. They then realized that Ḥasan had buried his father secretly and that he had put nothing in the coffin. Ḥasan tasted the result of his crime against family ties. God hastened his just deserts and removed from him that for which he had killed his father, brother and uncle. He lost both this world and the next – and that is a manifest loss indeed!

[414] Account of the conflict between Muslims and Georgians in Armenia

In Sha'bān of this year [September 1223] the lord of the castle of Surmārā,[3] which is a dependency of Armenia, went to Khilāṭ, because he was obedient to the lord of Khilāṭ, who was at that time Shihāb al-Dīn Ghāzī ibn al-'Ādil Abū Bakr ibn Ayyūb. He came to him and left one of his emirs as his deputy in his town. This emir gathered a body of men and marched to the lands of the Georgians, where he plundered a number of villages before returning.

The Georgians heard of this and the lord of Dvīn, whose name was Shalwa,[4] one

---

1 Above, p. [**401**].

2 Atsiz led a powerful armed pilgrimage from Yemen and took over Mecca (Abū Shāma, *Dhayl*, 132). Abū Shāma comments that he dealt with troublesome elements at Mecca and reduced prices by ample imports from Egypt. Under the year 621/1224–5 Sibṭ ibn al-Jawzī, 633, records that Aqsīs (sic) went to Cairo with gifts (including three elephants), hoping to receive Damascus etc. from his father.

3 Yāqūt, iii, 82: 'a great castle and an extensive territory between Tiflīs and Khilāṭ'.

4 He was defeated by Khwārazm Shāh Jalāl al-Dīn in 622/1225; see below, p. [**435**] and Juvainī, *History*, ii, 427–9. See also *EI(2)*, v, 490b.

of the great emirs of the Georgians, gathered his troops and marched to Surmārā. He besieged it for some days, plundered the town and the surrounding country and then retired.

When the lord of Surmārā heard the news, he returned home and arrived the day the Georgians departed. Taking his troops, he pursued them and fell upon their rearguard, killing them and taking booty. He recovered part of the booty that they had taken from his lands.

The lord of Dvīn then assembled his army and marched to Surmārā to put it under siege. News of this reached its lord, so he fortified it and collected stores and what he would need. Someone came to him with the information that the Georgians had camped in a valley between Dvīn and Surmārā, a narrow valley. He set out with all his troops without a baggage train and made swift progress to take the Georgians by surprise. He arrived at the valley where they were at daybreak and divided his army into two, one part [to attack] from the head of the valley and the other from the bottom end. They charged them when they were all unprepared and put them to the sword, [**415**] killing and taking prisoners. Among those taken was Shalwa, the emir of Dvīn, along with a large number of their captains. The Georgian survivors returned home in a wretched state.

The king of the Georgians then sent to al-Ashraf Mūsā ibn al-ʿĀdil, lord of the Jazīra, who was the one who had given Khilāṭ and its dependencies to Emir Shihāb al-Dīn, to say, 'We thought that we were at peace but now the lord of Surmārā has done these things. If we are at peace, we want the release of our men from captivity, but if peace between us has broken down, then let us know so that we may manage our affairs accordingly.' Al-Ashraf sent to the lord of Surmārā with orders to release the prisoners and renew the peace with the Georgians. This he did and peace was re-established and the prisoners released.

Account of the conflict between Ghiyāth al-Dīn and his maternal uncle

In Jumādā II this year [July 1223] Īghān Ṭā'īsī, the uncle of Ghiyāth al-Dīn ibn Khwārazm Shāh Muḥammad ibn Tekesh, was defeated. Ghiyāth al-Dīn was the lord of the Uplands, Rayy, Isfahan and elsewhere, and the land of Kirman was also his. It came about as follows. His uncle Īghān Ṭā'īsī was with him in his service, the greatest emir he had, without whose advice Ghiyāth al-Dīn would not initiate anything and whose authority spread through the whole kingdom. When his position became so great, he was tempted to seize rule for himself and others encouraged him in that and fed his ambition. It is said that the Caliph al-Nāṣir li-Dīn Allāh secretly assigned him lands and commanded him to act thus. [**416**] His heart was emboldened to rebel and he suborned and won over several in the army.

When his preparations were complete, he openly rebelled against Ghiyāth al-Dīn and renounced {his allegiance and went to Azerbayjan. There was a mamluke there belonging to its ruler Uzbek, named Bughdī, who had rebelled against his master.}[5] He began to cause disturbances and disrupt traffic, plundering whatever he could from towns and elsewhere. He was joined by a large body of evil troublemakers and had with him another mamluke, named Aybak al-Shāmī. {Their band became numerous and they made common cause with Ghiyath al-Dīn's uncle. All who wished to cause mayhem and pillage joined them and Ghiyāth al-Dīn's uncle was much strengthened by them and his following increased in number.} They all marched against Ghiyāth al-Dīn to bring him to battle, seize his lands and drive him out of them. Ghiyāth al-Dīn assembled his forces and they met in battle in the region of ...[6] Ghiyāth al-Dīn's uncle and his associates were defeated and many of his army were killed or taken prisoner. The defeated troops retired to Azerbayjan in a very wretched state. Ghiyāth al-Dīn remained in his lands and his hold on power became well established.

A strange turn of events without parallel

Of the ruling family in Georgia none remained but a woman. Sovereignty devolved to her and she duly assumed it. She exercised authority over them and ruled. They sought a man for her to be her husband and rule as her deputy, someone who would become a member of the ruling house. However, there was nobody who was fit for this task.

The lord of Erzurum at this time was Mughīth al-Dīn Ṭughril Shāh ibn [**417**] Qilij Arslān ibn Mas'ūd [ibn] Qilij Arslān, a member of the celebrated family of great princes of Islam, the Saljuq rulers. He had a grown-up son and he sent to the Georgians, requesting that his son might marry the queen. They refused to agree to this and said, 'We cannot do this because it is impossible that a Muslim should rule us.' He replied, 'My son will become a Christian and then marry her.' They accepted this, so, on his orders, his son converted and professed Christianity. He then married the queen, went to live with her and remained among the Georgians, ruling in their lands and continuing as a Christian. We seek refuge in God from being forsaken and we beseech Him to make the best of our works their last and the best of our works their conclusions and the best of our days the day we meet Him.

This Georgian queen was in love with a mamluke of hers. Her husband heard evil reports about her but was unable to speak out because of his weak position. One day he went into her chamber and saw her asleep on a bed with her mamluke.

---

[5] The two passages within curly brackets have been added from variant readings given in the text's footnotes. There can be no doubt that the additions are essential. Without them there is no sense in the paragraph. For example, how can 'another mamluke' make sense without mention of the first?

[6] The text has a lacuna here.

He could not accept this and faced her with the demand that she have nothing more to do with him. She replied, 'Either you condone this or you know well [what will happen].' He said, 'I cannot condone this,' so she moved him to another town. She handed him over to men who would control his movements and strictly confine him. She sent to the lands of the Alān, summoned two men who had been described as very handsome, and married one of them. He remained with her for a little and then she parted from him. She summoned another man from Ganja, a Muslim. She asked him to convert to Christianity and marry her but he refused. She then wanted to marry him, although he remained a Muslim. Several emirs, along with Īwānī,[7] who was the commander of the Georgian armies, stood up to her and said, 'We have been disgraced among princes by your actions. Now you want a Muslim to marry you! This we can never allow.' The situation remained unresolved between them. The man from Ganja remained among them but without agreeing to embrace Christianity, while she was still in love with him.

[418] Miscellaneous events

This year there were locusts in most countries, which ruined much of the cereal and vegetable crops in Iraq, the Jazīra, Diyār Bakr, much of Syria and elsewhere.

In Ramaḍān [October 1223] 'Abd al-Raḥmān ibn Hibat Allāh ibn 'Asākir, the Shāfi'ī lawyer from Damascus, died there. He was a man of great learning, knowledgeable in his school of law, very pious, ascetic and virtuous (God have mercy on him).[8]

This year the Bedouin in a great multitude waylaid the pilgrims from Syria. They wished to interrupt their passage and seize them. The emir in charge of the pilgrims was Sharaf al-Dīn Ya'qūb ibn Muḥammad, a man from Mosul who dwelt in Damascus and had become prominent there. He deterred them with threats and promises, eventually settling with them for some money, clothes and other items. He gave all from his own resources and did not take a single dirham from the pilgrims. This was a fine thing he did. He was a man of much learning and had the resource of a solid faith.

---

7 i.e. Ivane Mxargrdzeli. See Juvainī, *History*, ii, 440, note 10; Minorsky, *Studies*, 102–3.

8 A member of a leading Damascene family, Fakhr al-Dīn 'Abd al-Raḥmān ibn Muḥammad, a nephew of the historian Ibn 'Asākir, was born in 550/1155–6 (correct the 505 given by Abū Shāma) and died on Wednesday 10 Rajab/ 9 August 1223 (Abū Shāma, *Dhayl*, 136–9; Sibṭ ibn al-Jawzī, 630–31).

[**419**] The Year 621 [1224–1225]

Account of the return of a group of Tatars to Rayy, Hamadhan and elsewhere

At the beginning of this year [began 24 January 1224] a group of Tatars came from Chingiz Khan, different from the 'westward' group, whose doings before these arrived at Rayy we have already narrated. Those of Rayy's population who had survived had returned there and rebuilt it. The Tatars came upon them before they knew what was happening. They offered no resistance but the Tatars put the populace to the sword and killed them at will, plundering and destroying the town. They went to Saveh and acted in a similar fashion, and then on to Qumm and Qāshān, which had escaped the Tatars initially, for they had gone nowhere near them and inflicted no damage on their inhabitants. These, however, came and took both places, killed their people and destroyed both, adding them to [the list of] other ruined cities.

They then travelled through the land, destroying, murdering and plundering, and subsequently made for Hamadhan, where many of the surviving population had gathered. The Tatars eliminated them through massacre, capture and pillage, and razed the city.

When they arrived at Rayy, they saw there a large force of Khwārazmians, whom they surprised, killing some. The rest fled to Azerbayjan and settled on its borders. Before they were aware, the Tatars fell on them once more and put them to the sword. They fled in rout and some reached [**420**] Tabriz, to whose ruler Uzbek ibn Pahlawān the Tatars sent, saying, 'If you are with us, hand over the Khwārazmians you have; otherwise, tell us that you are not in agreement with us and not obedient to us.' Uzbek turned on the Khwārazmians with him and executed some and seized others. He carried the prisoners and the heads [of those executed] to the Tatars and also sent with them a large quantity of money, clothings and mounts. The Tatars then retired towards Khurasan. What they did was done by a small number, for they were about 3,000 horsemen, while the Khwārazmians, who were defeated by them, were about 6,000 strong. Uzbek's army was larger than both the others together and yet he could motivate neither himself nor the Khwārazmians to resist them.

We beseech God to provide for Islam and the Muslims someone to undertake to help them. They have already been reduced to a critical situation through the killing of people, the plunder of property, the enslavement of children, the killing and capture of womenfolk and the destruction of towns.

How Ghiyāth al-Dīn took the land of Fars

We have previously mentioned that Ghiyāth al-Dīn ibn Khwārazm Shāh was at Rayy. In addition he held Isfahan, Hamadhan and the territory between, and also Kirman was his. After the death of his father, as we have mentioned, the Tatars came to his land and he resisted in Isfahan. The Tatars besieged him there but could achieve nothing. When the Tatars left his lands and went to the lands of the Qipjaq, he again took control and reconstructed what he could. He remained there until towards the end of the year 620 [ended 23 January 1224]. There then happened to him what we have already narrated.[1]

At the end of the year 620 he marched to Fars and the first thing that its ruler was aware of, that is [**421**] Atabeg Sa'd ibn Dakalā, was the arrival of Ghiyāth al-Dīn at the borders of his land. He was unable to resist, so made his way to the citadel of Iṣṭakhr, where he took refuge. Ghiyāth al-Dīn proceeded to the city of Shiraz, the capital of Fars, its largest and most important city, and took it with no effort at the beginning of the year 621 [began 24 January 1224]. Ghiyāth al-Dīn stayed there and took control of most of the country. Only the strong fortresses remained in Sa'd's possession.

When Sa'd had endured this for some time, he came to terms with Ghiyāth al-Dīn on the basis that Sa'd should have an agreed part of the lands, while Ghiyāth al-Dīn had the remainder. Ghiyāth al-Dīn stayed at Shiraz and his period of residence there and his determination to remain grew when he heard that the Tatars had returned to Rayy and the lands he held and ruined them.

How Shihāb al-Dīn Ghāzī rebelled against his brother al-Ashraf and how Khilāṭ was taken from him

Al-Ashraf Mūsā, son of al-'Ādil Abū Bakr ibn Ayyūb, had assigned to his brother Shihāb al-Dīn Ghāzī the city of Khilāṭ and all the districts of Armenia, and had added to them Mayyāfāriqīn, Ḥānī and Jabal Jūr. That did not content Shihāb al-Dīn until he had been made his heir-apparent in all the lands al-Ashraf held and all the governors and troops in his lands had given him their oath.

When Armenia was handed to him, he made his way there, as we have related, and remained there until the end of the year 620 [ended 23 January 1224]. He made plain that he was angry with his brother al-Ashraf, openly accused him of wronging him, rebelled and threw off his allegiance. Al-Ashraf sent to conciliate him and to find fault with what he had done. However, he paid no notice and did not abandon his course but persisted in it. He, his brother al-Mu'aẓẓam 'Īsā, lord of Damascus, and Muẓaffar al-Dīn ibn Zayn al-Dīn, lord of Irbil, agreed [**422**] to oppose al-Ashraf and to unite to wage war on him. They made this public.

---

1 See pp. [**415–16**].

When he learnt this, al-Ashraf sent to his brother al-Kāmil in Egypt to inform him, for they were in alliance, and to ask him for aid. Al-Kāmil equipped [and despatched] troops and sent to his brother, the lord of Damascus, saying, 'If you move from your city, I shall come and take it.' He had already left to go to the Jazīra for the rendezvous that they had arranged, but when his brother's message reached him and he heard that he had dispatched troops, he returned to Damascus.

As for the lord of Irbil, he had assembled troops and set out for Mosul. What happened to him we shall relate later, God willing. Meanwhile, al-Ashraf, having confirmed that his brother had rebelled, assembled troops from Syria, the Jazīra and Mosul and proceeded to Khilāṭ. When he drew near, his brother Ghāzī became fearful, as he did not have the strength to meet him in battle, so he distributed his forces in his towns to garrison them. His brother, the lord of Damascus, expected that the lord of Irbil would send [troops] to the lands adjacent to him, Mosul and Sinjar, and that his brother [Shihāb al-Dīn] would move against al-Ashraf's lands near the Euphrates, Raqqa, Ḥarrān and others, so that al-Ashraf would then be compelled to withdraw from Khilāṭ.

However, al-Ashraf continued his march to attack Khilāṭ. Its populace were in favour of him and preferred his rule because of his good government they had known and Ghāzī's bad government. When he had put it under siege, its people surrendered it to him on Monday 12 Jumādā II [1 July 1224]. Ghāzī continued to defend the citadel but when night fell, he came down to his brother, making excuses and attempting vindication. Al-Ashraf rebuked him but spared him and did not punish him for his actions. He took the lands from him, however, and left him with Mayyāfāriqīn.

[423] Account of the lord of Irbil's siege of Mosul

We have already mentioned the agreement of Muẓaffar al-Dīn Kūkbūrī ibn Zayn al-Dīn 'Alī, lord of Irbil, Shihāb al-Dīn Ghāzī, lord of Khilāṭ, and al-Mu'aẓẓam 'Īsā, lord of Damascus, to attack the lands of al-Ashraf. After having travelled a few stages, the lord of Damascus returned home because his brother the lord of Egypt sent to threaten him that, if he left Damascus, he would attack and put it under siege. He therefore returned. Ghāzī was besieged in Khilāṭ, which was taken from him, as we have narrated.

The lord of Irbil assembled his army and marched to Mosul, which he put under siege on Tuesday 13 Jumādā II [2 July 1224], in the expectation that, when al-Ashraf heard that he had invested it, he would raise the siege of Khilāṭ, Ghāzī would emerge to pursue him, complicating his situation, and that the lord of Damascus would be emboldened to join them. When he began the siege of Mosul, its lord, Badr al-Dīn Lu'lu', had secured its position, enlisting soldiers to man the walls, preparing siege defences and issuing stores.

The lord of Irbil's ambition to besiege Mosul had been strengthened in particular because most of its regular forces had gone to join al-Ashraf at Khilāṭ and there were few troops left there. There was also a severe famine in all its lands and the price [of wheat] in Mosul was three *makkūk*s for a dinar. This was why he was bold enough to besiege it. After he descended upon it, he remained for ten days but then withdrew on Friday nine days remaining of Jumādā II [= 12 July 1224].

The reason for his withdrawal was that he saw how strong the city was, the great number of the inhabitants and that they had stores to suffice them for a long time. News also came to him that al-Ashraf had taken Khilāṭ. All his hopes from its lord and from Damascus were dashed. He was left **[424]** alone, embroiled in the situation. When these reports came to him, he was dismayed and saw that he had mistaken the right course. He withdrew back towards his own land and made a stop on the Zāb. During his siege of Mosul, he had made no assault on it. At moments some of his advance guard would just come to engage the city and some cavalry and some infantry come out to meet them. A clash that did not amount to much would ensue, then they would part and each side return to its lord.

Miscellaneous events

This year at the beginning of Āb [August] rain fell at Baghdad, accompanied by thunder and lightning. There was flooding in Basra Gate and al-Ḥarbiyya and likewise at al-Muḥawwal so that people were wading through water and mud at the latter.

This year the keeper of the Storeroom went to Ba'qūbā in Dhū'l-Qa'da [14 November–13 December 1224] and acted oppressively towards its inhabitants. It was reported to him that a man there was cursing him, so he summoned him and ordered him to be punished. He said to the man, 'Why do you curse me?' to which the reply was, 'You curse Abū Bakr and 'Umar for their taking Fadak, ten palm trees that belonged to Fāṭima (peace be upon her).[2] You then take one thousand palms from me and I am not to speak out!' He pardoned him.

This year discord broke out in Wāsiṭ between the Sunnis and the Shiites, as is their normal practice.

This year the rains were sparse in the lands. None came until February (Subāṭ). Then they came at scattered times over a short period but not sufficiently to irrigate the crops. The crops grew sparsely and then they were attacked by locusts. There was not enough [natural] vegetation in the country to keep the locusts busy, so they consumed all but a little of the crops. They were numerous, more than

2 One may assume from this that the official was a Shiite. There was a long-standing dispute over the status of Fadak, a formerly Jewish settlement near Khaybar in N. Hijaz. The Shiites claimed that was inherited by Fāṭima from Muḥammad as private property but for the Sunnis it was public charitable property, albeit used at times for the maintenance of the Prophet's family. For a full discussion, see *EI(2)*, ii, 725–7.

could possibly be counted. Prices rose in Iraq and Mosul and in the rest of the Jazīra and Diyār Bakr and elsewhere. Foodstuffs were in short supply, although the scarcity was worst in Mosul and the Jazīra.

[425] The Year 622 [1225–1226]

Account of the Georgians' siege of Ganja

This year the Georgians with all their forces went to the town of Ganja in Arran with the intention of besieging it. They prepared for it with all the strength they could because the people of Ganja were very numerous, militarily very powerful and of great valour from their long practice of warfare with the Georgians. When they arrived and camped about it, they engaged the defenders behind the city wall for several days. None of the defenders made an appearance. Then one day the people of Ganja and the soldiers among them sallied forth and engaged the Georgians outside the town in a violent and major battle. Seeing this, the Georgians realized that the town was too strong for them, so they withdrew after the people of Ganja had inflicted serious losses on them. 'God drove back the infidels in their raging. They achieved no good.'[1]

Account of the coming of Jalāl al-Dīn ibn Khwārazm Shāh to Khuzistan and Iraq

At the beginning of this year [began 13 January 1225] Jalāl al-Dīn ibn Khwārazm Shāh Muḥammad ibn Tekesh came to Khuzistan and Iraq. He came from Indian lands because he had gone there [**426**] when the Tatars invaded Ghazna. All of this we have mentioned already. When it became impossible for him to remain in India, he left, passing through Kirman, and came to Isfahan, which was in the hands of his brother Ghiyāth al-Dīn, an account of whose doings has been given before. He took Isfahan and from there proceeded to Fars, part of which had been taken over by his brother, as we have mentioned. He restored to Atabeg Sa'd, its ruler, what his brother had taken from him and made a treaty with him. Leaving him, he went on to Khuzistan and in Muḥarram [13 January–11 February 1225] besieged the town of Tustar, which was held as governor and emir by Emir Muẓaffar al-Dīn, known as Lion-Face, the Caliph al-Nāṣir li-Dīn Allāh's mamluke. Jalāl al-Dīn imposed a tight blockade on him but Lion-Face defended the town with a great deal of energy and care. The Khwārazmian forces scattered for pillage. They even reached as far as Bādurāyā[2] and Bākusāyā[3] among other places, and some went

[1] Koran, xxxiii, 25.

[2] Modern Badrah, east of Baghdad and north of Kut al-Amara. See Krawulsky, 464–5.

[3] At the modern town of Bagsaya, near the Iraqi border with Iran there are ruins of this small town, in the province of Maysan. See Yāqūt, i, 477; Krawulsky, 466.

south as far as the district of Basra, where they engaged in plunder. The prefect of Basra, namely Emir Multakīn, moved against them, fell on them and killed several. The siege [of Tustar] lasted about two months and then Jalāl al-Dīn departed suddenly.

The troops of the caliph were nearby with his mamluke, Jamāl al-Dīn Qashtimur. When Jalāl al-Dīn departed, the army was not able to stop him. He pressed on till he came to Ba'qūbā, a well-known settlement on the Khurasan Road about seven leagues distant from Baghdad. News of this came to Baghdad and preparations for a siege were undertaken. Armaments, such as arbalests, bows, arrows, naphtha and others, were made ready and the caliph's army returned to Baghdad.

Jalāl al-Dīn's army plundered and ruined the country. He and his army had arrived at Khuzistan in severe hardship and distress with few mounts and little baggage. He was in such a state of weakness that he was good for nothing, but they plundered all the country and became well provided. [**427**] In particular they took many horses and mules, for they were in extreme need of them.

From Ba'qūbā he went to Daqūqā, which he put under siege. Its citizens mounted the walls and fought him. They taunted him and gave many shouts of 'God is great!' This annoyed and irked him, so he exerted himself in his attacks on them. He took the place by force of arms and his troops sacked it, killing many of the inhabitants. Those that escaped being killed fled and were scattered throughout the lands.

When the Khwārazmians were at Daqūqā, a squadron of them went to al-Batt and al-Rādhān.[4] Their people fled to Takrīt. The Khwārazmians pursued them and a fierce battle took place between them and the army of Takrīt. They then retired to rejoin [the rest of] the army.

I met some of the notables of Daqūqā, namely the Banū Ya'lā, a rich family. They suffered in the sack, although one of them escaped along with two sons he had and a paltry part of his wealth. He sent what he managed to keep to Syria, along with his two sons to trade with it for income that they might employ for their own support. One of the sons died in Damascus and the authorities sequestered their property. I saw their father in a wretched state that God alone could comprehend. He used to say, 'Our money and properties have been seized, some of the family slain and the survivors fled our homeland with this paltry amount. We wished to use it to avoid the shame of begging and maintain ourselves, but now my son and my substance have both gone.' Later he travelled to Damascus to collect what was left with his other son. He did so and returned to Mosul. However, he did not survive more than a month before he died. 'A man in distress is throttled by every rope.'

---

4 Al-Batt is described as 'one of the dependencies (*a'māl*) of Baghdad' and 'near Rādhan'. There were upper and lower Rādhān, two districts (*kūra*s) of the Sawād of Baghdad, each containing many villages (Yāqūt, i, 488 and ii, 729–30).

After Jalāl al-Dīn had treated the people of Daqūqā as he did, the inhabitants of al-Bawāzīj, which belonged to the lord of Mosul, were fearful and sent to him, requesting him to send them a prefect to protect them, offering him a sum of money. He accepted this and dispatched someone to protect them. It is said that it was one of the sons of Chingiz Khan, ruler of the Tatars, who had been taken prisoner by Jalāl al-Dīn in one of his wars [**428**] with the Tatars and had been treated honourably. He gave them protection.

Jalāl al-Dīn remained in his position until the last days of Rabīʿ II [ended 10 May 1225], while messengers were going to and fro between him and Muẓaffar al-Dīn, lord of Irbil. They came to terms and Jalāl al-Dīn departed for Azerbayjan. During Jalāl al-Dīn's stay in Khuzistan and Iraq, the Arabs rose up throughout the land, interrupting communications, plundering villages and spreading fear on the roads. All and sundry suffered great hardship on account of them. They seized two large caravans on the Iraq highway that were going to Mosul. Nothing at all survived from either.

Account of the death of al-Afḍal and other princes

In Ṣafar of this year [12 February–12 March 1225] al-Afḍal, son of Saladin, died suddenly in the citadel of Sumaysāṭ.[5] He was about fifty-seven years old. We have mentioned under the year 589 [1193] at the time of the death of his father (God have mercy on him) how he became ruler of Damascus, Jerusalem and other parts of Syria. Under the year 592 [1195–6] we have mentioned how all was taken from him and then under the year 595 [1198–9] how he became ruler of Egypt and finally under the year 596 [1199–1200] how it was taken from him. He moved to Sumaysāṭ and took up residence there where he remained until the present time and died there.

He was (God have mercy on him) one of the ornaments of the age. There was no other prince like him. He was good, just, learned, mild and generous; rarely would he punish a fault and he never refused a petitioner. He wrote a handsome hand and excellent prose. In short, in him were united the excellencies [**429**] and virtues that were separately scattered among many princes. It is no wonder he was deprived of sovereignty and worldly success and that fate was hostile to him. With his death died every noble deed. May God have mercy on him and be pleased with him.

I have seen some excellent things that he has written. Among those that remain in my memory is the letter he wrote to one of his friends when Damascus was taken from him, one section of which has:

---

5 Ibn Wāṣil, iv, 155, agrees the date of his death, but Sibṭ ibn al-Jawzī, 637, and Abū Shāma, *Dhayl*, 145, give Rabīʿ I/13 March–11 April.

As for our friends in Damascus, I have no knowledge of any of them. This is because

Every friend I ask after is in disgrace and in obscurity at home;
Every enemy whose state I ask after, I hear what my ear likes not.

So I have given up asking about them.

This is a very excellent way to apologize for not enquiring about a friend. After his death his children and their uncle Quṭb al-Dīn Mūsā became in dispute but none of them was strong enough over the rest to seize power for himself.[6]

During this year the lord of Erzurum died, namely Mughīth al-Dīn Ṭughril ibn Qilij Arslān. He is the one who sent his son to the Georgians to become a Christian and marry the queen of Georgia. When he died, his son succeeded him as ruler.

There also died this year the ruler of Erzinjan.[7]

'Izz al-Dīn al-Khiḍr ibn Ibrāhīm ibn Abī Bakr ibn Qarā Arslān ibn Dā'ūd ibn Suqmān, the lord of Khartbirt, died this year. He was succeeded by his son Nūr al-Dīn Artuq Shāh. The administrator behind his and his father's throne was Mu'īn al-Dīn Badr ibn 'Abd al-Raḥmān, who was Baghdādī by origin and Mosulī by upbringing.

[430] Account of the deposition of Shirwān Shāh and the Muslims' victory over the Georgians

This year Shirwān Shāh's son[8] rebelled against him, removed him from power, banished him and took power as his successor. The reason for this was that Shirwān Shāh was a bad ruler, much given to wickedness and tyranny, laying his hands on his subjects' wealth and properties. It is also said that he used to interfere with women and children. His oppression became hard for people to bear. Some of the army conspired with the son and expelled his father. The son took power and ruled well, loved by the army and the people. He sent to his father to say, 'I wanted to leave you in one of the castles and to supply ample allowances for you and all whom you want to have around you. What brought me to what I did to you was your evil conduct and your oppression of the people and their hatred of you and your regime.'

---

6 After al-Afḍal's death his brother al-Mufaḍḍal Quṭb al-Dīn Mūsā took over Sumaysāṭ, according to Ibn Wāṣil, iv, 155. A later passage, based on *Kāmil*, states that al-Afḍal's 'sons and brothers' (sic) disputed Sumaysāṭ with no one gaining complete control (Ibn Wāṣil, iv, 158).

7 Bahrām Shāh was a member of a Turkoman dynasty dating from the early twelfth century, known as the Mangujakids and centred on Erzinjan and Divriği. See Cahen, *Pre-Ottoman Turkey*, 108–9, 127.

8 Complicated politics make identification of the persons concerned a problem. For a discussion, see *EI(2)*, ix, 489.

When the father saw this, he went to the Georgians and asked for their aid. He arranged with them that they would send an army with him to restore him to power and he would give them half the land. They therefore sent off a large force with him which drew near the city of Shirwān. His son assembled the army and informed them of the situation. He said, 'When the Georgians besiege us, perhaps they may overwhelm us and then my father will not spare one of us. The Georgians will take half the land. Perhaps they will take all. This is a great crisis. Our right course is to leave our baggage, advance and confront them. If we are victorious, then praise be to God, but if they are victorious, then we face a siege.' They agreed with him on this course.

He marched out with his army, which was small, about a thousand horse. They met the Georgians, who were three thousand fighting men strong. Battle was joined; the men of Shirwān held firm and the Georgians fled. Many of them were killed or taken. The survivors returned in a very bad state, with Shirwān Shāh, [**431**] the deposed, accompanying them.

The leaders of the Georgians said to him, 'You have been the cause of our coming to no good but we will not punish you for what you brought about. However, do not remain in our lands.' So he left them and continued a wandering life with no one to give him refuge. His son became well established in power and was good to the soldiery and the citizens. He restored to them their properties and what had been extorted from them. People were happy with his rule.

Account of another Muslim victory over the Georgians

Also in this year a body of Georgians left Tiflis, making for Azerbayjan and the lands in the possession of Uzbek. They camped beyond a narrow pass in the mountains, only passable by horsemen in single column, and they made camp there with no fear of the Muslims, because they thought them weak and were overconfident in the strength of their position and that there was no route to get to them.

A detachment of the Muslim forces rode out to meet them. They came to this pass, which they went through, taking great risks. The Muslims were upon them before the Georgians realized. They put them to the sword, killing them at will. The remnants turned their backs in flight with every man for himself.[9] A goodly number of them were taken prisoner, so with a feeling of outrage they determined to take their revenge and do their utmost to attack Azerbayjan and extirpate the Muslims. They began to make preparations commensurate with their plan.

While they were thus engaged, news came to them of Jalāl al-Dīn ibn Khwārazm Shāh's arrival at Marāgha, as we shall narrate, God willing. They abandoned their

9 The literal translation of the Arabic is 'with a father not concerned for his son, nor a brother for his brother'.

purpose and sent to Uzbek, lord of Azerbayjan, inviting him to cooperate in repelling Jalāl al-Dīn. They said, 'If we do not agree, we and you, he will overwhelm you and then us.' However, Jalāl al-Dīn forestalled them before they could agree and combine. What happened we shall narrate, if God Almighty wills.

[432] Account of Jalāl al-Dīn's taking of Azerbayjan

During this year Jalāl al-Dīn took control of Azerbayjan. This came about as follows. When he left Daqūqā, as we have mentioned, he made for Marāgha, which he seized and made his residence. He embarked upon the restoration of the town and found it to his liking. When he arrived there, news came to him that Emir Īghān Ṭā'īsī, the maternal uncle of his brother Ghiyāth al-Dīn, had attacked Hamadhan two days before his arrival.

This Īghān Ṭā'īsī had gathered a large army, as many as 5,000 cavalry, and plundered much of Azerbayjan. He travelled to the Caspian Sea from Arrān and wintered there because it was less cold. When he returned to Hamadhan he pillaged Azerbayjan again a second time. The reason for his expedition to Hamadhan was that the Caliph al-Nāṣir li-Dīn Allāh made contact with him and commanded him to attack it and assigned it and other places to him as a fief. He set out to take control of it, as he had been ordered. When Jalāl al-Dīn heard of this, he set out with a lightly equipped force and came to Īghān Ṭā'īsī at night. When the latter had made camp, he had placed around his troops all that they had plundered from Azerbayjan and Arrān, horses, mules, donkeys, cattle and sheep. When Jalāl al-Dīn arrived, he surrounded everything. In the morning when Īghān Ṭā'īsī's army saw the troops and the parasol that was carried over the sultan's head, they realized that it was Jalāl al-Dīn and were dismayed because they imagined him to be at Daqūqā. Īghān Ṭā'īsī sent his wife, Jalāl al-Dīn's sister, to ask for guarantees for him. They were granted and he was brought before Jalāl al-Dīn. His army was incorporated into that of Jalāl al-Dīn, leaving Īghān Ṭā'īsī with no following, until Jalāl al-Dīn assigned him an army, but not his [original] one. He then returned to Marāgha and was pleased to reside there.

Uzbek ibn Pahlawān, lord of Azerbayjan and Arrān, had left Tabriz [**433**] for Ganja in fear of Jalāl al-Dīn. The latter sent to those in Tabriz, governor, emir or headman, asking them that his troops might visit them to provision themselves. They allowed this and showed themselves obedient to him, so his troops entered the city and bought and sold foodstuffs, clothing and such-like, but they laid their hands on people's property. One of them would take something and give whatever he wanted as the price. Some of the inhabitants of Tabriz complained about them to Jalāl al-Dīn who sent a prefect to be with them and ordered him to remain in Tabriz and restrain his soldiers. Whoever mistreated anyone would be crucified. The prefect took up residence and the soldiers were stopped from mistreating any of the people.

The wife of Uzbek, that is, the daughter of Sultan Ṭughril ibn Arslān ibn Ṭughril ibn Muḥammad ibn Malikshāh, was resident in Tabriz and she was the [real] ruler in her husband's lands, while he was preoccupied with his pleasures, eating, drinking and dalliance.

Eventually the people of Tabriz complained of the prefect, saying, 'He demands from us more than we can manage.' Jalāl al-Dīn therefore ordered that he should be given only what he needed for his support and nothing more, so this is what they did. Jalāl al-Dīn then proceeded to Tabriz and besieged it for five days and fought a fierce battle with the inhabitants. He ordered an assault and his troops reached the city wall. The people then announced their submission and sent asking for his guarantee of security, for he was blaming them and saying, 'They killed our men, Muslims, and sent their heads to the Tatar infidels.' This incident has been mentioned before under the year 621 [1224].[10] This made them fear him and when they asked for terms, he reminded them of what they had done with his father's men and how they had killed them. They made the excuse that they had done none of that and that it was only their ruler's doing, while they had had no power to stop him. He accepted their excuse and granted them terms. They also asked him to give guarantees to Uzbek's wife and not to cause her difficulties over the property, money and the like in the parts of Azerbayjan she held, namely the town of Khoy and elsewhere. He granted that to them. He took the city on 17 Rajab of this year [25 July 1225] and sent Uzbek's wife to [**434**] Khoy, accompanied by a detachment of the army, led by an important man of high status, who was ordered to serve her. Once she had arrived at Khoy, they returned.[11]

When Jalāl al-Dīn came to Tabriz, he gave orders that none of the inhabitants should be kept away from him, so people came to greet him and were not denied access. He was generous to them, disseminated justice and promised them good treatment and more of it. He said to them, 'You have seen how I have been good to Marāgha and restored it after it was a ruin. You will see how I shall deal with you, giving you justice and restoring your land.' He stayed until it was Friday, when he attended the mosque. When the preacher named and prayed for the caliph, he rose to his feet and continued standing until the prayer was over and then sat down. He visited a pavilion that Uzbek had constructed and spent large sums of money on. It was extremely beautiful with a view over orchards. After he had wandered around it, he left and said, 'This is a dwelling of the idle. It is not fit for us.' He remained for several days, during which he gained control of other towns and dispatched troops to the land of the Georgians.

---

[10] See above, p. [**420**].

[11] For a version of the fall of Tabriz, see Nasawī, 194–6.

Account of the defeat of the Georgians by Jalāl al-Dīn

In previous years we have mentioned what the Georgians were doing in the lands of Islam, that is, Khilāṭ, Azerbayjan, Arran, Erzurum and Darband Shirwān, states which were bordering their lands, and how they were shedding Muslim blood, plundering their property and seizing their land, while the Muslims in these regions were being humbled and shamed by them. Every day they raided them, did slaughter among them and imposed upon them whatever they wanted [**435**] by way of tribute. Whenever we heard anything of this, we prayed God Almighty, we and [all] Muslims, to supply Islam and the Muslims with someone to defend and aid them and take revenge for them. Uzbek, lord of Azerbayjan, was devoted to the desires of his stomach and his private parts. He used not to sober up, but if he did, he would be preoccupied, gambling with eggs.[12]

It is unheard-of for a prince to act so, without being guided rightly to the public good or being outraged that his lands are seized, his troops avaricious and his subjects overweening. Everyone who wished to assemble a band and seize control of part of the country did so, as we have mentioned in the case of Bughdī, Aybak al-Shāmī and Īghān Ṭa'īsī. God Almighty looked upon the wretched people of these lands with a merciful eye, so he pitied them and sent them this Jalāl al-Dīn, who dealt with the Georgians as you will see and took revenge on them for Islam and the Muslims.

This year there was a battle between Jalāl al-Dīn ibn Khwārazm Shāh and the Georgians in the month of Sha'bān [8 August–5 September 1225]. Since Jalāl al-Dīn came to these regions he continued to say, 'I want to invade the Georgians, fight them and take their land.' After he had conquered Azerbayjan, he sent to them to declare war. Their answer was, 'We have been attacked by the Tatars who did to Uzbek what you are well aware of and he has a larger kingdom and a more numerous army than you and a stronger morale. They also took your lands. We, however, were not concerned about them and the most they could hope for was to get away from us in safety.' They began to collect troops and brought together more than 70,000 warriors. Jalāl al-Dīn marched against them and took the town of Dvīn, which was held by the Georgians, who had taken it from the Muslims, as we have narrated. He marched on and met them in a very fierce and great battle. Both sides held firm but eventually the Georgians fled. The order was given that they should be slain on every route and none of them spared. What we have ascertained is that 20,000 of them were killed. Some say more than that and others that all the Georgians were killed. They were scattered and many of their notables taken, among them Shalwa. Their rout was complete. Īwānī fled the field, the commander [**436**] of all the Georgians, the man they referred to and relied upon. They had no king; a woman ruled. The Prophet of God (God bless him and give

---

[12] See Rosenthal, *Gambling*, 61–2. What is described there sounds like 'conkers', played for stakes, using hard-boiled eggs.

him peace) spoke truly indeed when he said, 'No people will prosper who appoint a woman to rule over them.'[13]

When Īwānī fled, the pursuers caught up with him, so he went up into a castle of theirs on the route they followed and took refuge there. Jalāl al-Dīn posted some men to besiege it and prevent them from leaving and he sent parties of his soldiers throughout the lands of the Georgians to plunder, kill, take captives and ruin the land. Had it not been for the news from Tabriz that necessitated his return, he would have taken the country without fatigue or difficulty because its people were destroyed, either killed, captives or refugees.

Account of Jalāl al-Dīn's return to Tabriz, his conquest of the city of Ganja and his marriage with Uzbek's wife

Having completed the defeat of the Georgians, entered their lands and sent out his troops here and there, Jalāl al-Dīn ordered them to remain there with his brother Ghiyāth al-Dīn and himself returned to Tabriz. The reason for his return was that he had left his vizier Sharaf al-Dīn behind in Tabriz to hold the city and to investigate what was needed for the best interests of the population and what he had heard concerning the headman of Tabriz and concerning Shams al-Dīn al-Ṭughrā'ī, the leader of all in the city, and other prominent people that they had met together and taken an oath to oppose Jalāl al-Dīn and restore the city to Uzbek. They said, 'Jalāl al-Dīn has invaded the lands of the Georgians. If we rebel against him and summon Uzbek and the troops he has, Jalāl al-Dīn will be forced to withdraw and when he withdraws, the Georgians will pursue him. He will be unable to rest anywhere and Uzbek and the Georgians will unite to attack him. His position will unravel and his defeat will be complete.'

[**437**] Their plan was built on the premise that Jalāl al-Dīn would proceed slowly into the Georgians' lands and take his time on the route, being wary of them. When they had agreed on it, news of it reached the vizier, who sent to Jalāl al-Dīn to inform him of the situation. This intelligence came to him when he was already close to the Georgians' territory. He made none of this public but travelled with all speed towards the Georgians, whom he met and defeated. Having dealt with them, he then said to the army's emirs, 'Such and such information has come to my ears. Continue in this country to do what you are about, killing those you overcome and destroying all you can of their lands. I feared to inform you before the Georgians were defeated lest weakness and fear should come upon you.'

They continued as they were but he returned to Tabriz and arrested the headman, al-Ṭughrā'ī[14] and others. The headman he ordered to be paraded before

---

[13] See footnote to p. [**377**] above.

[14] According to Nasawī, 203–4, Shams al-Dīn al-Ṭughra'ī was falsely accused by the vizier Sharaf al-Dīn. Helped to escape by well-wishers, he went to Irbil and then Baghdad. In

the inhabitants and all who had suffered any wrong at his hands should take satisfaction for it, for he was an oppressor. This delighted the people and then he put him to death. The others were imprisoned. After they had been dealt with and order re-established in the city, he married Uzbek's wife, the daughter of Sultan Ṭughril. His marriage to her was valid because it was confirmed that Uzbek had sworn that he would not kill a mamluke of his, called ...,[15] otherwise he would divorce her. However, he had then killed him. When the divorce took place by virtue of this oath, Jalāl al-Dīn married her. He remained in Tabriz for a while and sent an army to Ganja, which was taken. Uzbek moved out to the fortress of Ganja in which he fortified himself.

I have heard that Jalāl al-Dīn's troops caused much damage to the dependent lands of this fortress by plunder and pillage. Uzbek sent to Jalāl al-Dīn to complain, saying, 'I was not in favour of this business which was due to some of my men. I request that aggressive acts against these districts be restrained.' Jalāl al-Dīn sent men to protect them from interference either from his followers or any others.

[438] Account of the death of the Caliph al-Nāṣir li-Dīn Allāh

This year the last night of Ramaḍān [5 October 1225] there died the Caliph al-Nāṣir li-Dīn Allāh Abū'l-'Abbās Aḥmad ibn al-Mustaḍī' bi-Amr Allāh.[16] ... **[439]** ... Al-Nāṣir's mother was a Turkish *umm walad*, called Zumurrud (Emerald). His caliphate lasted forty-six [lunar] years, ten months and twenty-eight days, and his age was about seventy years more or less. Nobody held the caliphate for a longer period than he, except for what is reported of al-Mustanṣir bi-Allāh the Alid, ruler of Egypt, for he was caliph for sixty years. However, he cannot be counted because he succeeded when he was seven years old and his caliphate was not genuine.

[**440**] For three years al-Nāṣir li-Dīn Allāh was left completely paralysed. Sight in one eye had gone and with the other he had weak vision. At the end he was afflicted with dysentery for twenty days and then he died.

Several viziers served him and they have been mentioned previously. Throughout his long illness he did not cancel any of the unjust taxes he had initiated. He was a bad ruler of his subjects, a tyrant. He ruined Iraq in his reign and its population was scattered far and wide. He seized people's properties and wealth and was capable of doing one thing and then its opposite. For example, he built 'hospitality homes' in Baghdad at whose expense people could break their fast

625/1228 he went to Mecca on pilgrimage and made public protestations of his innocence, which convinced Jalāl al-Dīn, who then brought him back to Tabriz.

[15] There is a lacuna in the text.

[16] The text continues with al-Nāṣir's full genealogy and details about the Abbasid family and their succession patterns which have been omitted. Al-Nāṣir was born in 553/ 1158 and became caliph in 575/1180 (Sibṭ ibn al-Jawzī, 635–7).

in Ramaḍān. They lasted a while and then he rescinded that arrangement. Next he built 'hospitality homes' for pilgrims. They also lasted a while and then he cancelled them. He waived some non-canonical taxes that he had introduced in Baghdad in particular but then he re-introduced them. His greatest care he bestowed on shooting with the crossbow, his pedigree pigeons and the *futuwwa* trousers.[17] Throughout all the lands he abolished the *futuwwa*, except for those who donned trousers at his hands and invitation.[18] Many rulers donned the *futuwwa* trousers, received from him.

Likewise he banned pedigree pigeons for anyone else, except for those bred from his birds, and he banned shooting with the crossbow except for men affiliated to him. People in Iraq and elsewhere accepted this, except for one man, called Ibn al-Saft, from Baghdad. He fled from Iraq to take refuge in Syria. The caliph sent tempting him with abundant cash to shoot for him, to be affiliated to him when he shot, but he would not do so. I have heard that one of his friends found fault with his refusal to take the money but his reply was, 'It is boast enough for me that there is nobody in the world who does not shoot for the caliph except me.' The caliph's passion for these things was a very serious matter.

His role in what the Persians attribute to him was correct, namely that he is the person who roused the Tatars' ambition for the lands of Islam and wrote to them about that. It was a very great disaster in comparison with which every serious sin becomes insignificant.[19]

[441] How al-Ẓāhir bi-Amr Allāh became caliph

We have mentioned under the year 585 [1189] that Emir Abū Naṣr Muḥammad, son of the Caliph al-Nāṣir li-Dīn Allāh, was proclaimed in the khutbah as heir-apparent in Iraq and other countries. Later the caliph removed him from the heir-apparentcy and sent to the countries that his name should be dropped from the khutbah. He did this because he inclined to favour his young son 'Alī, but it came about that the young son died in the year 612 [1215–16]. The caliph had no other son but his [original] heir apparent, so he was forced to reinstate him, although he was kept under surveillance and confined without any freedom of action.

---

17 The *futuwwa* had a long history as an order of social and moral action based on the idea of a perfect 'young man' (*fatā*), exemplified by 'Alī. See *EI(2)*, ii, 961–9. The putting-on of trousers (*sarāwīl*) was part of the initiation into the order. Al-Nāṣir tried to 'aristocratize' the organization, with himself as its 'grand master'. Keeping and racing homing pigeons became associated with the order at this period, as did shooting fowl with the pellet-bow (*bunduq*). The caliph was himself a pigeon enthusiast and at least one treatise on the subject was dedicated to him. See *EI(2)*, iii, 109.

18 *Yud'ā ilayhi*, rendered as 'at his … invitation', remains doubtful. If emended to *tud'ā* (with 'trousers' as the subject), one might hazard 'named for him', i.e. under his aegis.

19 See above, p. [**362**], where this charge is merely hinted at.

When his father passed away, he succeeded to the caliphate and summoned people to take the oath of allegiance. He took the title al-Ẓāhir bi-Amr Allāh, meaning [to show] that his father and all his officials had wanted to keep him from the succession but he triumphed (*ẓahara*) and became caliph by God's command (*bi-amr Allāh*), not by anyone's scheming.

After his accession he manifested such justice and kindness as revived the practice of the two 'Umars.[20] If one were to say that since 'Umar ibn 'Abd al-'Azīz no caliph like him had ruled, that would be the truth. He restored a large amount of property that had been seized in his father's reign and earlier, and cancelled non-canonical taxes throughout the land. He ordered the re-introduction of the old land tax in all Iraq and that all the innovations of his father be dropped. This represented a great sum beyond computation. To serve as an example, the village of Ba'qūbā in older times used to yield about 10,000 dinars. When al-Nāṣir li-Dīn Allāh ruled, 80,000 dinars used to be taken from it annually. The inhabitants came [to al-Ẓāhir] and pleaded for help. They told that their properties had been taken from them so that this sum could be realized, so he ordered that the old land tax be collected, which was 10,000 dinars. It was said to al-Ẓāhir, 'That sum comes to the Treasury. Where will replacement funds come from?' He produced the replacement from other sources. When the amount waived from just one source was 70,000 dinars, what would you expect in all the rest of the country?[21]

[**442**] One of his admirable measures was that he ordered the original land tax to be taken from all the rest of the lands. However, many of the people of Iraq came and told that in the properties from which the land tax was formerly taken most of their trees had dried up and were ruined. When the original land tax was demanded, the revenue from the rest would not suffice for the tax. He ordered that the tax be levied only on every healthy tree and that nothing be levied on any sick one. This was a very grand thing to do.

A further example is the following. The Storeroom had a standard weight for gold which was half a *qīrāṭ* heavier than the municipal weight. They would use it for receipt of money but, when paying out, use the city's weight which the people employed in their transactions. The caliph heard of this and his rescript was issued to the vizier, which began like this:

> 'Woe to those who give short measure, who, when they receive their measure from people, take it in full but, when they give measure or weight to them, fall short. Do they not imagine that they will be raised again on the terrible day?'[22] We have heard that such and such is the case. Let the Storeroom's

---

[20] i.e. the two ideal rulers, 'Umar I, the second caliph of Islam, and the 'good' Umayyad caliph, 'Umar ibn 'Abd al-'Azīz.

[21] The agricultural sector may well have benefited but one wonders which other sectors bore the 'replacement' cost.

[22] Koran, lxxxiii, 1–5.

standard weight be restored to the standard used by the Muslims, Jews and Christians for their transactions.

One of his deputies wrote to him, saying, 'This involves a large sum. We have calculated it and during last year it was 35,000 dinars.' He sent back a reply, rebuking the man concerned and saying, 'Even if it were 350,000 dinars, it shall be given up.' He also acted likewise in cancelling the addition to the standard weight that the Dīwān had, a *ḥabba*[23] in every dinar.

He ordered the cadi that all who presented a valid deed for a property should have it returned to them without further question. He also appointed a righteous man to control the escheats and the Treasury. He was a Ḥanbalī and he said, 'According to my school of law I will treat cognate relatives as heirs.[24] If the Commander of the Faithful will permit me to act accordingly, I shall take the job but otherwise, no.' The caliph replied, 'Give everyone with a rightful claim his due. Fear God and do not fear anyone else.'

[**443**] Another example is that it was the custom in Baghdad for the watchman in every quarter early in the morning to write a report to the caliph, recounting what meeting of friends with one another for entertainment or devotional exercises or such like had happened in his quarter and recording other things too, both minor and major. The people felt very restricted by this. When this caliph (God reward him well) succeeded, he received the reports as normal but he ordered them to be curtailed. He said, 'What is the purpose for us to know what people are about in their homes? Let nobody write to us anything other than what concerns the interests of the state.' It was objected, 'This will corrupt the common people and their wickedness will grow great.' He replied, 'We pray to God that He lead them to righteousness.'

Another of his measures is the following. When he became caliph, the head of the Dīwān came from Wāsiṭ. He had gone there during the reign of al-Nāṣir to collect money. He now came up to Baghdad with more than 100,000 dinars in cash. He wrote a report containing an account of what he had and a statement of how it was collected. The caliph replied that it should be returned to its owners, for he had no need of it, so it was duly restored to them.

Yet another is that he freed all who were in the prisons and ordered that what had been taken from them should be given back. He sent to the cadi 10,000 dinars

---

23 A *ḥabba* (literally 'grain') was mostly used for weighing coins. In round terms 100 *ḥabba* equalled one dinar. See Hinz, 1–2, 12.

24 The cognates (in Arabic *dhawū al-arḥām*) are those related to the deceased through a female. See Schacht, *Islamic Law*, 170–73. The point appears to be that, if there were no agnatic heirs (*'aṣaba*) and none entitled to fixed Koranic shares, the schools of law differed over whether it was then the cognates that inherited or whether the Treasury benefited. Despite his appointment to the Treasury, the present Ḥanbalī intended to prefer the cognates. See *EI(2)*, vii, 108–9, s.v. *mīrāth*.

to disburse on behalf of everyone held in the debtors' prison[25] who had no money.

The following is an example of his wanting the best for people. Prices [of cereals] in Mosul and the Jazīra were high but they came down. The caliph sanctioned the transport of foodstuffs there and that all who wished to sell grain could do so. Much, more than could be counted, was taken there. He was told, 'The price [in Baghdad?] has risen somewhat and the best course is to stop [export]', to which he replied, 'Those are Muslims and these are Muslims. Just as we must consider the situation of these, so we must consider those others.' He ordered that foodstuffs should be sold from the granaries he had at a lower price than that at which anyone else was selling. This was done and the prices with them [in the Jazīra?] fell more than they had at first.[26] When he became caliph, the price in Mosul was one dinar three *qīrāṭ*s for each *makkūk*. In a few days it became a dinar for every four *makkūk*s and it was the same for all other commodities, dates, treacle, [**444**] rice, sesame and such-like. May God Almighty strengthen and aid him and give him long life, for he is a rarity in this wicked age.

I have heard a report about him that pleased me greatly. Someone spoke to him about the money that he was spending or waiving, money that an individual might hesitate to give away even part of, and he said, 'I have opened my shop in the evening. Allow me to do some good. How long may I live?'[27] On the eve of the feast at the end of Ramaḍān this year he gave alms and distributed to the ulema and the men of religion 100,000 dinars.

How Badr al-Dīn took the two fortresses of al-'Imādiyya and Harūr[28]

This year Badr al-Dīn [Lu'lu'] took the fortress of al-'Imādiyya in the district of Mosul. Under the year 615 [1218–19] mention has already been made of its inhabitants' rebellion against him and its surrender to 'Imād al-Dīn Zankī, followed by their return to the allegiance of Badr al-Dīn and their dispute with 'Imād al-Dīn. When they returned to Badr al-Dīn, he treated them magnanimously, assigned them a large fief and gave them ownership of the villages, rewarding them with lavish gifts of money and splendid robes of honour. They remained like this for a little while.

---

[25] The text has *ḥabs al-shar'*, the Shariah prison. For the imprisonment of debtors, see Schacht, *Islamic Law*, 197.

[26] This section is not unconnected with the report of famine this year in the Jazīra. See below, p. [**447**].

[27] Cf. the version in Abū Shāma, *Dhayl*, 145: al-Ẓāhir became caliph at the age of fifty-two and 'He was asked, "Why do you not enjoy yourself?" He replied, "It is too late for sowing." It was said to him, "God bless your days," to which he said, "One who opens a shop in the evening, what profit will he have?"'

[28] It was a fortress thirty leagues north of Mosul and three 'miles' from al-'Imādiyya. Yāqūt, iv, 970, spells the name Harūr, as does *Kāmil* (Thornberg), xii, 289–90. The text has Harūz.

Then they started to make contact with ‘Imād al-Dīn, Muẓaffar al-Dīn, lord of Irbil, and Shihāb al-Dīn Ghāzī ibn al-‘Ādil, when he was at Khilāṭ, and to promise each of them that they would join with him and give him allegiance. They revealed the opposition to Badr al-Dīn that they had been harbouring. They only allowed to remain with them the adherents of Badr al-Dīn that they wanted and they shut out those they did not like. The situation continued for a long time, while he was tolerating their actions and courting them but they were only growing in boldness and contumacy.

They formed a group but they fell into dissension. Certain of them, namely the sons of Khwāja Ibrāhīm, his brother and their followers, became dominant over the others and expelled them from the fortress, which they now controlled, and persisted [**445**] in their course of hypocrisy.

When this year came, Badr al-Dīn marched against them with his troops and came upon them suddenly. He imposed a tight blockade and cut off their supplies. He himself remained there but positioned a detachment of his army at the fortress of Harūr to besiege it. It was one of the strongest and best-defended fortresses, quite without a peer. The people there had followed the same course of rebellion, obedience and deceit as those of al-‘Imādiyya. The troops arrived and put them under siege. They had little in store and after a siege of a few days the contents of the fortress were exhausted. Its defenders were forced to surrender, which they duly did and departed from it.

The troops returned to al-‘Imādiyya and joined in the siege there with Badr al-Dīn. After the taking of Harūr Badr al-Dīn remained for a little and then returned to Mosul. He left the army in its position with his son Amīn al-Dīn Lu’lu’. The siege lasted until the beginning of Dhū’l-Qa‘da [4 November 1225]. The defenders sent announcing their submission and asking to surrender it in return for a place in exchange. An arrangement was reached on a replacement castle where they could be secure, a fief and some cash and other things. Badr al-Dīn responded to their request and their representatives came to take an oath from him.

While he was about to swear to them, having summoned people to witness his oath, a carrier pigeon arrived from al-‘Imādiyya with a message from Amīn al-Dīn Lu’lu’ attached to its wing, with news that he had taken al-‘Imādiyya by force of arms and captured the Banū Khwāja, who had taken the dominant role there. Badr al-Dīn then refused to give his oath.

Amīn al-Dīn’s conquest of it came about as follows. When its people had returned to Badr al-Dīn’s allegiance, he had put him in charge of it. He remained there for a while and by good treatment he won over a group of them to use them as a force to wage war on those who had rebelled initially. Word of this was reported to them so they made it difficult for him to remain among them and asked to have him relieved of his post as governor. He left them and returned to Mosul. Those whom he had won over continued to write to him and keep in communication. When he besieged them, they [**446**] also sent messages to him on arrows, telling him all that the Banū Khwāja were doing, sending an envoy and such like, and what stores and other things they had. However, they were not sufficiently numerous to be able to overcome those others.

At this present moment when the agreement had been reached, the Banū Khwāja told none of the fortress's soldiers about the money mentioned in the draft of the oath, nor about anything else, the guarantees and fief. They were enraged at this and said to them, 'You have secured for yourselves an oath granting forts, villages and money, but we have had our homes ruined for your sake and you made no mention of us.' Nevertheless, they were slighted and ignored. Two of them came by night to Amīn al-Dīn and asked him to send them a body of men whom they would help to climb up into the fortress, surprise those others and seize them. He refused and said, 'I fear that this plan will not succeed and all that we have done will come to nothing. They replied, 'We shall lay hands on them early tomorrow. Let you and the troops be ready and when you hear us proclaim the name of Badr al-Dīn and his watchword, climb up to us.' He agreed to that.

He rode out early, he and his troops, as was his custom. Those men gathered together, arrested the Banū Khwāja and their followers and proclaimed Badr al-Dīn's watchword. While the troops were taking their position, suddenly there were shouts from the fortress calling out Badr al-Dīn's name. They ascended the fortress and seized it. Amīn al-Dīn took control of the Banū Khwāja and put them in prison. He then wrote the message, sent by the pigeon, with news of what had happened. The fortress had been taken with no difficulty and without giving anything in return. He had been willing to meet the cost of providing large sums of money, many fiefs and a strong castle, but he was saved all this. From them he took everything that they had bagged and stored. 'When God wills a matter, there is no avoiding it.'

[447] Miscellaneous events

This year on the eve of Sunday 20 Ṣafar [= 2 March 1225] there was an earthquake at Mosul, in the Jazīra, Iraq and elsewhere, of middling strength.

This year the famine at Mosul and in the whole of the Jazīra intensified. The people ate carrion and dogs and cats. Dogs and cats became scarce after they had been very numerous. One day I had entered my house and seen the servant girls cutting up meat for cooking. I was struck by the number of cats I saw, so I counted them and there were twelve. During this famine, however, I saw meat in the house with nobody nearby guarding it from the cats because there were none. There was not much time between these two occasions.

Along with food everything rose in price. A *raṭl*[29] of sesame oil was sold for two *qīrāṭ*s after it had been a half a *qīrāṭ* before the famine. Before that sixty *raṭl*s had

[29] In Iraq a *raṭl* equalled 130 dirhams in weight, that is 406.25 gm. (Hinz, 31).

cost a dinar.[30] It was remarkable that chard, carrots and turnips were sold at five *raṭl*s for a dirham and violets at six *raṭl*s for a dirham, at times seven *raṭl*s for a dirham. This was something unheard of. In former and recent times it had been the case when prices had risen that, when the rains came, prices went down but not this year. The rains were incessant from the beginning of the winter until the end of spring but the more it rained, the higher went prices. This too was something unheard of. Wheat reached a dinar and a *qīrāṭ* for one and a third *makkūk*s. This would weigh forty-five *raṭl*s of flour in Baghdad measures. Salt was a dirham a *makkūk* but became ten dirhams. Rice was twelve dirhams a *makkūk* and rose to fifty. [**448**] Dates were four or five *raṭl*s for a *qīrāṭ* but became two *raṭl*s for the same price.

Also surprising is the account that rare brown sugar used to be a dirham and a quarter for each *raṭl* and pure white Egyptian sugar was two dirhams a *raṭl*. Brown sugar became three and a half dirhams for a *raṭl* and white sugar three and a quarter dirhams each *raṭl*. The reason is that there was a lot of sickness. It became a serious epidemic. The women said, 'These illnesses are "cold", while brown sugar is "hot", so it is efficacious against them. The white is "cold" and exacerbates them.' Doctors followed them to put their minds at ease and because of their own ignorance. Brown sugar rose in price for this reason, all caused by extreme ignorance.

Things continued like this until the beginning of spring. The epidemic grew in intensity and there were many fatalities and much sickness among the people. Several corpses were carried on a single bier. One of those who died was our teacher, 'Abd al-Muḥsin ibn 'Abd Allāh, the preacher from Ṭūs, who was the preacher at Mosul. He was one of the most pious of Muslims. His age was eighty-three years and some months.

This year there was an eclipse of the moon on the eve of Tuesday 15 Ṣafar [= 24 February 1225].

Also during this year the emir of the Iraqi pilgrims, Ḥusām al-Dīn Abū Firās al-Ḥillī al-Kurdī al-Warrāmī, fled. He was the nephew of Shaykh Warrām and his uncle was one of the most pious and virtuous of Muslims, an inhabitant of al-Ḥilla al-Sayfiyya. He abandoned the pilgrims between Mecca and Medina and travelled to Egypt. One of his friends told me that he was led to flee owing to the great amount of expenditure on the route and the exiguous support from the caliph. The whole way they were disturbed by no alarms and they arrived safe and sound, except that [**449**] many of the camels perished. They were afflicted with large swellings and only a few survived.

In Āb [August] there was heavy rain, thunder and lightning. It continued until the wadis were flowing with water and the roads were full of mud. News came from Iraq, Syria, the Jazīra and Diyār Bakr that they had the same. Nobody came to us at Mosul without reporting that they had similar rains at that date.

---

30 This appears to be the equivalent of a *raṭl* for a third of a *qīrāṭ*.

This year in the winter there was also much snow. I came to stay in Iraq and heard that it had fallen throughout the country, even in Basra. As far as Wāsiṭ was concerned, there was no doubt about the snow, but as regards Basra, the reports that it had fallen there were not numerous.

This year the castle of al-Za'farān in the region of Mosul was destroyed. It was a famous fortress, know formerly as the Monastery of al-Za'farān, situated on a high hill near Farshābūr.[31]

Also this year the castle of al-Judayda in the Hakkāriyya lands, likewise part of the region of Mosul, was destroyed. Its dependent district and villages were added to al-'Imādiyya.

In Dhū'l-Ḥijja [December 1225] Jalāl al-Dīn, son of Khwārazm Shāh, marched from Tabriz to the country of the Georgians, intending to take their lands and extirpate them. The year ended without our having heard that he had achieved anything with them. We shall recount what he did to them under the year 623 [1226], God willing.

On 3 Shubāṭ [February] snow fell at Baghdad and water became extremely cold. The cold was so intense that it caused the death of a number of the poor.

During Rabī' I [13 March–11 April 1225] the Tigris rose to a very great extent and the people busied themselves with repairing the Qūraj dyke. They were very fearful. The flood regained almost its initial high level but then the water receded and the people rejoiced.

[31] Krawulsky, 434, s.v. Fīšābūr, 'a small town in the vicinty of Jazīrat Ibn 'Umar'.

[**450**]

The Year 623 [1226]

Account of Jalāl al-Dīn's taking of Tiflis

On 8 Rabīʿ I of this year [9 March 1226] Jalāl al-Dīn, son of Khwārazm Shāh, conquered the city of Tiflis from the Georgians. This came about in the following manner. We have already mentioned under the year 622 [1225] the hostilities between him and them, their defeat at his hands and his return to Tabriz because of the differences that broke out there. When affairs in Azerbayjan had been stabilized, he went back to Georgian lands in Dhū'l-Ḥijja that year [December 1225]. When the year 622 [1225] had passed and this present year had begun, he invaded their lands. They had once again raised troops and gathered men from the peoples who were their neighbours, Alān, Lakz, Qipjāq and others. They assembled together in a large multitude beyond counting and for this reason their expectations were high. Their hearts provided them with vain hopes and Satan promised them victory, but Satan promises them only delusion.

Jalāl al-Dīn confronted them and set ambushes for them in several places. Battle was joined and eventually the Georgians fled in rout, with every man for himself.[1] Each one of them cared only for his own life. From every side the swords of the Muslims overwhelmed them. None survived except the odd few of no account. Jalāl al-Dīn ordered his troops to spare nobody, but to kill all they found. They therefore pursued and killed the fugitives. His followers advised him to attack Tiflis, their capital, but he said, 'There is no need for us to kill our men beneath its walls. When I have annihilated the Georgians, I will take the city with no trouble at all.'

His troops continued to pursue them and seek them out thoroughly until they had all but eliminated them and then he moved against Tiflis and camped nearby. One day he went with a detachment of [**451**] the army with the intention of viewing the city to consider siege positions and how to engage it. When he drew near, he posted most of the troops that were with him in ambush in several places and then advanced further at the head of about 3,000 horsemen. When the Georgians within saw him, they were eager to attack him because of the fewness of those with him. They did not know that there were others with him. They made a sally and engaged him. When he retreated, their eagerness increased because of the small number of his men. They thought he was defeated, so they pursued him. When they advanced into the midst of the troops [in ambush], the latter emerged and put them to the sword. Most were slain. The rest fled to the city and entered

[1] The Arabic has the conventional phrase 'brother not turning aside for brother, nor father for son'.

it, pursued by the Muslims. As they came to the city, the Muslims among its inhabitants called out the watchword of Islam and the name of Jalāl al-Dīn. The Georgians threw up their hands and ceased to resist, because they had lost men in the battles we have mentioned and their numbers had dwindled. Their hearts were also full of fear and terror. The Muslims took the city by force of arms without granting terms and all the Georgians there were put to death. Neither young nor old was spared, except for those who accepted Islam and pronounced the two sentences[2] of the confession of faith. They were spared, circumcised by order and then left alone. The Muslims plundered property there, took the women captive and enslaved the children. However, the Muslims who were resident there suffered in part as well, being killed, pillaged or meeting other fates.

Tiflis is one of the strongest and best-defended cities, situated on both banks of the River Kura, a great river. This conquest was much celebrated and produced a great impression in the lands of Islam and amongst the Muslims, for the Georgians had been lording it over them and treating them as they wished. They were invading whichever lands of Azerbayjan they wanted and there was nobody to stop them or defend the lands against them. Such was also the case with Erzurum, so much so that its ruler donned a robe of honour from the king of the Georgians and raised above his head a banner crowned with a cross. His son converted to Christianity out of a desire to marry the queen of the Georgians and in fear of them, to defend himself from their evil. The story has already been told.[3] It was also the same with Darband Shirwān.

[**452**] Their threat became so great that Rukn al-Dīn, son of Qilij Arslān, the ruler of Konya, Aqsaray, Malaṭya and other Muslim lands of Anatolia, assembled his armies and enlisted others to join them in vast numbers and marched to Erzurum, which belonged to his brother Ṭughril Shāh, son of Qilij Arslān. The Georgians came against him and defeated him, inflicting on him and his troops every enormity. The inhabitants of Darband Shirwān were also in distress and hardship because of them.

In Armenia the Georgians entered the town of Arjīsh and took Kars and other places. They besieged Khilāṭ. Were it not that God (glory be to Him) showed favour to the Muslims through the capture of Īwānī, the commander of the Georgian troops, they would have seized it. The inhabitants were obliged to build a church for them in the citadel where the service bell was rung. Later they left them and departed. A detailed account of this incursion has already been given.[4]

This frontier region had always been one of the most dangerous for those living near it, the Persians before Islam and after them the Muslims from the beginning of Islam until now. Nobody had previously advanced so boldly against them and

---

2 i.e. 'There is no god but God' and 'Muḥammad is the Prophet of God'.

3 See above, pp. [**416–17**].

4 The Georgian capture of Kars and the surrender (sic) of Khilāṭ to them are mentioned under the year 603/1206–7 (see p. [**255**]) but there is nothing about the capture of Īwānī or other details. For their destruction of Arjīsh in 605 /1208–9, see p. [**279**].

done such great deeds. The Georgians took Tiflis in the year 515 [1121–2],[5] when the sultan was the Saljūq Maḥmūd ibn Muḥammad ibn Malikshāh, one of the greatest sultans with the most extensive kingdom and the most numerous armies. He was unable to defend it against them, despite his extensive lands, for he ruled Rayy and its dependencies, the Uplands, Isfahan, Fars, Khuzistan, Iraq, Azerbayjan, Arrān, Armenia, Diyār Bakr, the Jazīra, Mosul, Syria and more. His uncle Sultan Sanjar had Khurasan and Transoxania. Most of the lands of Islam were in their hands. Despite this, when he gathered his troops in the year 519 [1125] and marched against them after they had taken Tiflis, he was unable to overcome them. Later, his brother Sultan Mas'ūd succeeded him and Īldikiz became ruler of the Uplands, Rayy, Isfahan, Azerbayjan and Arrān. He received the obedience of the lord of Khilāṭ, the lord of Fars [**453**] and the lord of Khuzistan and gathered forces to confront the Georgians, but the best he could manage was to escape their clutches. Then came his son Pahlawān after him. The lands in the reigns of these rulers were flourishing with wealth and men in abundance but they had no ambition to win a victory over these Georgians. Finally this present sultan came when the lands were in ruin, having been initially weakened by the Georgians and then utterly destroyed by the Tatars (God curse them), as we have related, and yet he did these great exploits against them. Glory be to the One who, when He wills a matter, says, 'Be' and it comes about.

Account of the expedition of Muẓaffar al-Dīn, lord of Irbil, to Mosul and his withdrawal

This year in Jumādā II [June 1226] Muẓaffar al-Dīn ibn Zayn al-Dīn, lord of Irbil, marched towards the region of Mosul, intending to attack it. The reason for this was that he had reached an agreement with Jalāl al-Dīn ibn Khwārazm Shāh, al-Mu'aẓẓam, lord of Damascus, the lord of Āmid,[6] and Nāṣir al-Dīn lord of Mardin that they would attack the lands held by al-Ashraf, seize them by force and each take a stipulated share of them. The alliance was formed on that basis and Muẓaffar al-Dīn hastened against Mosul.

As for Jalāl al-Dīn, he left Tiflis, meaning to go to Khilāṭ. However, news came to him that his deputy in the land of Kirman, whose name was Balāq Ḥajib, had rebelled against him, as we shall relate. When he received this information, he ignored Khilāṭ and made no attack on it, except that his troops pillaged some of its territory and destroyed much of it. He made a forced march to Kirman and all that they had planned to do collapsed, although Muẓaffar al-Dīn did leave Irbil and camped on the bank of the Zāb but he was unable to cross into Mosul territory.

---

5 See *Chronicle of Ibn al-Athīr (1)*, 213–14.

6 This was the Artuqid al-Mas'ūd Rukn al-Dīn Mawdūd, who became ruler in 619/1222; see above, p. [**412**].

[**454**] From Mosul Badr al-Dīn had sent to al-Ashraf, who was at Raqqa, seeking assistance and asking that he come in person to Mosul to repel Muẓaffar al-Dīn. Al-Ashraf set out for Ḥarrān and from there went to Dunaysir. He ruined and pillaged the country of Mardin and its inhabitants.[7]

Meanwhile, al-Mu'aẓẓam, lord of Damascus, attacked Homs and Hama. He sent a message to his brother al-Ashraf to say, 'If you depart from Mardin and Aleppo, I shall leave Homs and Hama and I shall send to Muẓaffar al-Dīn that he should retire from Mosul.' Al-Ashraf then withdrew from Mardin and each of them returned to his own land. The region of Mosul and that of Mardin were ruined by this campaign. They had already been stricken by an unbroken famine of long duration and the flight of most of their population. This present disaster came upon them and things became yet worse with ruin upon ruin.

Account of Kirman's rebellion against Jalāl al-Dīn and his expedition there

In Jumādā II of this year [July 1226] Jalāl al-Dīn received a report that his deputy in Kirman, a great emir called Balāq Ḥājib, had rebelled against him and was ambitious to take over the country and monopolize it because Jalāl al-Dīn was far distant and occupied with the Georgians and others, as we have related, and also that he had written to the Tatars to inform them of Jalāl al-Dīn's strength and his taking power in much of the land and that, if he took the rest, his kingdom would be great, his armies numerous and he would take the lands that they held.

When Jalāl al-Dīn heard this, he had already set out for Khilāṭ but he forgot about that and marched to Kirman, hastening through the stages of the route. He sent on ahead a messenger to the governor of Kirman [**455**] with robes of honour to reassure him and to be able to come to him before he had taken precautions or prepared to resist. However, when the messenger arrived, he realized that this was an attempt to deceive him, because he was aware of Jalāl al-Dīn's normal practice. He therefore took what he held dear and went up into a strong citadel where he fortified himself. He placed his trusted men in the castles to hold out there and sent to Jalāl al-Dīn, saying, 'I am your slave and your mamluke. When I heard of your expedition to these lands, I vacated them for you because they are yours. If I knew that you would spare me, I would come in person to your presence, but I am afraid.' All the while the messenger was swearing to him that Jalāl al-Dīn was at Tiflis, although he paid no attention to his words. The messenger returned and Jalāl al-Dīn understood that he was unable to take the castles he held because that would require a long siege. He halted near Isfahan, sent him robes of honour and confirmed him in his office.

While the envoys were going to and fro, a messenger arrived from Jalāl al-Dīn's

---

7 Instead of *ahlahu* (its inhabitants), *Kāmil* (Thornberg), xii, 298, had *ahlakahu* (destroyed it), which seems rather tautologous.

vizier in Tiflis with the information that the army of al-Ashraf who was in Khilāṭ had defeated part of his army and inflicted heavy losses on them. He urged him to return to Tiflis, which he did with all speed.

Account of hostilities between al-Ashraf's troops and those of Jalāl al-Dīn

When Jalāl al-Dīn set out for Kirman, he left an army with his vizier, Sharaf al-Dīn, in the city of Tiflis. They became short of provisions, so they went to the region of Erzurum. On their arrival they pillaged it, enslaved the women and took booty, a great amount beyond counting. When they returned, their route took them through the confines of the principality of Khilāṭ. This came to the ears of al-Ashraf's deputy [**456**] in Khilāṭ, namely the Chamberlain Ḥusām al-Dīn 'Alī al-Mosulī,[8] who assembled his troops and marched against them. He inflicted a heavy defeat on them, recovered the booty they had taken and seized much from them before returning, he and his troops, safe and sound.

After this action Jalāl al-Dīn's vizier was fearful of them, so he sent to his master in Kirman to inform him of the situation and to urge him to return with a warning of the consequences of dilatoriness and negligence. Jalāl al-Dīn duly returned and we shall tell what happened next, God willing.

Account of the death of the Caliph al-Ẓāhir bi-Amr Allāh

This year on 14 Rajab [28 June–27 July 1226] there died the Imam al-Ẓāhir bi-Amr Allāh, the Commander of the Faithful, Abū Naṣr Muḥammad ibn al-Nāṣir li-Dīn Allāh Abī'l-'Abbās Aḥmad ibn al-Mustaḍī' bi-Amr Allāh. His full lineage has been given before[9] in the account of the death of his father (may God be pleased with them both). His caliphate lasted nine months and twenty-four days. He was an excellent caliph, who united humility with submission to his Lord, justice and good treatment of his subjects. In the account of his succession we have already recounted enough concerning his good works. Daily he continued to increase in goodness and kindness to his subjects. God was pleased with him and gratified him and gave him a good end and last resting-place. He had revived justice that was moribund. I shall mention examples of his goodness that have been forgotten.

Before his death he issued an order to the vizier, written in his own hand, to be read to the magnates of the state. The man that delivered the message said, 'The Commander of the Faithful says, "Our aim is not that one should say that a decree has been issued or that your desire has been effected and then there is no visible

---

[8] By error the text has al-Mosul.

[9] Above, pp. [**438–9**], but the full lineage and other comments have been omitted.

result; rather you need an imam of action more than you do an imam of words.'" They read out the order and found that it began as follows after the formula 'In the name of God etc.'

> Understand well that our delay is not a negligence, nor is our overlooking a condoning, but it is in order that we might test you, [**457**] to see which of you acts best. We pardon you the past ruining of lands, the eviction of subjects, the blackening of reputation, the deceitful and lying declaration of manifest falseness in the guise of hidden truth, the designation of extirpation and destruction as full payment and redress, for purposes the opportunities for which you seized, snatched from the claws of a bold beast and the teeth of an awesome lion. With varying words you agree on one idea and you are its keepers and trustees. You turn its notion to your preference and you confuse your falsity with its truth. It obeys you, although you rebel against it, and it agrees with you, although you oppose it. But now God (glorious is He) has replaced your fear with security, your poverty with riches and your falsity with truth. He has provided you with a ruling authority that excuses a stumble and accepts an apology, censures only the persistent and punishes none but the inveterate. He commands you to show justice and requires it from you. He forbids you to practise oppression and disapproves of it from you. He fears God Almighty and warns you of His devisings.[10] He longs for God Almighty and urges you to show Him obedience. Follow the path of God's caliphs on His earth and His trustees of His creatures, otherwise you are doomed. Greetings.

When he died, they found in a room of his palace thousands of sealed petitions that he had never opened. It had been suggested that he open them, but he said, 'We have no need of them. They are all slanders.'

Since his succession as caliph I had always feared (God Almighty knows it!) that he would rule for a short time because of the viciousness of the age and the corruption of those alive in it. To many of my friends did I say, 'How fearful I am that his caliphate will be curtailed, because our age and this generation do not deserve it,' and this is what came about.

[458] How his son, al-Mustanṣir bi-Allāh, became caliph

After the death of al-Ẓāhir bi-Amr Allāh his eldest son Abū Ja'far al-Manṣūr was proclaimed as caliph and given the title al-Mustanṣir bi-Allāh. In doing good and treating people well he followed the conduct of his father (may God be pleased with him). By proclamation in Baghdad he ordered that justice be widely

[10] Koran, iii, 54 (cf. viii, 30): 'They devised but God devised and God is the best of devisers.'

dispensed. Anyone who had a need or a complaint should report it and his need would be met and his complaint investigated.

On the first Friday to follow his succession he wished to pray the Friday prayer in the enclosure where the caliphs used to pray. He was told that the underground passage that gave access to it was ruined and impassable. He therefore mounted a horse and rode to the mosque, the Palace Mosque, publicly visible to the people in a white tunic and white turban with silk tassels. He did not allow anyone to process with him but ordered his attendants who had wanted to process with him to pray where he used to pray. He himself went with two servants and a groom, no more. It was the same on the second Friday until the passageway was repaired for him.

Grain prices had been fluctuating after the death of al-Ẓāhir bi-Amr Allāh (God be pleased with him). A *kāra* reached eighteen *qīrāṭ*s. The caliph ordered that the grain he had should be sold at thirteen *qīrāṭ*s for a *kāra*, so prices came down and affairs were stabilized.

Account of hostilities between Kayqubād and the lord of Āmid

In Sha'bān of this year [28 July–25 August 1226] 'Alā' al-Dīn Kayqubād ibn Kaykhusro ibn Qilij Arslān, the ruler of Anatolia, marched into the lands of al-Mas'ūd, ruler of Āmid, [**459**] and took several fortresses. The reason for this was the agreement, which we have mentioned, made by the lord of Āmid with Jalāl al-Dīn ibn Khwārazm Shāh, al-Mu'aẓẓam, the lord of Damascus, and others to oppose al-Ashraf. When al-Ashraf became aware of this, he sent to Kayqubād, ruler of Anatolia, for they were allies, to ask him to attack the land of the lord of Āmid and make war on him. At that time al-Ashraf was at Mardin. The ruler of Anatolia went to Malaṭya, which was his possession, camped nearby and sent his troops into the territory of the lord of Āmid. They conquered the Ḥiṣn Manṣūr, the castle of Shimsakāzād[11] and others. Seeing this, the lord of Āmid contacted al-Ashraf and renewed his alliance with him, so al-Ashraf sent to Kayqubād to tell him of this and to tell him to return to the lord of Āmid what he had taken from him. However, he refused to do so and said, 'I am not a deputy of al-Ashraf for him to tell me what to do and what not to do.'

It came about that al-Ashraf travelled to Damascus to make peace with his brother al-Mu'aẓẓam. He gave orders to his troops that he had in the Jazīra to aid the lord of Āmid, if the ruler of Anatolia persisted in his plan to attack him. Al-Ashraf's troops went to join the lord of Āmid, who had already assembled his forces and bestowed his lands on those fit to fight. He marched against the army of the ruler of Anatolia, who were besieging the castle of Kakhtā[12] {and they met

---

[11] The text has S.m.kārād. Shimsakāzād was a castle between Āmid and Malaṭya (Yāqūt, iii, 330).

[12] Modern Kahta (or Kölük), south of Malaṭya.

there in Shawwāl [25 September–23 October 1226]. The lord of Āmid and the troops with him suffered a great defeat. Many were wounded and many taken prisoner. The army of Kayqubād took the castle of Kakhtā}[13] after their defeat. It is one of the strongest castles and fortresses. After they had taken it, they returned to their master.

Account of Jalāl al-Dīn's siege of the two cities of Ānī and Kars

During Ramaḍān [26 August–24 September 1226] Jalāl al-Dīn returned from Kirman, as we have recounted, to Tiflis and from there went to Ānī, which was the Georgians' possession, where Īwānī was, the commander [**460**] of the Georgian forces, with the Georgian notables who remained with him. Jalāl al-Dīn put it under siege and dispatched a contingent of his army to the city of Kars, also a Georgian possession. Both places are among the strongest and most impregnable. He descended on both and besieged them, engaging their defenders and setting up trebuchets to attack them. He pressed the assaults vigorously but the Georgians held out, exercising extreme care and watchfulness because of their fear that he would treat them as he had previously treated their co-religionists in Tiflis. He maintained his position until half of Shawwāl had passed [9 October 1226] and then he left the army besieging both places, himself returning to Tiflis.

From Tiflis he proceeded by forced marches to the land of the Abkhāz and the rest of Georgia. He fell upon the people there, plundering, killing and taking captives. He ruined and burned the country and his troops took what was there as booty. He then left and returned to Tiflis.

How Jalāl al-Dīn besieged Khilāṭ

We have mentioned that Jalāl al-Dīn returned from the city of Ānī to Tiflis and entered the land of the Abkhāz. His journey was a ruse because he had heard that al-Ashraf's deputy in the city of Khilāṭ, the Chamberlain Ḥusām al-Dīn 'Alī, had taken precautions, taken affairs in hand to guard the city because of his being in the vicinity. He therefore returned to Tiflis, so that the people of Khilāt would feel secure and give up their precautionary and defensive measures and then he would attack them unexpectedly. His absence in Abkhazia lasted ten days. He then returned with forced marches, rolling up the stages of the journey, as was his wont. If he had not had with him people who were communicating intelligence to al-Ashraf's deputies, he would have surprised them in a state of unpreparedness. However, with his army there was one of al-Ashraf's trustworthy agents who kept

[13] The text between curly brackets is missing in *Kāmil*. For the correction, see *Kāmil* (Thornberg), xii, 300.

them informed of his moves. [**461**] He wrote to them and the information reached them two days before Jalāl al-Dīn's arrival.

When Jalāl al-Dīn arrived, he invested the city of Malazgird on Saturday 13 Dhū'l-Qa'da [= 7 November 1226]. He then raised the siege and descended upon the city of Khilāṭ on Monday 15 Dhū'l-Qa'da [= 9 November]. He immediately assaulted it and engaged the defenders in a fierce fight. His troops reached the city wall but many of them were killed. Then he made a second assault and engaged with the inhabitants in a mighty struggle. His troops caused great damage to the men of Khilāṭ, reached the wall and gained entry to the suburb, where they turned their hands to plunder and the capture of women. Seeing this, the citizens were outraged, urged one another on and again attacked the troops. They drove them out of the city with the loss of a great many on both sides. The Khwārazmian army took several emirs of Khilāṭ prisoner and many of them were killed. The Chamberlain 'Alī fought on foot, stood eyeball to eyeball before the enemy and did heroic deeds.

Jalāl al-Dīn then rested for a number of days before renewing the assault as on the first day. They fought him until they forced his troops to withdraw some distance from the city. The men of Khilāṭ were energetic fighters, eager to protect themselves, because of the evil behaviour of the Khwārazmians they saw, their pillaging and how wicked they were. They were fighting as do men who are defending themselves, their women and their property. Jalāl al-Dīn remained there until the cold became intense and a little snow had fallen, then he departed on Tuesday seven days from the end of Dhū'l-Ḥijja [15 December 1226]. In addition to his fear of snow his departure was caused by the reports he received of the depredations of the Īwā'ī Turkomans in his lands.

[462] Account of Jalāl al-Dīn's attack on the Īwā'ī Turkomans

The Īwā'ī Turkomans had seized control of the city of Ushnuh[14] and Urmiya in Azerbayjan and they levied the land tax from the people of Khoy in return for leaving them undisturbed. They were led astray by Jalāl al-Dīn's preoccupation with the Georgians and his[15] remoteness in Khilāṭ. Their ambitions grew and they felt free in Azerbayjan to pillage and waylay travellers on the road. News of this reached Khwārazm Shāh Jalāl al-Dīn, although he was putting them out of his mind because he was busy with what was the important matter in his opinion. Their ambition reached the point that they cut the highway near Tabriz and took a great deal from local merchants. In one instance the latter had bought sheep in

---

14 This town (read 'sh' for 's' in the edition), two days' journey from Urmiya and five from Irbil, was visited by Yāqūt in 618/1221 on a journey from Tabriz. He says that its ruined state was obvious (Yāqūt, i, 284–5).

15 The text has 'their'.

Erzurum and planned to bring them to Tabriz but the Turkomans seized all they had, including 20,000 head of sheep.

When this became serious and the evil had grown greatly, the wife of Jalāl al-Dīn, the daughter of Sultan Ṭughril, and his deputies in the city, sent to him, seeking assistance and telling him that the Īwā'īs had damaged the city and if he did not come soon, it would be ruined once and for all. This was a factor in addition to his fear of snow, so he left Khilāṭ and marched with all speed against the Īwā'īs, who felt themselves safe and secure, as they knew that Jalāl al-Dīn was besieging Khilāṭ and they thought that he would not leave it. Had it not been for this belief, they would have climbed into their impenetrable, soaring mountains which can only be ascended with difficulty and toil. Whenever they were fearful, they climbed up and took refuge in them. However, they were not aware of the troops of Jalāl al-Dīn until they were surrounded by them. They became a prey to the sword on every side. Much slaughter was done on them and booty and captives were taken in great quantities. Their women and children were enslaved and more than could ever be assessed taken from them. The troops saw much of the merchandise which [**463**] had been taken from the merchants, still untouched in its bales, apart from what had been untied and split up. When Jalāl al-Dīn had finished, he returned to Tabriz.

Account of the peace between al-Mu'aẓẓam and al-Ashraf

We shall begin by mentioning how their difference came about. When al-'Ādil Abū Bakr ibn Ayyūb died, his sons, the princes after him, cooperated very well together, namely al-Kāmil Muḥammad, ruler of Egypt, al-Mu'aẓẓam 'Īsā, ruler of Damascus, and al-Ashraf Mūsā, ruler of the Jazīra and Khilāṭ. They all acted as one to drive the Franks out of Egypt. When al-Kāmil retired from Damietta while the Franks were besieging it, his brother al-Mu'aẓẓam encountered him on the following day and his morale was strengthened and his position stabilized. Had that not been so, the situation would have been terrible, but we have related all this in detail.

Later al-Mu'aẓẓam returned from Egypt and travelled to his brother al-Ashraf in the Jazīra on two occasions to ask for his support against the Franks and to urge him to help their brother al-Kāmil. He persisted with him and eventually took him with him on the march to Egypt. They drove the Franks from Egypt, as we have told previously. Their cooperation against the Franks was the reason why the lands of Islam were kept safe and the people all rejoiced at that.

After the Franks had departed from Egypt and each of these princes, the sons of al-'Ādil, returned to his lands, they continued in the same way for a while. Later, al-Ashraf went to his brother al-Kāmil in Egypt. He passed by his brother al-Mu'aẓẓam in Damascus and did not take him with him. He made a long sojourn in Egypt and there is no doubt that this troubled al-Mu'aẓẓam. The latter subsequently marched to Hama and put it under siege. His two brothers sent to him from Egypt and obliged him against his will to raise the siege. This only increased his alienation. It is said that a report came to him that they had both formed an alliance against him. God knows best about this.

[**464**] In addition to this, the Caliph al-Nāṣir li-Dīn Allāh (may God be pleased with him) had become estranged in his relations with al-Kāmil because of the contempt with which his son, the ruler of Yemen, had treated the emir of the Iraqi pilgrims. He turned against al-Kāmil and also his brother al-Ashraf as they were allies and broke off relations with them both. He wrote to Muẓaffar al-Dīn Kūkbūrī ibn Zayn al-Dīn 'Alī, lord of Irbil, to inform him of his break with al-Ashraf and won his support. They agreed to contact al-Mu'aẓẓam and to stress their concern at the situation. Al-Mu'aẓẓam inclined to them and broke with his brothers.

Then the appearance of Jalāl al-Dīn on the scene with the large growth of his realm became a factor. Al-Ashraf's position became serious on account of the proximity of Jalāl al-Dīn Khwārazm Shāh to the territory of Khilāṭ and because al-Mu'aẓẓam in Damascus was preventing the troops of Egypt from reaching him and likewise the troops of Aleppo and other places in Syria. Al-Ashraf decided that he would go to his brother al-Mu'aẓẓam in Damascus, which he did in Shawwāl [25 September–23 October 1226], and won his support and settled their relationship. When al-Kāmil heard of this, he was very disturbed. They wrote to him, told him of Jalāl al-Dīn's descent on Khilāṭ and explained the seriousness of the situation. They also told him that this circumstance demanded their agreement for the sake of the prosperity of the house of al-'Ādil. The year came to an end with al-Ashraf in Damascus and other protaganists in their various places waiting to see what the Khwārazmians would do when the winter had passed. We shall relate the sequel under the year 624 [1227], if God Almighty wills.

Account of dissension between the Franks and the Armenians

This year the Frankish prince, lord of Antioch, assembled large bodies of troops and attacked the Armenians in the Passes, the land of the son of Leon. There were fierce hostilities between them.

The reason for this was that the son[16] of Leon the Armenian, lord of the Passes, had passed away and left no male child. He only left a daughter, whom the Armenians made their ruler. Subsequently they realized that rule cannot be maintained by a woman, so they proposed to marry her to the son of the prince.[17] He duly married her and moved to [**465**] their country, where he was established as ruler for about a year. They later regretted this and feared that the Franks would

[16] 'The son' is Leon II, ruled 1182–1219.

[17] The reference is to Philip, a son of Prince Bohemond IV, who married Isabella, daughter of Leon II.

take control of their lands, so they rose up against the son of the prince, arrested and imprisoned him.[18] His father sent asking for him to be released and restored to rule. They did not do this, so he sent to the Pope, the leader of the Franks at Great Rome, asking for permission to attack their lands. This prince of Rome's word was law to the Franks. He forbade the prince to attack them, saying, 'They are our fellow religionists. It is not allowed to attack their lands.' He disobeyed, however, and sent to 'Alā' al-Dīn Kayqubād, ruler of Konya, Malaṭya and the intervening Muslim lands, made peace with him and agreed with him to invade the lands of Leon's son and cooperate in this, which they did. The prince assembled his troops to march into Armenian lands. The Templars and the Hospitallers, the Franks' firebrands, opposed him and said, 'The prince of Rome has forbidden us to do this.' Nevertheless, others did obey the prince, who entered the fringes of the lands of the Armenians, which are narrow passes and rugged mountains. He was unable to effect what he wished.

Kayqubād[19] invaded Armenia from his direction, which gave easier access than the approach from Syria. He entered it in the year 622 [1225], pillaged and burned and besieged several fortresses, of which he conquered four. Winter then overtook him, so he withdrew.

When the Pope of Rome heard, he sent to the Franks in Syria to inform them that he had excommunicated the prince. The Templars, the Hospitallers and many of the knights would not meet with him or hear what he had to say. Whenever a religious feast came round for the people of his lands, Antioch and Tripoli, he would go away and, when they had completed their feast, return home.

Later he sent to the Pope complaining of the Armenians, that they had not released his son, and asking him to allow him to enter their lands and wage war on them if they did not release his son. The Pope sent to the Armenians, ordering them to free his son and restore him to power. If they did not, then he would allow him to attack their lands. When the message reached them, they still did not release his son, so the prince gathered his troops and invaded Armenia. The Armenians sent to Atabeg Shihāb al-Dīn in Aleppo to seek aid from him and to arouse his fear **[466]** of the prince, if he took control of their lands, because they were adjacent to the districts of Aleppo. In response Shihāb al-Dīn supplied them with soldiers and weapons.

When the prince heard this, he strengthened his determination to invade their lands. He marched to make war on them but did not achieve any useful aim, so he withdrew. I was told this by an intelligent Christian who had been in those regions and knew about them. I questioned another person. He knew some things but was unsure of others.

---

[18] Soon after 1224 Constantine, the head of the Hethoum family, arrested Philip and took power. After Philip's death, possibly by poison, Isabella married a son of Constantine. See Eddé, *Principauté ayyoubide*, 99.

[19] Kaykā'us is the reading of the text here but he had died at the end of 1220 (Cahen, *Pre-Ottoman Turkey*, 124). The expected Kayqubād is found in *Kāmil* (Thornberg), xii, 304.

Miscellaneous events

This year there were two eclipses of the moon, the first on the eve of 14 Ṣafar [14 February 1226].

In this year also there was a wonder in the vicinity of Mosul, a very hot spring, known as the Spring of al-Qayyāra, which the locals call the Spring of Maymūn. A little tar (*al-qār*) issues with the water and the people used to bathe there constantly during spring and autumn, because it was exceedingly efficacious for 'cold' illnesses, such as hemiphlegia. Those that swam in it underwent great pain from the heat of the water. However, this year the water cooled, so that any swimmer would now feel the cold. They gave it up and transferred to another spring.

This year there were numerous wolves, pigs and snakes, and many were killed. I have heard that a wolf entered Mosul and was killed there. A friend of mine who had an orchard outside Mosul told me that during the year 622 [1225] during the whole summer he killed two snakes there but this year by 1 Ḥayzurān [June] he had killed seven, so numerous they were.

[**467**] This year no rain fell on Mosul and most of the Jazīra from 5 Shubāṭ [February] until 12 Nīsān [April]. Nothing occurred according to custom but a little rain then fell in some of the villages and the crops were sparse. Then many locusts appeared and people's hardship increased. Prices had moderated a little but because of the great number of locusts they rose again. Furthermore, in most villages large hailstones fell which ruined and destroyed what the people had sown. Reports of what the largest size was differed. The weight of a hailstone was either 200 dirhams or, it was claimed, a *raṭl*. There were other claims made too. Nevertheless, the hail killed many animals and at the close of the year the famine still continued, most severely in Mosul.

A friend of ours caught a rabbit and saw that it had two testicles, a penis and a female's vulva. When they opened its belly, they saw inside two young.[20] I heard this from my friend and several others who were with him. They said, 'We have always heard that a rabbit is male for one year and female for the next. We did not believe it but when we saw this, we realized that it had become pregnant when a female and at the end of the year had become a male. Either this is so or otherwise it was among rabbits like a hermaphrodite among humans, for such a one has male and female private parts. It is also the case that a rabbit menstruates as women do. I lived at Jazīrat [Ibn 'Umar] and we had a neighbour who had a daughter called Ṣafiyya. She remained as she was for about fifteen years, when it appeared that a man's penis developed and her beard sprouted. 'He' came to have a vagina and a penis.

This year a man at our house butchered a sheep and found its flesh exceedingly

---

20 The text has *ḥ.rīfayn*, which gives no appropriate sense. One would like to read *janīnayn*, 'two foetuses' but as a copyist error it would be difficult to explain.

bitter, even its head, legs, pluck and all its offal (?). This is something that had never been heard of.

On Wednesday 25 Dhū'l-Qa'da [17 November 1226] at midday there was an earthquake at Mosul and in much of the Arab and Persian lands. It was strongest [**468**] at Shahrazūr, for most of it was damaged, especially the citadel, which was completely destroyed. In that area six fortresses were ruined. The aftershocks continued for a little more than thirty days and then God gave the people relief. As for the villages in that area, they were mostly ruined.

In Rajab [28 June–27 July 1226] the Cadi Ḥujjat al-Dīn Abū Manṣūr al-Muẓaffar ibn 'Abd al-Qāhir ibn al-Ḥasan ibn al-Qāsim al-Shahrazūrī, the cadi of Mosul, died there.[21] About two years before his death he had gone blind. He was knowledgable about the office of cadi and unblemished, respectable and possessed of great authority. He provided liberal grants for residents and visitors (God have mercy on him). He was one of the ornaments of this world. He left no issue other than a daughter who died three months after him.

---

[21] A member of the Shahrazūrī family that provided many cadis for Syria and the Jazīra. The founder of the dynasty was his great-grandfather, Abū Aḥmad al-Qāsim, who died at Mosul in 489/1096 (see *Wafayāt*, iv, 68–70).

[469] The Year 624 [1226–1227]

How the Georgians entered the city of Tiflis and put it to the torch

In Rabīʿ I this year [19 February–20 March 1227] the Georgians came to the city of Tiflis and there were no Muslim troops there to undertake its defence. The reason was that, after Jalāl al-Dīn had returned to Khilāṭ and fallen upon the Īwāʾīs, he sent his troops in groups to warm localities with plenty of pasture to winter there. His army had behaved badly towards the population of Tiflis, who were Muslims, and treated them unjustly, so they wrote to the Georgians to invite them to come and be accepted as rulers. The Georgians took advantage of this inclination of the populace in their favour and of the city's being devoid of troops. Having been in the cities of Kars and Ānī and other fortresses, they concentrated and marched to Tiflis, which was undefended, as we have said, because Jalāl al-Dīn had considered the Georgians to be weak owing to the great number of them he had slain and he did not think they were capable of any campaign. However, they took the city and put the remaining inhabitants to the sword. They recognised that they were unable to hold the city against Jalāl al-Dīn, so put it totally to the torch.

When this news reached Jalāl al-Dīn, he set out with the troops he had with him to come upon them but found none of them there, for they had abandoned Tiflis after setting it on fire.

[470] Account of Jalāl al-Dīn's pillaging of the lands of the Ismāʿīlīs

During this year the Ismāʿīlīs killed a great emir, one of Jalāl al-Dīn's emirs, to whom he had assigned the city of Ganja and its dependencies as a fief. He was an excellent emir, who did much good and ruled well, censuring Jalāl al-Dīn for the pillage and other wicked deeds perpetrated by his army. When this emir was slain, Jalāl al-Dīn was outraged at his assassination and very angry. He marched with his troops to the Ismāʿīlīs' lands from the confines of Alamut to Girdkūh in Khurasan and devastated them all, killing the inhabitants, plundering their property, capturing the women, enslaving the children and putting the men to death. He did terrible things to them and took his revenge on them. They had themselves done much evil and their depredations had increased. Their ambition had grown since the irruption of the Tatars into the lands of Islam until this present time. Jalāl al-Dīn stopped their aggression and subdued them. God made them face what they had done to the Muslims.

Account of hostilities between Jalāl al-Dīn and the Tatars

When Jalāl al-Dīn had finished with the Ismā'īlīs, he heard the news that a large body of Tatars had reached Dāmghān, in the vicinity of Rayy, intending an invasion of Islamic territory. He marched to meet them, brought them to battle and the fighting was very fierce. They were defeated and he inflicted substantial losses on them. For several days he pursued them, killing and taking prisoners. While this continued and he remained in the region of Rayy, fearing another gathering of Tatars, a report came to him that many of them were coming towards him. He held his position, awaiting them. We shall recount what they did under the year 625 [1227–28].

[471] Account of the entry of al-Ashraf's troops into Azerbayjan and the conquest of part of it

In Sha'bān of this year [17 July–14 August 1227] Chamberlain Ḥusām al-Dīn 'Alī, who was al-Ashraf's deputy in Khilāṭ and the commander of its forces, marched to Azerbayjan with the troops he had under him. The reason for this was that Jalāl al-Dīn's conduct was tyrannical and his troops were rapacious towards the population. His wife was the daughter of Sultan Ṭughril the Saljuq, who had been the wife of Uzbek ibn Pahlawān, the lord of Azerbayjan. She had become Jalāl al-Dīn's wife, as we have related. Alongside Uzbek she had ruled all those lands, leaving him and others no authority. However, after Jalāl al-Dīn married her, he ignored her and paid her no attention. She feared him, apart from the fact that he had deprived her of authority and the power to command and forbid. She and the people of Khoy sent to Ḥusam al-Dīn, the chamberlain, to invite him to come so that they could deliver the lands into his hands. He set out and entered Azerbayjan, where he took Khoy and the neighbouring fortresses which were still held by Jalāl al-Dīn's wife. He also took Marand. The people of Nakhchevan made contact with him, so he went to them and they yielded the city to him. Their aggressive capacity in those lands became great and had they continued, they would have taken them all, but they returned to Khilāṭ, taking with them Jalāl al-Dīn's wife, the daughter of Sultan Ṭughril. We shall relate the remainder of their story under the year 625 [1227–28], God willing.

Account of the death of al-Mu'aẓẓam, ruler of Damascus, and the succession of his son

In this year al-Mu'aẓẓam 'Īsā ibn al-'Ādil died on Friday the last day of Dhū'l-Qa'da [= 12 November 1227].[1] He had been ill with dysentery. His rule in

[1] Sibṭ ibn al-Jawzī, 648, confirms the day but has 1 Dhū'l-Ḥijja.

Damascus lasted from the time **[472]** of his father al-ʿĀdil's death for ten years, five months and twenty-three days.

He was learned and a good scholar in several disciplines, including jurisprudence according to the school of Abū Ḥanīfa, for he had studied it very much and became a distinguished exponent. Another discipline was grammar, which he also studied to a very advanced degree and excelled at. It was the same with lexicography and other subjects. He had commissioned the compilation of a large comprehensive book on lexicography to include *Kitāb al-Ṣiḥāḥ* by al-Jawharī[2] and supplements for what *al-Ṣiḥāḥ* had omitted, taken from *al-Tahdhīb* of al-Azharī, *al-Jamhara* of Ibn Durayd and others.[3] Likewise he commissioned an edition of the *Musnad* of Aḥmad ibn Ḥanbal, arranged by subject matter with each *ḥadīth* placed under the subject heading appropriate to its content.[4] Its pattern was that the *ḥadīth*s on 'ritual purity' should be collected together and that the same be done for 'prayer' and others, such as 'emotive exhortations' (*raqāʾiq*), 'Koran commentary' and 'accounts of the Prophet's expeditions', to make a comprehensive reference work. He had heard the *Musnad* from one of the pupils of Ibn al-Ḥaṣīn.

Learning was highly valued by him.[5] Ulema from distant places sought him out and he received them with honour and supported them with abundant pensions. He made them his intimates and would join their sessions, both benefiting from them and contributing to their discussions. He deferred to learning and put up with hearing what he disapproved of. Nobody who kept company with him ever heard a harmful word from him.

His creed was sound. He used to say, 'Concerning the fundamentals [of theology] what I believe is what Abū Jaʿfar al-Ṭaḥāwī[6] has recorded.' When near death he willed that he should be shrouded in white, that his grave clothes should not contain any garment with gold, that he should be buried in a simple grave, that no building should be erected over him but his grave should be in the open country beneath the sky. During his illness he used to say, 'I hope that I have sufficient merit with God from the Damietta affair for Him to show me mercy.'

After his death he was succeeded by his son Dāʾūd, who took the title al-Nāṣir. He was nearly twenty years of age.

---

2 Abū Naṣr Ismāʿīl al-Jawharī (died 393?/1003?) was a significant figure in classical lexicography. See *EI(2)*, ii, 495–7; *Encyclopedia of Arabic Literature*, i, 414.

3 Correct the edition's naming of al-Urmawī and Ibn Zayd (sic). Cf. *Kāmil* (Thornberg), xii, 308. Abū Manṣūr Muḥammad ibn Aḥmad al-Azharī was born at Herat in 282/895 and died there in 370/980 (see *EI(2)*, i, 822). Ibn Durayd, Abū Bakr Muḥammad ibn al-Ḥasan al-Azdī, was born in Basra in 223/ 847 and died at Baghdad in 321/933 (*EI(2)*, iii, 757–8).

4 In a *musnad* collection *ḥadīth*s were grouped according to their ultimate transmitting authority, irrespective of content.

5 The text has 'was in great demand in his market', but the commercial metaphor is difficult to express.

6 Abū Jaʿfar Aḥmad (d. 321/933) was the author of a well-known 'creed" (*ʿaqīda*); see Nogales, 'Sunni Theology', 14. In general, see Carter, 'Arabic Lexicography'.

[473] Miscellaneous events

During this year the famine persisted in the Jazīra. Prices continued to go up and down a little. There was no rain for all of Shubāṭ [February] and ten days of Ādhār [March] and the famine increased. Wheat reached a dinar and two *qīrāṭ*s for two *makkūk*s in Mosul and barley also a dinar and two *qīrāṭ*s for three *makkūk*s of the Mosulī standard. This year everything was in short supply and expensive.

In the spring there was little lamb to be had at Mosul and it became expensive, so that a Baghdadī *raṭl* of meat cost two *ḥabba*s by weight. For some days it possibly cost more than this. Those engaged in the sale of lamb at Mosul told me that one day they sold nothing more than a single lamb and on some days five or six head, sometimes more, sometimes less. This is something quite unheard of and something we have never witnessed in all our lives. We have never been told anything like it, because spring is when one expects meat to be cheap, as the Turkomans, Kurds and Kīlakān (?) move from the places where they have wintered to Zūzan and sell sheep cheaply. Every year at this season meat used to cost a *qīrāṭ* for every six or seven *raṭl*s. This year a *raṭl* rose to two *ḥabba*s.[7]

On 10 Ādhār [March], which was 20 Rabīʿ I, snow fell twice at Mosul. This was very strange and unheard of. It ruined the blossom that had come out, such as that of almonds, peaches, pears, quinces etc. News of the same was reported from all of Iraq, where their blossom and the fruit were ruined. This was more surprising than the situation in the Jazīra and Syria, because Iraq is much hotter than both of them.

This year a band of Turkomans, who were on the confines of the region of Aleppo, captured a celebrated Frankish knight of the Templars at Antioch and put him to death. The Templars heard of this, so they marched [**474**] and surprised the Turkomans, killing or capturing them and seizing their flocks. Word of this came to Atabeg Shihāb al-Dīn, the responsible authority at Aleppo, so he wrote to the Franks and threatened them with an attack on their territory. It chanced that the Aleppo troops also killed two great Templar knights, so the Templars declared their willingness to make peace and gave back to the Turkomans much of their flocks, their womenfolk and captives.[8]

In Rajab [17 June–16 July 1227] a large band from Diyār Bakr gathered and wished to raid Jazīrat ibn ʿUmar, where the ruler had been killed.[9] When they attacked Jazīrat [Ibn ʿUmar], the inhabitants of a large village within its region, called Salkūn, joined together and confronted them from morning until evening.

---

7 Based on data in Hinz, my fallible arithmetic suggests that this is at least a four-fold increase in price.

8 For these events see Eddé, *Principauté ayyoubide*, 100.

9 This appears to refer to the murder of Sanjar Shāh ibn Ghāzī II by a son of his (called Ghāzī), who failed to secure the succession, which passed to his brother Maḥmūd ibn Sanjar Shāh. This murder, however, took place in 605/1208–9. See above, pp. [**279–81**].

The fighting between them lasted a long time but in the end the villagers charged the Kurds, put them to flight and killed some. They ventured out, seized what they had and returned safely.

[475] The Year 625 [1227–1228]

Account of dissension between Jalāl al-Dīn and his brother

This year Ghiyāth al-Dīn ibn Khwārazm Shāh, the half-brother of Jalāl al-Dīn by his father, became fearful of his brother. Several emirs were also afraid of him. Apprehensive, they wished to escape from him but they were unable to do so before the irruption of the Tatars. Jalāl al-Dīn was then kept busy by the latter, so Ghiyāth al-Dīn and his followers fled and made for Khuzistan, part of the caliph's lands. They wanted to enter into allegiance to the caliph. However, the deputy there did not allow them to enter the town, fearing that this might be a ruse. Ghiyāth al-Dīn remained in the area and when the situation dragged on, he left Khuzistan and went to the lands of the Ismā'īlīs. After arriving he sought refuge and protection with them.

Jalāl al-Dīn had finished with the Tatars and returned to Tabriz, when news came to him, while he was playing polo in the Hippodrome, that his brother had attacked Isfahan. He threw the polo-stick from his hand and set out with all speed. Then he heard that his brother had approached the Ismā'īlīs to seek refuge with them and had not gone to Isfahan, so he returned to the Ismā'īlī lands to pillage them if they did not surrender his brother to him. He sent to demand his person from the leader of the Ismā'īlīs, who sent back a reply, saying, 'Your brother has sought us out. He is a sultan, son of a sultan. We cannot possibly give him up. However, we shall keep him with us and not allow him to take any of your lands. We ask you to allow me to be your intermediary with him and we guarantee [**476**] to hold to what we have said. If ever he does something you disapprove of in your lands, then our lands will be open to you to do there what you choose.' Jalāl al-Dīn agreed to this and took their oath to be faithful to it. He withdrew and went to Khilāṭ, as we shall recount, God willing.

Account of hostilities between Jalāl al-Dīn and the Tatars

During this year the Tatars again made moves towards Rayy and there followed many battles between them and Jalāl al-Dīn, how many there were being a matter of dispute. Most of them went against him but in the end he was victorious.

At the beginning of the warfare there were some strange wonders. Chingiz Khān, the ruler of these Tatars, had become angry with their commander, sent him away from his presence and banished him from his lands. The commander went to Khurasan and, having seen its ruined state, made for Rayy to conquer those regions and towns. Jalāl al-Dīn met him there and they fought fierce battles. Jalāl al-Dīn was defeated, came back and was defeated again. He set out towards Isfahan and remained between it and Rayy, where he gathered his troops and those subject to him. Among those who came to him was the ruler of Fars, namely the son of Atabeg Sa'd, who had come to power after the death of his father, as we have mentioned. Jalāl al-Dīn then returned to the Tatars and faced them again.

While they were forming their battle lines, each side facing the other, Jalāl al-Dīn's brother Ghiyāth al-Dīn defected with the emirs who had plotted with him to abandon Jalāl al-Dīn. They left the field and set off somewhere else. When the Tatars saw them leave the army, they thought they were planning to come upon them from their rear and fight them from two sides. Because of this assumption the Tatars retreated and were pursued by the lord of Fars. Jalāl al-Dīn, however, when he saw that he was abandoned by his brother and the emirs in league with him, thought [**477**] that the Tatars had retreated as a ruse to draw him forward out of position. He himself retreated and did not dare to enter Isfahan lest the Tatars besiege him there. He went on to Sumayram.

After the lord of Fars had gone far in pursuit of the Tatars but could see neither Jalāl al-Dīn nor his army with him, he became fearful of the Tatars and retraced his steps. The Tatars in their turn, when they saw nobody on their tracks, pursuing them, halted and later returned to Isfahan. On their way they found no one to oppose them and, having arrived at Isfahan, they put it under siege. The populace thought that Jalāl al-Dīn had perished. While under this impression and with the Tatar siege continuing, they received a messenger from Jalāl al-Dīn who told them that he was safe and saying, 'I shall remain in the field until the troops who are safe have rallied to me. Then I shall come to you and you and I shall act together to harass the Tartars and drive them away.'

They sent to urge him to come, promising him aid and that they would come out to meet the enemy with him, full of great valour. He went to them and joined forces. The men of Isfahan sallied forth with him and fought the Tatars, who suffered a most dreadful defeat. Jalāl al-Dīn pursued them to Rayy, killing and taking prisoners. When the Tatars had gone far from Rayy, he took up residence there. The son of Chingiz Khān sent him a letter, saying, 'These are not our followers. We banished them from our presence.' When Jalāl al-Dīn felt secure on the front with Chingiz Khān's son, he returned to Azerbayjan.[1]

Account of the Franks' incursion into Syria and their rebuilding of Sidon

This year many Franks came from their lands, which are west of Sicily and the countries beyond it, to their possessions in Syria, Acre, Tyre and other places on

---

1 The last sentence follows the wording in Ibn Wāṣil, iv, 233. The text in *Kāmil* and also in *Kāmil* (Thornberg), xii, 311, is odd and probably corrupt: 'When he was secure from Chingiz Khān's direction, he felt secure and returned to Azerbayjan.'

the Syrian coast, and a host of them had gathered. Before these another host had come [**478**] also, except that they had been unable to take any initiative or embark on any military activity owing to the fact that their ruler, who was their commander, was the king of the Germans,[2] whose title was emperor (said to mean 'king of emirs'), and because al-Mu'aẓẓam was still alive who was determined, brave and bold. When al-Mu'aẓẓam died, as we have related, and his son[3] succeeded and ruled Damascus, the Franks became ambitious and emerged from Acre, Tyre and Beirut to go to Sidon. They had an arrangement with the Muslims to share equally the revenues of Sidon, whose city wall was in ruins. They now rebuilt the city and took control of it.

They were able to manage that because of the destruction of the neighbouring fortresses, Tibnīn, Hūnīn and others. We have already mentioned that in full. The offensive capacity of the Franks became great and their ambitions grew strong. On his way [the emperor] took control of the island of Cyprus and became its ruler. From there he set out for Acre. The Muslims were full of foreboding but God Almighty will frustrate him and help the Muslims through Muḥammad and his family. In due course their ruler the emperor arrived in Syria.

How Kayqubād took power in Erzinjan

During this year 'Alā' al-Dīn Kayqubād ibn Kaykhusro ibn Qilij Arslān, the ruler of Konya, Aqsaray, Malaṭya and other Anatolian cities, took Erzinjan. His taking power there came about as follows. Its ruler Bahrām Shāh had ruled there for a long time and was past sixty years of age when he died.[4] He had not ceased to show allegiance to Qilij Arslān and his descendants. When he died, his son 'Alā' al-Dīn Dā'ūd Shāh succeeded him. Kayqubād sent to him asking for troops to march with him to Erzurum to put it under siege and for Dā'ūd Shah himself to accompany the army. He complied and marched to join him with his troops, but when he arrived, he was arrested and the city of Erzinjan taken [**479**] from him. Dā'ūd Shāh had a very strong fortress called Kamākh, held by a governor of his. The ruler of Anatolia sent to besiege it but the troops could not get close to it because of its high walls, lofty site and impregnable position. He then threatened Dā'ūd Shāh if he did not surrender Kamākh, so he sent to his deputy with orders to yield it and he duly gave up the fortress to Kayqubād.

Kayqubād intended to march to Erzurum to seize it. It was held by its lord, his uncle[5] Ṭughril Shāh ibn Qilij Arslān. When its ruler heard of this, he sent to Emir

---

2 i.e. Frederick II of Hohenstaufen.

3 This was al-Nāṣir Dā'ūd.

4 See above, p. [**429**] and footnote.

5 The text has *ibn 'amm* (cousin), but he was his uncle *('amm)*, as Ṭughril Shāh's brother was Kaykhusro.

Ḥusām al-Dīn 'Alī, al-Ashraf's lieutenant in Khilāṭ, to seek reinforcements and announced his allegiance to al-Ashraf. Ḥusām al-Dīn set out with the troops under him, whom he had gathered from Syria and the Jazīra in fear of the Anatolian ruler. They feared that, if he took Erzurum, he would go further and attack Khilāṭ, so the Chamberlain Ḥusām al-Dīn marched to Erzurum[6] and defended it.

When Kayqubād heard that troops had arrived there, he did not move directly to attack them. He left Erzinjan to go to his own lands. News had also reached him that the infidel Greeks[7] who were his neighbours had taken a fortress from him, called Sinope, one of the strongest of castles, looking towards the Black Sea, the Khazar Sea. After he arrived home, he sent the army there and besieged it by land and by sea, ultimately recovering it from the Greeks. He then went to Antalya[8] to winter there, according to his custom.[9]

Account of al-Kāmil's expedition

In Shāwwāl of this year [3 September–1 October 1228] al-Kāmil Muḥammad ibn al-'Ādil, ruler of Egypt, marched to Syria and arrived at Jerusalem (may God Almighty protect it and keep it Islamic territory for ever). He then left, took control of Nablus[10] and appointed prefects in all those regions. **[480]** They were part of Damascus's dependencies, so when its lord, the son of al-Mu'aẓẓam, heard of this, he feared that he would attack him and take Damascus from him. He therefore sent to his uncle al-Ashraf, asking for his aid and requesting him to come to him at Damascus. Al-Ashraf set out without heavy baggage and made his entry into Damascus.[11]

When al-Kāmil heard of this, he did not advance further because he knew that the city was well fortified and it now had men to defend and protect it. Al-Ashraf sent to him in conciliatory vein, telling him that he had only come in obedience to him and in sympathy with his aims, and agreeing with him to defend the land from

---

6 The edition reads al-Rūm here – with little sense. In *Kāmil* (Thornberg), xii, 312, the editor supplied what is needed to read the Arabic for Erzurum.

7 The reason for calling the Byzantine Greeks of Trebizond 'infidel' is that Ibn al-Athīr, when using the term *al-Rūm*, wished to distinguish between the Greeks and other Muslim inhabitants of Rūm (Anatolia/Asia Minor and its population).

8 Yet again the text has Anṭākiyya (Antioch).

9 For the events of this section, see the account (with slight differences) in Cahen, *Pre-Ottoman Turkey*, 126–7.

10 This phrase (*wa-tawallā bi-madīnat Nāblus*) is obscure. What appears to be a parallel passage in Ibn Wāṣil, iv, 227, has 'he sent his governors to Nablus, Jerusalem, Hebron and elsewhere'. Perhaps the present text should read *wa-wallā* in an absolute sense, i.e. 'he appointed a governor'.

11 According to Ibn Wāṣil, iv, 229, this was during the last third of Ramaḍān/24 August–2 September 1228. Ibn Wāṣil was in Damascus and witnessed his entry into the citadel.

the Franks. Al-Kāmil sent back his reply: 'I have only come to these lands because of the Franks, for there was nobody here to prevent them doing what they want. They have rebuilt Sidon and part of Caesarea and have not been stopped. You know that our uncle Sultan Saladin conquered Jerusalem and thereby we gained fair renown to outlast the elapsing of ages and the passing of days. If the Franks take it, we shall acquire such bad reputation and evil repute as will destroy the fair renown that our uncle stored up. What reputation will we retain in the eyes of the people and before God Almighty? The Franks will not be satisfied with their taking it. They will go further against other places. However, since you have arrived, I shall return to Egypt. Do you defend the land. I am not one to have it said of me that I fought my brother and besieged him. God forbid!'

He then withdrew from Nablus towards Egypt and made camp at Tell al-'Ajūl. Al-Ashraf and the people generally in Syria were fearful. They knew that, if he went home, the Franks would overcome Jerusalem and other places in its vicinity, for there was nobody to protect it. There followed an exchange of envoys and al-Ashraf went in person to al-Kāmil, his brother. He came to him, arriving on the eve of the Feast of Sacrifice [10 November 1228] and stopped him from returning to Egypt. They both then remained where they were.

[481] How Jalāl al-Dīn pillaged the lands of Armenia

During this year Jalāl al-Dīn Khwārazm Shāh arrived in the area of Khilāṭ and went by Khilāṭ into the desert of Mūsh and Jabal Jūr, all of which he ravaged, seizing women, enslaving children and killing men. He destroyed the villages and then returned to his own land.

When the news reached the lands of the Jazīra, Ḥarrān, Sarūj and other places, that he had gone past Khilāṭ into Jūr and that he had drawn near, the population feared that he would come to them, because the season was winter and they expected that he would aim at the Jazīra as a place to winter, as the cold there is not severe. They planned to migrate from their homes to Syria. Some of the inhabitants of Sarūj had reached Manbij in Syria when they received news that he had pillaged the area and then gone back, so they stayed where they were. The reason for Jalāl al-Dīn's return was that much snow fell around Khilāṭ. Nothing like it had been known before, so he was in a hurry to go back.

Miscellaneous events

This year in the whole of the Jazīra prices were low. The crops they had, wheat and barley, were excellent. Nevertheless, the low prices did not reach what they had originally been before the famine. Wheat became five *makkūk*s for a dinar and barley seventeen *makkūk*s of the Mosul standard for a dinar.

The Year 626 [1228–1229]

Account of the ceding of Jerusalem to the Franks

This year on 1 Rabīʿ II [27 February 1229][1] the Franks (God curse them) took over Jerusalem by treaty. May God restore it to Islam quickly! This came about because of what we have mentioned under the year 625 [1227–28], namely the coming of the emperor, the ruler of the Franks, by sea from the lands of the Franks to the Syrian coast. His troops, having preceded him, took up residence on the coast and caused ruin in the Muslim lands that were near them. A section of the Muslim population, who were dwelling in the mountains near the city of Tyre, went to the Franks, while they were in Tyre, and offered them their allegiance and joined them. The Franks also became bolder because of the death of al-Muʿaẓẓam ʿĪsā ibn al-ʿĀdil, the lord of Damascus.

When the emperor arrived on the coast, he resided in the city of Acre. Al-Kāmil[2] ibn al-ʿĀdil, the lord of Egypt, had marched out of Egypt to Syria after the death of his brother al-Muʿaẓẓam and was encamped at Tell al-ʿAjūl, planning to take Damascus from al-Nāṣir Dāʾūd, his brother al-Muʿaẓẓam's son, who was ruling there at that time. When Dāʾūd heard that his uncle al-Kāmil was intending to attack him, he had sent to his uncle al-Ashraf, lord of the Jazīra, to ask him for military support and to request aid to defend him from his [other] uncle. Al-Ashraf came to Damascus and then there was an exchange of envoys between him and his brother al-Kāmil to discuss peace. The two of them came to terms and made an agreement. Al-Ashraf travelled to al-Kāmil and met with him.

[483] After their meeting envoys went to and fro on many occasions between them and the emperor, ruler of the Franks, and a treaty was agreed according to which they would cede to him Jerusalem along with a few places nearby and the rest of the lands, such as Hebron, Nablus, the Jordan Valley, Tiberias[3] etc., would remain in Muslim hands.[4] Only Jerusalem and the places that had been specified

[1] The date is variously given, although Western sources agree on 18 February (e.g. Runciman, iii, 187; Stevenson, *Crusaders*, 312; Mayer, *The Crusades*, 227–8). Ibn Shaddād, *Liban*, 224, has 11 Rabīʿ I/7 February. If that were an error for 21 Rabīʿ I, the equivalent date would be 17 February, close enough to be adjusted to bring it into line with the Western sources.

[2] After his name the edition has 'May God Almighty have mercy on him', a formula for the deceased, but it must be a later copyist's insertion as al-Kāmil died in 635/ 1238, that is, after Ibn al-Athīr.

[3] Ṭabariyya (Tiberias) is the reading of *Kāmil* (Thornberg), xii, 315. Malaṭya (ancient Mitelene in Mesopotamia) is the rather unlikely reading of the edition and *Receuil*, ii, 176.

[4] For the negotiations, see Ibn Wāṣil, iv, 241–2; Abū Shāma, *Dhayl*, 154. Cf. Humphreys, 197–8, 202–3.

would be ceded to the Franks. The walls of Jerusalem had been razed. Al-Mu‘aẓẓam had razed them, as we have mentioned. Thereupon the Franks took over Jerusalem and the Muslims were outraged and thought it monstrous.[5] This caused them to feel such weakness and pain as are beyond description. May God facilitate its conquest and restoration to the Muslims by His grace and favour. Amen.[6]

How al-Ashraf took the city of Damascus

On Monday 2 Sha‘bān this year [= 25 June 1229] al-Ashraf ibn al-‘Ādil took Damascus from his nephew, [al-Nāṣir] Ṣalāḥ al-Dīn Dā’ūd ibn al-Mu‘aẓẓam. We have already mentioned how this came about. The lord of Damascus feared his uncle al-Kāmil and sent to his [other] uncle al-Ashraf to ask for support and for his help in defending him from al-Kāmil. He came to him from the Jazīra and entered Damascus. Its lord and its populace rejoiced at his coming. They had already taken precautions and were preparing for a siege, but al-Ashraf ordered that to stop and for their intention to take precautionary measures to be abandoned. He swore to its lord that he would give help and protect him and his lands. After he had contacted al-Kāmil, the two of them came to terms[7] while the lord of Damascus thought that he was included with them in these terms. Al-Ashraf travelled to see his brother al-Kāmil and they met in Dhū'l-Ḥijja 625 [**484**] on the day of the great feast[8] [10 November 1228]. The lord of Damascus proceeded to Baysān and waited there. Al-Ashraf returned from his visit to his brother and he and the lord of Damascus met together.[9] Al-Ashraf did not have a large number of troops with him. While they were sitting together in a tent they had, ‘Izz al-Dīn Aybak, a mamluke of al-Mu‘aẓẓam, the former lord of Damascus, who was a senior emir of the latter's son [Dā’ūd], entered and said to his master Dā’ūd, ‘Rise and leave, otherwise you will be arrested immediately,’ and he ushered him out. Al-Ashraf was unable to prevent him because Aybak had ordered all the troops they had to mount up and they were more numerous than those with al-Ashraf. Dā’ūd left and he and his troops rode to Damascus.

[5] Sibṭ ibn al-Jawzī preached a sermon at Damascus, which Ibn Wāṣil heard, that served al-Nāṣir's political purposes and aroused public anger towards al-Kāmil (see Ibn Wāṣil, iv, 245–6).

[6] A supportive account of al-Kāmil's policy is given by Ibn Abī al-Damm, especially 185–6.

[7] Ibn al-Athīr fails to make clear that they planned to make a new distribution of lands between members of the Ayyubid family, which involved depriving al-Nāṣir Dā’ūd of his chief possessions, including Damascus. For a full account, see Humphreys, 193–206.

[8] i.e. the Feast of Sacrifice, 10 Dhū'l-Ḥijja.

[9] According to Ibn Wāṣil, iv, 236–7, al-Nāṣir Dā’ūd had left Nablus for Damascus, having got wind of his uncles' plans, and the meeting with al-Ashraf took place at al-Qusayr, below the Pass of Fīq (or Afīq, east of Lake Tiberias), leading on to the Hauran plateau.

The reason for this was that Aybak had been told that al-Ashraf was intending to arrest his master and take Damascus from him, so he took this action. After they had departed, al-Kāmil's armies came to al-Ashraf, who marched to descend upon Damascus and put it under siege. He continued to besiege it until al-Kāmil joined him,[10] and then the siege was intensified and the situation became very serious for the citizens, whose hearts were in their mouths.

One of the most serious considerations for the lord of Damascus was that he had little money with him because his treasury was at Kerak and, as he had trusted his uncle al-Ashraf, he had brought none of it with him. He was obliged to sell his womenfolk's ornaments and clothing. He was in a very difficult situation, so he went out to his uncle al-Kāmil and offered to surrender Damascus and the castle of Shawbak to him on condition that he could have Kerak, the Jordan Valley, Baysān and Nablus, and that the castle of Ṣarkhad and its dependencies should be retained for Aybak.

Al-Kāmil duly took over Damascus and placed his deputy in the citadel until his brother al-Ashraf transferred to him Ḥarrān, Edessa, al-Raqqa, Sarūj and Ra's 'Ayn in the Jazīra. When he had taken them over, he gave up the citadel of Damascus to his brother al-Ashraf, who entered and took up residence there. Al-Kāmil proceeded to the Jazīra lands, where he remained until he summoned al-Ashraf because of Jalāl al-Dīn's siege [**485**] of the city of Khilāṭ. After he had presented himself before him at al-Raqqa, al-Kāmil returned to Egypt. What happened to al-Ashraf we shall relate, if God Almighty wills.[11]

Account of the arrest and execution of the Chamberlain 'Alī

This year al-Ashraf sent his mamluke 'Izz al-Dīn Aybak,[12] a great emir in his state, to the city of Khilāṭ and ordered him to arrest the Chamberlain Ḥusām al-Dīn 'Alī ibn Ḥammād, who was the governor of Khilāṭ and the ruling authority there on behalf of al-Ashraf. We have not learnt of anything to cause his arrest, because he was in sympathy with him and a true adviser, guarding his lands and ruling well over the subjects. Through this long period he had faced Khwārazm Shāh Jalāl al-Dīn and protected Khilāṭ in a way that no one else was capable of. He took great care to hold and defend al-Ashraf's territory. Reference has already been made to his attack on Jalāl al-Dīn's lands and his conquest of part of them, which is enough

---

[10] Al-Kāmil joined the siege in Jumādā I/ 28 March–26 April, after the treaty with Frederick II had been concluded (Ibn Wāṣil, iv, 252).

[11] See below, pp. [**487**] and [**489**]. Al-Nāṣir had written to Jalāl al-Dīn, urging him to press his siege of Khilāṭ to distract al-Ashraf from his ambitions for Damascus (see Ibn Wāṣil, iv, 240).

[12] Not to be confused with 'Izz al-Dīn Aybak, a mamluke of al-Mu'aẓẓam and then of al-Nāṣir Dā'ūd; see p. [**484**].

to demonstrate his high zeal and perfect bravery. His master gained great standing through him. Indeed, people used to say, 'One of the mamlukes of al-Ashraf can stand against Khwārazm Shāh.'

He was (God have mercy on him) a good and generous man, who allowed no injustice. He carried out many pious building works, such as caravanserais on the highways and mosques in the towns, and at Khilāṭ constructed a hospital and a Friday mosque. He did much to the roads and repaired those on which it was difficult to travel.

When Aybak came to Khilāṭ, he arrested him and then had him murdered, for he was an enemy of his.[13] After his death, how effective he had been became plain to see. Jalāl al-Dīn besieged Khilāṭ after his arrest and took the city, as we shall narrate, God willing. God did not give long respite to Aybak but punished him speedily, for Jalāl al-Dīn [**486**] took Aybak prisoner along with other emirs after he had taken Khilāṭ. When al-Ashraf and Jalāl al-Dīn made peace, the latter freed them all, but it is related that he put Aybak to death.

The reason why he was killed was that a mamluke of the Chamberlain 'Alī had fled to Jalāl al-Dīn and, when Aybak was taken prisoner, this mamluke requested Jalāl al-Dīn to kill him to avenge his master the Chamberlain Alī. Jalāl al-Dīn handed him over and he killed him. I heard that al-Ashraf in a dream saw 'Alī enter an assembly where Aybak was, take a kerchief and place it on Aybak's neck. He then took it and left. When he awoke, al-Ashraf said, 'Aybak is dead. In my dream I saw such and such.'[14]

How al-Kāmil gained possession of the city of Hama

This year towards the end of Ramaḍān [ended 22 August 1229] al-Kāmil took possession of Hama.[15] This came about as follows. We have mentioned that al-Manṣūr Muḥammad ibn Taqī al-Dīn, the lord of Hama, died.[16] When he was on the point of death, he had made the soldiers and the leading men of the city swear

---

13 According to al-Ḥamawī, 183a, Aybak arrested 'Alī because he found the castles devoid of treasure etc. and 'Alī could not give a satisfactory explanation. A little later his death from dysentery is reported but the author comments 'The facts were otherwise,' and then refers the reader to his major history, unfortunately lost.

14 Ḥusām al-Dīn 'Alī's obituary notice, in which the year of his death is stated as 627/1229–30, is given in Sibṭ ibn al-Jawzī, 664–5. The significance of the dream is not fully understood. Often putting on or receiving a kerchief (*mandīl*) is associated with submission or pardon; e.g. Nasawī, 230: 'He gave him his *mandīl* as a sign of safe conduct.' Cf. also *Chronicle of Ibn al-Athīr (2)*, p. [**373**]. Perhaps the significance here is in its being taken away.

15 For the campaign, see Humphreys, 207–8.

16 Al-Manṣur died in 617/ 1221, so the edition's 'as we shall relate' is inappropriate. One obviously expects 'as we have mentioned', but in fact there is no reference to his death under the appropriate year.

an oath to his oldest son, who took the title al-Muẓaffar.[17] His father had sent him to al-Kāmil, the lord of Egypt, because he had married his daughter. Muḥammad had another son, whose name was Qilij Arslān and his title Ṣalāḥ al-Dīn. He was at Damascus. He came to Hama and the city was surrendered to him and he took control of it and its citadel. Al-Kāmil sent to him, ordering him to give up the city to his older brother, for his father had named him for it in his will. He refused to do so and envoys went backwards and forwards on this matter to al-Mu'aẓẓam, ruler of Damascus, but no positive response followed.[18]

After al-Mu'aẓẓam died and al-Kāmil came into Syria and took Damascus, the latter sent a force [**487**] to Hama and besieged it on 3 Ramaḍān [26 July 1229]. Commanding this force was Asad al-Dīn Shīrkūh, lord of Homs, and a great emir in his army, called Fakhr al-Dīn 'Umar. With them was the son of Muḥammad ibn Taqī al-Dīn, Maḥmūd[19] who had been at al-Kāmil's court. The siege of the city continued for several days.

Al-Kāmil had marched from Damascus and made camp at Salamiyya, intending to proceed to the Jazīra lands, Ḥarrān and others. When he had Hama put under siege, the lord of Hama, Ṣalāḥ al-Dīn [Qilij Arslān] sought him out and came down from his citadel to visit him. There was no reason for this other than God Almighty's decree. Ṣalāḥ al-Dīn said to his advisers, 'I wish to leave and go to meet al-Kāmil.' They replied, 'In Syria there is no citadel stronger than yours and you have gathered unlimited stores. Why should you go down to him? This is not a good idea.' However, he insisted on doing so and in the end said, 'Allow me to descend, otherwise I shall throw myself from the citadel.' At that they held their peace and he descended with a small body of men. He came to al-Kāmil, who imprisoned him until he surrendered the city of Hama and its citadel to his older brother al-Muẓaffar. The castle of Barin, which was his, remained in his hands.[20] He was like 'one seeking his destruction with his own hoof'.[21]

Account of Jalāl al-Dīn's siege and capture of Khilāṭ

Early in Shawwāl [began 23 August 1229] Jalāl al-Dīn besieged the city of Khilāṭ, a possession of al-Ashraf, where his troops were. They held out, being aided by the

---

[17] Al-Muẓaffar Taqī al-Dīn Maḥmūd had already been made heir-apparent in 616/1218–19 (Ibn Wāṣil, iv, 64, 272).

[18] In fact, up to this present year al-Nāṣir Qilij Arslān had held Hama for almost nine years (Ibn Wāṣil, iv, 272).

[19] Correct the 'Muḥammad' in the edition.

[20] For the whole of this dispute over Hama, see the account of a participant, Ibn Abī al-Damm, especially 184–5.

[21] For this proverbial saying, see al-Yūsī, i, 177, where a story is told of some Arabs, who wished to slaughter a she-goat but could find no knife, until the animal, digging in the soil, uncovered one they had lost.

populace out of fear of Jalāl al-Dīn, because of his evil conduct. They indulged to excess in their vilification of him and their impudent remarks. He was seized by a determination to deal with them and continued his siege the whole winter. He distributed much of his army in the neighbouring villages and towns owing to the severe cold and the quantity of snow, for Khilāṭ is one of the coldest places and one with the most snow.[22]

Jalāl al-Dīn showed strong resolution and a patience that was astounding. He set up [**488**] several trebuchets to attack it and continued to launch stones at it until they had demolished part of the wall. The citizens helped to repair it but he continued his relentless confrontations with them until the final days of Jumādā II 627 [mid-April 1230]. He then carried out a series of assaults and took the city by force on Sunday 28 Jumādā I [14 April 1230]. It was treacherously yielded to him by some of the emirs.

After the city fell, the emirs there went up into its citadel and continued to resist, while Jalāl al-Dīn besieged them. He put the population to the sword, killing all he found, although they were few for some had left in fear and others had departed because of severe hunger, while yet others had already perished from want and lack of food. The people of Khilāṭ ate the sheep, then the cattle, then the buffaloes, then the horses, then the donkeys, then the mules, then the dogs and cats. We heard that they were catching rats and eating them. They showed endurance that nobody could match.

Khilāṭ alone was taken by him; they did not take any other towns. Nevertheless, they razed Khilāṭ and slaughtered many there. Any survivors fled to the country. The womenfolk were made captives and the children enslaved. All were sold and scattered to the four winds, dispersed throughout the lands. Property was pillaged and what the people endured was unheard of. No wonder that God Almighty did not spare him for long and he suffered his defeats at the hands of both Muslims and Tatars which we shall tell of, God willing.

Miscellaneous events

Towards the end of this year the Franks attacked the castle of Barin in Syria. They plundered the town and its dependencies, taking men and women captive. Among those they seized was a large body of Turkomans, all of whom they captured. Only the rare fugitive escaped. God knows best![23]

---

22 Note that on p. [**481**] Ibn al-Athīr had written of an unparalleled heavy snowfall in Khilāṭ.

23 In 1229 the Hospitallers made a raid on Barin in response to a raid by al-Kāmil on Ḥiṣn al-Akrād in the previous year (Runciman, iii, 207). For this raid and a series of minor engagements in following years, see Stevenson, *Crusaders*, 314, note 4.

The Year 627 [1229–1230]

Account of the defeat of Jalāl al-Dīn by Kayqubād and al-Ashraf

This year on Saturday 28 Ramaḍān [10 August 1230][1] Jalāl al-Dīn, the son of Khwārazm Shāh, suffered a defeat at the hands of 'Alā' al-Dīn[2] Kayqubād ibn Kaykhusro ibn Qilij Arslān, the ruler of Anatolia, Konya, Aqsaray, Sivas, Malaṭya etc., and al-Ashraf, the ruler of Damascus, the Jazīra and Khilāṭ.

This came about as follows. The ruler of Erzurum,[3] that is, the cousin of 'Alā' al-Dīn, ruler of Anatolia, had offered allegiance to Jalāl al-Dīn. Between the latter and the ruler of Anatolia there was an entrenched enmity. The ruler of Erzurum presented himself before Jalāl al-Dīn at Khilāṭ and gave him aid in his siege of it. 'Alā' al-Dīn feared them both, so sent to al-Kāmil, who was then at Ḥarrān, asking him to summon his brother al-Ashraf from Damascus, for he was now residing there after becoming its ruler. 'Alā' al-Dīn sent a series of messengers on that matter because he feared Jalāl al-Dīn. Al-Kāmil summoned his brother al-Ashraf from Damascus. He came to him, while 'Alā' al-Dīn's messengers were arriving one after another with his urgings for al-Ashraf to come and join with him. It is even said that on a single day al-Kāmil and al-Ashraf received five messengers from 'Alā' al-Dīn, all of them asking for al-Ashraf to come, even if he were alone.

Al-Ashraf united the armies of the Jazīra and Syria and marched to join 'Alā' al-Dīn. They met at Sivas and proceeded towards Khilāṭ. Jalāl al-Dīn heard [**490**] of their approach and moved to meet them with all speed. He came upon them at a place called Yāsī-chimen in the region of Erzinjan, where they clashed.[4]

'Alā' al-Dīn had a great host with him, said to be 20,000 cavalry, and al-Ashraf led about 5,000, although these were excellent, brave troops, fully armed and mounted on lively Arab steeds. All of them had been tested in battle and their commander was an emir from the Aleppan forces, called 'Izz al-Dīn 'Umar ibn Mujallī,[5] an Hakkārī Kurd, brave to the highest degree and possessed of fine qualities and noble characteristics.

---

[1] Abū Shāma, *Dhayl*, 159, gives the date Saturday 18 Ramaḍān but the equivalent, 31 July, fell on a Wednesday. He also refers to the *Kāmil* and the date given by Ibn al-Athīr.

[2] This is the reading of *Kāmil* (Thornberg), xii, 319. Inexplicably, the edition reads: 'Abd Allāh ibn.

[3] i.e. the Saljuqid, Rukn al-Dīn Jahān Shāh (ruled 622–7/1225–30), son of Mughīth al-Dīn Ṭughril Shāh. See Humphreys, 217; Zambaur, 144; above, p. [**429**].

[4] In the text the site of the battle is written as B.basī Ḥ.mār. For an account of the campaign, see Humphreys, 218–20.

[5] Here and just below the text reads 'Alī, in Arabic script a likely error for Mujallī, which is found in Ibn Wāṣil, iv 298 (where he is commander of the Aleppan contingent only), *Zubdat al-ḥalab*, iii, 209, and Eddé, *Principauté ayyoubide*, 102.

When they came face to face, Jalāl al-Dīn was startled by the great number of troops he saw, especially when he saw the Syrian detachment, for their fine appearance, their weaponry and their mounts that he saw filled his breast with terror. 'Izz al-Dīn ibn Mujallī initiated the battle along with the troops of Aleppo. Jalāl al-Dīn did not stand against them or hold firm, but departed in flight, he and his army. They were torn to pieces with every man for himself. They returned to Khilāṭ and then, taking with them their comrades who were there, they returned to Azerbayjan and made camp at the city of Khoy. Nothing of the region of Khilāṭ had been conquered by them apart from the city of Khilāṭ itself.[6] Al-Ashraf arrived, after they had [left and] taken their comrades there with them. It was left in a ruined state, devoid of inhabitants and residents. We have related before what happened to them.[7]

Account of 'Alā' al-Dīn's taking of Erzurum

We have mentioned that the lord of Erzurum was with Jalāl al-Dīn at Khilāṭ, stayed with him and witnessed with him the battle that has been mentioned. After Jalāl al-Dīn's defeat, the lord of Erzurum was taken **[491]** prisoner and brought before 'Alā' al-Dīn Kayqubād, his cousin. Taking him with him, he set out for Erzurum, where its lord surrendered to him the city and the castles and treasuries etc. that belong to it. It was as the saying goes, 'the ostrich set out to seek horns and returned with no ears'. Just so, this poor wretch came to Jalāl al-Dīn, seeking more, and he promised him some of 'Alā' al-Dīn's lands, but his wealth and the lands he already possessed were taken and he was left a captive.[8] Glory be to Him whose dominion is everlasting.

Account of al-Ashraf and 'Alā' al-Dīn's peace with Jalāl al-Dīn

After al-Ashraf returned to Khilāṭ and Jalāl al-Dīn went, defeated, to Khoy, there followed an exchange of ambassadors. Each of them settled for what he held and terms were arrived at on that basis and sworn to. When peace was established and oaths had been given, al-Ashraf returned to Sinjar and from there went on to Damascus. Jalāl al-Dīn remained in his own lands in Azerbayjan until the Tatars made a move against him, as we shall relate, if God Almighty wills.

---

6 Ibn Wāṣil, iv, 298, stresses that no local fortresses had been taken by Jalāl al-Dīn, presumably fortresses that would have provided refuge.

7 See p. [**488**].

8 He remained in prison until he died (Ibn Wāṣil, iv, 300).

How Shihāb al-Dīn Ghāzī became ruler of Arzan

Ḥusām al-Dīn, the lord of Arzan[9] in Diyār Bakr, had continued to be an ally of al-Ashraf, {giving him loyal advice},[10] participating in all his wars and his adventures, spending money in his service and offering his person and his troops in his support. To his enemies he was an enemy and to his friends a friend.

As part of his cooperation he was in Khilāṭ when Jalāl al-Dīn besieged it {and he suffered the hardship and fear that he experienced there but endured until Jalāl al-Dīn conquered the city}.[11] He was taken prisoner [**492**] by the latter, who wished to take the town of Arzan from him. Someone said to him, 'This man is from an ancient house, with long traditions of rule. He inherited Arzan from his ancestors, who had other lands besides but they lost all of them.' So Jalāl al-Dīn, feeling sympathetic towards him and taking pity on him, allowed him to retain his town but took oaths and undertakings from him that he would not take arms against him.

When al-Ashraf and 'Alā' al-Dīn came to make war on Jalāl al-Dīn, he did not take the field with them. Later, when Jalāl al-Dīn was defeated, Shihāb al-Dīn Ghāzī ibn al-'Ādil, al-Ashraf's brother, who held Mayyāfāriqīn and Ḥānī, came and besieged him in Arzan, which he subsequently took on terms. In exchange he gave him Ḥānī, part of Diyār Bakr.

This Ḥusām al-Dīn was an excellent man, of good conduct, noble and liberal. His door was never free of crowds coming to seek his bounty. His conduct in government and towards his subjects was admirable. He was of an ancient family, called the house of Ṭughān Arslān. In addition to Arzan he held Badlīs, Wasṭān and other places. They were also known as the house of the hunchback. These lands had been in their hands since the days of Malikshāh ibn Alp Arslān the Saljuq. Baktimur, the lord of Khilāṭ, took Badlīs from them, taking it from the uncle of this Ḥusām al-Dīn, because he was an ally of Saladin. That is why Baktimur attacked him. This present man kept Arzan until now and then it was taken from him. For every beginning there is an end. Glory be to Him who has no beginning and who continues without end.

[493] How Savinj Qush-yalwa took the castle of Rūyīndiz

During this year there came to prominence a Turkoman emir called Savinj. His title was Shams al-Dīn and Qush-yalwa was the name of his tribe. His power grew, he acted as a brigand and his following increased. He operated between Irbil and Hamadhan, he and his men interrupting traffic and disturbing the land. Then he went further to attack a strong fortress, the name of which was Sārū,[12] a possession

[9] See *EI(2)*, i, 679–80.

[10] Additional text in curly brackets from *Kāmil* (Thornberg), xii, 321.

[11] Additional text in curly brackets from *Kāmil* (Thornberg), xii, 321.

[12] This place remains unidentified. Given its stated position, it is unlikely to be a mistake

of Muẓaffar al-Dīn in the region of Irbil. He captured it and killed there a great emir, one of Muẓaffar al-Dīn's emirs, {called 'Izz al-Dīn al-Ḥumaydī}.[13] Muẓaffar al-Dīn gathered troops and wished to recover it from him, but was unable to do so because it was so well defended and because of the large following of this man. They made peace on the understanding that the castle would be left in his hands.

Jalāl al-Dīn's army was besieging the castle of Rūyīndiz, one of Azerbayjan's castles and one of the strongest and most impregnable fortresses, the like of which was not to be found. The siege of the inhabitants had lasted a long time, so they announced that they would surrender. Jalāl al-Dīn sent one of his closest followers and trusted advisers to take it over, sending with him robes of honour and money for those within. When the envoy climbed up to the castle and took it over, he gave to some of the defenders but did not give to others, whom he slighted and exploited, as he now had control of the fortress. When those to whom he gave no robes or money saw how he treated them, they sent to Savinj, asking him to come so that they could surrender the castle to them. He came with his men and they yielded it to him. Glory be to Him who, when He wills a thing, provides the means.

This castle of Rūyīndiz had always been too much for the capacities of great and mighty princes in former and recent times and it became proverbial for its impregnability. When God (glorious and mighty is He) willed to make this weak man ruler of it, He facilitated matters for him, so that he took it without a fight and with no trouble and dispossessed the followers of such a one as Jalāl al-Dīn whom all the princes on earth held in awe and feared. As for Jalāl al-Dīn's men, it was like the saying, 'Many a man strives for one who sits idly by.'

[**494**] After Savinj had taken it, he became ambitious to take others, especially as Jalāl al-Dīn was preoccupied with the defeat he had suffered and with the coming of the Tatars. He left the castle to go to Marāgha, which was nearby. He put it under siege but he was hit by a stray arrow and killed. After his death his brother became ruler of Rūyīndiz. This second brother left the castle and attacked and plundered the region of Tabriz. He returned to the castle to deposit that plunder and booty there as a store in fear of the Tatars, who had already appeared. He was surprised by a body of Tatars, who slew him and took the plunder that he had with him. After his death the castle was ruled by a nephew of his.[14] All this happened in a period of two years. Fie on a world which always makes a sorrow follow a joy and some evil follow some good.

---

for Sarāv (modern Sarāb), a town situated between Ardabil and Tabriz. Cf. above, p. [**382**].

[13] Additional text in curly brackets from *Kāmil* (Thornberg), xii, 322.

[14] At this point, Ibn Wāsil, iv, 308, who otherwise reproduces Ibn al-Athīr's text in this section, has 'a sister of his became ruler of the castle'.

[495] The Year 628 [1230–1231]

Account of the incursion of the Tatars into Azerbayjan and what they did

During this year the Tatars arrived in Azerbayjan from Transoxania. We have already related how they conquered Transoxania and what they did in Khurasan and other lands by way of pillage, destruction and massacre. Their rule became established in Transoxania and the cities there began to be re-populated. They built a large city that was almost the equivalent of[1] the city of Khwārazm. The cities of Khurasan, however, remained in ruins, no Muslims daring to dwell in them. As for the Tatars, every now and then a band would make a raid and plunder what they could find. The country was in a totally ruined state. They kept on like this until, in the year 625 [1227–8], a horde of them appeared and there ensued between them and Jalāl al-Dīn the events we have already narrated. Their situation remained unchanged until at this present time Jalāl al-Dīn met with defeat at the hands of 'Alā' al-Dīn Kayqubād and al-Ashraf, as we have mentioned under the year 627 [1229–30]. The leader of the Ismā'īlī heretics then sent to the Tatars to inform them of Jalāl al-Dīn's weakness owing to the defeat he had suffered and to urge them to attack him, following on his weakness, and to guarantee them victory over him because of the enfeebled state he had come to.

Jalāl al-Dīn was a bad ruler who administered his realm abominably. Among the princes who were his neighbours he did not leave one without showing hostility to him and challenging him for his kingdom, acting as a bad neighbour. As an example of that, as soon as he appeared in Isfahan and gathered an army, he invaded Khuzistan and besieged Tustar, a possession of the caliph. He marched to Daqūqā, which he sacked and where he killed many people. It too belonged to the caliph. **[496]** Then he took Azerbayjan, which was held by Uzbek, and attacked the Georgians, whom he defeated and harassed. Later he made war on al-Ashraf, lord of Khilāṭ, and then on 'Alā' al-Dīn, ruler of Anatolia, and on the Ismā'īlīs, whose lands he ravaged and many of whom he killed. He imposed upon them an annual tribute in money and also on others. Every prince abandoned him and would not take his hand.

When the letters of the leader of the Ismā'īlīs came to the Tatars, calling upon them to attack Jalāl al-Dīn, a horde of them hastened to enter their lands, where they seized Rayy and Hamadhan and the territory between them. Then they invaded Azerbayjan, where they caused havoc, plundered and killed the inhabitants they captured. Meanwhile, Jalāl al-Dīn did not dare to confront them, nor was he able to defend the country from them, being overcome with panic and

[1] A possible meaning is 'that was near [the site of]'. Cf. Barthold, *Turkestan*, 457.

fear. Furthermore his troops had turned against him and his vizier, along with a large section of the army, had cast off their loyalty.

The cause of this was strange and revealed an unparalleled lack of good sense on Jalāl al-Dīn's part. It was the case that Jalāl al-Dīn had a eunuch servant, called Qilij, whom he loved greatly. It so happened that this eunuch died and Jalāl al-Dīn exhibited such sorrow and grief for him as had never been heard of, not even from Majnūn for Laylā.[2] He ordered the soldiers and emirs to walk on foot in his funeral cortege. His death occurred at a place that was several leagues from Tabriz. The troops proceeded on foot, as did he himself for part of the road, but then his emirs and vizier prevailed on him to ride. When he reached Tabriz, he sent to the inhabitants, ordering them to leave the city to meet the eunuch's coffin, which they did. However, he blamed them for not going far and not showing more sorrow and tears than they did. He wanted to punish them for that, but his emirs interceded for them, so he let them be.

Furthermore, this eunuch was not buried but Jalāl al-Dīn took him with him wherever he went, beating his breast and weeping. He refused food and drink; when food was offered to him, he would say, 'Take some of this to so-and-so,' naming the eunuch, and nobody dared to say that he was dead. On one occasion someone did say to him [**497**] that he was dead and he killed the man that said it. They continued to take food to him, come back and say, 'He kisses the earth and says, "I am now better than I was."' His emirs were overcome with exasperation and disgust at this situation. It led them, along with his vizier, to abandon their allegiance and turn away from him. He was left out of his mind, not knowing what to do, especially when the Tatars made their incursion. At that time the eunuch servant was buried and Jalāl al-Dīn contacted the vizier, won him over and tricked him into coming back to him. After his arrival he survived a few days and then Jalāl al-Dīn put him to death. This is indeed a strange and rare occurrence, the like of which had never been heard of.

How the Tatars took Marāgha

This year the Tatars besieged Marāgha in Azerbayjan. The population resisted and then declared that they would surrender in return for a guarantee which they asked for. The Tatars offered them the guarantee and took over the city, where they did kill some people, although not very many. They appointed a prefect there and the position of the Tatars became very strong. Throughout Azerbayjan the people's fear of them increased greatly. God Almighty will Himself provide aid for Islam and the Muslims, but for now we do not see among the princes of Islam one who has a desire to wage the Jihad or to aid the religion. On the contrary, each of them

[2] These two are the archetypal desperate lovers of poetry and romances, the Romeo and Juliet of the Middle East.

looks to his pleasures, his sport and the oppression of his subjects. For me this is more frightening than the enemy. God Almighty said, 'Fear temptation that will not only come upon those of you who are wicked.'[3]

Account of Jalāl al-Dīn's arrival at Āmid, his defeat there and what befell him

Jalāl al-Dīn saw what the Tatars were doing in Azerbayjan and that they were remaining there, killing, plundering, taking captives, ruining the country and levying money, [**498**] while planning to attack him. He saw too his own feeble and weak state, so he left Azerbayjan for Khilāṭ and sent to al-Ashraf's deputy there to say, 'We have not come to make war or to cause harm. Fear of this enemy has alone brought us to seek out your city.' His plan was to make for Diyār Bakr and the Jazīra and to visit the caliph's court to ask for aid from him and all the princes against the Tatars and to request their help to repel them and to warn them of the result of their failure to act. He arrived at Khilāṭ and heard that the Tatars were pursuing him, hard on his tracks, so he went to Āmid. He posted scouts at several places in fear of a night attack. A detachment of Tatars came, following his tracks, and arrived by a different route from the one where the scouts were. They fell on him at night in his position outside the city of Āmid. He left, fleeing for his life, and the troops with him were dispersed and scattered in all directions.[4] One group from his army made for Ḥarrān, where the Emir Ṣawāb and the troops of al-Kāmil who were with him at Ḥarrān fell upon them and took the money, weapons and mounts they had. Another group made for Nisibis, Mosul, Sinjar, Irbil and other places. The local rulers and their subjects harassed them and everyone was eager to attack them, even the peasants, Kurds and Bedouin etc. They took revenge on them and requited them for their evil deeds, their wicked behaviour at Khilāṭ and elsewhere and for all the destruction they had wreaked in the land. 'God does not love those that do evil.'[5] Jalāl al-Dīn grew more and more weak and more and more feeble owing to the dispersal of his army and what had befallen them.

After the Tatars had treated them in this manner and he had fled from them in defeat, they came into Diyār Bakr in pursuit of him, because they did not know which destination he had sought nor which route he had travelled. Glory be to Him who replaced their security with fear, their might with humiliation and their great numbers with few. Blessed be God, the Lord of the Universe, who does what He wills.

---

3 Koran, viii, 25.

4 The historian al-Nasawī, who was in Jalāl al-Dīn's camp, had spent the night on secretarial work and had dozed off just before the attack. He fled, leaving all his possessions but having witnessed the dramatic rescue of the sultan, who was drunk at the time (Nasawī, 378–9).

5 Koran, iii, 64.

[499] Account of the entry of the Tatars into Diyār Bakr and the Jazīra and the wicked deeds that they perpetrated there

After the defeat of Jalāl al-Dīn by the Tatars at Āmid, they ravaged the hinterland there, Arzan and Mayyāfāriqīn and then set out for Is'ard, where the populace resisted them. The Tatars offered them a guarantee, so they trusted them and surrendered. When the Tatars had them in their power, however, they put them to the sword. They slew them [in such numbers] that they almost annihilated them. The only survivors were people who hid themselves, and few there were of them.

A merchant, who had gone to Āmid, told me that they estimated the dead at more than 15,000. With this merchant was a slave girl from Is'ard, who related that her master had gone out to fight. His mother had stopped him, as she had no son other than him, but he did not listen to what she said, so she went with him and both of them were killed. A nephew of the mother inherited the girl and sold her to this merchant. She had a terrible story to tell about the number of the slain and how the siege had lasted five days.

From there the Tatars went to the town of Ṭanza, where they acted in the same way, and then from Ṭanza to a valley nearby called the Valley of al-Qurayshiyya,[6] where there were flowing streams and many orchards. The road leading there was narrow and the inhabitants of al-Qurayshiyya fought the Tatars and denied then access. They held out against them and many were killed on both sides. The Tatars withdrew without having gained any success against them. They then roamed through country where they met no resistance and nobody stood to face them. Having reached Mardin, they plundered what they found in the town, while the lord of Mardin[7] and the people of Dunaysir took refuge in the citadel of Mardin, as did others who lived near the citadel.

Next they came to Nisibis in the Jazīra,[8] which they threatened for part of a day. They ravaged the hinterland [**500**] and slew any persons they seized. The gates remained shut, so they retired and went to Sinjar. They came to the mountains in the region of Sinjar, which they pillaged and then entered Khābūr. Having then reached 'Arābān,[9] they again plundered and massacred before withdrawing.

Another group followed the Mosul road. They came to a village, called al-Mu'nisa, which is a day's journey from Nisibis, lying between it and Mosul. They sacked it while the inhabitants and others hid in a caravanseray there. All were killed.

I was told the following by a man from there:

---

6 See Yāqūt, iv, 79: 'a village near Jazīrat Ibn 'Umar'.

7 i.e. a member of the Artuqid dynasty, al-Manṣūr Nāṣir al-Dīn Artuq Arslān ibn Īl-Ghāzī (ruled 599–637/1203–39). See Bosworth, *New Islamic Dynasties*, 194.

8 This is the main town of this name, the modern Nusaybin, in upper Mesopotamia. See Krawulsky, 448; *EI(2)*, vii, 983–4.

9 A small town on the River Khābūr (Yāqūt, iii, 632–3; Krawulsky, 427–8).

> I hid from them in a building where there was straw, so they did not capture me. I was watching them through a window in the building. Every time they were going to kill someone, he would say, 'No, for God's sake,' but they killed him nevertheless. When they had finished with the village, plundered what there was there and seized the women as captives, I saw them sporting on horseback, laughing and singing in their language, and repeating the words 'No, for God's sake.'

Yet another group went to Nisibis of the Greeks[10] on the Euphrates, part of the region of Āmid. Having plundered and massacred there, they returned to Āmid and then went on to Badlīs, where the populace took refuge in the citadel and in the hills. They killed a small number there and set fire to the town. One of the local inhabitants said to me, 'If we had had 500 cavalry, not one of the Tatars would have survived, because the road is narrow between the hills and a few men can repel many.'

From Badlīs they went to Khilāṭ. They descended upon a town, one of Khilāṭ's dependencies, called B.r.k.rī (?),[11] a very strong place, and took it by force of arms, killing all within. They then made for Arjīsh, also a dependency of Khilāṭ and a large and important town. They acted in the same way here. This took place in Dhū'l-Ḥijja [October 1231].

I have been told stories about them, that the hearer can scarcely credit, about the fear of them that God Almighty cast into people's hearts. It has even been said that one of them would enter a village or a quarter, where there was a large number of people, and he would continue to kill them [**501**] one by one, while nobody dared to raise his hand against that horseman.

I have heard that one of them captured a man but the Tatar had nothing to kill him with, so he said to him, 'Put your head on the ground and do not move.' The man put his head on the ground, the Tatar left, fetched a sword and killed him with it.

Another man told me the following:

> I was travelling on a road with seventeen men. A Tatar horseman came to us and told us to tie one another up. My companions began to do what he had ordered them. I said to them, 'This is one man. Why do we not kill him and run away?' They said, 'We are afraid.' I replied, 'This man is intending to kill you this minute. Let us kill him. Perhaps God will save us.' By God, not one

[10] Mentioned separately by Yāqūt, iv, 789: situated on the Euphrates, three or four days from Āmid and the same from Ḥarrān.

[11] The text has Bāk.rī. This fortress appears as B.r.k.wī (Ms. variant B.r.k.rī) in *Kāmil*, ix, 437, and as Bākazā in *Kāmil*, xi, 15, in a list of toponyms (mostly unidentified, see *Chronicle of Ibn al-Athīr (1)*, 308, where a correction should probably be made). In Nasawī (see especially Nasawī, 374, which refers to this passage of the Mongols) the spelling is invariably B.r.k.rī.

of them dared to act, so I took a knife and slew him. We ran away and were safe.

There were many incidents like this.

Account of the arrival of a group of Tatars at Irbil and Daqūqā

In Dhū'l-Ḥijja this year [October 1231] a group of Tatars came from Azerbayjan to the region of Irbil. They killed the Īwā'ī Turkomans, the Jūzqān Kurds and others on their route before they entered Irbil. They sacked the villages and slew all the inhabitants of those regions whom they seized. They perpetrated abominable deeds that had not been heard of from others.

The ruler of Irbil, Muẓaffar al-Dīn, took the field with his troops. He asked for reinforcements from the troops of Mosul, who went to join him. When he heard that the Tatars had returned to Azerbayjan, he remained in his lands and did not follow them. They reached the village of al-Karkhīnī,[12] the town of Daqūqā and others and returned safely, [**502**] nobody having caused them any alarm and no soldier having stood to face them.

These are misfortunes and crises, the like of which had never been seen by people in former or recent times. May God (glorious and mighty is He) be gracious to the Muslims and have mercy on them and drive this enemy away from them. This year came to an end and we had no confirmed information about Jalāl al-Dīn. We do not know whether he has been killed or is in hiding, not having revealed himself for fear of the Tatars, or whether he has left the country to go elsewhere. God knows best!

How the people of Azerbayjan submitted to the Tatars

Towards the end of this year the people of all Azerbayjan submitted to the Tatars and supplied them with money, 'Chinese', Khoy and Attabi[13] textiles and other items. The reason for their submission was that Jalāl al-Dīn had been defeated by the Tatars, his army dispersed and utterly torn apart, the stragglers seized by the people, and the Tatars in Diyār Bakr, the Jazīra, Irbil and Khilāṭ did what they did with nobody to stop them and no one to stand and face them and the princes of

[12] A fortress and a small suburb between Daqūqā and Irbil (Yāqūt, iv, 257).

[13] Attabi fabrics (cf. English 'tabby'), of watered silk, derived their name from a quarter in West Baghdad. According to Yāqūt, i, 822, Tabriz produced various textiles, including *Khiṭā'ī* ('Chinese'), as in this present text. See Serjeant, 'Islamic Textiles', xv–xvi (1951), 81: 'The importation of Chinese silks into Islamic countries was continuous and the authors frequently mention "Chinese silk" (ḥarīr Ṣīnī) … Many of the stuffs, however, which were called "Chinese silks" came from neighbouring countries and not from China proper.'

Islam skulked in their burrows. Add to this the interruption of information about what had happened to Jalāl al-Dīn, for there was no news forthcoming about him. People did not know what his situation was. They despaired, declared their submission to the Tatars and supplied them whatever money and garments they demanded of them.[14]

This was the case with the city of Tabriz, which is the core of Azerbayjan, to which all look, as also to its people, for a lead. The chief of the Tatars camped with his armies near the city and sent to its inhabitants inviting them to submit and threatening them if they refused. They sent him much money and rare textiles of all kinds, silks among others, and all sort of things, even wine, and they offered him their submission. He replied, thanking them and asking that their leaders should come before him. The city's cadi and headman and several of the local notables went to see him, but [**503**] Shams al-Dīn al-Ṭughrā'ī[15] failed to join them and he was the one that everybody looked to, although he did not make this obvious at all.

When these others presented themselves, he asked them about al-Ṭughrā'ī's refusal to attend. They said, 'He is a man who lives in pious seclusion. He has no connection with princes. We are the people that matter.'[16] He made no reply but then asked them to assemble before him some makers of 'Chinese' textiles and the like, so that they could be put to work for their great ruler, for this man was one of that ruler's subjects.

The craftsmen were summoned and he employed them to produce what it was they wanted. The people of Tabriz met the cost. He then asked them for a tent, also for his ruler, so they made a tent unlike any that had ever been made. Its covering they made of fine embroidered satin and the interior they made of sable and beaver skins.[17] It cost them a great amount. He imposed on them an annual tribute in cash. The Tatar envoys travelled back and forth to the caliphal Diwan and to several princes demanding that they should give no aid to Khwārazm Shāh.

I have read a letter that came from a merchant, an inhabitant of Rayy, last year before the incursion of the Tatars. When the Tatars came to Rayy and the populace there submitted to them and they then went on to Azerbayjan, he travelled with

---

[14] The Mongols had a high regard and demand for gold brocade and other luxury textiles. They were used as a 'political commodity' and distributed to acquire and maintain loyal followers (Allsen, *Commodity and exchange*, 11–13, 27 and 103–4).

[15] See above, pp. [**382**] and [**436**].

[16] At this time Shams al-Dīn exerted himself to suppress mob violence and maintain Khwārazmian authority. It also seems to be suggested that he died before the surrender of Tabriz to the Mongols (Nasawī, 309). The comment in Nasawī, 196, helps to explain Shams al-Dīn's role, namely that through his personal standing and family traditions he had great influence in Tabriz without any formal office. His character and efforts for the people are also mentioned in Nasawī, 210. See above, p. [**436**].

[17] For the large and elaborate tents of the Mongols, see Allsen, *Commodity and exchange*, 13–15.

them to Tabriz and wrote to his colleagues in Mosul as follows:

> We cannot describe the infidel (God curse him) nor tell of his hordes lest the hearts of the Muslims be broken, for the situation is very grave. Do not imagine that the aim of this group which came to Nisibis and Khābūr and the other group which reached Irbil and Daqūqā was plunder. They simply wanted to learn whether there was in this country anyone who could resist them or not. When they returned, they told their ruler of the country's lack of any protector or defender and that the land is devoid of any authority or troops. Their eager ambition has increased and in the spring they will attack you. There is nowhere left for you to remain, unless it be in the lands of the west, for their purpose is to invade all the lands. Look out for yourselves.

[**504**] This was the content of the letter. Verily we belong to God and to Him do we return. There is no power or might except in God the High, the Mighty.

As for Jalāl al-Dīn, up to the end of the year 628 [ended 28 October 1231] no news of him was forthcoming and likewise until the end of Ṣafar 629 [26 December 1231] we had learnt nothing of his doings.[18] God is the One from whom help comes.

Miscellaneous events

This year there was little rain in the Jazīra and Syria, especially at Aleppo and its dependencies, for there it was exceedingly sparse.[19] Prices rose and the rise in prices at Aleppo was the worst, although it was not as serious as has been mentioned in past years. The Atabeg Shihāb al-Dīn, who was in charge of affairs at Aleppo, the source of commands and prohibitions, the regent and guardian for its sultan, al-'Azīz ibn al-Ẓāhir, produced much of his own money and corn and bestowed plentiful alms. He administered the city so well that there was no obvious sign of the shortages and high prices. May God reward him with a goodly reward.[20]

---

[18] According to Ibn Wāṣil, iv, 322, Jalāl al-Dīn hoped to take refuge with the Ayyubid Shihāb al-Dīn Ghāzī in Mayyāfāriqīn. He outstripped his companions, came to a village nearby and was there killed by a Kurd whose father and brother had been killed by Khwārazmian troops. Later, fugitives from the army identified certain effects as belonging to the sultan.

Despite criticism of his bloodthirsty and destructive career, it was recognized that Jalāl al-Dīn was like a barrier holding back the Mongols. After him the way was open into Iraq, the Jazīra and Asia Minor (Ibn Wāṣil, iv, 296, 323–4). Sibṭ ibn al-Jawzī, 667–71, has similar mixed views and dates his death to 628 or 629.

[19] The population of Aleppo went out to the hill of Bānqūsā and prayed for rain (*Zubdat al-ḥalab*, iii, 210).

[20] In mid-Ramaḍān/mid-July 1231, after acting for about fifteen years as regent, Shihāb

During this year Asad al-Dīn Shīrkūh, lord of Homs and al-Raḥba, constructed a castle at Salamiyya, which he called Sumaymis. When al-Kāmil left Egypt to go to Syria, Asad al-Dīn gave him true service. His loyalty and his fighting for him gained him an important result. Al-Kāmil assigned him Salamiyya as a fief and he built this castle nearby on a high hill.

This year the Franks in Syria attacked the town of Jabala,[21] which is one of the towns belonging to Aleppo. They entered it and took booty and prisoners from it. The Atabeg Shihāb al-Dīn sent troops against them with an emir[22] who had been assigned it as a fief. He engaged the Franks, killed many of them and recovered the prisoners and the booty.

[505] This year the Cadi Ibn Ghanā'im ibn al-'Adīm, the pious shaykh, died. He was one who put great effort into his worship and his spiritual exercises and put his learning into practice. If someone were to assert that there was nobody more pious in his lifetime, he would be speaking the truth. May God be pleased with him and give him satisfaction. He was one of our teachers. We studied Ḥadīth with him and benefited from observing him and hearing his words.

In this year also, on 12 Rabī' I [18 January 1231], there died our friend Abū'l-Qāsim 'Abd al-Majīd ibn al-'Ajamī al-Ḥalabī. He and his family were the leading exponents of the Sunna at Aleppo. He was a man of ample virtue, good character, abundant forbearance and great leadership qualities. He loved to provide meals and the people he loved best were those who ate his food and accepted his charity. He used to receive his guests with a cheerful face and would not rest until he had made them comfortable and satisfied their wants. May God extend to him abundant mercy.

---

al-Dīn handed power to the Ayyubid al-'Azīz Muḥammad, who had now reached eighteen years of age (Eddé, *Principauté ayyoubide*, 102). His loyal service is explicitly contrasted with the conduct of Badr al-Dīn Lu'lu' at Mosul, who displaced the Zankid house there. Note too that Ibn Wāṣil spent most of this year at Aleppo, studying and making the acquaintance of Bahā' al-Dīn Ibn Shaddād, the historian of Saladin. See Ibn Wāsil, iv, 309–12.

[21] Situated on the Syrian coast between Lattakia and Bāniyās.

[22] The troops left Aleppo on 15 Rabī' II/21 January 1231 and raided Marqab and Bāniyās. The emir was Badr al-Dīn Aydamur, a former governor of the citadel of Aleppo. On 20 Sha'bān this year/23 June 1231, a truce was signed between Aleppo and the Hospitallers and Templars (*Zubdat al-ḥalab*, iii, 209–10; Eddé, *Principauté ayyoubide*, 101).

Bibliographical References

Primary sources

Abū Shāma, *Dhayl*: Abū Shāma, *Tarājim al-qarnayn al-sādis wa'l-sābi' (al-ma'rūf bi'l-dhayl 'alā al-rawḍatayn)*, ed. Muḥammad Zāhid al-Ḥasan al-Kawtharī, Cairo, 1366/1947.

al-Aghānī: Abū'l-Faraj al-Isfahānī, *Kitāb al-Aghānī*, 24 vols, Cairo, Dār al-Kutub, 1927–74.

Ansāb: al-Sam'ānī, *Kitāb al-ansāb*, ed. Abd al-Rahman ibn Yahya et al., 13 vols, Hyderabad, 1962–82.

Bāhir: Ibn al-Athīr, *al-Ta'rīkh al-bāhir fī'l-dawla al-atābakiyya*, ed. A. A. Tolaymat, Cairo, 1963.

Bukhārī, *Ṣaḥīḥ*: al-Bukhārī, *al-Jāmi' al-ṣaḥīḥ*, ed. M. L. Krehl, 4 vols, Leiden, 1862–1908.

al-Fayrūzabādī: Majd al-Dīn al-Fayrūzābādī, *al-Qāmūs al-muḥīṭ*, 4 vols, Cairo, 1913.

al-Ḥamawī: Muḥammad ibn 'Alī al-Ḥamawī, *al-Ta'rīkh al-manṣūrī*, facsimile ed. P. A. Gryaznevich, Moscow, 1960.

Ibn Abī al-Damm: D. S. Richards, 'The Crusade of Frederick II and the Ḥamāh succession. Extracts from the Chronicle of Ibn Abī al-Damm', *Bulletin d'Etudes Orientales*, xlv (1993), 183–200.

Ibn al-Sā'ī: 'Alī ibn Anjab ibn al-Sā'ī, *al-Jāmi' al-mukhtaṣar*, ed. Mustafa Jawad, vol. ix, Baghdad, 1934.

Ibn Shaddād, *Damas*: 'Izz al-Dīn Ibn Shaddād, *La Description de Damas d'Ibn Šaddād*, ed. Sami Dahan, Damascus, 1956.

Ibn Shaddād, *Liban*: 'Izz al-Dīn Ibn Shaddād, *Liban, Jordanie, Palestine: Topographie historique d'Ibn Šaddād*, ed. Sami Dahan, Damascus, 1963.

Ibn Wāṣil: Jamāl al-Dīn Muḥammad ibn Wāṣil, *Mufarrij al-kurūb fī akhbār Banī Ayyūb*, ed. Jamal al-Din al-Shayyal et al., 5 vols, Cairo, 1953–77.

Kāmil: Ibn al-Athīr, *al-Kāmil fī'l-ta'rīkh*, 12 vols, Dār Ṣādir ed., Beirut, 1965–7.

Kāmil (Thornberg): C. J. Thornberg ed., *Ibn-el-Athiri Chronicon quod Perfectissimum Inscribitur*, 14 vols, Leiden, 1851–76.

al-Maydānī, *Amthāl al-'arab*: al-Maydānī, *Amthāl al-'arab (Arabum Proverbia)*, ed. G. W. Freytag, 2 vols, Bonn, 1838–43.

Mustaqṣā: al-Zamakhsharī, *al-Mustaqṣā fī amthāl al-'arab*, 2 vols, Beirut, 1977.

al-Mutanabbī, *Dīwān*: al-Mutanabbī, *Dīwān (Kitāb al-'arf al-ṭayyib fī sharḥ dīwān*

Abī'l-Ṭayyib), ed. Nāṣīf al-Yāzijī, Beirut, 1882.
Nasawī: Muḥammad ibn Aḥmad al-Nasawī, *Sīrat al-Sulṭān Jalāl al-Dīn Mankubirtī*, ed. Ḥāfiẓ Aḥmad Ḥamdī, Cairo, 1953.
Qalqashandī, *Ansāb al-'arab*: al-Qalqashandī, Aḥmad ibn 'Alī, *Nihāyat al-arab fī ma'rifat ansāb al-'arab*, ed. Ibrahim al-Ibyari, Cairo, 1959.
Rawḍatayn: Abū Shāma, *Kitāb al-rawḍatayn fī akhbār al-dawlatayn*, ed. Ibrahim al-Zibaq, 5 vols, Beirut, 1418/1997.
Sibṭ ibn al-Jawzī: Sibṭ ibn al-Jawzī, *Mir'āt al-zamān*, vol. viii, Hyderabad, 1951.
Simṭ al-ghālī: Badr al-Dīn Muḥammad ibn Ḥātim al-Hamdānī, *Kitāb al-simṭ al-ghālī fī akhbār al-mulūk min al-Ghuzz bi'l-Yaman*, ed. Rex Smith, Cambridge, 1974.
Ta'rīkh Irbil: Ibn al-Mustawfī, *Ta'rīkh Irbil*, ed. Sāmī ibn al-Sayyid Khamās al-Ṣaqar, 2 vols, Baghdad, 1980.
Wafayāt: Ibn Khallikān, *Wafayāt al-a'yān wa-anbā' abnā' al-zamān*, ed. Ihsan Abbas, 8 vols., Beirut, 1977.
Wāfī: al-Ṣafadī, *al-Wāfī bi'l-wafayāt*, ed. H. Ritter et al., 1931–in progress.
Yāqūt: Shihāb al-Dīn Yāqūt al-Rūmī, *Kitāb mu'jam al-buldān*, ed. F. Wüstenfeld, 6 vols, Leipzig, 1866–70.
Yāqūt, *Irshād*: Yāqūt al-Rūmī, *Irshād al-arīb ilā ma'rifat al-adīb*, ed. D. S. Margoliouth, 7 vols, London, 1923–31.
al-Yūsī: al-Ḥasan ibn Mas'ūd al-Yūsī, *Zahr al-akam fī'l-amthāl wa'l-ḥikam*, 3 vols, Casablanca, 1981.
Zubdat al-ḥalab: Kamāl al-Dīn Ibn al-'Adīm, *Zubdat al-ḥalab min ta'rīkh Ḥalab*, ed. Sami al-Dahhan, 3 vols, Damascus, 1954–68.

Primary material in translation

Blochet, 'Patriarches': E. Blochet, 'Extraits de l'Histoire des Patriarches d'Alexandrie relatifs au siège de Damiette sous le règne d'al-Malik al-Kamil', *Revue de l'Orient latin*, xi, 1908, 240–60.
Chronicle of Ibn al-Athīr (1): *The Chronicle of Ibn al-Athīr for the Crusading Period from* al-Kāmil fī'l-ta'rīkh, Part 1; The Years 491–541/1097–1146. *The Coming of the Franks and the Muslim Response*, trans. D. S. Richards, Aldershot, 2006.
Chronicle of Ibn al-Athīr (2): *The Chronicle of Ibn al-Athīr for the Crusading Period from* al-Kāmil fī'l-ta'rīkh, Part 2; The Years 541–589/1146–1193. *The Age of Nūr al-Dīn and Saladin*, trans. D. S. Richards, Aldershot, 2007.
Eddé, *Description*: 'Izz al-Dīn Ibn Šaddād, *Description de la Syrie du Nord*, trad. Anne-Marie Eddé-Terrasse, Damascus, 1984.
Juvainī, *History*: Juvaini, *The History of the World-Conqueror*, trans. John Andrew Boyle, 2 vols, Manchester University Press, 1958.
Recueil: *Recueil des Historiens des Croisades, Historiens orientaux*, eds. J. T.

Reinaud, S. de Sacy et al., 5 vols, Paris, 1872–1906.

Ṭabaqāt-i Nāṣirī: Major H. G. Raverty (trans.), *Ṭabaqāt-i Nāṣirī; a General History of the Muḥammadan Dynasties of Asia etc*, reprint Delhi, 1970.

Secondary material

Abun-Nasr, *Maghrib*: Jamil M. Abun-Nasr, *A History of the Maghrib*, Cambridge, 1975.

Adle, 'Le pays du Zuzan': Chahryar Adle, 'Une contreé redécouverte: le pays du Zuzan à la veille de l'invasion mongole', in *L'Iran face à la domination mongole*, ed. Denise Aigle, Tehran, 1997, 23–36.

Allsen, *Commodity and exchange*: Thomas T. Allsen, *Commodity and exchange in the Mongol empire: A cultural history of Islamic textiles*, Cambridge, 1997.

Barthold, *Turkestan*: W. Barthold, *Turkestan down to the Mongol Invasion*, ed. C. E. Bosworth, 3rd edn, London, 1968.

Biran, *Empire of the Qara Khitai*: Michal Biran, *The Empire of the Qara Khitai in Eurasian History. Between China and the Islamic World*, Cambridge, 2005.

Borgomale, 'Dynasties du Mâzandarân': Rabino di Borgomale, 'Les Dynasties du Mâzandarân', *Journal Asiatique*, ccxxviii (1936), 409–37.

Bosworth, *New Islamic Dynasties*: C. E. Bosworth, *The New Islamic Dynasties: A chronological and genealogical manual*, Edinburgh, 1996 (paperback 2004).

Bosworth, *Saffarids of Sistan*: C. E. Bosworth, *The History of the Saffarids of Sistan and the Maliks of Nimruz (247/861 to 949/1542–3)*, California and New York, 1994.

Bosworth, 'The Iranian World': C. E. Bosworth, 'The Political and Dynastic History of the Iranian World (A.D. 1000–1217)', in J. A. Boyle, ed., *The Cambridge History of Iran*, vol. 5: *The Saljuq and Mongol Periods*, Cambridge, 1968, 1–202.

Buell, 'Early Mongol expansion': Paul D. Buell, 'Early Mongol expansion in Western Siberia and Turkestan (1207–1219): a reconstruction', *Central Asiatic Journal*, xxxvi (1992), 1–32.

Cahen, *Pre-Ottoman Turkey*: Claude Cahen, *Pre-Ottoman Turkey: A general survey of the material and spiritual culture and history c. 1071–1330*, trans. J. Jones-Williams, London, 1968.

Carter, 'Arabic Lexicography': M. G. Carter, 'Arabic Lexicography', *CHALRLS*, 106–17.

CHALRLS: *The Cambridge History of Arabic Literature: Religion, Learning and Science in the 'Abbasid Period*, ed. M. J. L. Young et al., Cambridge, 1990.

Cornu, *Atlas*: Georgette Cornu, *Atlas du Monde Arabo-Islamique à l'époque classique, IXe–Xe siècles*, Leiden, 1985.

Dozy, *Supplément*: R. Dozy, *Supplément aux dictionnaires arabes*, 2 vols, Leiden, 1881, reprint Beirut, 1968.

Eddé, *Principauté ayyoubide*: Anne-Marie Eddé, *La Principauté ayyoubide d'Alep (570/1183–658/1260),* Stuttgart, 1999.

EIr: *Encyclopaedia Iranica*, ed. Ehsan Yarshater, London, Boston and Henley, 1985–in progress.

EI(2): *The Encyclopaedia of Islam*, eds. H. A. R. Gibb et al., 11 vols, 2nd edn, Leiden, 1960–2002.

Elisséeff: Nikita Elisséeff, *Nūr ad-Dīn. Un grand prince musulman de Syrie au temps des Croisades (511–569 H./1118–1174)*, 3 vols, Damascus, 1967.

Encyclopedia of Arabic Literature: Julie Scott Meisami and Paul Starkey, eds, *Encyclopedia of Arabic Literature*, 2 vols, London and New York, 1998.

GAL: Carl Brockelmann, *Geschichte der arabischen Litteratur,* 2 vols and 3 Supplement vols, Leiden, 1943–49.

Gibb, 'Armies of Saladin': H. A. R. Gibb, 'Armies of Saladin', *Cahiers d'Histoire égyptienne*, iii, Cairo, 1951, 304–20 (reprinted in *Studies on the Civilization of Islam*, eds S. J. Shaw and W. R. Polk, London, 1962).

Gottschalk, *al-Malik al-Kāmil*: Hans L. Gottschalk, *al-Malik al-Kāmil von Egypten und seine Zeit: Eine Studie zur Geschichte Vorderasiens und Egypten in der ersten Hälfte des 7./13. Jahrhunderts*, Wiesbaden, 1958.

Hinz: Walther Hinz, *Islamische Masse und Gewichte*, Leiden/Köln, 1970.

Hodgson, *Order of Assassins*: Marshall G. S. Hodgson, *The Order of the Assassins*, The Hague, 1955.

Humphreys: R. Stephen Humphreys, *From Saladin to the Mongols: the Ayyubids of Damascus, 1193–1260*, Albany, 1977.

Jackson, *Delhi Sultanate*: Peter Jackson, *The Delhi Sultanate: A Political and Military History*, Cambridge, 1999.

Jackson, 'Fall of the Ghurid dynasty': Peter Jackson, 'The Fall of the Ghurid dynasty', in *The Sultan's Turret. Studies in Persian and Turkish Culture* (Studies in Honour of Clifford Edmund Bosworth, vol. ii), ed. Carole Hillenbrand, Leiden etc., 2000, 201–37.

Krawulsky: Dorothea Krawulsky, *Īrān – Das Reich der Īlḫāne: Eine topographisch-historische Studie*, Wiesbaden, 1978.

Le Strange, *Baghdad*: G. Le Strange, *Baghdad during the Abbasid Caliphate*, Oxford, 1900.

Le Strange, *Caliphate*: G. Le Strange, *The Lands of the Eastern Caliphate*, Cambridge, 1930.

Makdisi, *Colleges*: George Makdisi, *The Rise of Colleges. Institutions of Learning in Islam and the West*, Edinburgh, 1981.

Mayer, *The Crusades*: Hans Eberhard Mayer, *The Crusades*, trans. John Gillingham, Oxford, 1972.

Mayer, 'Syrian Earthquake': Hans Eberhard Mayer, 'Two unpublished letters on the Syrian Earthquake of 1202', in *Medieval and Middle Eastern Studies in Honor of Aziz Suryal Atiya*, ed. Sami A. Hanna, Leiden, 1972, 295–310.

Michot, 'Ibn Taymiyya on Astrology': Yahya J. Michot, 'Ibn Taymiyya on

Astrology: Annotated Translation of Three Fatwas', in *Magic and Divination in Early Islam*, ed. Emilie Savage-Smith, Ashgate, 2004, 277–340.

Minorsky, *Sharvān and Darband*: V. Minorsky, *A History of Sharvān and Darband in the 10th–11th centuries*, Cambridge, 1958.

Minorsky, *Studies*: V. Minorsky, *Studies in Caucasian History*, London, 1953.

Morgan, *Mongols*: David Morgan, *The Mongols*, Blackwell, 1986.

Nizami, 'Ghurids': K. A. Nizami, 'The Ghurids', in *HCCA*, iv, Part One, 177–90.

Nogales, 'Sunni Theology': S. G. Nogales, 'Sunni Theology', *CHALRLS*, 1–14.

O'Callaghan, *Medieval Spain*: Joseph F. O'Callaghan, *A History of Medieval Spain*, Ithaca and London, 1975.

Phillips, *Fourth Crusade*: Jonathan Phillips, *The Fourth Crusade and the Sack of Constantinople*, London, New York, etc., 2004.

Pingree, 'Al-Ṭabarī': D. Pingree, 'Al-Ṭabarī on the prayers to the planets', *Bulletin d'études orientales*, xliv, 1993, 105–17.

Pringle, *Churches*: Denys Pringle, *The Churches of the Crusader Kingdom of Jerusalem: A Corpus*, 2 vols., Cambridge, 1993–8.

Pringle, *Secular buildings*: Denys Pringle, *Secular buildings in the Crusader Kingdom of Jerusalem: An archaeological gazetteer*, Cambridge, 1997.

Queller and Madden, *Fourth Crusade*: Donald E. Queller and Thomas F. Madden, *The Fourth Crusade. The conquest of Constantinople*, 2nd edn, Philadelphia, 1997.

Queller et al., 'The neglected majority': Donald E. Queller, Thomas K. Compton and Donald A. Campbell, 'The Fourth Crusade: the neglected majority', *Speculum*, xlix (1974), 441– 65.

Rachewiltz, 'The title Činggis Qan': Igor de Rachewiltz, 'The title Činggis Qan/Qaγan re-examined', in *Gedanke und Wirkung: Festschrift zum 90. Geburtstag von Nikolaus Poppe*, eds. Walther Heissig and Klaus Sagaster, Wiesbaden, 1989, 281–98.

Rosenthal, *Gambling*: Franz Rosenthal, *Gambling in Islam*, Leiden, 1975.

Runciman: Steven Runciman, *A History of the Crusades*, 3 vols, Cambridge, 1951–4.

Schacht, *Islamic Law*: Joseph Schacht, *An Introduction to Islamic Law*, Oxford, 1964.

Serjeant, 'Islamic Textiles': R. B. Serjeant, 'Material for a History of Islamic Textiles up to the Mongol Conquest', *Ars Islamica*, ix–xvi (1943–51).

Smith, *Ayyubids and Early Rasulids*: G. R. Smith, *The Ayyubids and Early Rasulids in the Yemen (567–649/1173–1395)*, 2 vols, London, 1978.

Stevenson, *Crusaders*: W. B. Stevenson, *The Crusaders in the East*, Cambridge, 1907, reprinted Lebanon, 1958.

Vasiliev, *Byzantine Empire*: A. A. Vasiliev, *History of the Byzantine Empire 324–1453*, 2 vols, Madison and Milwaukee, 1964.

Wiet, *L'Egypte arabe*: Gaston Wiet, *L'Egypte arabe etc.*, vol. 5 of *Histoire de la Nation Égyptienne*, Paris, 1937.

Zambaur: E. von Zambaur, *Manuel de Généalogie et de Chronologie pour l'Histoire de l'Islam*, Hanover, 1927.

Index

The definite article (al-) is ignored for purposes of alphabetical order